NEW CAMBRIDGE SHAKESPEARE
STUDIES AND SUPPLEMENTARY TEXTS

The Problem of *The Reign of King Edward III*:
A Statistical Approach

The Reign of King Edward III (1596) is a little-known Elizabethan play of uncertain authorship, some or all of which has long been considered possibly to have been Shakespeare's work. In assessing the origins of *King Edward III*, Slater's book is pioneering in its use and extension of vocabulary tests to solve problems of authorship. The author reviews the debate regarding the creation of *Edward III*. Following a survey of applications of quantitative methods to literary problems, he examines the authorship of *Edward III* by means of a statistical study of the play's rare words, and their links with rare words in Shakespeare's canonical plays. This is a technique developed by Slater himself and is of particular interest to literary scholars and stylometrists. The investigation indicates that the play was written by Shakespeare. The book therefore provides important new evidence to suggest that an exciting and much-neglected play should be admitted into the canon of Shakespeare's early history plays.

The rewards of Slater's research range beyond the provenance of only one work. He offers a persuasive set of adjustments to the traditional chronological order of Shakespeare's plays, based on his study of the rare-word links between them. The word lists and appendices assemble invaluable raw materials from which further tests can be carried out on Shakespeare's plays, poems, and apocrypha, to help resolve questions of chronology and authorship.

Dr Eliot Slater enjoyed an internationally eminent career in psychiatry and for many years served as Editor-in-Chief of the *British Journal of Psychiatry*. In retirement he pursued his longstanding interest in Shakespeare, publishing in *Notes and Queries* and *The Bard* before bringing his research into a book-length study.

The Problem of
The Reign of King Edward III:
A Statistical Approach

ELIOT SLATER

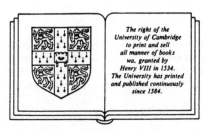

The right of the
University of Cambridge
to print and sell
all manner of books
wa. granted by
Henry VIII in 1534.
The University has printed
and published continuously
since 1584.

CAMBRIDGE UNIVERSITY PRESS

CAMBRIDGE

NEW YORK   NEW ROCHELLE   MELBOURNE   SYDNEY

CAMBRIDGE UNIVERSITY PRESS
Cambridge, New York, Melbourne, Madrid, Cape Town, Singapore,
São Paulo, Delhi, Dubai, Tokyo

Cambridge University Press
The Edinburgh Building, Cambridge CB2 8RU, UK

Published in the United States of America by Cambridge University Press, New York

www.cambridge.org
Information on this title: www.cambridge.org/9780521123488

First published 1988
This digitally printed version 2009

A catalogue record for this publication is available from the British Library

Library of Congress Cataloguing in Publication data
Slater, Eliot, 1904–83
The problem of the reign of King Edward III: a statistical
approach/Eliot Slater.
p.   cm. – (New Cambridge Shakespeare studies and
supplementary texts)
Originally presented as the author's thesis
Bibliography p.
ISBN 0-521-34353-4
1. Edward III (Drama – Language. 2. Shakespeare, William,
1564–1616 – Spurious and doubtful works.   3. Edward III (Drama) –
Authorship.   4. Shakespeare, William, 1564–1616 – Language – Word
frequency.   5. Shakespeare, William, 1564–1616 – Authorship.
6. Style. Literary – Statistical methods.   7. Edward III, King of
England, 1312–1377, in fiction, drama, poetry, etc.   I. Title.
II. Series.
PR2859. S54 1988
822.3 – dc 19   87-36837 CIP

ISBN 978-0-521-34353-4 Hardback
ISBN 978-0-521-12348-8 Paperback

It was sad that Cambridge University Press should have accepted this work for publication shortly after my father's death in May 1983. Since he was not able to see the book through the press himself, it has been reproduced from his original doctoral dissertation without alteration, save for the excision of one chapter of general literary criticism of *Edward III*, and the addition of an appendix on word links between *Edmund Ironside, Edward III, Henry VI* Parts 1 to 3, and *Titus Andronicus*. This appendix is drawn from a letter published by *The Times Literary Supplement* on 18 March 1983, and a corrected word list found among my father's papers after his death.

Ann Pasternak Slater

Contents

Tables

Figures

Preface

DR ELIOT TREVOR OAKESHOTT SLATER

The late Dr Eliot Slater registered as a postgraduate student in the Department of English at King's College, London in the autumn of 1977. He was awarded the London PhD in February 1982 for his statistical work on the vocabulary of the anonymous Elizabethan play *The Reign of King Edward III* (1596). These facts might seem unremarkable, were it not that this graduate student entered professional English studies in his seventy-fourth year and in his retirement from an internationally eminent career in psychiatry.

Dr Slater's interest in Shakespeare was sustained and deeply personal. Before he came to King's he had already published articles and notes in *Notes and Queries* and in *The Bard* on the subject of the chronology of Shakespeare's works, based on analysis of the rarer elements in their vocabulary. With the encouragement of the late James Maxwell, then editor of *Notes and Queries*, Dr Slater decided to devote himself to more sustained study in his retirement. Unlike many other amateurs of Shakespearean scholarship, he resolutely set on one side his deep curiosity about the personality and psychology of Shakespeare and asked to be given a useful job to do. On my suggestion, he turned back to the work of Alfred Hart on the vocabulary of plays attributed to Shakespeare. He soon decided that the authorship of *Edward III* offered a suitable case for his treatment.

With increasing difficulty as his health deteriorated and in face of a number of disappointments and set-backs – most dauntingly, his reluctant acceptance that computer-aided analysis of vocabulary could not alone determine the chronology of Shakespeare's works – Eliot Slater completed his PhD thesis, 'The Problem of *The Reign of King Edward III* (1596): a Statistical Approach'. He took his own line of enquiry as far as it could go. His findings, though in the nature of the case they could not be decisive in favour of Shakespeare's authorship of the play, will remain an important point of reference for future investigators. His study bears the print of a rare personality, whose sharp observation and dry wit impart life to the dry bones of a statistical argument. Not least, it offers a trenchant critique of some earlier methods used in the attempt to solve the question of attribution.

As a final, personal note I wish to record my gratitude to a remarkable student for his patient forbearance with a supervisor many years his junior in years, experience and wisdom. Guiding, and following, his work was an educative experience I should have been sorry to miss.

Richard Proudfoot
King's College, London
26 October 1987

Acknowledgements

My first thanks go to my Supervisor at King's College, Dr. Richard Proudfoot, who has guided my progress throughout (apart from the more purely statistical work). His comments, based on a scholarship to which the writer can lay no claim, though silently accepted as a rule, have been subjoined in footnotes to the text, where that was called for. I have received indispensable help from the Computer Unit at King's College, and especially from Miss Margaret Skinner and Mrs Christine Brown. I have had much help from the London Library and the Senate House Library of the University of London. Lastly my daughter, Dr. Ann Pasternak of St Anne's College, Oxford, has given me unfailing support, in assembling sources, reading and commenting on the text, and correcting lapses or errors in the written word.

The Raigne of King Edward the third

*Edward III** first appeared as an entry in the Stationers' Register on 1 December 1595.
The First Quarto was published in the following year: *The Raigne of King Edward the
third: As it hath bin sundrie times plaied about the Citie of London. London. Printed for
Cuthbert Burby. 1596.*[1] A second quarto, also printed for Burby, appeared in 1599.
There is a good deal of difference of opinion about when the play was most
probably written. According to Farmer, on the title page of his facsimile edition of
the first quarto, the play was written about 1589. However, Muir[16] thinks it likely it
was written after 1593, because of its allusion to *Lucrece* in lines 1019–22:

> Arise true English Ladie, whom our Ile
> May better boast of then ever Romaine might,
> Of her whose ransackt treasurie hath taskt,
> The vaine indevor of so many pens:

No other critic has made much of this. Both Ribner[21] and Scharr[22] think the play
was written 1592–3; Østerberg[19] before 1592; Jackson[12] about 1590; Wentersdorf[27]
1589–90; and Lapides[14] any time between 1588 and 1592.

For purposes of comparison we may note that there is general agreement that all
three parts of *King Henry VI* were written before the end of 1591. Chambers,
Harrison and the Arden editors place *Richard III* and *Titus Andronicus* closely
following in 1592–3. If it were Shakespeare's, then, *Edward III* would be among his
earliest creations. By the end of 1595 *The Taming of the Shrew*, *The Comedy of Errors*,
The Two Gentlemen of Verona, *Love's Labour's Lost*, *Romeo and Juliet*, *A
Midsummer Night's Dream* and *Richard II* had all been staged. The first and second
parts of *Tamburlaine* had been produced a number of years earlier, in 1587 and 1588.
So if *Edward III* were Marlowe's, it would be a work of his maturity.

Capell published *Edward III* in 1760 as 'a Play thought to be writ by Shakespeare'.
It has been reprinted a number of times, the first quarto of 1596 being taken as
authoritative. Since 1760 the question of Shakespearean authorship has been batted
to and fro by editors and critics. Some have maintained that the whole of the play is
by Shakespeare, and some that none of it is. Others to whom parts or the whole
have been attributed include Drayton, Greene, Lodge and Peele. No general
agreement has yet been reached. The balance of opinion has tended to favour

---

*For this book the Tudor Facsimile Text, edited by John S. Farmer, published in 1910, has been relied on; with
reference, for a modern scholarly edition, to that edited by R. L. Armstrong in *Six Early Plays Related to the
Shakespeare Canon*, ed. E. A. Everitt, Copenhagen, 1965.

divided authorship, the Countess scenes in particular being allotted to Shakespeare.

In the present century the history of criticism begins with Tucker Brooke's edition of the play in his book *The Shakespeare Apocrypha*, 1908[4]. Brooke included in the *Apocrypha* edited texts of fourteen plays or parts of plays, but as candidates for acceptance into the canon he dismissed them all. The selection made for the First Folio cannot be faulted. We have the genuine articles – and the apocrypha, mostly poor stuff. Though some have merits, even great merits, they are not Shakespearean merits. In short, they can never pass Shakespearean standards and must be judged by apocryphal standards. *Edward III* fails along with the others.

The play is 'broken-backed', falling into two irreconcilable halves. The first two acts are a love intrigue. The beginning of Act III brings a complete change of plot and a considerable dimunition of dramatic force. The last acts, 'though full of fine dramatic poetry', are not Shakespeare (p. xxi). And looking again at the Countess scenes, 'so much more Shakespearean at first sight', one sees they are in reality by the same author as the rest of the drama. The two references to the Countess story in III.iii and III.v show that the author of Act III must have had the contents of I and II before his mind (ibid.). Brooke finds other reasons for favouring singleness of authorship. Wherever in the last three acts the necessity of portraying actual events disappears, there is a return to the style of the earlier unhistoric scenes. Such parts actually 'give more pleasure to the true student and lover of the play than the brilliant intrigue scenes of the first acts which have . . . a rather cloying sweetness' (p. xxii). These scenes will hardly bear reading frequently:

Tried by the test of what they say, not how they say it, these passages sound hollow and insincere; the sophistry of nearly all the arguments becomes more objectionable . . . as one comes to feel . . . how much the characters guide their actions by the dictates of complex academic reasoning and how little by the inner voice of nature (pp. xxi–xxiii).

Brooke, in fact, finds the military scenes of the last three acts more to his taste than 'the quibbling mawkishness' of Warwick and the Countess. He singles out for high praise IV.viii.6–8 (in his edition; Farmer, ll. 2275–7) and V.27–30 (2376–80):

We recognize the writer's love of noble situations and his sympathy with high-minded characters, but the continual inferiority of his hand to his heart is equally obvious. The inability to grasp strongly the realities of life produces in the historical scenes a woodenness and restraint, which mark these portions of the play as distinctly un-Shakespearean, despite several bursts of magnificent poetry (p. xxii).

Tucker Brooke's verdict is, then, that all of the play is by one author, and that author not Shakespeare. He says he would like to see 'this fine though very imperfect play recognized as the crown and conclusion of the work of George Peele', a thesis which he then argues to maintain.

Brooke believed that the sources of the play were, for the Countess scenes, Painter's *Palace of Pleasure*, and for most of the rest Holinshed's *Chronicles*, with an unknown source for the Villiers–Salisbury episode in Act IV. However, in 1911 R. M. Smith[24] showed with chapter and verse that the whole of Act I, scene i, and the whole of the main part of the play from III.i to the end of Act v, had been taken from Froissart; and finally that the Countess episode was described in detail by Froissart, taken over by Bandello and from him by Painter, and so finally back to *Edward III*:

Many critics, who insist that the Countess episode interrupts the main play, urge the fact as proof that the episode was thrust into an earlier version by Shakespeare. But this episode holds in the French chronicle the same position which the dramatic version of it holds in the play. It is evident, therefore, that the dramatist merely followed the order of events that Froissart had established, and selected only certain details from Painter for the Countess scenes (p. 101).

On the possibly Shakespearean authorship of the play Smith says that the contention that Shakespeare wrote the entire play can be dismissed at once. None of the critics offer reasons other than aesthetic to support the theory:

The whole drama is by no means up to Shakespeare's level. There is an absence of comedy, and a general want of characterization. Furthermore, the drama was never considered Shakespeare's until the eighteenth century, nor is there external evidence in favor of his authorship. Finally, the whole play was written at one time by one dramatist who took nearly all of his material from Froissart's Chronicles; and Shakespere probably never consulted Froissart for chronicle history plays (p. 103).

On the Marlovian possibility Smith continues:

It is equally difficult to believe that Marlowe wrote the play. Aside from the Marlowesque blank verse and bombast which were employed in all drama after the appearance of Tamburlaine in 1587, *Edward III* bears none of that dramatist's well known characteristics. There is no protagonist, no attempt at such plot construction as is found in *Edward II*; nothing but the presentation of an interesting chronicle narrative taken wholly from one source. Furthermore, the portrayal of such a woman character as the Countess was totally foreign to Marlowe's genius. These facts, with others, make it probable that the whole drama was written by one playwright three or four years earlier than Mr. Fleay's date 1594, perhaps 1590, before Marlowe had put his final stamp upon Chronicle History Plays (p. 104).

Who that one playwright might have been, Professor Smith does not venture to conjecture.

Smith laid a firm foundation for our present understanding of the sources of *Edward III*, in plot and sub-plots, which has not subsequently been undermined; but, against his hopes, it seems to have had no effect at all on the debate about the authorship. This has remained as conjectural as ever. By far the most critical evidence has come from the work of Alfred Hart.[9] This is statistical in nature and will be considered later. At this point we may notice the opinions advanced by Golding, Crundell and Østerberg. Of these only the last is worth serious attention.

Golding[8] reports that from his perusal of the play he soon became 'convinced' then its author was 'undoubtedly' Robert Wilson (p. 313); and he noted and lists 30 parallels with *A Larum for London* totalling 125 lines of verse. Of these Nos. 5 to 11 are with *Edward III*, I.ii to II.ii. Golding has been alone in his attribution, and no other critic has reported being impressed by his parallel. Parallelisms, it would seem, are more or less convincing as evidence of community of authorship by their

3

appeal to a subjective judgment. Moreover, the quality of that judgment is dependent on the discriminatory powers of the controversialist and the intimacy of his knowledge of a whole epoch of creative writing. The extent to which his arguments may also be found acceptable by others may be affected by current critical fashions and academic stereotypes. This sort of evidence is certainly not such with which the unlearned should venture to concern himself.

The arguments of Crundell[5] are somewhat more widely based than those of Golding. He claims that there is a general likeness of *Edward III* (in both parts) to the work of Michael Drayton, and that it is more reasonable to regard it as an early work of Drayton's than to ascribe the play to Shakespeare or Greene. The 'likeness' is to be found in incidents, rhetoric, style, borrowings, and the comparison of certain passages.

Østerberg[19] considers only the Countess scenes, i.ii and Act II, and expresses no opinion about the rest of the play. These scenes are of the highest poetic and dramatic merit, and Shakespearean in *character*. The balance of the evidence is decidedly in favour of Shakespearean *authorship*.

Østerberg bases his appreciation on the following qualities of the 'Countess' scenes:

1. their technical mastery;
2. dependence for dramatic tension on character rather than action;
3. the human earnestness as well as artistic excellence;
4. sound though limited psychology;
5. the union of linguistic and rhythmic power, poetic imagination and thought;
6. the ethical standard maintained throughout.

He then proceeds to examine parallels between passages in *Edward III* and others in *Venus, Lucrece, Romeo, Love's Labour's Lost* and the Sonnets. These are numerous and extensive, and some of them are striking. Østerberg also makes comparisons of sentiment, phraseology and rhythm, and tricks of word repetition.

He finds communalities of vocabulary between *Edward III* and Shakespeare's poems, observable in common usages, but also 'striking coincidences in the use of rarer and even "remarkable" ones' (p. 65). He lists: *scornful* (i.e. scorned), *wistly, reverent, cloak* (vb), *stain, let* (i.e. hindrance), *forbidding, untuned, insulting, lament* (n), *languishment, misdeed, mote, oratory, cabinet*. He also records combinations. 'Fly it a pitch above the soar of praise' of *Edward III* shows the combination soar–above–pitch found also in *Romeo, Julius Caesar* and *Richard II*. *Love's Labour's Lost* furnishes a number of uncommon words held in common with *Edward III*: *mote, muster, via, unseen wind, solicitor, immure, barbarism, cadence, foragement, faceless*. Communalities are also found with a number of the Sonnets, *A Midsummer Night's Dream, John, Merchant of Venice, Taming of the Shrew*, 2 Henry IV, Henry V (*gimmal, ordure, fluent*), *Hamlet, Measure for Measure, Lear* (*dislodge, grained ash*), *Coriolanus* (*twist*, n), *Antony* (*snaffle, tissue, treasurer*), *Timon* (*solder, wither*, trans. vb).

Østerberg examines parallelisms pointed out by others, e.g. by Robertson in

Greene, but believes them to be mainly delusive. He has counted, and names, a number of words found in *Edward III* but not elsewhere in Shakespeare, and he argues against giving them importance. On this point Muir's discussion (see pp. 5–7 below) is greatly to be preferred. Østerberg enters on some other matters, such as versification, which need not concern us. He concludes by advancing his theory of authorship. This is that there was an early play, written by several authors in conjunction, probably Marlowe, Kyd and Greene. About the time of the re-opening of the theatres in 1594 the play was acquired by the company to which Shakespeare belonged, and '*as usual*' (p. 90) Shakespeare was employed in dressing up the play. He then inserted his own vivid and spirited piece of poetry.

We are indebted to Kenneth Muir for the most recent full and scholarly review of the authorship problem. His first essay,[16] 'A reconsideration of *Edward III*', appeared in *Shakespeare Survey* in 1953. In a revised form[17] it was re-published as Chapter 2, 'Shakespeare's hand in *Edward III*', in his book, *Shakespeare as Collaborator*, 1960. The third chapter, '*Edward III*', examines the play's merits and demerits. Muir notes that some of the imagery in the Countess scenes recalls that of the Sonnets, *Romeo and Juliet* and *Love's Labour's Lost*. He concludes that if one were to follow Tucker Brooke in attributing the play, or parts of it, to Peele, one could account for the great unevenness in the quality of the poetry by supposing that Shakespeare revised a play by Peele, re-writing the Countess scenes and making extensive alterations in Act IV. But the evidence for Peele's hand in *Edward III* is slight, he thinks.

In his 1953 essay[16] Muir discusses the vocabulary tests published by Hart,[9] which we will examine later. Muir is particularly impressed by the frequency of compound and participial words, conspicuously high both in *Edward III* and in the works of Shakespeare, where they are two or three times as frequent as in Marlowe, Greene and Peele. Muir seems to consider this test alone as sufficient to dismiss these three as candidates for the authorship.

Muir then offers his own counts for one of Hart's tests, not applied by the latter to *Edward III*. This is the occurrence of words not used before in Shakespeare's plays. Muir divides *Edward III* into two parts, hypothetically Shakespearean and non-Shakespearean. The former, part A, is selected to include Act I scene ii, lines 90 and following, the whole of Act II and Act IV scene iv. Part B, the non-Shakespearean part, is the rest of the play. This excludes a substantial piece, including a soliloquy by the Countess, but starts with her re-entry at line 276 and goes down to the end of Act II with line 1037. Of Act IV it includes lines 1914 to 2079 inclusive. The entire play runs to 2600 lines, and by Muir's division part A has 928 lines and part B 1672. He tabulates the numbers of new words in parts A and B in six different counts: (a) when only Shakespeare's plays are taken into account, and (b) when the poems are also comprehended; and by date: if *Edward III* was written in 1597 (before *1 Henry IV*), if in 1596 (before *King John*), or in 1594 (before *Richard II*). In all six presentations the number of new words in part A outnumbers the new words in part B; and in terms of lines per new word, almost exactly twice as many lines on average are required for a new word in part B as in part A. We may note that the difference between the two parts is statistically significant in all six presentations. We need instance only one of them. As we are considering Shakespeare as a writer, or a total personality, rather than as mere playwright, it seems well to take Muir's count, which includes both poems and plays; and as *Edward III* was published in 1595, Muir's counts for 1594 seem to be the most appropriate. In this count he found a total of 145 new words, 78 in part A, 67 in part B. The number to be expected, on the supposition of a single writer for both parts, would be proportionate to the number of lines available, 928:1672, i.e. not 78:67 but 51.75:93.25. The difference between observation and expectation is 26.25, and χ^2, the sum of $(0-E)^2/E$, where O is the observed and E the expected number, is $13.315 + 7.389 = 20.704$. This is far larger than any number which could plausibly be attained even by an exceedingly remote chance. We can say, then, that on this criterion, there is a large and real difference between the two parts of the play – from whatever cause.

Muir then proceeds to a study of the imagery. He says there are about twice as many images in proportion to the number of lines in A as in B, one image per 3.8 lines as compared with one per 7 lines. An observation of this kind is not susceptible to statistical tests without a rigid if arbitrary definition of what constitutes an 'image'. The same limitation applies to Muir's observations on iterative imagery and image-clusters. Muir then has a short passage on parallels, finding them in *As You Like It, Hamlet, Richard III, Love's Labour's Lost, Twelfth Night, Winter's Tale, Much Ado, 2 Henry IV, Macbeth, Antony, 3 Henry VI, Henry V, Measure for Measure.*

Muir concludes by admitting that his arguments may not be conclusive. If Shakespeare was not the author of *Edward III*, he was at least intimately acquainted with it and deeply influenced by it. A theory which would cover all the facts is that Shakespeare, as perhaps in *Pericles*, was hastily revising a play by another dramatist, certain scenes being entirely re-written, and the remainder being left with comparatively few alterations.

In the revised edition of this essay, which he published in 1960 as Chapter 2 of his book *Shakespeare as Collaborator*, Muir changed his views and their presentation very little. He lists as inconclusive the following statistical observations reported by Alfred Hart:

(a) the average number of words used in some of Shakespeare's Histories is not very different from the number used in *Edward III*, not very different from the number used in some of Marlowe's plays;

(b) the vocabulary common to *Edward III* and some of Shakespeare's Histories is not very different in proportion to the vocabulary common to *Edward III* and some of Marlowe's plays (this objection is not well founded, as we shall see);

(c) nor is there any significant difference in the use of certain prefixes and suffixes in *Edward III* in comparison with some of Shakespeare's Histories and some of Marlowe's plays.

We shall come later to a detailed discussion of Hart's work.

Muir then takes note of Mary Bell's thesis[3] on *Edward III*, in which she included a concordance. He is impressed by the compounds: *light borne, under garnished, summer leaping, sole reigning, bed blotting, honey gathering, poison sucking,* in part A; and in part B *ever bibbing, Bayard-like, high-swollen, iron-harted, sweet-flowering, stiff-grown, .imble jointed, swift-starting,* and *just-dooming* 'to mention only a few'. Yet while all the '-like' compounds appear in Part B, all the six 'thrice-' formations are in part A. Mary Bell reported a close resemblance between the vocabularies of the three *Henry VI* plays and *Edward III;* many words used once only in *Henry VI* are to be found also in *Edward III.* 'This evidence', says Muir, 'is ambiguous, since some critics still believe that *Henry VI* is not wholly Shakespearean.' Surely what the critics still believe is subjective and non-evidential. If it can be said that Mary Bell has disclosed communalities and resemblances between the vocabularies of *1 Henry VI* and *Edward III,* this is objective factual evidence connecting two plays, whoever their Authors may have been. Muir then develops his commentary on the imagery of *Edward III* with greater depth and variety than in his essay of 1953.

In concluding his chapter Muir inclines to the theory of double authorship, with the Countess scenes and IV.iv allotted to Shakespeare. The strongest support for this judgment is the presence of close parallels with *Henry V* and *Measure for Measure.* He then, as in the 1953 essay, suggests a Shakespearean revision of another dramatist's work. This theory has the weakness that no named playwright, certainly not Greene or Marlowe or Peele, can be suggested for the job.

Over the years from the fifties to the seventies of the present century there seems to have been a variable tendency to shift from the theory of multiple authorship to that of single authorship. In a University of Texas dissertation of 1956, W. B. Dobson[6] engaged in an elaborate discussion of the sources of each scene, the Author's habits of composition, the possibilities of single or multiple authorship, and the probable date of composition. He thinks there is sufficient evidence to conclude that the Countess scenes are interpolations by a second author. In comparison with other scenes, these passages have a firmer plot structure and are superior in originality. They introduce the character of Lodowick, who does not reappear in later scenes. They portray the Countess and the King in a manner inconsistent with characterisation in the rest of the play. They make more frequent and noticeably different use of imagery. They are somewhat less rigid in metre, and have a higher percentage of rhyming lines, and in general a more lyrical and rhetorical style. The Countess scenes may echo the style of Shakespeare's lyrical plays and narrative poems – but are not necessarily written by Shakespeare.

A few years later, in 1960, in a dissertation presented to the University of Cincinnati, K. P. Wentersdorf[26] takes an almost diametrically opposite point of view. Similar arguments are also advanced in his article of 1965.[27] He shows how Shakespeare's imagery differs from that of his contemporaries. The homogeneity of *Edward III* militates against any theory of multiple authorship. Main groups of imagery are drawn from the same areas of experience as those Shakespeare drew on. The Author of *Edward III* used the same kind of images in the same proportions from the same mental standpoint as Shakespeare. The possibility that the parallels of *Edward III* and the canon result from borrowing is untenable, as many relate to later work:

The view that Shakespeare is the borrower is not forbidden by chronology; to accept it, however, one must assume that Shakespeare was well acquainted with *Edward III* at a very early stage in his career, since there are many parallels in the narrative poems, and that he either possessed or developed the same artistic tastes as the unknown Author in the matter of image-subjects. Furthermore that the play impressed itself on his mind so powerfully that he reproduced multiple echoes from it throughout the rest of his long career.

A hypothesis requiring all these assumptions has little to recommend it in the face of the natural interpretation of the clusters, namely that these thoughts and images developed in the mind of one man – William Shakespeare.

In his study of the imagery of *Edward III* (1965), Wentersdorf[27] quoted other authors. He noted that Tillyard (1944)[25] regarded the play as 'evidently written' not by a professional dramatist, but by a university-trained courtier who had been greatly influenced by Shakespeare's idiom. Irving Ribner (1957),[20] Wentersdorf thought, read not only the love element but a great deal more of the play as Shakespearean in origin; and Frank O'Connor (1961)[18] considered the whole play of single authorship, manifesting clear evidence of Shakespeare's draftsmanship throughout. Wentersdorf dates the play at any time between 1588 and 1595, but most likely near the earlier of these two dates. The play breathes the nationalistic feeling that was strong in the years before the Armada. Wentersdorf sees many resemblances between *Edward III* and the first part of *Henry VI*. 'Quite apart from the similarity of tone, *Edward III* has many points of resemblance in diction, imagery and the treatment of subject matter in the play about Talbot' (p. 231). The latter was written not later than 1591–2, possibly a year or two earlier, as it has plausibly been asserted that it preceded *Henry VI* Parts 2 and 3. 'It seems ... most likely that *Edward III* was written, as the topical allusions to the Armada and to the *Nonpareil* indicate, about 1589–90' (ibid).

Wentersdorf considers that arguments against Shakespearean authorship have been based on its stylistic inferiority, especially when compared with *Henry V*. If it was written in 1594–5, the argument that Shakespeare could not have been the author is stronger than if the play was written in 1589–90. The account of the sea-battle is modelled on reports of the English triumph over the Spanish in 1588. The account in Froissart of the Battle of Sluys, 1340, described ships grappled together and hand to hand fighting. The account in *Edward III* has the anachronistic use of artillery. The highly imaginative description of the artillery effects is evidently one of the dramatist's additions.

The contributions of Claes Schaar (1962)[22] was to analyse the parallelisms between *Edward III*, Act II, and Shakespearean Sonnets, especially 7, 94, 127. Like other critics Schaar was greatly struck by identities of 'scarlet ornaments' and 'lilies that fester smell far worse than weeds'. As long ago as 1911, Arthur Platt[20] pointed out that the reference to lilies that fester is appropriate in the Sonnet, but in *Edward*

III is irrelevant. 'Scarlet ornaments' passes in the Sonnet, but applied to the cheeks of King Edward is quite ridiculous. The Sonnets were antecedent to the play, and must have been available to the author before the publication date of 1596. Platt writes 'after repeated readings of the play ... I feel more and more convinced that the whole of it is due to one hand alone', (p. 513) – and that not Shakespeare's.

Schaar thinks the whole of Lodowick's description of the behaviour of King Edward bears comparison with a series of passages in canonical works (*TGV*, *Shr*, *R2*, *1H4*). The notorious identities discussed by Platt above have their full force only in the Sonnets, and where they occur in the plays they do not ring naturally. Likewise parallel phrases in *Edward III* and *Measure for Measure* are better expressed and are more appropriate in the Shakespearean play than in the apocryphal one. The better versions are likely to be the later ones. Schaar writes

I have come to visualise the [Author] as having at his elbow a manuscript copy of Shakespeare's sonnets, or of some of them, dipping occasionally into the slender volume to appropriate an image or a phrase. [The present writer finds this imagined way of composing quite unthinkable.] If so he had access only while composing the last part of I.ii, and the first part of Act II. Sonnets 7, 33, 94, 127 and 143 were available to the [Author]. The iterative imagery in these parts of *Edwrd III* suggest Shakespeare's authentic work.

Schaar concludes that if Shakespeare had a finger in the main part of *Edward III*, he had at least a hand in the Countess scenes.

Koskenniemi (1964)[13] differs from the majority of critics in objecting to the tendency to divide the play into two parts, one about twice the magnitude of the smaller. He quotes both Tillyard (1944)[25] and Ribner (1957)[21] in support of the view that the Countess scenes play an integral part in the education of the King. Tillyard saw a main theme in the education of those that have power: in the education of the King to self-mastery, and in that of the Black Prince to enter battle in hand to hand fighting, together with his education, through the wise words of Audley, to face death with equanimity. Queen Philippa teaches the King to show mercy to hostages; and she herself is given a moral lesson in what should be a royal attitude to the exceptional bravery of a subject (Sir John Copeland). Respect for marriage and respect for an oath are inculated in more than one episode. Numerous images are supplied to support the emotional background of these teachings: school, learning, teaching, law, justice, crime and punishment. This presentation, which is taken up again by William Armstrong (1966),[2] makes the play something of a sermon.

Koskenniemi examines the case for other possible candidates for the authorship, including Peele, proposed by Tucker Brooke.[4] He thinks there is no similarity in imagery. He also examines the candidacy of Thomas Kyd (proposed by G. Lambrechts), but here objects that a common imagery, with striking parallels, has little evidential value, since it all comes from a stock of imagery common to and used by many dramatists of the time. Koskenniemi concludes that Shakespeare wrote at least some parts of *Edward III* and revised the whole. King Edward III is mentioned fifteen times in Shakespeare's history plays: and the King and the Black Prince are held up as models of military and political virtue.

McD. P. Jackson has contributed two notes. The second (1971)[12] is of minor interest to us here: he argues that the Author's foul papers served as copy for the Quarto. In an earlier work (1965),[11] he states categorically: 'It is now virtually certain that Shakespeare had at least a share in the writing of *Edward III*', and that 'there are excellent reasons for believing he wrote it all'. To support this emphatic judgment he calls upon Muir and Wentersdorf to stand at his side. Jackson gives an early dating to *Edward III*, confirming Wentersdorf: about 1590.

The debate about this play has ranged far and wide; but the conclusions of any one critic are usually taken seriously only by members of his own party. Schoenbaum (1966)[23] takes the play as a text for a sermon on the need for caution in appraising internal evidence. His dismissive résumé of the work of Alfred Hart (very generally ignored by others) amounts to little more than allowing him to show that the Author of *Edward III* had in common with Shakespeare 'a remarkably rich vocabulary' (p 126). Schoenbaum also gives some attention to image-clusters, mentioning that some acceptedly Shakespearean clusters appear in the works of other writers. 'No matter how promising a new test may seem, it behooves the investigator to proceed with extreme caution' (p. 189).

F. R. Lapides (1966)[14] prepared a new critical edition of *The Raigne of Edward III* as a Rutgers Dissertation. He collected and collated his text from all available copies of the Quarto. He tries to show that in image-parallels, associational clusters and vocabulary tests, Shakespeare is the only Elizabethan who could have written the play. It was written no earlier than 1588 and no later than 1592. His thesis includes a theatrical history of the play, a study of the sources, Froissart and Painter, and a critical study of the plotting, of the character drawing, and of the poetry. Finally he examines the efforts of the printer(s), working from Author's foul papers, and marks and discusses the variant readings. This thesis would seem to be a useful source-book for textual criticism (which, however, is not the main focus of my study).

F. D. Horn (1969)[10] also produced a critical edition of the play as a dissertation for the University of Delaware. He undertook a careful image study and discovered no fewer than twelve clusters. He concludes that the play could only have been the work of Shakespeare:

Charges of faulty structure and poor characterisation are found unconvincing after close study. There is a sense of unity throughout the play, strengthened by a strong central theme. Even though this dominant theme tends to cast all Englishmen in roles as strong, prudent and generous warriors, and all Frenchmen as boastful, imprudent and ultimately craven individuals, the [Author] has created an entire play, not only of persons, but also of personalities, especially important figures such as King Edward, the Countess of Salisbury, Prince Edward, Warwick and Artois ... [*Edward III*] dramatizes the dangers of frivolous deeds and the rewards of noble behavior, and demonstrates that the appropriate response to potential tyranny is wise and understanding counsel.

As the latest addition to the critical literature we have Georgio Melchiori's book (1976),[15] *Shakespeare's Dramatic Meditations*. Dealt with in depth are four of the Sonnets of most equivocal mood and many-sided interpretation, Sonnets 94, 121,

129 and 146. Sonnet 94 is held to provide the most intimate parallels with *Edward III* (also with *Measure for Measure* and *Hamlet*). It is the mighty who are the lords and masters of their faces: this means the King and not Warwick. The mighty, only apparently just, have absolute control over their outer forms. The others, their stewards, may be honest, like Warwick, and masters of their honour, but are in honour bound to serve the 'excellence', that is to say the superior status, of their lords and masters, whatever the form their superiority may take. Melchiori thinks that Sonnet 94 (and many others) was written after, not before *Edward III*.

The present writer cannot accept the line of argument and the comparisons adduced by Melchiori. Shakespeare distinguishes between the lords and masters and the 'others'. Those others, however honest, have a contemptible status in Shakespeare's scheme of things, and, in his view, deserve no attention at all. The first seven lines of the octave are given entirely to the dominance of those that *have* power; and of course the whole of *Edward III* is given to the supreme aim of the conquest of power. Melchiori is right in thinking and saying that Shakespeare has a highly critical attitude towards them. But they are still the only persons of consequence in his world. The masters, by having the power and compelling their stewards, such as Warwick, to exercise it, divest themselves of responsibility, and in so escaping the consequences, become dehumanised, and 'moving others are themselves as stone, / Unmoved, cold and to temptation slow'. But the analogy fails at many points. King Edward's blood is on fire. Temptation has such a grip on him that he has become its slave. It is made clear that King Edward tries to have at least a companion in villainy, and to move Warwick to do his business for him. The appositeness of the Sonnet to *Edward III* consists only in this, that the Author, in each case, is completely aware of the extent to which they that have power to hurt and will do none can attain their ends by devious means.

Many and various are the views that have been taken by scholars about *Edward III*. On the whole they tend to be critical and to feel that the play falls below the level of the canonical work. But there is no agreement on what the faults are. Even the phrases used in criticising it could be read in another context as expressions of appreciation. Great attention is paid to metaphor and imagery, and industrious search is made for parallels in other works, by both Shakespeare and others. But there is no criterion of what is a parallel and what is not. If a parallel is found (e.g. 'scarlet ornaments'), commonly no conclusion can be drawn on whether A borrowed from B, or B from A, or whether B and A are one and the same person. There is no agreement among the scholars on whether the play is or is not by a single author. There is no agreement on whether the play does or does not fall into two parts, the Countess scenes and the others, either by difference in authorship, or in time or mood of composition. It would not seem that the work of disintegration has been effectively done. In their preoccupation with poetic and dramatic values, the critics have paid but scant attention to the mind of the playwright.

Once one does call him into view one sees the evidence of a formidable intellect. Here is a man who has constructed for himself a highly individual Weltanschauung which (for what the impression is worth), underlying both parts of the play, speaks for a single authorship. This man's view of life, informed by a wide and mature experience, is essentially realistic and pessimistic. But the vision which sees the world is guarded by distance and objectivity. There is a powerful and compassionate awareness of human suffering, but the author reserves his own integrity by personal non-involvement. He will not permit the emotions either of his characters or of his audience to touch that ironic internal serenity. As is often the case with pessimists, there is a wry sense of humour and a grasp of the comic aspects of human pretensions, failures and absurdities. The author has not merely played with but has felt his way into the human problems of the great institutions, statecraft, kingship, war and peace. He sees them in the terms of a philosophy which, though not profound, is universal and all-embracing. In the writer's world the stage is vast; and on it, eternal and unequal protagonists, Man stands in confrontation with Destiny.

2

The statistical study of
literary vocabulary

Udny Yule, the Cambridge statistician, published his book with this title in 1944.[4]
At the time when he had nearly finished his work he believed he was an all-time
pioneer. 'It seems almost strange', he wrote, 'that no statistician, so far as I am
aware, should have specially devoted himself to this branch of work during the past
half-century of rapid advance in statistical method' (p. 7). He then discovered that
he had had predecessors, though the most important, G. K. Zipf, seems to have
been a linguist rather than a statistician. Zipf's work,[5] according to Yule, contained
three tables of word distribution, for Latin, for English and for Chinese. There was
a very important difference between Yule and Zipf. Zipf entered every inflection
separately (as is the practice in a concordance), whereas Yule classified inflections
with the stem from which they derived (as is the practice in a dictionary). A less
important difference is that Yule concerned himself almost exclusively with nouns,
but Zipf with all parts of speech. Nevertheless both workers found out that
wherever word-frequency distributions were examined (whatever the language,
whoever the author, whatever the length of the sample), they showed three cardinal
features:

1. Unique words, used only once by the author in a given substantial sample of his
   writing, greatly outnumbered those used twice, and they in their turn outnumbered
   those used thrice, and so on. If x is the number of times a given word is used, and f_x is
   the number of that category of words, then f_x tends to diminish as x increases*.
2. While f_x diminishes as x increases, the rate of decrement gets less and less. The
   distribution curve flattens out.
3. The once-words (for which $x = 1$) remain a high proportion, however one increases the
   size of the sample. However long a man goes on writing, his mind seems to remain as
   well stocked as ever of words he has never used before.

To show these features as they actually appeared, Yule's tabulation of the nouns
appearing in the *De Imitatione Christi* is quoted below in an abbreviated form. The
top and tail ends of the distribution are shown in exact numbers, but over the
middle of the range the numbers of words of middling frequency are grouped
together in groups of ten x-values.

---

* Zipf speculated that the value of x multiplied by the number of its exemplars tended to vary about a constant.
Yule could not agree. In fact Yule could not convince himself he had found a satisfactory mathematical model,
though he inclined to think complex or multiple Poisson curves looked most like the observed data. This point will
not be discussed here. But beyond this Yule found himself unable to suggest why the mind of man, in its use of a
treasury of words, should fall into such a strange and such a constant pattern.

Table 2.1. *Distribution of nouns in* De Imitatione Christi *(extracted from Yule, Table 11.1).*

x	f_x	x	f_x	x	f_x
1	520	10–19	76	102	1
2	174	20–29	28	104	1
3	111	30–39	22	135	1
4	70	40–49	9	146	1
5	37	50–59	9	172	1
6	33	60–69	6	196	1
7	20	70–79	3	210	1
8	28	80–89	—	242	1
9	11	90–99	2	418	1

Note: Total nouns = 1168   Total occurences = 8225

The rare words are many; the 520 once-words constitute over 44% of the total of 1168 different words. The common nouns are few. There are only 9 that appear a hundred or more times, but together they account for 1725 occurrences or over one fifth of the total of 8225. There are only 60 nouns, 5% of the total of 1168, occurring thirty times or more; but they contribute 4185 occurrences, or over half the total. The commoner the noun, the more characteristic of the book, it seemed to Yule, 'until the final dozen or so seemed almost a brief epitome of the book itself – ANIMA: SPIRITUS: VERBUM: PAX: AMOR: CONSOLATIO: MUNDUS: VITA: NIHIL: COR: GRATIA: DOMINUS: HOMO: DEUS.

Yule hopes to use these features of word-frequency samples as an aid to the problems of disputed or doubtful authorship. He determined to restrict himself to nouns; but he began by showing that substantial samples of both adjectives and verbs showed exactly the same features as nouns: once-words outnumbered others, and groups of higher denomination diminished in size regularly but ever more slowly (see Table 2.2). He decided to ignore other parts of speech: 'My object was in part simply the limitation of the material and the exclusion of words of little or no significance as regards style, such as prepositions, pronouns, etc.' It is an irony of fate that modern computer-based 'stylometry' has concerned itself precisely with the words of 'little or no significance'. Yule notes that he occasionally got into difficulty deciding what was a noun. Verbal nouns in *-ing* were one difficulty; such formations as 'every thing' and 'every body', hyphenated nouns, and homonyms of different meanings were others. He set arbitrary rules for his guidance where possible; but sometimes an element of subjectivity in the judgment could not be avoided. He says that these were minor troubles; and differences of treatment would make very little difference in the final results.

Yule wanted to get at the heart of a man's command and use of language. He took as his experimental object the problem of the authorship of *De Imitatione Christi* (for short, *Imitatio*). The two principal candidates, each with a number of scholarly supporters, were Thomas à Kempis and Jean Charlier de Gerson. The *Imitatio* is a short work of some 42,000 words; and a concordance to it is available. Current arguments about the authorship seemed to Yule in the greater part inane, concerning themselves with such details as words used in unusual senses. Such minutiae are capable of giving an answer of sorts, as finger-prints may identify a criminal without telling us anything of substance about him. But Yule wanted a method of characterising the style of a writer as a whole; and a man's vocabulary seemed to him an eminently interesting and informative characteristic. He went ahead to draw up comparative noun-vocabularies for the *Imitatio*, for the other works of Thomas à Kempis, and for the religious works of Gerson. The programme broadened as it progressed, so that he was led into extending his base into Macaulay's many essays, the four main works of John Bunyan, words classified alphabetically or etymologically, and estimating the total number of nouns, adjectives and verbs in the Vulgate, the *Concise* and the *Shorter Oxford English Dictionary*. And on the other hand he plunged into more and more complex statistical theory and argument.

Very much more interesting are the speculative conclusions that Yule drew about the way one calls a word to mind. He showed that however many samples of a man's work are added, one to another, once-words continue to appear with undiminishing frequency. Their supply, available in the treasure-house of memory, may be by several orders of magnitude greater than the number that ever come to be employed. Just how great, for a man like Macaulay, one might make a rough guess from Yule's estimate of the numbers of words in the *Oxford Dictionaries*: in the *Concise Oxford* 24,600 nouns, 13,000 adjectives and 7700 verbs; in the *Shorter Oxford* 58,000 nouns, 27,000 adjectives and 13,500 verbs. Turning over the pages of a dictionary one becomes aware what a small proportion of the words it is that one actually uses or is likely to use. The number of those one recognises and would understand if encountered is far greater; and greater still is the number of those that stand in a penumbra where there is some understanding though vague and imprecise. What is the liability of a word available to the writer to be actually used? Yule denotes this probability value by the symbol v_λ:

In order to estimate v_λ we have to estimate w, the number of words at risk, the total number of words in the author's 'treasure-chest'. This number is, I believe, likely to be much larger, even very much larger, than the estimate usually given for an author's vocabulary, but the conception is an entirely different one. It is not a question of the number of words the author has in fact used in the finite field of his writings, but of how many words he had at call for purposes of use, and the phrase 'had at call' should be understood in the widest possible sense. It is, I think, true that every word one has ever read is in some sense stored in the mind: if one says one cannot *remember* the word for this or the other, one usually means no more than that one cannot at the moment *recall* it. That there *was* a record in the memory is shown by the fact of 'recognition' when the word does turn up, as was pointed out by St. Augustine over 1500 years ago (Conf. x, xix) . . . Capacity to recall is subject not only to secular change, to that all too familiar deterioration with age which often renders it impossible to recall when wanted even a well-known name or word, but to fluctuation from day to day, hour to hour, and second to second. At one instant we may be quite unable to recall a word that is wanted; a moment or two later, for no assignable reason, it may suddenly toss up ... No sharp line, I submit, can be drawn between such ill-trained dogs of words, which will not come when we whistle for them but soon appear from nowhere with a disarming smile, and those words which we fail to recall for some considerable period of time and then describe as 'completely forgotten'. Some casual, some exceptional stimulus may bring them back. So that, as I picture it, the writer's treasury really does contain all the words he has ever read, and for any man of wide reading they are bound to add up to a very impressive total.

[4.16.] To use a metaphor ... the writer's treasure-chest may be pictured as containing, beneath the top layers of words in daily and hourly use, lower layers of less frequently but still fairly frequently used words, words also fairly readily at call and in numbers greatly exceeding those in daily use. Below these again will be layers of words in still less frequent use, and more difficult to recall, but amounting in all to a still larger total. And right at the bottom of the chest there will be layer on dusty layer, but rarely disturbed, of words very infrequently used and very hard to recall. The xs for words in the top layers will be relatively large; for words in the bottom layers microscopically small, but not zero

(pp. 69–70).

To the present writer Yule's graphic metaphor reads in every way as true to life. In the textbooks of normal and abnormal psychology there are innumerable records of observations, both clinical and experimental, that bear it out. There is only one reservation. Memories for events, and so probably also for words, may on occasion be blotted out, apparently beyond any possibility of restitution, by actual physical damage to the brain.

The immensity of the resources of the treasure-house is shown by the fact that even huge samples will not exhaust a large treasury. In a sample from the Vulgate, a book of some 750,000 words or more, 'we still have as large a proportion of the nouns as 24 per cent occurring only once, and the most frequent words occur several thousand times'. Yule concludes that w, the treasure-chest, is in fact of incommensurable capacity; and a comparison between the used vocabularies of two writers may give no satisfactory answer or be quite misleading. So much depends on the differing proportions of rare and common words in any treasury.

Yule was able to show to his own satisfaction that Thomas à Kempis was the probable author of the *Imitatio*, and that the candidature of Gerson could be dismissed. His grounds seem quite adequate and will not be discussed here. What are, for our purposes, the most interesting parts of his observations are shown in the table below, and along with them a number of ratios calculated by the present writer. The word output of the authors studied by Yule is shown under T in the first column; all are of comparable magnitude, but dwarfed by Spevack's computer count for Shakespeare. The proportion of once-words is remarkably steady throughout the table; for Shakespeare this was calculated with the help of data from Hart.[2] The ratio T/V is the average number of times a vocabulary (dictionary type) word appears in the given text; the higher the number, the more words have been repeated and the more restricted the range; Gerson used a wider range, on average, than à Kempis, and Macaulay than Bunyan. The findings in the Shakespeare rows are staggeringly high, and need special discussion.

Yule occupied himself almost exclusively with nouns, though he took passing

Table 2.2 *Vocabulary analysis for* Imitatio, Bunyan, Macaulay, Shakespeare

	T	V	O	O/V	T/V	M	P
Imitatio							
nouns	8225	1168	520	0.45	7.0	30	0.0497
adjectives	5053	529	203	0.38	9.6	38	0.0491
verbs	8116	1157	407	0.35	7.0	18	0.0847
Theologians' nouns							
Imitatio	8225	1168	520	0.45	7.0	30	0.0497
à Kempis	8203	1406	621	0.44	5.8	19	0.0612
Gerson	8196	1754	804	0.46	4.7	14	0.0724
Bunyan and Macaulay							
Bunyan	16,056	2246	931	0.41	7.1	26	0.0503
Macaulay	20,178	3543	1460	0.41	5.7	16	0.0756
Shakespeare							
Total	884,647	17,677	7219	0.41	50.0	1796	0.0044
1/20 Concdce	27,852	1576	719	0.45	17.7	208	0.0140
1000 nouns	31,701	1000	346	0.35	31.7	400	0.0130

Columns: T=total number of words (usually nouns) counted in sample. V=vocabulary, i.e. total number of independent dictionary words in sample. O=number of once-words. O/V=proportion of once-words in vocabulary; note that this proportion varies very little, whatever the source. T/V=average number of occurrences of vocabulary word. M=median, i.e. number of appearances of word half-way between first and last; half of T has occurred with words of lower frequency, half at higher frequency. This number is always greater, sometimes very much greater, than T/V, the average, because of the extreme skewing of the distribution. P=that proportion of the V words, i.e. the very commonest, which account for half of the total output (T). *Rows:* Counts for different parts of speech in *Imitatio*. Distribution of counts of nouns in other works of Thomas à Kempis, and in religious works of Gerson, *Imitatio* excluded. Noun counts for Bunyan and Macaulay: Bunyan, *Pilgrim's Progress, Parts I and II, Life and Death of Mr. Badman, Holy War*; Macaulay, essays on Milton, Hampden, Bacon and Frederick the Great. Shakespeare: 884,647 is the number given by Spevack for the total number of words in the works of Shakespeare included in the *Harvard Concordance*, this is, then, a measure of Shakespeare's output. 17,677 is Hart's total for all independent dictionary words in Shakespeare. 7219 is Hart's total of 'one-play', or 'peculiar' words, which may be a slight over-estimate of the total once-words. 1796 is the number reached at 'go', 78th in order of frequency, half of T being contributed by still commoner words. For the next row every 20th entry in the *Concordance* was taken into the reckoning to provide corresponding figures to the above. For the last row a consecutive series of 1000 nouns was taken, to get a random sample of nouns.

notice of the adjectives and the verbs in the *Imitatio*. This restriction reduced the problems of definition. In considering Shakespearean vocabulary, however, other parts of speech will have to be taken into account. For psychological purposes, and for most linguistic and statistical purposes, the only satisfactory definition of a word is to follow dictionary usage*. A concordance word is a statistical entity in only a limited and incompletely defined sense. In his Preface to the *Harvard Concordance to*

* In this book, *The Shorter Oxford English Dictionary*, third edition, revised, 1969.

Shakespeare, Marvin Spevack[3] states that the complete works contain 884, 647 'words'. But to take one example, the word 'will' is included as a melee of three homographs, a verb, a noun and a name. There are 5306 occurrences of 'will', too many to be provided with a context, so that it is *impossible* to discover from the *Concordance* how many there are of each of the homographs. If we regard 884,647 words as constituting Shakespeare's 'vocabulary', in the special sense of total word output, we shall be over-estimating it in terms of current usage, which excludes proper names from the class of dictionary words. In abiding by dictionary criteria, homographs of radically different meanings or derivations are regarded as distinct words. So also are different parts of speech. On the other hand, inflections and contractions are regarded as variants of the stem word and are not held to be distinct entities. This is the practice that was followed by Yule, as also by Alfred Hart, whose work will shortly come up for discussion, and again by the present writer. Unless otherwise stated, in this book 'word' is always intended in the dictionary sense.

Distinct concepts are also combined, and sometimes confused, in 'vocabulary'. It has been said, for instance, that Shakespeare has 'a larger vocabulary' than Milton. This would be generally understood to mean that Shakespeare had at his command a larger treasury of words to draw on, a larger w in Yule's notation. As Yule convincingly showed, such a statement is exceedingly dangerous, since it can never be confirmed. The upper limit of w for any writer is always beyond computation. Its lower limit can be denominated and counted, however, since it must equal or exceed the actual number of words (in the dictionary sense) which the writer used. This is what we shall call his vocabulary. The majority of these vocabulary words will have been used, of course, again and again and again. The total number of words a writer has written can be termed his output. In this sense Spevack's number, 884,647, is an estimate of Shakespeare's output.

We must now consider how closely Shakespeare's output and vocabulary follow the patterns that were traced by Yule. Yule found that, however large a sample of a writer's work one took, one found no sign that the proportion of once-words tended to thin out or fail in frequency. Alfred Hart[1,2] conducted a systematic enumeration of the number of words (dictionary or D-words) in Shakespeare's plays and poems, which he published in 1943. He provided counts for 37 plays, including *Henry VIII*, and also *Venus*, *Lucrece* and the Sonnets and Poems, i.e. 40 rows of figures arranged in a standard chronology. The columns under which the numbers were listed included the length in lines, the number of (different D-) words, and a column of 'peculiar' words, also called 'one-play' words, i.e. words only found in a single opus, though whether once only or more than once is unstated. This is the nearest we get in Hart to Yule's once-words. Presumably all the once-words would be included under this heading, but there might be a few others in addition.

For the convenience of a rough test we may divide Hart's 40 rows into 4 epochs. In abbreviated notation Group 1 includes *2H6*, *3H6*, *1H6*, *R3*, *Err*, *Ven*, *Tit*, *Luc*, *TGV*, *Shr*; Group 2 includes *LLL*, *Rom*, *R2*, *MND*, *Jo*, *MV*, *1H4*, *2H4*, *Ado*, *H5*;

Table 2.3. *Vocabulary analysis (Hart) for Shakespeare (4 epochs)*

	No. of lines	Words	All new words	One-play words
Group 1	24,316	26,307	5244	1252
Group 2	27,467	28,172	3815	1870
Group 3	28,820	28,615	3056	2067
Group 4	27,225	28,534	2256	2030
Totals	107,828	111,628	14,371	7219

Group 3 Poems and Sonnets, *JC, Wiv, AYL, TN, Ham, Tro, Oth, AWW, MM*; and Group 4 *Lr, Mac, Tim, Per, Ant, Cor, Cym, WT, Tmp, H8*. This leads to a convenient tabulation: – 2.3.

Looking down the columns in Table 2.3 one sees that Group 1, including such short works as *Err, Ven, Luc* and *TGV*, is approximately less by the equivalent of one play than the other three groups, in both number of lines and number of words. Each of the totals of these two columns is an expression of total output. The third column shows the number of new words Shakespeare was adding to his repertoire. It was highest at the beginning of his career and gradually tailed off, being less than half as much in the last group as in the first. The need for new additions might perhaps be expected to diminish as his vocabulary grew and as he became more skilled in making use of its resources. The total, 14,371, may be regarded as an approximation to the magnitude of his D-word vocabulary. Hart's specific count of the total number of different words in Shakespeare is 17,677; but he does not seem to like it and modifies it in several ways, e.g. by excluding words from parts of plays which he does not think are assuredly Shakespearean. It seems best not to follow him, but to accept his 17,677 as a best guess. The fourth column of one-play words shows the feature which Yule would have predicted. It shows no sign of a dimunition in numbers as Shakespeare went on writing and writing. However much his vocabulary had grown, these singularities continued to well up out of the depths where they had been stored. Shakespeare's treasury of words that had not been used shows absolutely no sign of depletion. We note the enormous number of these unique words. Their total, 7219, is over half of 14,371, the sum of all new words in this table, and is 41% of 17,677, Hart's estimate of the grand total of all Shakespeare's dictionary words. Looking back to Table 2.2, we see it is a typical number for a variety of writers besides Shakespeare.

But Table 2.2 shows us that Shakespeare differs radically in practically all other respects from the other writers contained there. The crucial factor is the immensity of the 'sample' of nearly a million words of output. A vocabulary of 17,677 D-words, large though it is, is exiguous in comparison with the amount of text it was called on to create. These words have had to be used, on average (T/V, Table 2.2), 50 times to achieve the task. Of course, as many are rare words and 41% are once-words, other words have been used many hundreds and thousands of times to make up the balance. Spevack gives the following list of concordance words so frequent in occurrence as to be recorded simply as a number, without context. Dictionary equivalents, such as 'th'' for 'the', are separately recorded and find no place in this list. A dictionary list of these words would make them much more numerous than they appear here, even though a few of them are homographs, and therefore include two or more D-words. Homographs are marked with *.

This trifling number of the 43 commonest (concordance) words has a total of 364,823 occurrences, accounting therefore for 41% of the gross output of 884,647. Spevack started to print contexts for words only with fewer than 3000 occurrences. Nevertheless it is a matter of interest to take the list down to words appearing a thousand times and over. In this continuation we begin to find a few of the commonest nouns appearing: *lord* 2748, *man* 1878, *king* 1375, *time* 1144, *heart* 1076. If we look back to Yule's list (p. 14) of the commonest nouns in *Imitatio*, and the way they seem to epitomise the themes of the book, we may feel like regarding these five nouns of Shakespeare as likewise significant of his predominant concerns. These additional 72 words add 132,069, which, together with the 43 uncontexted words, make up a total of 496,892, which is 56% of the entire word output. We reach the median of this bizarre distribution with the word 'go', which occurs 1796 times. The long tail-end, with 443,464 output words, is provided by a mere 78 words, a mere 0.44% of Hart's count of 17,677.

I thought it worth while to make an independent count of the commonest nouns, i.e. those exceeding a count of 500 (including those marked with a slash), and now including plurals and possessives made with added s or 's, but omitting all other inflected and contracted forms. 'Man' includes 'men', etc., 'lady' includes 'ladies', etc., 'wife' includes 'wives', etc., 'woman' includes 'women', etc.; but 'life' does not include 'lives', as this last is most usually a verb. However, the contexts have not been read through to distinguish meanings and obtain a list of dictionary words. Some of the nouns have been used as verbs, but not to a substantial extent. This list, then, is our counterpart to Yule's list of the highest-frequency nouns in *Imitatio*, providing a sketch of the themes of the book. Looking at Shakespeare's list, one notices how concrete, how objective, how familiar, how domestic it is. There is only a handful of abstract nouns – *time, god, word, honour, name, nothing, grace, soul, peace, fortune* – and all the rest are physical, even tangible, objects. These 43 nouns provide the greater part of Shakespeare's world, and it is mainly through their metaphorical application that his subtler meanings are conveyed.

We still have not considered the word frequencies of Shakespeare's output along the lines of Yule's analysis of the nouns in *Imitatio*. Unfortunately there is no practicable possibility of showing a distribution of dictionary words, either for nouns alone or more comprehensively. We must try to learn what we can from concordance words. The table below shows the frequencies of every twentieth word in Spevack's *Concordance*, which, by chance, did not include a single example of the 43 uncontexted words. As in Table 2.1, the extremes of the distribution are

Table 2.4. *Shakespeare: the 43 commonest concordance words*

the	27,735	with	7908	thy	4360
and	26,560	*be	7379	no	4090
*I	21,358	his	7285	all	4037
to	20,114	this	7138	by	4028
of	17,276	your	7065	*do	3998
*a	14,821	*he	6725	shall	3870
you	14,432	but	6712	if	3790
my	13,192	have	6282	are	3746
that	11,838	*as	6134	we	3569
in	11,642	thou	5855	thee	3423
is	9678	so	5463	our	3305
not	9080	him	5448	on	3179
me	8281	*will	5306	now	3031
for	8164	what	4834		
it	8123	*her	4499	Total	364,823

Table 2.5. *Shakespeare: concordance words with 2999 to 1001 appearances*

good	2985	hath	2069	'tis	1520
from	2835	than	2021	out	1430
lord	2748	there	1959	give	1425
she	2711	one	1944	these	1419
come	2638	*like	1917	some	1418
they	2618	I'll	1891	where	1409
sir	2613	man	1878	king	1375
*or	2604	upon	1850	too	1351
at	2597	*may	1801	who	1341
which	2560	go	1796	*can	1315
would	2498	did	1794	take	1280
*more	2497	*make	1780	*mine	1264
*o	2464	*say	1769	most	1242
was	2443	yet	1766	speak	1207
then	2380	know	1760	never	1145
how	2328	us	1751	time	1144
their	2315	were	1712	tell	1126
am	2302	should	1704	up	1125
*well	2300	must	1641	think	1107
love	2271	*an	1572	much	1098
here	2249	why	1571	doth	1084
when	2246	had	1555	heart	1076
*let	2238	*see	1549	nor	1061
them	2075	such	1531	*art	1011

Note: Very common concordance words (including those with slash), between 2999 and 1001 occurrences, without including contracted and inflected forms. N=72; sum 132,069.

Table 2.6. *Shakespeare: the commonest nouns*

lord	3150	thing	920	woman	630
man	2972	master	905	soul	613
sir	2656	heaven	855	part	600
king	1662	lady	846	duke	584
time	1404	son	802	peace	571
god	1325	honour	798	wife	568
heart	1317	night	782	face	538
eye	1311	name	759	madam	527
hand	1221	world	738	fool	524
father	1143	blood	710	tongue	522
day	1016	way	696	prince	520
death	985	brother	695	fortune	516
word	969	nothing	682	daughter	515
friend	963	grace	676		
life	921	head	633		

Table 2.7. *Shakespeare: analysis of concordance words in a 1 in 20 sample*

x	f_x	x	f_x	x	f_x	x	f_x	x	f_x
		10	24	20	7	30–9	16	445	1
1	715	11	22	21	6	40–9	15	448	1
2	226	12	9	22	5	50–9	8	536	1
3	114	13	15	23	7	60–9	10	622	1
4	75	14	6	24	8	70–9	6	1139	1
5	57	15	11	25	4	80–9	3	1698	1
6	47	16	9	26	1	90–9	7	2591	1
7	34	17	12	27	4	100–99	21	2696	1
8	17	18	6	28	2	200–99	10		
9	18	19	6	29	1	300–99	4		

Note: Vocabulary (total number of words included) 1576. Total output (occurrences) 27,852. Average frequency 17.7. Median frequency 208. Proportion of once-words 0.454. One half of output contributed by 22 words of 200+ frequency.

shown in exact numbers, while words in the middle of the range have been grouped.

This table emphasises once again what an overwhelming proportion of Shakespeare's text is made up by extremely common and commonplace words of high frequency. The unique, the rare and the unusual words play a very small role – however dramatically and thematically important they may be. Such a work might be likened to a great edifice constructed out of innumerable small bricks, with only here and there sizeable blocks of stone. One might think that commonplace words might have tied Shakespeare to commonplace utterance; this would be to adopt *2* mistaken view of the nature of language. But there are many writers who strain for an unusual word in order to produce an impressive effect. Compare the means employed with the everyday material used by Shakespeare for one of his more flamboyant images (Sonnet 13):

Who lets so fair a house fall to decay,
Which husbandry in honour might uphold,

Against	619
the	27735
stormy	7
gusts	8
of	17276
winter's	22
day	771
And	26560
barren	43
rage	135
of	17276
death's	35
eternal	39
cold?	217

Here 'stormy gusts' are the only unusual words, and they are far from out of the way. The rhetorical effect comes from the content, the imagery, and particularly from the contrast between concrete and abstract, and a certain ambiguity of meaning. The other side of Shakespeare's abundant use of the most commonplace words to produce far from commonplace effects is that he falls at times into a repetitiveness that makes one grit one's teeth.

3

The advent of the computer

It was inevitable that when the computer appeared on the scene it should be mobilised in the attack on problems of disputed authorship. But in the early years there had to be many advances in a variety of directions before effective use could be made of it. Computers of adequate capacity and complexity had to be developed and established at many centres. Computer 'languages' had to be perfected. Programs had to be written by workers trained for the job, and applied under the direction of literati aware of the problems and how they might be faced. In the world of Shakespeare scholarship, a major computer achievement was the *Harvard Concordance* planned and directed by Marvin Spevack.[12] The huge work itself indicates the limitations of computer logic. The computer can only work on a text – in the case of Shakespeare a text that is full of internal inconsistencies, archaisms, and passages open to doubts and disputes. When, some time in the 1950s, Ellegård (1962)[5] went to work on finding the answer to the question 'Who was Junius?', he had to do nearly all the slave labour personally by hand and eye; and only when he had accumulated all his counts could he turn to the computer for help with the arithmetic. Nevertheless the principles on which he worked were an advance on the earlier theoretical studies of Udny Yule, at least for limited practical tasks.

The first of the Junius letters appeared in the *Public Advertiser* (London) on 21 January 1769; and they continued at the rate of one or two a month for three years. They ceased abruptly and for ever on 21 January 1772. From the start they created a sensation, and one which grew and grew with time. They were by far the ablest, the best informed and the most vitriolic of the political writings of the day. The writer wrote from firm convictions as a Whig, defending the rights of the people against both King and Parliament. His tone of omniscience and haughty arrogance gave punch to his attack. William Lecky wrote of him that as a political theorist he was second-rate; but as literature the letters had merits of the highest order:

Their style is entirely different from that of any of the great models of the time ... No writer ever excelled Junius in condensed and virulent invective ... His letters are perfectly adapted to the purposes for which they were intended. There is nothing in them superfluous or obscure, and nothing that fails to tell.

(Ellegård, 1962, p. 88)

When the graphologist Charles Chabot published in 1871 'The handwriting of Junius professionally investigated', with 217 lithographic plates of specimens of the handwriting of Junius on the one part and Sir Philip Francis on the other, the handwriting of Junius could be seen to be as calligraphically beautiful, as distinguished and as individual as his literary style. Sir Philip Francis was widely suspected of being the unknown Junius. His handwriting (like his personal style in private correspondence) was much more ordinary. Nevertheless Chabot found enough in the way of particular correspondences to assign both hands to a single writer. Other people were less convinced.

The debate whether Francis or another was the Unknown behind Junius continued, decade by decade, through endless re-publications of the letters, up till the death of Francis in 1818. And beyond, since he left no clue behind him, into the twentieth century. The letters, collected into book form, were re-published thirty-seven times before the end of the 1790s, many times in the first decades of the nineteenth century, in 1927, and again in 1978. Through all this time alternative candidates were being promoted, though never accepted; and even in 1960 the *Oxford History of England* records: 'the identity of Junius is still a puzzle'.

Philip Francis was born in Dublin in 1740, the son of a distinguished churchman, who later removed to London. He was educated at St Paul's and became a good classical scholar. At the age of sixteen, through family influence, he got a junior clerkship in the office of the Secretary of State. He was immensely industrious, spent his free time with books, and learned French, Portuguese and Spanish. He stayed in the Foreign Office till 1763, and then moved to the War Office, where he remained in the important post of Chief Clerk till 1772. 'Accordingly he had no less than 16 years' experience of two of the most important public offices – an excellent qualification for a Junian candidate' (Ellegård 1963, p. 44). He resigned his post in 1772, and in June 1773 he was made a member of the Council appointed for the government of Bengal. His fortune was made. The post carried with it a salary of £10,000 p.a. and abundant opportunities for patronage. Francis was not only immensely energetic in official work and the duties of his post: he was also a very active letter-writer, using both his own name and pseudonyms. He led the campaign against Warren Hastings. Though he had married early, happily and fruitfully, he remained a lover of beautiful women, a failing which led him into scrapes. He was severely wounded in a duel. He had a liaison with a lovely girl of sixteen, who left her husband to put herself under his protection (and eventually became the wife of Talleyrand). He was a bold and successful gambler, and when he returned to England in 1784 he had made a fortune worth £3000 a year. He did not then get the advancement he had hoped for, but was given the sop of a KCB in 1805. He had a number of years as a Member of Parliament, but was ineffective as a speaker. He lost his wife and two of his daughters in 1802–5; but he married for the second time in 1814, a bride of twenty-six, when he was seventy-four. Leslie Stephen, his biographer in the *Dictionary of National Biography*, characterises him as a man of great ability and unflagging industry, arrogant, vindictive in the extreme, an unscrupulous enemy, but motivated by noble principles and courageous in attacking great men.

This was the man who wrote 'I am the sole depositary of my own secret, and it shall die with me.' For two hundred years no one knew for sure who Junius was. No fewer than forty candidates have been dragged under the spotlight of enquiry. But this freakish genius was the man who became the prime suspect, and who now has been proved by the efforts of Alvar Ellegård to have been the true author. At the end of his laborious analysis, in which all the external evidence had been fairly appraised, Ellegård wrote: 'The "one new fact" demanded by Dilke has been produced. The Franciscan hypothesis is proved as conclusively as any empirical hypothesis can be proved. The statement that Sir Philip Francis was Junius may henceforth be allowed to stand without a question-mark' (Ellegård 1962, p. 119). This must be conceded. Ellegård was the man who revealed the truth; and the statistical study of literary vocabulary – what he called stylo-statistics – was his tool.

The study of handwriting, of which much might have been expected, proved a disappointment. Scientific graphology has come a long way since 1871. Re-examination now might add another element of certainty. Although Chabot claimed that the two handwritings came from the same writer, people at that time did not generally accept it. The writings were *too* different. The handwriting of Francis was sloping, angular, without distinction, on a pattern with that of a hundred others, the normal clerical hand of the time. The handwriting of Junius was upright, rounded, eminently beautiful and quite unique. Apart from the pseudonymous letters accepted as those of Junius, there exists but a single envelope in that handwriting and not another word: not one in all the voluminous matter left behind by Francis. Some people have found it difficult to believe that anybody could write so fluently and elegantly in a feigned hand. Yet it should not be forgotten that formalised calligraphic scripts can be learned and, once familiar, can then flow very naturally. What would be an unacceptable miracle would have been for a man whose natural hand was Junian to have artificially developed for himself the angularities and the imperfections of the Franciscan hand. A slovenly handwriting must come naturally; it cannot be feigned. Junius, self-confessedly, composed his letters with great labour. It would have gone well with his mood to have embodied his highly polished prose in a deliberately elegant handwriting.

Ellegård was a pioneer in applying linguistic analysis to an authorship problem. He did not succeed in bringing the method to a high level of finish, or even to the ordinarily economical use of time and labour. There was material and to spare for the task, approximately 150,000 words of text, and also an abundance of authentic work by Francis. Ellegård aimed at developing a test which would have discriminant powers within a small compass, say a few thousand words. He familiarised himself with a great mass of political writings, pamphlets, newspaper correspondence of the time, and then read the Junius letters with particular attention. He was on the look out for 'plus', 'minus' and 'neutral' words. The neutral words would have an average frequency, not varying very greatly from author to author; the 'plus' words would be often used by X, seldom by others, and the 'minus' words would be those not infrequent in other writers, but rarely used by X. He was particularly interested in 'highly characteristic' words, which were, naturally and inconveniently, rather infrequent. He reflected that the words most commonly used, articles, prepositions, conjunctions and pronouns, as well as the commonest verbs, nouns, adjectives and adverbs, were 'necessarily' about equally frequent in all texts, whoever the author. (In this, he was almost certainly in error.) He thought the majority of the most (positively or negatively) distinctive words would belong to frequency ranges below 0.0001, or one per ten thousand. Liability to sampling errors would mean that a battery of plus and minus words would be required in the comparison of two texts. Though in this battery single words might be uninformative or even misleading, the battery as a whole should give one the right answer. He instances the word *uniform*, adj. In Junius its frequency is around 0.000280; in a comparative sample of a million words it was 0.000065. The Junian distinctiveness ratio was accordingly 280/65 or 4.3. It is, then, a Junius plus word, coming high up in the 4th group from the top. But, by itself, it might not help much, since in a sample of 10,000 words of Junius text it might appear a number of times (average 2.8), or not at all. In the search for variation between authors, which is the goal of the investigation, there are other sources of possible mistakes of judgment besides sampling error. One must make allowance for within-author variation, such as differences of subject and changes in style.

For comparison with the Junius texts Ellegård considered he needed at least a million words of comparative material derived from about a hundred authors contributing about 10,000 words each. He then proceeded as follows. He read the entire Junius material with an eye to picking out the words which seemed to him to occur with remarkable frequency. He then did the same with the million-word sample of comparative contemporary political material, now noting also those words which he could not remember having seen in Junius. In this way he obtained a preliminary list of Junius-plus words and Junius-minus words. He then got the entire lists of both sorts of words by heart. He then read through the entire text material (Junius and comparative), recording each occurrence of each word. It then remained only to calculate the distinctiveness ratio (Junius-frequency divided by comparative frequency), and the final testing list could be drawn up. Of course first impressions were not always borne out by exact counts, and many target words had to be abandoned when their distinctiveness ratio was too near unity. The preliminary list contained 458 expressions, i.e. words, related formations (e.g. *absurd, absurdly, absurdity*), words plus their forms negated by *im-* or *in-*, stereotyped phrases and clichés; some syntactical peculiarities were also registered. All these 458 units had to be sufficiently well fixed in memory for Ellegård to stop whenever they came up in the text. Every page of the texts was read through twice; and Ellegård feels able to assure us that the consistency of the results show that occurrences missed by inadvertence have not seriously affected the classification. From the preliminary list two separate final testing lists were constructed. The first was used in Program 1, the second list in Program 2. The comparative material consisted of 109 text items by 98 different authors; political pamphlets and speeches 386,700 words; other political writings 363,000 words; and non-political literature 428,000 words. Together with the works by Junius and Francis the investigation covered

1,604,800 words. All the candidates for whom Ellegård could get literary remains were included in the comparative material. On an average the writers in the comparative sample contributed about 10,000 words each. In order to get an idea of within-author variability the 10,000 word samples were subdivided into five 2000 word samples. The final tabulation was, in essence, a structure with 458 rows (the items of the preliminary word list); the columns were the various 2000 word text portions. Intersections of row and column provided cells in which word counts were entered. The final calculations were based on a 458 × 265 table, i.e. about 120,000 cells. The task of dealing with this vast material arithmetically then arose, adding, multiplying, dividing. 'The labour involved was considerable. It seemed obvious that a modern electronic computer would be of great help in this respect.' So at last the indefatigable researcher handed his material over to a machine.

When he came to match his comparison samples against the 'distinctiveness' standards set by the Junius material, Ellegård found only two of the 88 texts by 79 authors falling within the Junius range on the positive side, ten texts on the negative side, but no text within the Junius range on both sides. On the other hand the eight texts written by Philip Francis included only one with a negative value outside the Junian range, two on the positive side; but all Francis text samples were within the Junian range on the positive side or the negative side or both. With a test using the extreme-valued test words, negative and positive, Junius and Francis distributions coincided, all others being left outside the pale.

This gives a general picture of the way Ellegård went to work. It is perhaps unnecessary to go into further detail about his progress in perfectionism: how he added another 100,000 words from Junius's own newspaper to the comparison material; how he added to his Francis text results; how he modified his classification; how he added personal letters to the printer to the Junius material; how he sifted out his test words to get ones of greater distinctiveness; how he did special calculations on pairs and triplets of words contrasted with alternatives. And how finally he went through another battery of operations with Program 2.

Ellegård solved his problem. He showed that his word list satisfactorily accepted Sir Philip Francis into the Junius range, and rejected all the other candidates with near certainty in text samples of 10,000 words and more; that it was effective down to texts of 4000 words; and that it had considerable discriminant capacity even down to text samples of about 2000 words. Sir Philip Francis was the man. The amount of work undertaken by the unfortunate Ellegård was unspeakably laborious; his exposition of its many stages (1962) hardly less so; and his statistical methods could hardly be called elegant. But he reached the end of the journey, one might say by a feat of brute diligence.

'As if it could matter the value of a brass farthing to any living human being who was the author of Junius,' said Carlyle.[3] To be sure, knowing who was helps us no whit with the problems offered us by *Edward III*. The relevance of the Junius quest lies in how it was achieved. The historical and biographical facts are in every detail compatible with Francis, and give no support for any other. The 'stylo-statistics' fit

Francis like a glove and clash with any other authorship. The combination of two extreme improbabilities makes it certain that no other man than Francis could have been the author. It is the negative statement that is proved. Not the result but the methodology is what concerns us. If we are to apply statistical methods to the unsolved problems of authorship, do we have to follow the stony track trodden by Ellegård? Certainly some of his preliminary labours were unavoidable. He could not have made a beginning in getting away from a literary and subjective study towards logical rigour without collecting his comparative million-word sample. (To use an equally rigorous technique with, say, Shakespeare, we would need not only a satisfactory Shakespeare word list (for what we need are dictionary words, not concordance words), but also corresponding word lists for all his contemporary playwrights and poets.) But once the 'plus words' and 'minus words' had been collected, and their 'distinctiveness' had been given mathematical form, the rest would have been the application of the very simplest routine statistical procedures. Plus words, rated by their distinctiveness, would be assigned weights from $+10$ down to $+1$; neutral words would have a zero rating; and minus words would be assigned weights from -10 for the most distinctively anti-Junian to -1 for the least so. In any sample plus and minus numbers would be summed, averaged against the total of words in the sample, with the calculation of standard deviations, standard errors and the other simple measures used universally in science to compare populations one with another. Half a dozen numbers would have given all the information needed to describe each and any sample adequately for comparison and discrimination. It would have been a schoolboy's exercise.

Unfortunately Ellegård did not make any practical use of his simple clarifying concept of variation along a single dimension between Junian and anti-Junian poles. Perhaps his advisers did not permit him to. He kept his material split up into 18 groups. On the 'plus' side at the extreme is Group 1, with a distinctiveness ratio of 10 or more, Group 2, with distinctiveness ratio from 9.9 to 7, and so on down to Group 9, with distinctiveness ratio 1.5 to 1.4 (below which words are classified as 'neutral'). Then he breaks continuity, and starts Group 10 with the most anti-Junian words of all, words never used by Junius though used by others, distinctiveness ratio therefore zero. Thereafter the groups ascend towards neutrality and Group 17, with distinctiveness ratio 0.7. This illogical arrangement bedevils all that follows. The total material is never unified, but remains fragmented throughout the exposition.

One guesses that Ellegård put himself into the hands of advisers, namely into the hands of a mathematician who could not or would not accept such simplification as was suggested above, and is now standard practice. For him each single point, such as the 4.3 for *uniform*, adj. mentioned on p. 27 above, had to be regarded as the centre of a probability area. An elaborate model of dispersion in a multi-dimensional space was developed. The different groups of words were kept separate. And instead of two or three tables the reader is faced with forty-seven pages of tables (defying the comprehension of at least one reader) whose meaning is distilled into eight histograms (diagrams), far from easily read. The complex and subtle mathematics and the simple crudity of the basic data stand against one another in horrid disproportion.

Logically, Ellegård's results were conclusive within an astronomically high probability band. However, historians are not statisticians and are liable to ignore statistical evidence or receive it dismissively and with a total absence of confidence. It is, then, interesting that the whole subject was opened again with the 1978 re-publication of the Letters of Junius, edited by John Cannon.[8] Great care was given to providing an exact and reliable text of the letters themselves, with their attendant bibliographic data. Extraneous sources of evidence were examined, and Cannon shows that the historical evidence for Francis as the author is much stronger than Ellegård realised. Cannon gives exact references for seven critical reviews of Ellegård's statistical work, namely *Times Literary Supplement*, January 1963, March 1963; *Language*, 1964; *Studia Neophilologica*, 36, 203–6; *English Studies*, 44, 376–81; *English Historical Review*, 79, 862–3; *Journal of English and German Philology*, 62, 688–9; *Modern Language Review*, 58, 412–13. He finds that 'no fundamental criticisms are offered of either Ellegård's method or his statistical accuracy'.

From Cannon's work, on top of all that has been accumulated previously, the authorship of the Letters of Junius can surely now be regarded as solved. There is no contradiction or inconsistency in the entire evidence; it all tends in one direction, and at no point does it run up against an impossibility. Stylo-linguistically the case is overwhelming; historically it achieves consistency, reliability and high probability; in terms of the personality of Junius on the one hand, Francis on the other, the clothing fits the man to a nicety that Savile Row could not outdo. Sir James Mackintosh dined with Philip Francis in the last year of his life, and noted: 'the vigourous hatreds which seem to keep Francis alive were very amusing'.

Ellegård's work gave an enormous boost to stylometry, and with the increasing knowledge of computer technology – how and where it could be applied – led to a succession of works, some of which lead in the direction eventually taken by the present writer. A fascinating problem was the uncovering of the authorship of the *Federalist* papers (Mosteller and Wallace 1964).[10] These were a series of anonymous political articles appearing in the United States in the years 1787–8. They were attributed by current opinion to two political writers, Alexander Hamilton and James Madison. The question was, which? The investigators took a very different line from that of Ellegård, and decided to dispense entirely with thematic words with a high content in meaning as possibly tendentious and liable to mislead. They restricted themselves to 'non-contextual' or 'filler' words of moderate to high frequency that would be natural constituents of almost any kind of message. They were able to start from a body of political papers of known authorship by the two writers in question. According to the summary provided by Bailey (1968),[1] they found marked differences between them in the frequency of use of certain common words, as shown in Table 3.1. Some of the other words that came into consideration

Table 3.1. *'Filler' words in the* Federalist *papers*

word	No. of Hamilton papers	No. of Madison papers
enough	14	0
commonly	9	1
whilst	0	13
language	2	10

were *an, any, upon, may, his*. Supposing such words to be distributed according to a negative binomial model, one can calculate from the known frequency of any stated one of them what are the expected numbers of appearances of 0, 1, 2 etc. in any text of a stated number of words. The actually observed number of appearances can be related to the theoretical expectation to provide a probability, separately calculated for Hamilton and Madison, for each index word, and, seriatim, for each of the papers of unknown authorship. For each paper, individually, the Hamilton probabilities provided by the index words can be multiplied together, as also the Madison probabilites, and the products used to provide a Hamilton:Madison probability ratio. To quote Bailey's résumé:

When a considerable body of known writings is considered, we have the opportunity to give a precise formulation of the odds in favour of one of the candidates when the unknown texts are approached. Thus, the odds are about 800 to 1 in favor of Madison's authorship of paper number 56 – and this is one of the weaker predictions in the authors' opinion. For most of the other papers in question, the odds are found to be even greater in Madison's favor. Mosteller and Wallace are therefore able to conclude beyond any reasonable doubt that Madison was the author of the twelve disputed papers (p. 227).

Bailey continues by commenting: 'The technique developed in the studies of Ellegård and Mosteller–Wallace can be taken as models for authorship-determination tests ...' (ibid). But he makes the important points that there must be an abundant test material and abundant comparison material, and, finally, abundant historical evidence must be combined with the stylistic investigations if really safe predictions are to be made. To take the case of *Edward III*, the whole play, let alone its two hypothetical 'parts', might not be sufficient material for a conclusive stylo-linguistic argument in the present state of the art.

The anthology edited by Doležel and Bailey, *Statistics and Style* (1969),[4] contains a number of papers, and a number of comments, which should be of interest to literary scholars. The very first paper, by Doležel ('A framework for the statistical analysis of style', pp. 10–25) begins: 'The foundations of the statistical theory of style can be summarised in a simple statement: *style is a probabilistic concept.*' This is, of course, a challenge. If it is to be held unjustified or untrue, then one is called on to define style in some other way which will allow it to be recognised and identified. Dictionary definitions will not do, and it is hard to see what this other way might be. Stylistics, the editors say, have become a crossroads for the interests of literary scholars and critics, linguists, psychologists, sociologists and mathematicians.

'Statistical stylistics has not acquired the scientific authority that it deserves [due to] communication barriers that separate the scholars in the field.' In his historical survey ('Statistics and style: a historical survey', pp. 217–36) Bailey notes that there are 'few cases in which genuine expertise in language, literature and statistics have been combined in one investigator' (p. 218). The required competence in three fields is to be obtained only by the collective efforts by specialists in each discipline. P. J. Wexler, we are told, has noted, in works of statistical sophistication, 'the unfathomable naiveté, from the linguistic point of view, of the units being counted – for example, the "word"' (p. 219). Work by other specialists similarly shows serious statistical deficiencies. As a warning to the literary scholar concerning himself with attribution studies, Bailey writes: 'Without some rigorous definition of style and a notion of the factors that influence it, the critic will find that even the most sophisticated extraction of verbal parallels may fail to produce the desired discrimination of authorship' (p. 222). This has certainly been the case with *Edward III*. As the reader will have noted from Chapter 1 of this book, no firm conclusion, or general agreement, about the authorship of the work has yet been reached, despite much diligent study. The single solid piece of statistical work by Alfred Hart (1934)[7] has been treated dismissively where it has not been totally ignored, and has not received the close scrutiny it deserves.

One of the studies in the Doležel–Bailey anthology is worth particular notice. Paul Bennett's 'The statistical measurement of a stylistic trait in *Julius Caesar* and *As You Like It*'[2] was originally published in 1957, a work by a Shakespearean scholar which seems to have been fairly widely ignored. Bennett was much struck by Yule's statistical methods and wrote: 'Yule was able to measure a significant aspect of literary style, something which has never been done before' (Doležel and Bailey, p. 30). Yule's book was published in 1944.[15] It was apparently passed over in silence by Shakespearean scholars, with the single exception of H. G. McCurdy (1953).[9] When Bennett's paper of 1957 was re-published (with omission of its word lists) by Doležel and Bailey in 1969, Bennett still had to report that 'I know of no studies of vocabulary or style which have employed Yule's method other than those of Yule himself' (p. 41, n. 3). This is, however, what Bennett did, with a view to explaining the method to Shakespeareans by publication in the *Shakespeare Quarterly* (8, 1957, 33–50). His explanation is illustrated by extracting the necessary data from two Shakespeare plays and showing exactly how they should be handled to arrive at a measurement of Yule's K. This is done for each act of each play, and for each of the two plays as a whole. He chose *Julius Caesar* and *As You Like It*, firstly to test the method by comparing Shakespeare against himself, secondly to see whether the results attained were constant to the author when two such different plays were compared:

Julius Caesar is a tragedy, without sub-plots, primarily in blank verse; *As You Like It* is a comedy, largely in prose, abounding in sub-plots, and there are other differences between the plays as well. Moreover, the First Folio offered the same sole textual authority for both plays, both of which are relatively free from editorial cruxes (p. 31).

The labour involved in this relatively limited exercise was very considerable. Bennett, following Yule, drew up a complete card index of all the nouns appearing in each of the plays, recording the number of appearances, disregarding inflexional forms. He checked his counts against Bartlett's *Concordance*, and found to his dismay that Bartlett had inexplicably omitted dozens of occurrences. Of course it was Bartlett and not Bennett who was in error. There is no doubt that Bartlett sometimes allowed himself a certain selectivity with very common words. Bennett also found the chore of checking words laborious. He had 'a sufficiently difficult time deciding, with the aid of the *OED*, just which words were nouns, especially in regard to substantives used attributively, and the quasi-substantives' (p. 30). 'Yule *longa, vita brevis*', he says (p. 31), and two plays were as much as he could bear. Bennett provides twelve tables of word-frequency distributions, one for each of the five acts of each play, and one for each of the plays as a whole, together with the corresponding K values. Theoretically the magnitude of K is independent of the size of the sample, but it will be seen that it is usually lower for the play as a whole than for any single act. Yule's $K = 10,000 \, (s_2 - s_1)/(s_1)^2$. Its meaning will be clear if the reader refers to Table 2.1 of Chapter 2. s_1 is the sum of the products of x and f_x, and is therefore the total number of nouns; s_2 is the sum of the products of x^2 and f_x and is a measure of their dispersion. In fact K is a measure of repetitiveness. The smaller it is, the greater is the number of different nouns, i.e. the variety of the nouns used by the author. The more the author uses the same words over and over again, the greater will the value of K be in the piece analysed. The values of K calculated by Bennett for the two plays are shown in Table 3.2

Bennett quotes the estimations of K which Yule made for some other authors, e.g. for Macaulay (four essays) 17.9, 21.8, 27.2 and 34.1, all of which are relatively low; John Bunyan (four works) 56.5, 66.9, 80.6 and 88.0; and St John's Gospel, 177.9. The two-play Ks for Shakespeare are of intermediate magnitude and approximate to those of Bunyan. In concluding his essay, Bennett remarks:

I believe that students of literature must master and employ Yule's method if they are to go on comparing and contrasting the styles of various Elizabethan playwrights in the hope of attributing the plays correctly. Indeed, Yule's method is only one step in the direction that research must take, for it cannot be overemphasized that Yule's method measures only *one* aspect of style, namely, repetitiveness. There certainly must be other significant aspects of style which scholars can devise means of measuring. And it is desirable that they should do so, for repetitiveness is influenced not only by the individuality of the author but also, as we have seen from variations in the characteristic among the different acts of *Julius Caesar* and *As You Like It*, by subject matter. I should not care to suggest that the characteristic is going to provide an infallible test of authorship, for it may well turn out that some of Shakespeare's plays will have the same characteristic as some, say, of Jonson's plays, whereas other of his plays might yield the same characteristic as, perhaps, one of Marlowe's. The real desideratum is to develop objective measures of several different significant aspects of style; authorship might then confidently be ascribed when two or three or four of these measures were in substantial agreement. All that is claimed for Yule's characteristic is that it provides an objective measurement of one significant aspect of literary style (pp. 39–41).

Despite Bennett's recommendation, students of literature have gone on

Table 3.2. *Values of Yule's* K *in* Julius Caesar *and* As You Like It

Julius Caesar		As You Like It	
Act I	61.3	Act I	79.9
Act II	45.7	Act II	42.0
Act III	77.5	Act III	52.9
Act IV	50.6	Act IV	54.6
Act V	72.3	Act V + Epi.	55.2
Play as whole	49.2	Play as whole	40.5

comparing and contrasting the styles of various Elizabethan playwrights (whether or not in the hope of attributing the plays correctly) without making any attempt to master or employ Yule's method. However, attempts have been made to devise other objective methods, to which we will come. This is not entirely surprising. The amount of labour involved, though considerable, ought not to have been discouraging. A student, being assigned such a task, would have the satisfaction of adding one solid and permanent brick to a scientific structure which would grow ever more imposing. What does put one off, however, from following in Bennett's footsteps is the combination of high variability in K within authors and the likelihood that estimates of its mean value in different authors might lie uncomfortably close together. Macaulay's largest K is nearly twice his smallest; and if we take the twelve estimates Bennett provides for Shakespeare, the largest, 79.9, is again very nearly twice the smallest, 40.5. These disadvantages should not have proved final. The mean of Bennett's Shakespeare Ks is 56.81 with standard deviation 13.31, less than a quarter of the mean. It is indeed a pity that no one has bothered to make counts for other Elizabethan playwrights. One would guess that Ben Jonson would be found to have a smaller average K than Shakespeare, Marlowe perhaps a larger one.

A later symposium of 1971 on the use of the computer in literary and linguistic research, edited by Wisbey,[14] is disappointing. In the great diversity of papers, mostly of a highly technical kind, there is only one, that by Tallentire,[13] which is relevant to our topic; and this demands retreat rather than advance. Tallentire takes a generally pessimistic view of any mathematical approach, and ends by recommending a return to subjective ancient and standard modes of study. He writes:

That an author is variable rather than absolute in his stylistic characteristics is probably true, but it is ironic that the most lauded statistical study to date... owes its deservedly high reputation to the discovery that, in admittedly limited samples from two authors, certain linguistic preferences were absolutely fixed. Frederick Mosteller and David L. Wallace resolved the disputed authorship of *The Federalist* papers by showing that function words (those that occur very frequently and are generally independent of context) exhibit a surprising power to discriminate among authors. In fact, certain words were *never* found in samples known to be by one of the two candidates, while these words frequently occurred in the work of the other and vice versa (p. 126).

This does not mean, he argues, that in general we are concerned with anything other than probabilities. Doležel has committed himself to a probabilistic approach to style, and this means that

there is little hope that Doležel will isolate 'specified, exactly measurable style components' using statistical techniques. What is more important, subsequent studies, attracted by Doležel's apparently sophisticated and mathematically rigorous 'specified text-style formula', could perpetuate his fundamental misconception that statistical methods can both describe a probabilistic trend, and determine the specific determinants of that trend. It should be evident that these demands are mutually contradictory (p. 127).

He goes on to say that analysts of style have now fashioned or adapted each of the possible mathematical approaches. And the result has been that people are now very much less optimistic than they used to be. What now is the justification for the use of mathematics in stylistics at all? Tallentire offers a defence against this criticism, and then rebuts it. Mathematics can at best offer *analogues* of literary style; statistics can arrive only at probabilities and never at proof. His final paragraph would drown the puppy before it could ever become a dog:

It is evident that mathematical paradigms of style are becoming more diverse and sophisticated, but it is fair to say that their practical applications have been only moderately successful. Therefore, for the present at least, the most potent tool for stylistic evaluation remains the most basic, that of intuition. In the foreseeable future it is likely to remain the scholar's most valuable aid in stylistic research (p. 128).

The present writer is not a mathematician and he is not competent to oppose Tallentire's presentation, discussion and dismissal of the available mathematical approaches to stylistics. Nevertheless it seems to him, as a statistics-user, that Tallentire adopts too rigid an attitude. Tallentire's logical and mathematical purism leads him to nihilism. In effect he asserts that nothing can be achieved by a statistical approach, since it does not lie within the limits of that approach to arrive at proof. This is a strange conclusion to reach, when Tallentire has before him the massive and convincing evidence provided by the researches of Yule, Ellegård and Mosteller–Wallace. It is not in the nature of empirical questions to admit of proofs. What one can achieve is an estimate of probabilities. It may be that on one side they diminish to vanishing point. It then becomes unreasonable not to accept its alternative. Tallentire's other point, that the statistical approach cannot 'both describe a probabilistic trend, and determine the specific determinants of that trend' seems to betray ignorance of how the statistician actually goes about a particular complex task. Having accumulated the statistical evidence that leads to a probability in favour of a particular conclusion, we can start afresh from that point, on that basis. We then formulate a new hypothesis, e.g. about one or another possible determinant of the trend we have discovered, and then look for the evidence which might rebut it, or possibly be compatible with it. The logical foundation for this approach is the logic of scientific discovery, as has been abundantly established by Karl Popper.[11]

Tallentire's belief 'that the most potent tool for stylistic evaluation remains the most basic, that of intuition' is well enough. But his willingness for the scholar to rely on that, and on that alone, amounts to a counsel of despair. Intuition, especially intuition based on profound knowledge and sensitive discrimination, is indispensable as a source of the impetus that leads to a voyage of discovery. But that voyage must be guided by a hypothesis which can be stated in unambiguous terms, and predicts conclusions which can be checked against objectively verifiable observations. It is only what is objectively verifiable which can survive critical scrutiny. In the history of the literary research into *Edward III* we can see the free play of many intuitions, but, unhappily, no conclusions which have been raised above the arena of possible dispute.

4

Style and stylometry

What is style? And how is it to be measured? More particularly, what is Shakespeare's style? And is it to be discovered in *Edward III*? In attempting an answer to these difficult questions we should be able to get some help from a recent symposium of essays by Shakespeare scholars of great experience: *Shakespeare's Styles: Essays in honour of Kenneth Muir*.[5] Unfortunately the plural adds to our difficulties; for if style is the man, one man should have only his one particular individual style. If he seems to have many styles, they should all be facets of one unity, harmonious, and at no point incompatible with one another. If the 'style' seems to change with time, it is still part of one man's life development, and its evolution will be one self-consistent story. It must be possible to establish criteria for distinguishing one man's style from another's, say Shakespeare's from Marlowe's. Indeed, if one is to proceed by the logic of science, studies of style must be comparative studies. Some time there must be a definition of 'style', at least an operational definition, however arbitrary, of what it is that one is going to study.

Referring to the work of previous critics, R. A. Foakes says:[6]

What has been written relates mainly to four aspects of Shakespeare's style; one is what characterises his work in distinction from that of his contemporaries; another is the way his style changes and develops, as in his exploration of the use of prose in the period from about 1598 to 1603, or his stretching of the boundaries of blank verse in the late plays; a third is the use of a particularly marked style in a given play, such as the latinate vocabulary that is a feature of *Troilus and Cressida*; and a fourth is what John Russell Brown calls his 'dramatic style', in seeking to illustrate the 'theatrical life' of a text

(p. 83).

Shakespeare, says G. R. Hibbard,[8] has a 'talent for conferring life and individuality on a character by endowing him with a distinctive and often idiosyncratic idiom, and way of speaking which is peculiarly his own' (p. 100). On the other hand, Nicholas Brooke[2] remarks of *Macbeth* that the play has a language of its own, spoken equally by Macbeth, Lady Macbeth, Old Man, First Murderer, etc. 'Throughout his working life,' writes Anne Barton[1], 'Shakespeare displayed a marked predilection for analysing situations by way of contraries or antitheses. Dualities and polar opposites are a striking feature of his style' (p. 144). Wolfgang Clemen[3] observes:

style being a highly complex phenomenon, many aspects would have to be taken into consideration if a balanced assessment of language and style in these plays were to be attempted. For this would have to include not only the figures of rhetoric but also grammar and syntax, forms of address, tempo and versification ... [Shakespeare] had many styles ... We find straightforward language side by side with richly adorned speech, or brisk dialogue followed by formal and slowly moving declamation (pp. 15–16).

Other critics refer to what might well be regarded as faults or deficiencies. L. C. Knights[9] points out how Shakespeare's sophisticated use of the arts of rhetoric leads him to persuasions which are not, even not intended to be, fully persuasive. Philip Edwards[4] senses 'the scepticism of a great master of language about the reliability of his own stock-in-trade as the voice of feeling' (p. 39). Shakespeare's male lovers show 'a tendency to cheapen a sincere affection in the effort to affirm it in words . . . In there declarations the best become confused with the words; their language is indistinguishable' (p. 50). (It is well to remember that words are not the language of love.) Anne Barton[1] notes the 'twisted rhythms and tortured syntax of the Last Plays' (p. 136), and quotes James Sutherland who, confronting the opening lines of *Cymbeline*, suspected that 'the person who is thinking rapidly, breaking off, making fresh starts and so on, is not the character, but Shakespeare himself' (ibid.). This calls to mind what Partridge wrote in 1949:[20]

On the track of the telling and indelible image, he may leave behind anacoluthons and hanging relative clauses in the most inconsequent fashion; he compresses his meaning and tortures his syntax, so that while the effect of the passage may be poetically grand, the meaning is wrung from it with extreme difficulty (p. 16).

Some of the causes of difficulty in interpreting Shakespeare are peculiar to his age, but some to the dramatist. Shakespeare's imagination needed 'rapid transitions of feeling, thought and figure, and for these the syntax of the time, of any time, was too halting' (ibid.). Narrative, which requires an orderly development of details and events, 'is naturally tortuous in Shakespeare *unlike most of his contemporaries*' (my italics). Shakespeare tends to lose track of his relative clauses, 'especially in continuative function and in proximity to participial phrases, or adverbial clauses, of time'. So he may lapse into 'apparently anacoluthic constructions'.

All these are very interesting observations, and they give us some picture of the 'style' of the poet. Their weakness is systematic: they concentrate almost wholly on the mind of one man. We note the comparisons between early, mature and late Shakespeare. The indications of psychopathology will almost certainly be unique to Shakespeare; they are of extreme interest to the psychiatrist.[21] Particular aspects or elements of style are identified. But for systematic purposes they need to be defined and charted through the works of contemporary playwrights. What was uniquely, distinctively, idiosyncratically Shakespearean in all that great corpus of poems and plays? We may be sure it will not be any single quality, but only a spread or spectrum of qualities whose uniqueness will lie in their combination in one person. Impressions, examples and illustrations are the starting point of a descriptive science. They must be taken on into comparisons, counts and statistical analysis.

STYLISTIC ANALYSIS

The Edinburgh stylometrists, of whom more anon, distinguish between 'modern stylometry' on the one side, and 'stylistics' or 'stylistic analysis' on the other. But they all have a common stem; and for a comprehensive exposition of the logical and philosophical basis from which these sciences have evolved one may turn to Herdan's classic work of 1956, *Language as Choice and Chance*.[7] Herdan relates his general theory to Schopenhauer's concepts, 'World as Will and Appearance', in which 'Appearance' is subject to causality while 'Will' is free. The study of language involves the 'whittling down of the supposedly all-powerful contribution of choice to language'. If I understand Herdan correctly, it would seem that Chance involves all the constraints, language, vocabulary, syntax, within which the writer has to write. Choice corresponds only to what he chooses to write about. The first is subject to statistical laws, capable of analysis, producing stylo-statistics and enabling the analyst to define the nexus of probabilities which constitutes a writer's style. The more one analyses, and the more successful one's analysis, the larger becomes the area governed by causative factors attributable to chance, and the more restricted the motive that led that individual writer to that individual choice.

Herdan adopts Saussure's dichotomy of *langue* and *parole*. Language, *langue*, is the total of wordengrams plus their probability of occurrence in individual speech, their relative frequencies in actual use, in total therefore the statistical population of such events, constituting a statistical universe. Any individual speech utterance (*parole* in Saussure's terminology) then plays the role of a sample from that universe. From this it would seem that one can come to learn the universe, *langue*, only by accumulating samples; but the individual samples, *parole*, have to be accepted as irreducible primary elements. The logical processes of analysis and comparison can be applied only in the wider field. Herdan proceeds to describe the primary observations of statistical linguistics in terms of syllables, phonemes, morphemes, etc., but above all of words. In an interesting section he discusses correlation between writers in a total vocabulary, where one is in a position to enumerate the number of words used by both A and B, by A not B, by B not A, and by neither. An application of this idea appears in the next chapter when some word counts by Hart are discussed.

A later work of general exposition takes us a big step further and is of much closer relevance to problems related to the Shakespeare canon. Carrington Bonsor Williams, one gathers from his extensive bibliography, is a biologist. His book, *Style and Vocabulary*[22] (see especially pp. 15–16), shows a number of parallels between the statistics applicable to biological populations and populations of linguistic events. He has resurrected for us the work of T. C. Mendenhall, a professor of physics, who published in 1887 (in a statistical journal) a paper on the different lengths of words. In 1901, apparently motivated by the Shakespeare–Bacon controversy, he produced results from a count of 400,000 words from Shakespeare, 200,000 from Bacon and smaller samples from other writers. In every single separate count from Shakespeare there were more words with four letters than words with three (or two or one); in every sample from Bacon there were more with three than four. Later he found in Marlowe a 4-letter peak, and in J. S. Mill a 2-letter peak. Williams shows that these skewed curves correspond to log-normal distributions.

Williams took 100 consecutive words from each of ten of Shakespeare's plays, randomised samples but all of them verse. He found that all nouns, adjectives, verbs and adverbs peaked at four letters; articles, conjunctions, pronouns and and interjections peaked at three; and prepositions at two. He also made counts of the distribution of 2-, 3-, 4-letter and longer words in Dickens and Mill as well as Shakespeare.

The distribution of the length (word number) of sentences is also log-normal. Quoting data from Yule, Williams notes that Bacon's peak is at 31–5, Coleridge's at 21–5, Macaulay's at 11–15.

Much attention has been paid, though rather unsystematically, to the idiosyncrasies of a dramatist's style in terms of verse-rhythm. Thus Langworthy[10] in 1931 attempted a chronology of Shakespeare's plays by tabulating the proportions of blank verse lines with feminine endings, of run-on lines, of speeches ending with the line, and light and weak endings. He found, for instance, a fairly steady progression in the proportion of run-on lines from 12.4% in *Two Gentlemen* to 46.0% in *Cymbeline*. On the basis of his counts and calculations he came to the following conclusions:

1. *Shrew* is either a very early play, or there is a large measure of non Shakespearean authorship in it;
2. *All's Well* is not 'Love's Labour Won'; it is nearer to *Lear* and *Macbeth* than to *Twelfth Night*;
3. The authorship of the last three acts of *Pericles* is confirmed as Shakespeare's; the two authors of the two parts are very distinct;
4. The authorship of *Henry VIII* is divided: one author has I.i and ii, II.ii and iv, III.ii as far as the exit of the King, and v.i; another author wrote the rest; the first was Shakespeare.

Langworthy promises a great mass of work to come on Shakespeare's contemporaries by the methods he has devised. One assumes it never saw the light of day.

Williams quotes work, along rather similar lines to those of Langworthy but statistically more sophisticated, published by Yardi in 1946 in the *Indian Journal of Statistics*: 'A statistical approach to the problem of the chronology of Shakespeare's plays.' The work depended on enumerating a number of independent features: the number of 'full split lines', the number of lines with 'redundant final syllables' and the number of 'unsplit lines with pauses', in relation to the total number of speech lines. The appropriate weighting of each of these features was combined in a 'discriminant function' designed to produce the most consistent result in assigning Shakespeare's plays each to its own position in a total chronology. All these features are ways of breaking free from formality and regularity of rhythm; and the index increases in magnitude as Shakespeare grows older. Age, or chronological order, is not the only factor to influence rhythmical patterns. Other observers, including Williams himself, have shown that the percentages of run-on and end-stopped lines, etc., vary between classes of play, the tragedies, serious comedies, histories and light comedies.

To the present writer the most interesting statistical innovation offered by Williams is his 'index of diversity' (pp. 97–104). It has been repeatedly shown that estimates of a writer's total vocabulary (or 'treasury' of words, as posited by Yule) depend on the size of the sample taken. Williams points out that there tends to be a linear relation between the log of the total number of words in the sample and the size of the vocabulary. The larger the sample, the larger the size of the 'treasury' from which it appears to be taken. 'A constant multiplication of the sample is associated with a constant arithmetical increase in the vocabulary.' Yule was much troubled by the disturbing effect of sample size on one's appreciation of the size of a writer's 'treasury'. He proposed therefore his characteristic K $(= \Sigma n(n-1)/N^2)$, which is not affected by sample size. In this n is the magnitude of the group to which a word belongs, i.e. 1 in the case of words which have been used once only, 2 in the case of words which have been used twice only, etc. $\Sigma n(n-1)/2$ is the total number of possible pairings of any given word with itself. N is the total number of words in the sample; and $N(N-1)/2$ is the total number of pairs that can be made by linking any one word with any other. As N is always large, $N(N-1)$ can be replaced by N^2. Yule's characteristic (originally so small that he multiplied it by 10,000) is accordingly ten thousand times the chance that any sample of two nouns selected at random will be identical. It is, accordingly, a measure of the homogeneity, or uniformity, of the vocabulary, indeed of the *smallness* of the treasury. But what we want is an estimate of the magnitude, the diversity of the vocabulary; and this is obtained by turning Yule's K upside-down. Simpson's index of diversity, $N(N-1)/\Sigma n(n-1)$, proposed in 1949, is what we need. It has been usefully applied to the relative abundance of species of animals with different numbers of individuals in mixed wild populations in the field. The number of random pairs that must be selected from a sample to give an even chance of getting an identical pair is the total possible pairs divided by the total identical pairs, i.e. the mathematical expression shown. The fact that it is unaffected by size of sample is demonstrated by Williams on four samples of approximately 2000 words (nouns) from Macaulay's essay on Francis Bacon. The index of diversity varied between 347 and 397 with an average of 363; totalling the four samples, i.e. shifting the total vocabulary from about 2011 to four times that figure, 8045, left the index of diversity practically unchanged at 368.

Williams shows that different parts of speech have different diversities. Taking the Macaulay samples the diversities are: nouns 368, adjectives 116, pronouns 13.6, prepositions 4.3, conjunctions 2.7. But samples from Shakespeare and from Osbert Sitwell show material differences, e.g. in conjunctions Macaulay 2.7, Shakespeare 4.5, Sitwell 5.9. It is clear that in estimating diversities one must take good-sized samples of specified parts of speech, e.g. 350 nouns or 100 adjectives. Williams observes that 'within a single part of speech, diversity can be a very definite characteristic of an author and an additional factor in determining questions of disputed authorship'. It would be good to see systematic work on Shakespeare along this line, taking chronology into account, and comparing him with his contemporaries. Williams goes on to say that there may be other good measures of diversity (in samples of comparable size), e.g. the numbers of words used once only, and the rate of increase of vocabulary with sample size.

Diversity, one would think, would be related to richness of vocabulary, and through that with the writer's capacity to step outside the range of cliché. A writer's ability to find the unusual but particularly appropriate word, the striking image or metaphor, would also depend on the command of a wide diversity. There do not seem to be any studies directed to these points. Unfortunately estimates of diversity depend on voluminous word counts, which nowadays would demand the help of a computer. Williams is, of course, aware of the great amount of work done with computer aid in stylistic studies; but he is equally aware of their likely limitations. 'I have yet to see the machine that will sort the different parts of speech, or the different meanings of the same letter sequence. Machines often answer questions, but seldom ask them.'

STYLOMETRY AND THE SCHOLARS

On the whole literary scholars have not welcomed purely statistical studies with unadulterated enthusiasm. Dr A. Q. Morton,[17] for instance, has felt moved to protest at the chilly reception his work has met, and the general lack of understanding of its *raison d'être*. Important results have been obtained by observing the conjunctions of certain common 'filler' words (such as *and, the*). These observations have their probative value regardless of any explanation of the occurrence of the conjunction. Morton writes:

This is an elementary point but an important one and it keeps being raised by literary critics of the occurrence of proportionate pairs of words. They seem to feel that until some convincing reason is given for the coupling of these words, they are in some sense unreliable as tests of authorship, when the truth is that they have been demonstrated to be reliable tests. It is only the reason why they should be so that is in doubt.

And again:

The occurrence of proportional word pairs is based upon a number of observations made by different people for different reasons. Some critics, especially those who are anxious to resist the conclusions that follow from the evidence, will attack the pairings as being nonsensical on grammatical or linguistic grounds. They see no reason why the occurrence of the pair should be linked. But for each pair of words all that is claimed is that their occurrence is proportional, and this is a matter of evidence and not opinion (p. 148).

Morton is a terse writer, and he sees no reason to be otherwise when presenting cogent evidence. He recommends a summary of the problem and an analysis. If the

Table 4.1. them *and* 'em *in Fletcher and Shakespeare*

Shakespeare		Fletcher		Henry VIII	
Cymbeline	64:3	Woman's Prize	4:60	Shakespeare	23:5
Winter's Tale	37:8	Bonduca	6:83	Fletcher	7:59
Tempest	38:13	Last two of Four Plays in One	1:15		

summary is well done and the course of the analysis is made clear by it, then all that need be added is a summary of the conclusions:

No doubt some critics will refuse to read the summary as well as the analysis and will continue to suggest that another book on a different subject would have been more congenial to them, or even remind their readers that no evidence will embarrass their firm stance, but the summary is not for them (p. 154).

However, not all literary scholars have found statistical evidence incomprehensible, inconclusive or antipathetic. In his edition of *Henry VIII* J. C. Maxwell[12] writes:

A much more satisfactory type of evidence [than metrical analysis] is that afforded by trivial habits of syntax and accidence which a writer is not likely to be aware of, or to vary deliberately (or even unconsciously) in different parts of work about the same period. It is in this field that twentieth-century investigation has confirmed Spedding's findings in several mutually independent ways; I find it quite impossible to regard the convergence of these results as fortuitous (pp. xxi–xxii).

Maxwell then mentions the work of Thorndike (1901), who investigated the relative frequency of the pronominal forms *them* and *'em* in late plays by Shakespeare, in plays by Fletcher of about the same date as *Henry VIII* and in *Henry VIII* itself. The relative numbers of *them:'em* are tabulated in Table 4.1. Maxwell says that for *has* and *hath* the results are comparable, the first being Shakespeare's and the second Fletcher's preference. Contractions, such as *'t* and *th'*, frequent in Shakespeare, also come into consideration. In a postscript Maxwell refers to work by Jackson (1962) showing Shakespeare's preference of *ay* over *yes*, Fletcher's of *yes* over *ay*; and to work by Lake (1969) showing the absence in Fletcher, and in the Fletcherian part of *Henry VIII*, of the contraction of *more* to *mo*, common in Shakespeare.

It will be conceded that Maxwell's entire line of thought, as well as that of the workers he quotes, is in complete harmony with that of Dr Morton and his colleagues at Edinburgh. It is perhaps no wonder that Maxwell took a sympathetic attitude towards the statistical approach to problems of authorship, since he had himself engaged in just such an essay. In his article on Peele and Shakespeare,[11] published in 1950, he showed that a certain grammatical construction is more than usually common in the first act of *Titus Andronicus* and in Peele. This is the use of a possessive (a) adjective or (b) pronoun as the antecedent of a relative clause. He

Table 4.2. *Shakespeare: repetition of the first word in the line*

First word repeated in	*1 Henry VI*	*Winter's Tale*	*Tempest*
2 successive lines	28	49	35
3 successive lines	5	4	2
4 successive lines	1	—	—
Total repetitions	41	57	39
No. of lines	2644	2110	1515
Repetitions per 100 lines	1.507	2.701	2.574

gives examples. He conducted a count, not only in *Titus*, where in this respect Act I distinguished itself from Acts II to V, but also in *Venus and Adonis* and *Rape of Lucrece*, for Shakespeare; and on the other side Peele's poems, *David and Bethsabe*, *Edward I*, *The Old Wives' Tale* and *The Arraignment of Paris*. The count is extended to eight further Shakespeare plays, Marlowe's *Tamburlaine* plays and *Edward II*, two plays of Kyd, three of Greene, one of Lodge, and ten plays of doubtful authorship. Maxwell found six examples of the construction he specifies in *Edward III*, 'not too low for Peele or too high for Shakespeare'.

Unfortunately this characteristic is unpromising as a test of authorship. It does not occur frequently enough to provide numbers sufficient for statistical testing; and it would seem to require close attention to pick it up in reading. Moreover its frequency shows a lot of random variation. It is only really common in Peele's poems, in his one reasonably well preserved late play, and in the first Act of *Titus*.

The impressionistic observations made by scholars may be delusive; and it is not everyone who, like Maxwell, goes to extraordinary pains to verify them. Professor Wolfgang Clemen[3] quotes from a Belgrade periodical* a statement by Professor Kenneth Muir which is a case in point. Quoting Muir verbatim, Clemen reports him as saying:

'He [Shakespeare, in his later work] came to use more metaphors and fewer similes, and he abandoned some of the more obtrusive figures [of rhetoric]. There is less obvious alliteration. He no longer begins successive lines with the same word. He compromises more with colloquial speech. But to say he abandoned rhetoric is a misuse of term.'

In among these impressionistic statements there is one statistical one which can be verified. Counting only the blank verse lines and omitting prose and lyrics, and dropping one line from the count for each change of scene, we have the numbers given in Table 4.2 &or one early play and two late ones. Purely for interest we may give the figures for *Edward III*, part A (I.ii, II.i, II.ii, IV.iv) and part B (the rest). For A we have the first word repeated in successive lines for 2, 3, 4 and 5 lines respectively on 23,

* *Filoloski Pregled*, Beograd, 1964.

2, 1 and 1 occasions with total of 34, i.e. 3.427 repeats per 100 lines. For part B the corresponding numbers are 21, 3 and 1, totalling 30, or 2.022 per 100 lines. We see that Muir's statement (if Clemen quoted him aright) is not borne out by the facts.

MODERN STYLOMETRY

Great difficulties stand in the way of literary scholarship when faced by problems of disputed authorship. There does not seem to be any way through, in the majority of cases, other than by statistical methods. Dr A. Q. Morton and his colleagues at Edinburgh have devised sophisticated but straightforward methods of great generality, involving computer aid, applicable to most languages and most texts, for providing that way through. Dr Morton is primarily a classicist and Greek scholar; but he has joined forces with Professor Sidney Michaelson and Mr Hamilton-Smith of the Department of Computer Science at Edinburgh. They have been fortunate in receiving adequate funds to carry out a very diverse programme of investigations. A general account of their ideas and their work, up till quite recent years, has been given us in Morton's book, *Literary Detection*,[17] from which some quotations have already been made.

In 1971 Morton and Winspear, in a little book, *It's Greek to the Computer*,[19] reported work done on Greek texts of doubtful authorship. They said (even in 1971!) that 'during the last ten years' there had been a revolution in philological studies as a result of computer analysis. The older stylometry concentrated on the study of uncommon words and words used once only. The new method concentrates on the small common words. It has been variously called the study of 'unconscious habits of style' and of the 'skeletal structure of language'. The first term was thought too reminiscent of Freud, but the latter has also been abandoned. In fact, one would say, the small 'filler' words do not provide a skeleton so much as a cement (p. 9).

The work under investigation has to be typed into a computer, which will then provide a print-out, total or selective, on command. It is interesting that it has been found impossible to get a totally error-free print-out. The first version, compared with the original, shows in every 10,000 characters, i.e. about 2000 words of text, between 10 and 20 errors. These are detected and marked for correction. This will get rid of all but 2 or 3 errors per million characters. But if these are detected (a phenomenally difficult task) and corrected, the new print-out will throw up as many new errors. In fact, like all high-precision work in engineering, perfection is unattainable and can only be approached within a given level of 'tolerance'. This is not a bar to getting a text adequate for testing.

The achievements of Morton and his colleagues are very impressive. In *Literary Detection*[17] he describes the methods by which they were attained. Attention is concentrated on the small filler words of very common occurrence, devoid of thematic content, used by all writers but by all in individually differing patterns. It can be shown that, as a rule, in these patterns there is much more variation between writers than within writers between their selves in one stage, or mood, or mode, at one time or another. These individual elements of style are called 'habits'. The main types of habit studied are (1) preferred position in the sentence (e.g. as first word, or last word, or last word but one), (2) proportionate pairs (e.g. the relative frequency of *a* and *an*, or *no* and *not*), (3) collocations (e.g. *and* followed by *the*). In this scheme code abbreviations are used for tabulations, and will be used here, i.e. fws = first word in sentence, lws = last word in sentence, fb = followed by. Sentence length, in terms of words in sentences ended by full stop, query or exclamation mark, has also been found useful.

The first study to claim our attention here is that devoted to the Homeric poems, *Iliad* and *Odyssey*. Did 'Homer' write them, either or both? One must first say, 'Who do you define Homer to be?' The first step is taken when Morton answers, 'the writer of the *Odyssey*, book 15'.* Is there anything in either poem which would not fit in with the hypothesis of its having been written by the writer of *Odyssey* 15? In particular, are there any post-Homeric sections in the poems? In the event, these questions proved to be unanswerable by the means available. There is no comparative material. Sentence length is so much influenced by line endings that there is an enormous excess of sentences exactly one, or two, or three, etc., lines long. So that the position of small very common words in a sentence is subject to artificial constraints and no longer useful as a test of identity of authorship. Proportionate pairs and collocations are affected by the poet's habit of repeating again and again and again incantatory phrases, e.g. adjectives applied to Hector, of just such a length, whether appropriate or not, to fill out the line. Nothing can be identified as post-Homeric, though some sections, e.g. the names of ships or cities, are probably pre-Homeric. Finally, the strongest argument in favour of regarding the authorship of the poems as single is the oldest: 'No one knows what the population of "Greece" was in Homer's day, but that the country should nourish two geniuses of such stature at much the same time is a coincidence beyond acceptance.'

Passing from Homer to the Pauline Epistles, the problems are much easier. The discriminant factors used in the analysis are distributions of sentence lengths and the occurrences of certain common words (*kai, de, gar, ei*) in preferred positions (first or second word in sentence). *Romans* I and II, *Corinthians* and *Galatians* form one group, and the others are separate from it.

Turning to Shakespeare, Morton and his colleagues could find no significant difference between the first two and the last three acts of *Pericles* in respect of three sets of tests: (1) the occurrence in preferred positions of *a, and, as, but, for, if, in, it, no, of, that, the*; (2) the collocations *and a, and the, as the, by the, in a, in the, it is, of a, of all, of the, the* adj., *to* vb; (3) proportionate pairs $a/(a+an)$, $all/(all+any)$, $no/(no+not)$. The fact that not a single one of these 27 independent tests exhibits a statistically significant difference between the two parts of the play is put forward as a massive

---

* A. Q. M. notes: 'Lines 1–300, defined for us by J. Chadwick.'

piece of evidence that cannot easily be dismissed. It may be regarded as supporting the view of a minority of Shakespearean scholars (including Professor Philip Edwards) that, despite the great difference in poetic and dramatic quality between the two parts, they are both Shakespeare's. However Morton, elsewhere, has stressed the fact that statistical agreements are not conclusive, but only disagreements. It is open to those who believe that the first two acts of *Pericles* are not by Shakespeare to object that the critical test, though it has not been found, is yet to be discovered.

That Morton's methods are adequate to distinguish Shakespeare's work from that of two contemporaries, Bacon and Marlowe, is shown by common words in preferred positions and by collocations. The statistical differences between Shakespeare and Bacon are actually of little interest; one can hardly expect dramatic dialogue in blank verse to be comparable with philosophic essays in prose. The Marlowe–Shakespeare comparison is more appealing. However, *Pericles* is the sole representative for Shakespeare; and while samples have been taken for Marlowe from *Tamburlaine*, *Faustus* and *Jew of Malta*, they total to a smaller material than the one play of Shakespeare's. The numbers of *as*, *and*s, *of*s total 1183 for *Pericles*, but only 658 for Marlowe's four plays. It would have been much more satisfactory if one whole play had been taken from each poet, say *Richard II* and *Edward II*.

Morton's tests have been tried out over a wide field. They have proved their power to distinguish between genuine Jane Austen and pastiche, between a Conan Doyle Sherlock Holmes story and an imitation by two Holmes fanatics. They have been upheld in courts of law in this country, and in Sweden when applied to texts in Swedish. The team believe that their methods could be applied to almost any language (including Chinese?), and to almost any spoken or written material (including genuine folk nursery rhymes and modern imitations?). They believe that these methods, which could of course be extended to words and word couplings almost without limit, are adequate for the solution of almost any dispute about authorship, provided the material is adequate in amount and provided also that comparative material is available. Nothing they say goes to show that other methods, depending on observations of other kinds, could not also be used for the same range of problems. It will be maintained in a later chapter that rare words can also be made use of for such a purpose.

'The techniques we use are those of modern stylometry, not of stylistics nor of stylistic analysis' (p. 1).[16] Stylometry measures habits displayed by a person in his utterances, and recognised as his and not another's. As a science it belongs to the general class of recognition systems, such as are applied, for instance, in the recognition of the identity of suspects or criminals. The point is developed more particularly in their article, 'Fingerprinting the mind'.[15] We are all quite unique. We are prisoners of our habits and reveal ourselves in all we say or write. Progress in stylometry has resulted from cutting free from the categories used in literary, linguistic, philological, and all other kinds of studies. Stylometry is now a descriptive science. We take the point. Stylometry is, purely, a recognition system.

It has nothing to do with 'style' as that word is understood (or, perhaps one should say, as it is vaguely apprehended) by students of literature. An efficient recognition system can identify an individual while telling us absolutely nothing about his character and personality, his education and culture, his cast of mind – saturnine, jovial or melancholic, – his occupations and interests, his attitude to life, death, humanity and God. A single finger-print has such an immense number of particularities, all at set angles and distances in relation to one another, that its origin (even though it be a forgery) can be established with absolute certainty. But the finger-print of an accused person, which effectively ties him to the locus of the crime, tells nothing else about him which the scientist, the jurist or the juryman can possibly want to know. The same is true of other recognition systems, equally decisive of identity and equally uninformative of anything else – the blood-groups, the antigenic systems of the body tissues, the pattern of the blood vessels in the retina of the eyes, the sound spectrum of the vibrations of the voice. As the archaeologist goes to the physicist for a carbon dating of some significant *objet trouvé*, so must the literary scholar go to the stylometrists if he wishes to establish, say, the authorship of *Sir Thomas More*.

In their University of Edinburgh Report of 1978,[14] Michaelson, Morton and Hamilton-Smith attempt to formulate a scientific basis for their system which would bring it into an intelligible relationship with the physiology of the brain. The stylometry of English was based on a stylometry of Greek. Investigations in Sanskrit and Swedish have produced comparable results. A stylometry of Latin is under development. This suggests the existence of a larger pattern which can only come from the human brain and reflects how it arranges and retrieves the words it stores. The authors refer to Wernicke's and Broca's areas in the brain, damage to which produces speech disturbances of different kinds. Relevant to this theory is an investigation they carried out on two works of Sir Walter Scott.

Sir Walter Scott had a series of strokes, in 1823, two in 1830, a fourth in 1831 and a last one in 1832. There were other vicissitudes which intervened between the publication of *The Antiquary* in 1816 and of *Castle Dangerous* in 1831. Accordingly the first of these books was written when Scott's brain was presumably intact, and the second after he had had at least one, and perhaps two or three strokes. Scott's medical history is unknown to the present writer, but it seems inconceivable that he could have had serious local damage to the speech centres of the brain and have gone on to produce *Castle Dangerous*. What one must suppose, however, is that the cerebral vascular disease which killed him most probably did have some general intellectual effect years before he died. An interesting study would have been an investigation *à la* Yule of his treasury of words, the number of unique words and the diversity of his vocabulary, as suggested by Williams,[22] as sampled before and after the cerebral insults. It is not this that the stylometrists give us, of course, but a study along the lines they have made their own. Statistically the work is very thorough, taking repeated samples of each book, so that each can be compared with itself as well as with the other. In the end they give us a table of 27 discriminatory tests of which the great majority show no significant difference between the two works. The table (p. 50) shows the raw numbers converted into percentages, correct to the second significant figure, to help the eye in making comparisons. The denominators for these percentages are relatively large numbers running from hundreds into thousands, so that some differences, though seemingly not very great ones, attain statistical significance. The table shows the value of χ^2 if it has reached statistical significance (for one degree of freedom: see Table 4.3).

No explicit explanation is offered by the authors for the other significant differences, which are put down to non-normal distributions of the words. The argument is not easily understood. Whether a distribution is binomial or Poisson, the χ^2 test is applicable; and in these tests its value is far too high to be dismissed. The total χ^2 of 152.26 for all tests together is out at an astronomical distance from ordinary ranges of improbability. In their summing up the authors write: 'The conclusion is that Scott's habits did not change from the writing of The Antiquary to the composition of Castle Dangerous.' How can this be acceptable? A number of very largely significant differences are shown; brain damage affected Scott between the writing of the first book and the second; it is part of the authors' theory that stylometry measures habits which depend on brain functions; it is entirely plausible that the change in habits could be accounted for by the brain damage. The findings in the case of Walter Scott are, in fact, substantial evidence in favour of the neurophysiological hypothesis which the authors have themselves advanced. Then why not accept them, instead of trying to invalidate them by single unconnected arguments ad rem?

Dr Morton has recently circulated in manuscript a series of papers of particular interest to students of Shakespeare.[18] In the first of these three plays of Shakespeare, Julius Caesar, Pericles and Titus Andronicus, are compared. Allowing two degrees of freedom for the three-fold comparison, the value of χ^2 must exceed 5.99 for p <0.05. In the fifty or more habits analysed there are only 5 which reach this level. They are shown in Table 4.4, Morton's raw numbers being recalculated as percents correct to the second significant figure.

The 52 tests yield a total χ^2 of 174.18 for 104 degrees of freedom. For large values of d.f. the expression $\sqrt{2\chi^2} - \sqrt{2n-1}$ can be used as a normal deviate with unit variance; here it is $18.6644 - 14.3875 = 4.2769$. The value of the expression is accordingly more than four times its standard error, and must be regarded as highly significant.*

Dr Morton feels that these large values of χ^2 should be explained away, but it is not necessary to enquire into his explanations. These large differences can hardly come as a surprise, even to those who would be willing to accept the totally Shakespearean authorship of all three plays. Titus Andronicus is one of Shakespeare's very earliest plays, written in the Senecan mode; Julius Caesar, a play of the middle period, is one with a relatively impoverished vocabulary, and one in which

*For 104 d.f., p=0.00050, χ^2=158.086 (Geigy).

Table 4.3. *Change in habits in Sir Walter Scott*

Test			Percentages in		
Preferred positions			*Antiquary*	*Castle D.*	χ^2
1	BUT	fws	27	22	
2	I	,,	16	18	
3	IT	,,	7.9	11	
4	THE	,,	4.8	4.3	
5	IT	lws	4.8	6.2	
6	THE	last but one	5.7	3.5	19.11
Proportionate pairs					
7	A	A + AN	85	84	
8	ANY	ALL + ANY	27	48	17.63
9	IN	IN + INTO	91	90	
10	MORE	MORE + MOST	44	22	16.83
11	NO	NO + NOT	41	30	14.62
12	THIS	THIS + THAT	37	36	
Collocations					
13	A	fb adj.	35	41	6.75
14	AND	,, THE	6.2	9.0	9.73
15	,,	,, adj.	15	10	16.26
16	AS	,, THE	8.9	8.4	
17	AT	,, ,,	23	34	11.10
18	BE	preceded by TO	25	27	
19	BY	fb THE	27	25	
20	FOR	,, ,,	16	21	
21	IN	,, ,,	25	22	
22	OF	,, ,,	25	23	
23	ON	,, ,,	35	37	
24	THE	,, adj.	23	27	20.39
25	TO	,, BE	5.5	6.0	
26	,,	,, THE	13	14	
		Total χ^2			152.26

Note: The 26 tests include 9 in which there is a highly significant difference in habits between the two books, in tests numbered 6, 8, 10, 11, 13, 14, 15, 17, 24. The authors make the following comments: *Test 6.* Analysis of variance shows the difference is one within one work rather than between works; and in Chapter 23 of *The Antiquary* it is largely concentrated in passages of direct speech. *Test 8.* Difference due to passages in *Castle Dangerous* in Scottish dialect in which *all* is replaced by *a'*. If *a'* is added to *all*, the difference between the two books disappears. *Test 11.* Difference due to passages in *The Antiquary* in which *no'* replaces final *t* of *not* with glottal stop.

Shakespeare kept exceptionally close to his source; while *Pericles* is one of his last plays, and (although the stylometric tests show no incompatibilities) it is so different in its first two and its last three acts that most scholars reject the Shakespearean authorship of the first two acts, and all hypothesise a major disturbing factor affecting their language. Indeed, it is a matter for some wonder

Table 4.4. *Differences in habits:* Caesar, Pericles, Titus

Habit	*Julius Caesar*	*Pericles*	*Titus*	χ^2
IS fb THE	2.8	5.6	9.4	8.36
IT fb IS	19	7.0	8.6	13.02
THE fws	6.8	4.6	1.7	19.14
„ last but one	17	11	8.4	21.61
„ fb adj.	17	20	24	8.64

that the Shakespearean thumb-print is so consistently displayed in 47 out of the total 52 tests.

However, Dr Morton has made other observations which transform the situation. Six of the 52 tests relate to preferred position, and they produce the largest χ^2s. Dr Morton counts sentences as ending with a full stop, question mark or mark of exclamation. The numbers of these punctuation marks for the three plays counted by Morton are shown below, underneath the count of lines in the plays as published by Alfred Hart, and finally the average length of a sentence in terms of lines (Table 4.5). By this computation *Titus* has on the average much longer sentences than either of the other plays. This still remains so if we add the colon to other stops: the three average lengths then become 2.20, 1.30 and 1.58. It seems that the preferred position habits should not be taken into account. If they are dropped the total χ^2 loses its two largest components in Table 4.4, and drops to 119.78 for 92 d.f., but $\sqrt{2\chi^2} - \sqrt{2n-1}$ is 1.95, which is still significant (p=0.027).*

In his next comparison Morton examines two plays of George Peele. Habits involving 25 degrees of freedom showed only three differences exceeding the p <0.05 level of significance, two of them involving *I* and *the* as first word of sentence, and therefore subject to the arbitrary influence of punctuation. The third shows a sharp difference between the two plays (p <0.005) in the frequency of *and*

Table 4.5. *Differences in punctuation:* Titus, Caesar, Pericles

	Titus	*Caesar*	*Pericles*
Total no. of lines	2522	2450	2331
full stops	815	1256	1034
question marks	131	292	199
exclamation marks	2	208	156
total punctuations	948	1756	1389
average sentence length	2.66	1.40	1.68

*For 92 d.f., p=0.05 χ^2=115.39, p=0.025 χ^2=120.43 (Geigy)

fb adj. Omitting tests of preferred position, which seem to be unreliable in Elizabethan texts, we have a total χ^2 of 34.03 with 0.05 > p > 0.02 for 20 tests (and 20 d.f.). On the whole, then, one cannot agree with Morton in concluding that there 'is no reason to doubt the homogeneity of these plays when combined to make a single sample for comparison with Shakespeare'.

When Morton compares Peele with Shakespeare he finds seven significant differences in habits (none of them relating to preferred position in sentence), six of them with probabilities of less than 0.01, 0.001 or very much less than that. His conclusion that 'Peele is not a candidate for having written any Shakespearean texts' would very likely be quite justified, if we had full stylometric data for all those texts regarded as Shakespeare's where Peele might conceivably have intruded. Morton comments: 'the two writers resemble each other in many habits and so, from a literary point of view, to argue that they are similar is not ridiculous'. However, 'unless the critic is aware that resemblance proves nothing [see the stylometric data on *Pericles*] and only differences matter, he can easily mislead himself'.

An interesting application of Edinburgh stylometry has been made by Thomas Merriam.[13] He was interested in the authorship of *Henry VIII*, which, since James Spedding's article of 1850, has been generally regarded as the work in part of Shakespeare and in part of Fletcher. Merriam had the collaboration of John Dorricott at Basingstoke Technical College. The text of *Henry VIII* was typed into the computer and then submitted to 20 stylometric tests. It was found that dividing

Table 4.6. *Spedding and Merriam on* Henry VIII

	Fletcher (F) Spedding agree	or Shakespeare (S) Merriam disagree
Prologue	F	
Act I scenes i and ii	S	
scene iii	F	
scene iv		F/S
Act II scene i		F/S
scene ii	F	
scene iii		S/F
scene iv	S	
Act III scene i		F/S
scene ii to line 202	S	
scene ii from line 203	F	
Act IV scene i	F	
scene ii to line 82		F/S
scene ii from line 83	F	
Act V scene i		S/F
scenes ii–v	F	
Epilogue	F	

the play into Shakespearean and Fletcherian parts in the way recommended by Spedding gave an inconclusive result (χ^2 23.85, 20 d.f., 0.30 > p >0.20). It seemed that the play did fall into two parts, but that Spedding probably had not got the division just right. An ingenious programme was devised to find the most distinctive division, which was found to follow Spedding in the main, but to correct him at six places, as shown in Table 4.6.

With these corrections the stylometric tests gave a much more decisive statistical result, χ^2 being raised by the first revision from the previous 23.85 to 64.42, and then, after the subdivision of an equivocal Act IV scene ii, to 72.90. This is far beyond the limits of what is thinkable as a chance phenomenon; and with the previous evidence available, one must regard the play as certainly heterogeneous. The stylometric tests do not in themselves establish who were the two authors who

Table 4.7. *Fletcher/Shakespeare:* Henry VIII *and* Winter's Tale *(adapted from Merriam's data)*

Habit		χ^2	Percentages in			χ^2
			Henry VIII		*Winter's*	
			Fletcher	Shakespeare	*Tale*	
A	fws	4.38	4.1	9.1	13	ns
AND	,,	ns	8.1	9.0	14	,,
AS	,,	5.80	15	3.2	7.0	,,
BUT	,,	ns	38	36	32	,,
FOR	,,	9.90	8.2	24	27	,,
IF	,,	ns	42	46	54	,,
IN	,,	,,	5.1	4.4	5.9	,,
IT	,,	14.00	29	13	10	,,
,,	lws	ns	19	23	20	,,
NO	fws	,,	27	16	14	,,
OF	,,		insufficient numbers			,,
THAT	,,	4.05	11	5.1	9.2	,,
THE	,,	ns	9.8	12	12	,,
AN/A	,,	,,	12	11	10	,,
ALL/(ALL + ANY)		7.67	96	83	80	,,
NO/(NO + NOT)		ns	37	35	29	,,
BY fb THE		,,	3.8	9.7	11	,,
IN ,, ,,		,,	14	14	22	,,
IT ,, IS		22.32	37	14	18	,,
TO ,, THE		ns	12	13	16	,,
Total χ^2		72.90				12.96

Note: The first columns of χ^2 figures relates to the differences between the two parts of *Henry VIII*, Fletcher's and Shakespeare's. The last column also relates to χ^2, but here the numbers are all too small to achieve significance at p < 0.05, for which χ^2 must exceed 3.841. ns = not significant. It shows that there is no significant stylometric difference between the hypothetically Shakespearean part of *Henry VIII* and Shakespeare's *Winter's Tale*.

collaborated. The whole of Maxwell's argument identifying one of them as Shakespeare and the other as Fletcher remains in possession of the field. Merriam's improvement on Spedding should be considered by literary scholars, for them to say whether the new allocations are felt to be satisfying.

Although Merriam did not pursue the Fletcherian part of the authorship, he carried out a comparison of the Shakespearean part of *Henry VIII* (as determined by him) with Acts II and III of *The Winter's Tale*. The result was a very satisfactory fit. The figures are shown in Table 4.7. For demonstration purposes Merriam's percentages have been reduced to two significant places, and the values of χ^2 have been entered where they attained significance at the $p < 0.05$ level. While the total χ^2 reaches the very high value of 72.9 in distinguishing Shakespeare's *Henry VIII* from Fletcher's, it is held to the low value of 12.96 in distinguishing Shakespeare (*Henry VIII*) from Shakespeare (*Winter's Tale*). Here the fit is excellent with $0.90 > p > 0.80$.

CONCLUSION

This account of the important modern developments in computer-aided stylistic and recognition systems in literature must suffice for the purposes of this book. The problem of the authorship of *The Reign of King Edward III* is one of identification, and would have been well suited to analysis by stylometry. How is it then that these methods have not been used? The short answer is that the writer has been travelling along a very different path for a number of years, one, moreover, in which a series of interesting findings were made. It was natural, then, that he should wish to apply his own techniques rather than those of others of which he has only recently become aware. Extensive aid from computers and highly expert program-writers were in any case beyond his reach.

But there is also a longer answer. Stylometrists will agree that their methods tell us no more about the mind of the poet and dramatist than finger-prints tell the criminologist about the mind of the criminal. Moreover, even as a recognition system, the habits studied by stylometry are much the less reliable material. Finger-prints are precise, exact and are immune to variation from infancy to the grave. Habits are probabilities, and are subject to 'errors' both random and systematic. The frequency of coupling between two words, such as *and* and *the*, varies, to some degree at least, from one work to another of the same author. How much variation is there? Is variation greater in some habits than others? In some authors than others? Is there an interaction, so that habit A is more variable than habit B in X, but the other way round in Y? How do habits change with age? or theme? or type of product? Are there secular changes in habits from generation to generation? Clearly we shall not be in a position to appreciate fully the significance of this new field of enquiry until a whole regiment of writers have been systematically worked over. Like the intrepid Captain Cook, Dr Morton has discovered Australia, and the exploration of a continent remains.

Recognition systems such as stylometry enable us to identify text with author. The identification is essential, but only to provide a footing for further study. Such study may be impersonal, but generally it will include a personal element. If we aim at a deeper understanding of the mind and thought of a writer we shall have recourse to comparisons with others. If we try to describe his personal style, the qualities that make him unique, we shall need many avenues of approach. Each of these will lead to some facet of his individuality in which he differs, though only in degree, from associates and rivals and peers. What we have in the end, then, is not a single discrete unity, but a figure in many dimensions, unique not in any single quality but in the singularity of the total combination.

SUMMARY

1. In 1980 a symposium in honour of Kenneth Muir was published on the subject of 'Shakespeare's styles'. This gave the opportunity of seeking what would be a scholarly consensus on the distinctive features of Shakespeare's writing. No consensus emerged. Variations in expression were noted between early, mature and late Shakespeare; sometimes between plays; sometimes between characters. More personal, perhaps, is the mobility of the mind behind the writing. 'Rapid transitions of feeling, thought and figure' might be too much for the syntax. Spontaneous images burst through coherence. Shakespeare's world of ideas is very odd indeed, but that was beyond the scope of the symposium. His ways of expressing his ideas proved too various to be confined within the limits of literary formulae. Any literary judgment has an element of subjectivity; it is very hard to *demonstrate* its truth. Unaided by some objective test, it is unlikely to reach a conclusive answer to a question of authorship.

2. Stylistic analysis appears as an offshoot of linguistics in the basic text of Herdan. It is developed along readily practicable lines by C. B. Williams. Differences between authors can be found in a number of measures: the peak number of letters in a word, of words in a sentence, etc. In verse, percentages of end-stopped and run-on lines have been called in aid in Shakespearean chronology. Williams has proposed an interesting index of diversity $N^2/\Sigma n(n-1)$, in which the numerator is the square of the total number of words (e.g. nouns) in the sample, and the denominator is the total number of pairings of any given word with itself. The index has the great advantage of insensitivity to the size of the sample; and its significance is important as an indication of the richness of the vocabulary available to the author.

3. Stylometry is yet another and quite different field of study made possible by the availability of large computers. It has been extensively applied by Dr A. Q. Morton and his colleagues at the Department of Computer Science at Edinburgh. The method consists in reading an extended text into the computer, and then recording on the print-out the frequency of conjunction of two supposedly independent common events. It is much concerned with the very commonest filler words, *and,*

the, etc. Individual writers have been shown to have their own patterns of frequency. The method has been applied to the Homeric poems, the Pauline Epistles, certain novels, certain plays of Shakespeare. The method has a good record of successes in admitting or rebutting an authorship; but it has certain limitations and disadvantages.

5

The statistical work of Alfred Hart

The work of Alfred Hart, an Australian scholar, has already been touched on in Chapter 1, pp. 3–6, and Chapter 2, pp. 18–20. One of his articles[1] was specifically concerned with *Edward III*. It does not seem that either this or his other work has received much attention from scholars in Europe or America. But he was a pioneer in the statistical approach to problems of authorship to whom the present writer is deeply indebted.

The first of his works to concern us is actually the later in date of publication. This comprises the two articles he contributed to the *Review of English Studies* in 1943: 'The vocabularies of Shakespeare's plays'[2] and 'The growth of Shakespeare's vocabulary';[3] and we deal with them here because in the first of the two he describes in detail his method of work, a matter of central importance. He opens with the sentence: 'When I decided to count the words in each play and long poem of Shakespeare, the first thing needful was a concordance suited to my purpose' (p. 128). He does not say why he took such an extraordinary decision, nor what he hoped to gain by undertaking what he must have realised was a dauntingly laborious task. His work on *Edward III*[1] was published in 1934 in a book, *Shakespeare and the Homilies*. This contains a number of articles e.g. on play abridgement and on the vocabulary of *Two Noble Kinsmen*, for which he made extensive enumerations; so he must have embarked on meticulous enumerative work many years before 1934. In fact, this solitary pioneer must have entered on his stony track long before the statistician Udny Yule conceived the approach which led to the publication of his book *The Statistical Study of Literary Vocabulary* in 1944. Yule explains why and how he went to work the way he did; Hart leaves his motivation in utter obscurity. Without any such explanation his work must have struck many readers as pointless, boring and barely comprehensible. Perhaps, for some, it still does.

In looking for a suitable concordance, Hart examined the *Complete Concordance to Shakespeare* compiled by Mrs Cowden Clarke nearly a century earlier, Schmidt's *Shakespeare Lexicon* of 1874, and Bartlett's *A New and Complete Concordance* first published twenty years later. It was only Schmidt's *Lexicon* that suited his needs. Both Clarke and Bartlett omitted pronouns and pronominal adjectives, auxiliary verbs and nearly all prepositions, conjunctions and interjections, some adjectives, some adverbs and even some verbs. On the other hand, both gave separate artiles to the inflexions of many verbs, adjectives and even nouns, but not uniformly. Homonyms differing in origin, meaning and functions were confounded; different parts of speech written alike were not distinguished. Both compilers used nineteenth-century editions of the plays, 'and in consequence admitted into their concordances words not used by Shakespeare but emendations made by some critic, and omitted variant readings found in the early quartos and folios' (p. 128).[2] Schmidt's *Lexicon*, says Hart, is free of these defects, and was gathered from the early quartos and folios. His faults are due to insufficient knowledge of idiomatic English. Homonyms of different meanings were at times included under a single heading. So, as Hart found, the counting of words in the vocabulary of a play could not be a mechanical process. He continues his explanation in the words quoted below (p. 129). The present writer takes this opportunity of defining his own practice, closely similar to that of Hart, by detailing in square brackets those of his own practices which differ from Hart's:

My method of enumeration was, in the main, based on the principles adopted by the editors of *The Oxford English Dictionary* (O.E.D.). I counted as one word a noun used adjectivally, an adjective used as a noun or an adverb, an adverb used as a preposition, or a preposition used as a conjunction or adverb. [Different parts of speech taken to be distinct words.] A verb uniform in stem with a noun or an adjective was treated as a distinct word. In general I did not count inflected forms of a verb, e.g. present participle, past participle or gerund, as distinct from the parent verb. If a participle had acquired a specialized sense or represented a substantive with the addition of *-ed* or *-ing*, it was reckoned as a distinct word. Much though was given to the position in our speech of the verbal noun, which in some instances came into our language before the finite verb. In O.E.D. the editors seem to accept the gerund as a distinct word by treating it in a separate article. Most hesitatingly I decided, in counting the vocabularies, against following this practice, and did not usually give the gerund the status of an independent word. [Word checked against the *Shorter* O.E.D. and taken as distinct if given its own article with heading in bold.] Certain gerunds in common use for centuries, e.g. 'breathing', 'breeding', 'hearing', 'hunting', 'learning', 'offering', 'opening', 'reading', 'writing', etc., words long denizened in our speech, were included as separate words in my count, because for some of them there are no exact synonyms. Gerunds used in the plural were usually counted as distinct words. The total number of these formations included in the poet's vocabulary would not much exceed a hundred. Names of persons or of characters in the plays, and place-names of villages, towns, counties, countries, seas, etc., have been omitted in my totals. Some adjectives formed from the names of counties, countries and towns, e.g. 'English', 'French', 'German', 'Welsh', 'Scottish', 'Irish', 'Kentish', 'Greek', 'Roman', 'Londoner', Athenian', 'Venetian', etc., are included, but they are not numerous. [All words with initial capital were omitted.] No word taken from living languages other than English has been counted unless it was then in common use or has been naturalized since. [No word from any other language than English admitted.]

Hart's statement in explication of his method must also be read as a statement of the method of the present writer, with the modifications noted. In addition, hyphenated words have been taken as unities. The guiding principle, when in doubt, of taking that decision which will increase the total material available for statistical analysis rather than that one which will restrict it, has also been relied on. As an example we may take the word *eyne*, an archaic plural for *eyes*. *Eye* and *eyes* appear too frequently for inclusion in a rare-word vocabulary; but the use of *eyne* represents an act of choice on the part of the writer, and may therefore be characteristic of him or of him at one stage of his writing. Accordingly it is included.

With his own list of words, gathered in the way he has described, Hart drew up a Table embracing the 37 plays of Shakespeare (including *Henry VIII*), the two long poems *Venus and Adonis* and *The Rape of Lucrece*, and the Poems and Sonnets, i.e. a total of 40 items. Unfortunately he lumped the Sonnets (2155 lines) together with *The Phoenix and the Turtle* (67 lines), *A Lover's Complaint* (329 lines) and *The Passionate Pilgrim* (410 lines), making the total 2981 lines [2961]. He took no account of the fact that a number of poems in the last-named collection are known not to be by Shakespeare.

Hart tabulated (1) title of play or poem, (2) number of lines, (3) number of different dictionary or lexical words, (4) 'peculiar' words, i.e. words appearing once or more in the work named and not elsewhere, by number, and (5) as a proportion per cent of the number of lexical words. This tabulation is given twice, in Table I of 'Vocabularies of Shakespeare's plays'[2] (p. 132), and again as Table IV in 'The growth of Shakespeare's vocabulary'[3] (p. 249). Unfortunately the numbers in column III of Table I and the column 'No. of Words' in Table IV do not agree in every particular. As the second article is presumably later than the first, we must assume that the alterations* represent corrections: it is these corrected numbers which have been entered in our Table 5.1.

This table adopts some of Hart's counts (as shown), but has been rearranged slightly in chronology, and omits the poems and *Henry VIII*. The 2442 words counted by Hart for *Pericles* have been divided into two parts, for Acts I and II, and Acts III to v, proportionately to the numbers of lines in those two parts. Column 1 shows Hart's counts for the numbers of different words in the plays, column 2 the numbers of lines, and column 8 Hart's estimates of the proportion of 'peculiar' words to all words in the play, not as per cent, but as parts per thousand. The other columns are new, and have been calculated by myself. The whole vocabulary sums to 100,934 distributed over 98,991 lines, and column 3 shows the number of different words (to the nearest whole number) to be expected in a play if it had its due proportion corresponding to its number of lines. The proportion of Observed to Expected is shown in column 4, and it will be seen how widely the ratio varies, all the way from 1.25 down to 0.89:

1.20 + *Mac*, *1mp*;
1.15 +   —
1.10 + *1H6, Err, MND, Jo*;
1.05 + *LLL, Tim*;
1.00 + *2H6, Tit, R2, 1H4, TN, Ham, Lr, Per, WT*;
0.95 + *Shr, TGV, Rom, MV, 2H4, H5, AYL, Tro, AWW, MM, Ant, Cym*;
0.90 + *3H6, Wiv, Ado, Oth, Cor*;
0.85 + *R3, JC*

* These are (numbers in brackets are those of Table I, i.e. superseded) *R3* (3224) 3218, *Shr* (2462) 2463, *H5* (3147) 3162, *AYL* (2623) 2578, *TN* (2524) 2534, *Tro* (3260) 3360, *Oth* (3075) 3015, *AWW* (2697) 2703.

Table 5.1. *Shakespeare: vocabulary analysis (Hart–Slater)*

0	1	2	3	4	5	6	7	8
2H6	3146	3069	3129	1.01	+ 17	.09	17	50
3H6	2790	2902	2959	.94	-169	9.65	-152	41
1H6	3014	2676	2729	1.10	+285	29.76	+133	48
R3	3218	3600	3671	.88	-453	55.90	-320	45
Err	2037	1753	1787	1.14	+250	34.97	- 70	41
Tit	2578	2522	2572	1.00	+ 6	.01	- 64	44
Shr	2463	2552	2602	.95	-139	7.43	-203	61
TGV	2153	2193	2236	.96	- 83	3.08	-286	33
LLL	2872	2651	2703	1.06	+169	10.57	-117	88
Rom	2916	2986	3045	.96	-129	5.47	-246	96
R2	2833	2755	2809	1.01	+ 24	.21	-222	47
MND	2363	2102	2143	1.10	+220	22.59	- 2	68
Ja	2901	2570	2620	1.11	+281	30.14	+279	48
MV	2571	2554	2604	.99	- 33	.42	+246	45
1H4	3028	2968	3026	1.00	+ 2	.00	+248	80
2H4	3130	3180	3242	.97	-112	3.87	+136	78
Wiv	2527	2634	2686	.94	-159	9.41	- 23	91
Ado	2396	2535	2585	.93	-189	13.82	-212	46
H5	3162	3166	3228	.98	- 66	1.35	-278	78
JC	2218	2450	2498	.89	-280	31.39	-558	32
AYL	2578	2608	2659	.97	- 81	2.47	-639	60
TN	2534	2429	2477	1.02	+ 57	1.31	-582	62
Ham	3882	3762	3836	1.01	+ 46	.55	-536	102
Tro	3360	3329	3394	.99	- 34	.34	-570	93
AWW	2705	2738	2792	.97	- 87	2.71	-657	59
MM	2669	2660	2712	.98	- 43	.68	-700	61
Oth	3015	3229	3292	.92	-277	23.31	-977	72
Tim	2521	2299	2344	1.08	+177	13.37	-800	56
Lr	3339	3205	3268	1.02	+ 71	1.54	-729	104
Mac	2652	2084	2125	1.25	+527	130.70	-202	74
Ant	3004	3016	3075	.98	- 71	1.64	-273	78
Cor	3130	3279	3343	.94	-213	13.57	-486	78
Per¹	1049	2331	2377	1.03	+ 65	1.78	-421	43
,, ²	1393							
Cym	3260	3264	3328	.98	- 68	1.39	-489	67
WT	2965	2925	2982	.99	- 17	.10	-506	74
Tmp	2562	2015	2055	1.25	+507	125.08	+ 1	79
	100934	98991	100933			590.67		

Note: Columns: o:play, Per¹=first 2 acts, Per²=rest. *Henry VIII* has been omitted. 1: number of different words, count by Hart. 2: number of lines (Hart). 3: number of words expected, correct to nearest whole number. 4: ratio of 1:3. 5: difference 1–3. 6: χ^2. 7: cumulative sum of 5. 8: ratio of 'peculiar' words to 1 (Hart) proportion per 1000.

It is not easy to suggest a reason why *Macbeth* and *The Tempest* should so far outdistance the other plays in the richness of their vocabulary. It is clear, of course, that the number of words per play runs roughly parallel with the number of lines; but the large spread shown in the distribution exhibited above tells us that there must be other major factors involved. There is much too much variation to be ascribed to chance.

Hart noticed this. He writes:

Factors other than length... influence the number of words used, especially variety of theme, incidental episodes, characterization, and the amount of prose. In general a comedy has a smaller vocabulary than a tragedy or history of equal length. This is due partly to the circumstance that comedy must keep closer to the language of every-day life and partly to the fact that it moves ordinarily on a lower emotional plane (p. 136).

These seem to have been impressions, without evidential backing. The figures of column 4 in Table 5.1 are measures of excesses or deficiencies of words per unit length. They show that the average figure for the Histories (*2H6, 3H6, 1H6, R3, R2, Jo, 1H4, 2H4, H5*) is 1.001; the Tragedies (*Tit, Rom, JC, Ham, Oth, Tim, Lr, Mac, Ant, Cor*) average slightly more, 1.005; while the Comedies (the remainder) have actually the largest vocabularies, with an average of 1.016. Hart's other suggestions for factors influencing the number of words are not capable of objective definition apart from 'amount of prose', which he might have tested but didn't.

The relation between number of words observed and number of words proportionally expected is also shown in columns 5, 6 and 7. Column 5 shows the arithmetical difference Observed (o) minus Expected (E), with the two totals of positive and of negative differences equalling one another (± 1). Column 6 shows the values of χ^2. The numbers here run to very large ones indeed, indicating the magnitude of the effects of factors unknown. Column 7 shows the accumulated total, positive or negative, of these differences as one proceeds down the table from early to late plays. This figure (commonly called the 'cusum') is a sensitive indicator of differences between one part or parts of a series and others. We see here that the cusum varies between positive and negative down to *2H4* and thereafter is consistently negative down to *Tmp*. More precisely, the numbers show three eras: *2H6* to *Jo*, totalling $+279$, *MV* to *Oth*, totalling -1256, and *Tim* to *Tmp*, totalling $+978$. We test the significance by analysis of variance. (Sum of squares $= 1,464,489$, 35 degrees of freedom; variance between eras $= 277^2/13 + 1256^2/14 + 978^2/9 = 224,945$, 2 d.f.; residual variance $= 1,239,544$, 33 d.f.; F $=$ ratio of mean squares $= 2.994$, p > 0.05, ns.

We may suspect that there was some factor affecting Shakespeare's facility with words over the middle part of his career. This could be connected with a mood change; and there are scholars, as for instance Chambers, who have postulated a melancholic phase, a view also taken by myself.[4] Nevertheless this is unproven, and does not help us very much. The variance, as shown by a χ^2 value of 590, in this matter of word-per-line productivity, must have many sources; with the variation (between the three eras) we have not identified any significant part.

Hart's principal conclusions, based on his statistical analysis, are given in the following words:

(i) Shakespeare was continually changing portions of his vocabulary. (ii) Certain words, representing from three to over ten per cent of the vocabulary of a play [see Table 5.1, column 8], were used only in that play, i.e. he discarded them after using them once or more in that play. (iii) He gradually increased, not the size of the vocabulary of a play, but the number of once-used words in the vocabulary [of that play] (p. 138).

These conclusions are somewhat misleading. There is no justification for saying Shakespeare 'discarded' words he had once used. The mental process cannot have been so deliberate and voluntary. Certain words simply happened not to be used again (see Fig. 5.1). We can understand this very well from the model offered by Yule of words being overlaid and, with the passage of time, less easy of access (see Chapter 2, p. 16). Let us put the point more precisely. In working from opus 1 towards the final opus, when Shakespeare had reached opus N he would have accumulated a total of x words which at that stage he had used once and once only. In moving on from opus N to opus $N+1$, some of these once-used words would be used a second time and so have to be dropped from the list, diminishing x by that amount. But this diminution would be more than made up by an accretion of new words, never used before. The effect of both processes together would be to increase the magnitude of x from opus to succeeding opus. As Hart's final count of the total of one-play words (7219 in Table III[3], p. 243) shows, the rate of growth was surprisingly large throughout his career.

In his second paper Hart made a start on estimating the rate of inflow of new words into Shakespeare's vocabulary, i.e. to start with, 3146 words in *2H6*, an additional 1141 appearing with *3H6*, a further 921 with *1H6*, and a further 824 with *R3*. The method of accounting for the growth of the vocabulary became too laborious; and Hart substituted for it a count extending over the whole of the canon, enumerating the totals of 'one-play words', 'two-play words' and so on down to 'ten-play words'. We can safely suppose that these numbers would be a little greater than words used once only, twice only, etc., but the two series would be very closely correlated and run parallel. Hart's totals for one- and two-play words, etc., dropping from 7219 and 2206 all the way down to 262 for the ten-play group, have exactly the limp-flag-hanging-from-a-flag-pole shape of curve that we met with in the work of Yule in Chapter 2, p. 13.

When Hart concludes that Shakespeare 'gradually increased' the number of one-play (i.e., in effect the once-used) words in the later plays, he misunderstands what was the inevitable consequence of once-used words getting used again. The greater the number of plays still to be written, the higher the probability that a once-used word would get used again; and the later the play, the smaller is the chance it will be repeated. So it is that the probabilities, quoted from Hart, in column 8 of Table 5.1, show clear signs of increasing from top to bottom of the Table. Dividing the whole series into six groups each of six plays, we have as the average number of 'peculiar' words per 1000 of all different words: Group 1, earliest plays, *2H6* to *Tit*, 45; Group

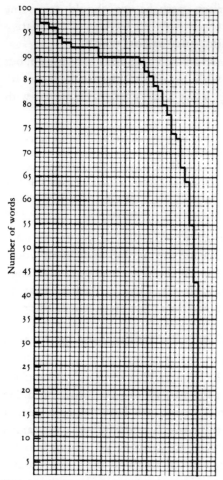

Play *1H6   Tit*   *R2*   *2H4 AYL MM   Ant   Tmp*

Figure 5.1. Drop out of words with time. Fate of 100 consecutive rare words (*quaint* to *retain*) appearing first in *1 Henry VI*. Figure shows their final appearance over the course of subsequent plays. In *The Tempest* 43 of them are still to be found. (Counts by Slater from the *Harvard Concordance*).

2, *Shr* to *MND*, 65; Group 3, *Jo* to *Ado*, 65; Group 4, *H5* to *Tim*, 71; Group 5, *AWW* to *Mac*, 71; last plays, *Ant* to *Tmp*, 70. Submitted to a statistical check, there is a highly significant difference between the first half and the last half of the series; but the trend towards progression in a straight line from first to last is not significant. However, let us suppose that a continuous trend from first to last should be taken into account. We should then divide the numbers of column 8 by a number corresponding to their position in the early to late dimension. After this adjustment we should get numbers showing a truer idea of the degree of richness in 'peculiar' words of each of the plays, as follows:

27 *Rom*, 26 *Ham*, 25 *LLL*, *Lr*, 24 *Wiv*, 23 *Tro*, 22 —,21 *1H4*, *2H4*, 20 *H5*, 19. *MND*, 18 *Tmp*, 17 *Shr*, *Oth*, *Mac*, *Ant*, *Cor*, 16 *TN*, *WT*, 15 *2H6*, *1H6*, *AYL*, *Cym*, 14 *R3*, *Tit*, *AWW*, *MM*, 13. *3H6*, *Err*, *R2*, *Jo*, *Tim*, 12 *MV*, *Ado*, 11 —,10 *Per*, 9 *TGV*, 8 *JC*.

This tabulation certainly has some surprises, perhaps we should say some implausibilities; but it is not entirely out of touch with our feelings of the relative diversity and inventiveness of language, rating play against play.*

Hart has some interesting comments to make on the vocabulary of Marlowe; but in comparing it, greatly to its disadvantage, with that of Shakespeare, he makes no allowance for the fact that he is comparing 14,805 lines of dramatic output with 101,798. He writes, for instance:

> Ever since Malone suggested that Shakespeare did not write the plays on Henry VI critics have been discovering reasons for ascribing them to Marlowe. It seems to me a sufficient refutation of such an ascription to state the simple fact that *1 Henry VI* is of almost the same length as *Edward II* but contains 600 words more. Had Marlowe written a play of 3075 lines on the subject of *2 Henry VI*, his vocabulary would not have exceeded 2750 words, if we judge, as we must, on the figures given for his longest plays, *Jew of Malta* and *Edward II* (p. 139).

In fact, the comparison is not a fair one. Hart provides the figures for 11 non-Shakespearean and Marlovian plays. If we calculate the number of different words per 100 lines for these eleven and for the first four Shakespearean plays, and arrange them in order we get the results shown in Table 5.2. Clearly, Marlowe is at no disadvantage in comparison with Shakespeare, and their plays bracket one another in the respect noted.

There are several ways in which Hart's work leaves deficiencies unfilled, which his successors must regret. It would have been of great interest if he could have continued his account of the 'fresh' words which entered Shakespeare's vocabulary at each successive play, which he took as far as *Richard III* and then abandoned. He provides a count of 'one-play words', 'two-play words', etc. How valuable, then, it would have been if he had assembled lists of these words, and left them on file at his University for consultation by others. However, we must be grateful to him for pioneer work whose value has hardly yet been realised. Certainly the further studies which have gone into this book would not have been possible without the foundation supplied by Hart.

HART'S WORK ON *EDWARD III*

In his work of 1934 on *Shakespeare and the Homilies*,[1] Hart included two studies of vocabulary, one of them on the vocabulary of *Two Noble Kinsmen*, the other on that of *Edward III*. In the latter he reported the results of a great number of enumerations carried out on the vocabularies of plays by Shakespeare, Marlowe, Greene, Peele and others, comparing them with the vocabulary of *Edward III* (*E3*). He came to the conclusion that, in the directions he investigated, *E3* was more similar to the work of Shakespeare than to any of the others. He embodied his results in a number of tables; but he was not able to subject them to tests of statistical significance, which were necessary to show that differences had probability values which would enable

---

* Note by Richard Proudfoot: 'Or, the untypical linguistic character of the play, e.g. *Wiv.*'

Table 5.2. *Marlowe/Shakespeare: words per 100 lines*

Play	Different words per 100 lines
Dido	120.6
Edward III	118.0
Massacre at Paris	113.3
1 Henry VI	112.6
1 Tamburlaine	107.6
Soliman and Perseda	106.3
2 Tamburlaine	103.3
2 Henry VI	102.5
Doctor Faustus	101.4
3 Henry VI	96.1
Arden of Feversham	93.2
Spanish Tragedy	93.1
Jew of Malta	91.5
Richard III	89.4
Edward II	88.9

one to evaluate them as evidence. Fortunately he gave his data in sufficient detail to enable such tests to be made, as follows.

In his first table (p. 220) Hart shows the numbers of lines and numbers of different words in *Edward III*, in six non-Shakespearean and eleven Shakespeare plays. The numbers agree fairly well, but not always exactly, with the counts he reported in 1943;[1,2] the main part of this information has already been shown in Table 5.2. As Hart sees it, these counts show *E3* coming high up the scale in terms both of number of different words in the play, and in number of different words per 100 lines. Hart used Crawford's Concordances to Marlowe and Kyd, and Schmidt's *Shakespeare Lexicon*. The latter is complete, and was used by Hart for his Shakespeare counts. But Crawford's Concordances omit a number of very common filler words. These do not make up a large proportion of a writer's vocabulary (though a very large proportion of his output); but this does mean that Hart under-estimated the total number of different words in the non-Shakespearean plays. Hart considers that the vocabulary of a play in relation to its length is distinctive of the author. Table 5.2 shows that this is not so. In fact he entirely overrates the importance of this characteristic.

He argues that the great size of the vocabulary of *E3*

makes it impossible for us to accept joint authorship as a reasonable explanation of the variations in the quality of various parts. Elizabethan collaboration in play-writing usually meant that each man wrote a few scenes. Accordingly the total number of words used by two, three or more collaborators in writing a play could not possibly exceed the number that would have been used by the author with the largest vocabulary if he had written the whole of a play instead of a part (p. 222).

Hart's idea is that the vocabulary of a composite play would be a kind of average of the vocabularies of the various writers. This is mistaken. The vocabularies of the writers would differ from one another, some of the words being frequent in the works of X but rare in those of Y, and vice versa. Each man would dip into his own word treasury, with the result that a composite work would sample a wider and more heterogeneous population of words than that of any single one of the collaborators. Hart himself made a note of a number of Marlowe's words not used by Shakespeare (Hart 1943, p. 139), and very colourful words they are:

aghast [*TNK*], antarctic, anti-Christian, arctic, base-bred, basso, contributory, empyreal, final [finally *Wiv*], half-dead, hugy, inviolate [inviolable *3H6, R3, Jo*], lustless, papal, piece-meal [peecemeale *E3* line 104], pro-rex, terrify, transitory, triple-headed, etc. [sic!].

In his Table II, p. 223, Hart shows the number of words held in common by various pairs of plays, but he does not make the most effective use of this material. He notes that Crawford remarked in his introduction to his *Concordance to Marlowe* on the close resemblance of the vocabulary of *E3* to that of *1H6*, but he has reservations about the reliability of vocabulary as a characteristic. He writes with reference to his Table II:

All our early dramatists seem to have drawn upon what amounted to a common dramatic vocabulary; in fact, the extraordinary similarity of the language used in the tragedies and histories written during the period 1587–1594 tends to cover up and make almost useless for critical purposes the small differences in the use of words due to difference of authorship. Consequently attempts made to find an author or authors for any of the anonymous plays printed during these years or shortly afterwards must ultimately rest, not on clues from vocabulary or phrases, but on the most variable and elusive of tests, the subjective impression of the critic (p. 224).

This is an interesting idea. But it is in part a truism, and it cannot be more than partly true. Speaking a common language, living and working in the same era and a common culture, the Elizabethan playwrights must necessarily have shared a great part of their vocabularies. But this means only a difficulty, perhaps an exceptional difficulty, in distinguishing differences of vocabulary. It does not mean that differences, once found, are particularly likely to be fallacious or misleading. What logically follows is that resemblances between plays may be weak evidence of community of authorship, whereas differences remain as crucial as ever in the opposite sense. If that were not the case, all the work that Hart devoted to Shakespeare's vocabulary would have been spent in vain. The empirical facts show that this is not so. The resemblances between the first part of *Tamburlaine*, the *Henry VI* plays and *Edward III* may be regarded with reservation; but the statistically significant differences between these and other contemporary plays have to be taken as seriously as ever.

Hart's Table II (Hart 1934, p. 223) provides the count of the number of words held in common between seventeen pairs of plays; the number of different words in each of the fourteen plays involved is also given. A simple calculation will now give us a measure of the degree of kinship within pairs. If there are x different words in play X and y different words in play Y, and there are a words in both lists, it is clear that the total number of different words in both plays taken together is $x + y - a$;

Table 5.3. *Communities of vocabulary between pairs of plays (Hart)*

	Plays paired		a	x+y−a	ratio	variance
1	1 Tam	2 Tam	1482	3468	0.4273	70563
2	2H6	3H6	1614	4188	0.3861	56596
3	E3	2H6	1679	4359	0.3852	54329
4	E3	3H6	1571	4145	0.3790	56781
5	E3	1H6	1604	4280	0.3748	54748
6	1H6	2H6	1603	4367	0.3671	53203
7	E3	R2	1558	4288	0.3633	53949
8	1H6	3H6	1480	4168	0.3551	54943
9	E3	Jo	1539	4371	0.3521	52191
10	1 Tam	E2	1280	3650	0.3507	62386
11	E3	1 Tam	1412	4096	0.3447	55147
12	E3	E2	1352	4022	0.3362	55487
13	MND	Tmp	1046	3945	0.2651	49385

Note: a = number of words held in common between the members of the pair. $x+y-a$ = total number of different words in the pair of plays combined. ratio = proportion of words held in common to total vocabulary of pair. variance = $p.q/N$ where p is the ratio, $q = 1-p$, and $N = x+y-a$.

and furthermore that $a/(x+y-a)$ will be a measure of the degree of community between the two members of the pair, a measure, one might say, of kinship in vocabulary. If we take all the pairs for which Hart gives the necessary figures, 17 pairs in all, and arrange them in order of degree of community, we find a highly meaningful arrangement, with the two parts of *Tamburlaine* the most closely connected pair; and *A Midsummer Night's Dream* and *The Tempest* (separated by some sixteen years of Shakespeare's writing life and by 23 other plays), the most distantly related. We do not need to give Hart's figures for the *Henry IV* and *Henry V* plays, nor the *R2:Jo* pair, and so can reduce his 17 pairs to 13. They are shown in Table 5.3.

In this table three of the columns of figures are given for the record only, but the reader should look carefully at the column headed 'ratio', i.e. $a/(x+y-a)$, the proportion of community of vocabulary. The first pair, *1 Tam:2 Tam*, has by far the highest degree of community; the ratio 0.4273 is greater than any of the other ratios by a statistically very significant margin. In the same way, all the higher-placed ratios in the table exceed the *MND:Tmp* ratio by a statistically highly significant difference. The other pairs, numbered from 2 to 12, are bunched more closely together. However, although they are all included in the range 0.386 to 0.336, the differences between the more widely separated members of this group are still big enough, in many cases, to achieve a high degree of statistical significance.*

* As the t values are not independent, the whole tabulation would have been more properly submitted to analysis of variance.

The calculation of statistical significance is made by taking into account the figures in the last column of Table 5.3, the data on variance. The variance of a proportion p, which is less than 1, is pq/N where $q = 1 - p$ and N is the total number of observations on which p is based. So for the pair 3, $E3:2H6$, its variance is $0.3852 \times 0.6148/4359 = 0.000054329$. Similarly for the pair 11, $E3:1Tam$, its variance is 0.3447×0.6553 divided by $4096 = 0.000055147$. The difference between pair 3 and pair 11 is $0.3852 - 0.3447 = 0.0405$. The standard error of this difference is the square root of the sum of the variances, i.e. the square root of $0.000109476 = 0.010463$. The ratio of the difference to its standard error is $0.0405/0.010463 = 3.87$. This is the value of t. Consulting statistical tables we find that the 0.01 probability point for t when the numbers involved are large ones is less than 2.58. Our value for t of 3.87 is very far indeed beyond any acceptable chance probability, and must be taken as statistically highly significant.

What our example proves, in fact, is that, in the matter of vocabulary, $E3$ is much closer to $2H6$ than it is to 1 *Tam*. Indeed, $E3$ is closer to all the *Henry VI* plays than it is to plays in the pairings numbered from 9 down. This is exhibited in Table 5.4; the numbers entered in the table are the values of t, whose 0.05, 0.02 and 0.01 probability values are respectively 1.96, 2.33 and 2.58. Where no number is entered the value of t is not statistically significant. From the table one can read, looking down the columns, that both pair $2H6:3H6$ and pair $E3:2H6$ have significantly more community of vocabulary than any other pair from 7 down; that pair 4, $E3:3H6$, has significantly more community than any other pair from 8 down; etc. The total effect of these figures is to bring *Edward III* into significantly closer relationships with Shakespeare's *Henry VI* plays, all three of them, than with any play of Marlowe's. This is, so far, the weightiest evidence we have found against Marlowe's hand in *Edward III*.

Hart next examines the numbers of occurrences of words with certain prefixes, in *Edward III*, in five Shakespeare plays, and in three Marlowe plays. The prefixes were: *ad-, be-, con-, de-, dis-, en-, ex-, for-, in-, out-, over-, per-, pre-, pro-, re-, sub-, un-,* with the variants occurring before varying consonants. It is possible that an adventitious factor, caused by the differences between ancient and modernized spellings, may have influenced Hart's counts; but if so, it can hardly have introduced any systematic bias. Hart's counts are shown in his Table III, p. 227. This table shows along the rows 16 prefix forms (*out-* and *over-* being taken together), and separate columns for 9 plays (together with three columns for averages). There are, then, 144 independent items of information out of which some sense has to be made. Hart's own attempts to do so are not satisfactory, as he makes no use of statistical tests; but he is right in suggesting that the proportion of prefix words in *Edward III* is high, and fits better with Shakespeare than with Marlowe (see Table 5.5). However, little weight can be laid on the separation of *Edward III* from the Marlowe plays, since the difference between $E3$ and $E2$, the nearest Marlowe play, is not statistically significant.

When one looks more closely at the counts for individual prefixes, one finds that seven of them (*ad-, ex-, in-, out-, over-, per-, re-*) are so much dead wood, showing little variation from play to play. Hart was hypnotized by the lower frequencies found in Marlowe, compared to Shakespeare or $E3$, because he was judging by the

Table 5.4. *Communities of vocabulary: differences between pairs*

			Play pair 2(2H6:3H6)	3	4	5	6	
3	*E3*	*2H6*	(0.1)					
4	*E3*	*3H6*	(0.7	0.6)				
5	*E3*	*1H6*	(1.1	1.0	0.4)			
6	*1H6*	*2H6*	(1.8	1.7	1.1	0.7)		
7	*E3*	*R2*	2.2	2.1	(1.5	1.1	0.4)	
8	*1H6*	*3H6*	2.9	2.9	2.3	(1.9	1.2	0.8)
9	*E3*	*Jo*	3.3	3.2	2.6	2.2	(1.5	1.1)
10	*1 Tam*	*E2*	3.2	3.2	2.6	2.2	(1.5	1.0)
11	*E3*	*1 Tam*	3.9	3.9	3.2	2.9	2.2	1.5)
12	*E3*	*E2*	4.7	4.7	4.0	3.7	3.0	2.6

Note: The table shows statistically significant differences (*t* values) between degrees of community of vocabulary.

Table 5.5. *Frequency of certain prefix words in Shakespeare and Marlowe plays: counts by Hart*

		Words	Prefix words	Per cent
1	*1H6*	2908	569	19.57
2	*R2*	2875	526	18.33
3	*E3*	2976	535	17.98
4	*2H6*	3062	522	17.07
5	*3H6*	2740	465	16.97
6	*Jo*	2934	496	16.91
7	*E2*	2398	387	16.14
8	*1 Tam*	2532	405	16.00
9	*2 Tam*	2418	354	14.64

number of lines, rather than the total number of words, in the plays. It seems well, then, to simplify our labours by confining our calculations to the remaining prefixes, and the most significant comparative material for *E3*, namely the *Henry VI* and *Tamburlaine* plays. When this is done, one can distribute the observed totals of prefix words of any one kind between the six target plays proportionally to the total number of words in each of them. The difference between Observation and Expectation is then measured by χ^2. Adding together the values of χ^2 for all six plays, we find that 4 of the 10 prefixes we have left to us are quite inadequate to distinguish play from play. These values are, correct to the first place of decimals:

Table 5.6. *Prefix words in* Tamburlaine *and* Henry VI: χ^2 *values*

	1H6	2H6	3H6	1 Tam	2 Tam	E3
1H6	—	6.634	9.446	11.011	*21.168*	5.038
2H6	6.634	—	3.494	10.613	*13.334*	*14.938*
3H6	9.446	3.494	—	*16.630*	*18.500*	*20.623*
1 Tam	11.011	10.613	*16.630*	—	4.277	9.667
2 Tam	*21.168*	*13.334*	*18.500*	4.277	—	10.265
E3	5.038	*14.938*	*20.623*	9.667	10.265	—

Note: χ^2 values for differences within pairs of plays taken two at a time, in respect of frequencies of 6 groups of prefix words (beginning with *de-*, *dis-*, *en-*, *for-*, *pro-*, and *un-*). χ^2 values for which p <0.05 are in italics. Primary counts by Hart.

be- 9.8, *con-* 8.8, *de-* 11.5, *dis-* 18.1, *en-* 26.5, *for-* 16.8, *pre-* 4.8, *pro-* 16.5, *sub-* 4.2, *un-* 23.6. We can now safely discard the four smallest-ranking prefixes, *be-*, *con-*, *pre-* and *sub-*, and concentrate our attention on the others. These are *de-*, *dis-*, *en-*, *for-*, *pro-* and *un-*, and we use the numbers of their occurrences in the six target plays, taken in pairs, matching each against each of the others. The results are shown in Table 5.6, in which statistically significant values of χ^2 for 6 degrees of freedom are underlined. The differences within pairs *2H6:3H6* (0.80>p>0.70), *1Tam:2Tam* (0.70 >p >0.50) and *1H6:E3* (0.50 > p >0.30) are all very small. Neither of the other *Henry VI* pairings with one another shows statistically significant difference, but both *2H6* and *3H6* are significantly different from *E3*. In fact, in respect of these six prefix-word groups, *Edward III* shows itself close only to the first, and not to the second or third, parts of *Henry VI*. The relation of *Edward III* to the *Tamburlaine* plays is left in an ambiguous probability area, and has not been decided by this test.

The prefix which, 'with the variants occurring with varying consonants', gave the largest individual χ^2 was *en-*. It seemed worth while accordingly to put on record the counts of *em-*, *en-*, *im-* and *in-* in the six target plays, word by word. They are shown in Table 5.7 (taken from Crawford's Concordance, i.e. all modernised spellings).

Looking through these lists, one sees that in the *em-* and *en-* words, *Edward III* exceeds all other plays, with an advantage persisting, but less, in the *im-* and *in-* words. We can also count the numbers of times a prefix group appears in *Edward III* and also in another play, i.e. if *m* times in *E3* and *n* times in another play, the magnitude of *mn*. Confining ourselves to the *em-* and *en-* words, as the most distinctive, we find the combination of *E3* with *1H6* substantially the commonest:

E3 with	*1H6*	125	times
„	„ 2H6	98	„
„	„ 3H6	92	„
„	„ 1 Tam	102	„
„	„ 2 Tam	50	„

Table 5.7. Tamburlaine, Henry VI *and* Edward III: *occurrences of prefix words in* em-, en-, in- *(count by present writer)*

	1H6	2H6	3H6	E3	1Tam	2Tam
embalmed					1	
embassade			1			
embassage				2	1	
embattled				1		
embellished					1	
emblaze		1				
embossed				1	1	
embrace/d/ment/th/ing	4	3	4	8	3	1
embroidered			1			
[emperess, etc., omitted]						
employ/ed	3	2	1	4	1	
empyreal					2	3
emulates/ion	2			1		
Totals	9	6	7	17	10	4
enamoured				1		
encamp/ed			1	1		
enchant/ed/ment/ress	2			3		
enchased		1			3	3
enclose/d/ing	1	1		2		
encompass/ed	2		2	3	3	
encouch				1		
encounter/ed/ing	4	2	4	2	5	5
encroach/ing		1		1		
endamage/ment	1			1		
endeavour/ed	1	1		3	1	
endow					1	
endure/d	3	5		2	3	3
enfeebled	1					
enforce/d/ing	1	1	2		2	1
enfranchisement		1				
engage/d				2		
engender/ed	2		1	1		1
engirt		2		1	1	
engraved	1			1		
enjoin/ed				2		3
enjoy/ed/ing	4	3	6	3	3	1
enkindled				1		
enlarge/d/ment	2		1	1	2	
enraged	1					1
enrank	1					
nrich/ed	1			2	2	
enrol/led			1		1	
enshrines	1					
ensign	1			2	2	1
ensnared				2		
ensue/ing	1	1		1		
entail/ed			2	1		
entangled				1		
[enter... omitted]						
enthralled	1				2	

Table 5.7 (*cont.*)

	1H6	2H6	3H6	E3	1Tam	2Tam
enthrone				1		
entice/ing	2	1			1	
entirely				1		
entomb/ed				1	1	
entrails			1	1	1	1
entrance	2			1		
entrap/ped	1			1	1	
entreat/ed/y	3	5	3	4	5	3
envenom/ed/eth		1		1		
envy, envies, emvious	5	6	3	2		
envired				1		
environ/ed/ing	1		3		3	1
Totals	40	32	30	55	48	25
immured				1		
impale/d			3	1		
impart/ing		1				1
impeach			1			
implored	1					
import/ant/ing	2				4	1
importune				2		
imposed						1
imprecations					1	
impression			1			1
imprison/ment	3	1	2			
impugns		1				
Totals	6	3	7	4	5	4
incaged			1			
incense/d	1		1		2	1
incline/d/ation	1	2	2	1		
include	1					
increase/d/ing		2	1	3		
incur					1	
indebted		1				
indulgences	1					
industry			1			
infect/ed/ing/ion		1	1	2	2	1
infer/reth/ring			2			
inflame/d/ing/s	1			1		2
inflict/ions		1			1	1
influence					2	3
inform/ed	4		1	3		
infringe/d			1	3		1
infuse/ion	1		1			1
ingraffed						1
inhabit/ants/ed/ing				3	1	4
inhearsed	1					
inherit/ance/or	2	2	1	3		
injure/d/ies/ious	1	2	4	1	2	2
inner				1		
innovation					1	
insinuate/ing	1			1		

Table 5.7 (*cont.*)

	1H6	2H6	3H6	E3	1Tam	2Tam
insomuch				2		
inspire/d/ation	3	1			1	
install/ed	3		1	1		
instance		1				
instant/ly		1		2		
instead.	3	3	2	1		
instigate/ion		2				
instinct		1			1	
instruct/ions	2				1	1
instrument	2		2	1	1	3
insult/ing	3		4	1		
intend/ed/est/ing	5	8	4	4	5	2
intent	3	2	2			1
intrench/ed	1			1		3
intricate				2		
intrusion				2		
invade, invasion				1		1
invectives			1	1		
inveigle					1	
invent/ed/ing/ion	1	2	1		1	3
invest/ed/ers/eth/ion					8	3
invite/d		1		1		
invocate	1			1		
inward/ly				1	1	1
Totals	42	33	34	44	32	35

These numbers are not suitable for statistical testing, since the more commonly occurring words are given too much weight, or, in statistical terms, where m and n appearances are combined, the degrees of freedom available are not mn but $m+n$. However, the finding does indicate a closer association of *E3* with *1H6* than with any other of the target plays.

Hart's counts of prefix words, given in his Table III, p. 227, can be subjected to another and an independent test, i.e. in differences between plays in respect of the total frequency of the six most critical prefix-word groups, *de-, dis-, en-, for-, pro-, un-*, taking all of them together. These frequencies are shown in Table 5.8.

It can be seen that the frequencies of the chosen prefix words in the *Tamburlaine* plays is substantially lower than in the *Henry VI* plays, and also that *E3* is richest in these words, exceeding its nearest rival, *1H6*. The plays are now taken in pairs, and the difference in frequency between one and the other is set against its standard error (the square root of the sum of the variances of the two plays in question). The relation between the difference and its standard error is the statistic t, and tables are available to show the probability value of the ratio difference/s.e. of difference. The value of t are set out in Table 5.9.

This table marks a substantial advance. The difference between *Edward III* and the *Tamburlaine* plays, which was left undecided by the data of Table 5.6, is now

Table 5.8. Tamburlaine and *Henry VI*: frequencies of 6 prefix words

	No. of words in play	Proportion of prefix words	variance 0.0000
1H6	2908	0.0663686	213080
2H6	3062	0.0548661	169353
3H6	2740	0.0572993	197139
1 Tam	2532	0.0481833	181128
2 Tam	2418	0.0392887	156100
E3	2976	0.0665323	208689

Table 5.9. Tamburlaine *and* Henry VI: *prefix words, t values*

	1H6	*2H6*	*3H6*	*1 Tam*	*2 Tam*	*E3*
1H6	—	1.860	1.416	*2.896*	*4.457*	0.025
2H6	1.860	—	0.402	1.129	*2.731*	1.897
3H6	1.416	0.402	—	1.482	*3.030*	1.449
1Tam	*2.896*	1.129	1.482	—	1.532	*2.939*
2Tam	*4.457*	*2.731*	*3.030*	1.532	—	*4.511*
E3	0.025	1.897	1.449	*2.939*	*4.511*	—

Note: Values of *t*, i.e. ratio of difference between two plays in frequency of prefix words to its standard error; numbers in italics are statistically significant.

clarified. With the high *t* values of 2.9 and 4.5 the vocabulary of *E3*, in respect of the 6 named prefix word groups, has been shown to differ very sharply from *1Tam* and still more from *2Tam*. However, in Table 5.9, the sharp difference between *E3* and both *2H6* and *3H6*, shown in Table 5.6, is now left unclear. The relation of *E3* and *1H6*, however, has now become more pronounced than ever. The miniscule *t* value of 0.025 is the equivalent of no difference at all. Both these tables, relating to prefix words, are compatible with one another; taken together they provide highly significant differences from both the *Tamburlaine* plays on the one hand, and the second and third parts of *Henry VI* on the other hand; moreover both agree in revealing a very close similarity in vocabulary between *Edward III* and *1 Henry VI*.

Hart next proceeds in his Table IV (p. 230) to examine the frequency of certain suffixes. These are adjectives ending in *-able, -ant, -ary, -ate, -ent, -ful, -ible, -ish, -ive, -less, -ous* and *-y*; nouns ending in the suffixes *-ance, -ence, -er, -ment, -or* and *-tion*; adverbs ending in *-ly*. And counts are provided for *1Tim, 2Tam, E2, 1H6, 2H6, 3H6, E3, R2, Jo, 1H4, 2H4, H5*. The data can be condensed into Table 5.10.

This section is far from satisfactory. Hart should have been on the look out for small but distinctive differences between authors; and he could not with any reason have hoped to find them in broad categories of suffixes distinguished by their *grammatical* classification. As we have found in the analysis of prefix words, it is only certain prefixes that proved of evidential value. In the same way suffixes,

Table 5.10. *Frequency of certain suffix words (Hart), three parts of speech combined*

	Total vocabulary	Suffix words	Per cent
Three Marlowe plays	7348	845	11.50
Edward III	2976	385	12.94
Three *Henry VI* plays	8710	1148	13.18

distinguished into *individual* forms, *-ance*, *ence*, etc., might well have thrown into relief habits differing between author and author. When they are all jumbled together, it is hardly surprising that statistically significant differences, which would almost certainly have been found if looked for, almost wholly fail to emerge from the general confusion. Checking through Hart's Table IV (p. 230), the frequencies of adjectival suffixes show no statistically significant differences between the members of any single pair of plays. The noun suffixes show only two significant differences: their frequency is less in *2Tam* than in either *1H6* or *2H6*. The adverbs in *-ly* show no statistically significant differences within any pair of plays. Throughout the whole table the frequencies of these suffix words, measured against the total vocabularies of the plays, is remarkably uniform. Taking all suffix words together, once again we find that only *2Tam* differs sufficiently from other plays for a statistically significant effect to be produced, here between *2Tam* and the second and third parts of *Henry VI*. All other pairs show uninformative results.

In his Table V (p. 233) and his Table VI (p. 235) Hart compares the frequency of compound words in the vocabularies of Shakespeare, Marlowe, Greene and Peele. Hart does not define the term 'compound word', nor give examples. In Table V dramatic works are lumped together, being distinguished from poems; and the base is in terms of number of lines, not words. Although Hart shows that Shakespeare makes more liberal use of these compounds than the other writers, the material is not suitable for statistical testing. It is not satisfactory to compare a single play (*E3*) with the average of many plays by any other author, since in these averages individual variation from play to play passes unrecognised. In Table VI (p. 235), Hart provides us with counts for 9 separate plays, and he distinguishes compound words into 'adjectival' and 'other'. Counts tend to be low in Marlowe plays, and about 50% higher in the Shakespeare plays instanced and in *Edward III*; but the numbers are rather small and the only four statistically significant differences are between all the three parts of *Henry VI* and *Edward III* on the one hand as against *2 Tamburlaine* on the other. The frequency of compound words in *Edward III* is closer to what it is in *1 Henry VI* than in *2H6* or *3H6*. There is one odd feature about these compound words. While the adjectival compounds separate all the Shakespeare plays, carrying *E3* with them, from the Marlovian ones, the same is not true of the non-adjectival forms. Here *Edward II* ranks higher than *3H6*, *Jo* and *R2*. The rank orders in the two lists bear no relation to one another. The two orders are, in fact, independent and uncorrelated. Nevertheless, each list brings *Edward III* into the immediate neighbourhood of *1Henry VI* and *2Henry VI* with *3Henry VI* further off.

Hart's next table, VII, exhibiting compound participial adjectives, is not suitable for statistical testing, for the same reasons as for Table V: whole groups of plays or poems are thrown together, and make no suitable comparison for a single play (*E3*), and number of lines is taken as the base instead of number of words, as should have been.

This practically concludes our consideration of Hart's work on *Edward III* taken as a single unit, but before passing on to another most important and distinct question we might briefly review the relation of *Edward III* to *Edward II*. Of all Marlowe's plays this might well seem the most obviously comparable work. So far it has hardly appeared in our statistical analyses – for the very good reason that in practically all vocabulary tests it shows itself to be a very different piece of work. On the other hand, the play *1 Henry VI* has shown itself again and again to be the nearest to *Edward III* in all the respects examined. The unlikeness of *Edward II* and the likeness of *1 Henry VI* to our problem play is brought out in the following table, 5.11. There is, in fact, only one respect in which all Hart's counts show a statistically significant difference between *Edward III* and *1 Henry VI*: the number of different words per 100 lines of text, in which *Edward III* is the richer play. This point, however, is not a very telling one, since in respect of it there are very great differences between plays by the same author.

In his concluding paragraphs Hart briefly considers the homogeneity of *Edward III*. He says that many critics of his time were inclined to accept the second scene of Act I and the whole of Act II as Shakespeare's work. This is now thought to be too crude a division, the fourth scene of Act IV having as good claims to be Shakespearean. However, we may still examine Hart's argument, since his error, if error it was, would be to obscure a difference between two parts of the play rather than to create an artificial difference where none existed in reality. These scenes, I.ii, II.i and II.ii, 'part A', contain by Hart's count 836 lines; the remaining two-thirds of the play, 'part B', has 1662. For any particular sort of word, Hart argues, there should be proportionately 1662 to 836, or very nearly two to one, chances of finding it represented in part B rather than part A. This is almost exactly matched by the distribution of adjectival participial compounds (A 13, B 24), but fails to meet the case with unique words, not found elsewhere in Shakespeare (A 54, B 70), words appearing in only one other place (A 49, B 63), and words new to our language (A 24, B 26). In all these three respects part B is proportionately less well endowed than part A. Hart finds himself baffled by these differences. Though part B is less rich in these formations than part A, it is still richer than any works by other authors examined by Hart. 'Accordingly, if we must father B upon some author known to us we are forced to suggest Shakespeare. The other possibility is to accept the facts, confess our ignorance, and permit the play to remain authorless' (pp. 240–1). It would certainly be unwise to place any reliance on Hart's evidence. He is committing the cardinal statistical sin of muddling his units, i.e. setting numbers of words as numerators with numbers of lines as denominators.

Table 5.11. *Comparisons between* 1 Henry VI, Edward III, Edward II

		E3	1H6	E2
No. of different words		2976	2908	2398
Different words per 100 lines of text			119.135	108.670	89.813

		E3:1H6		E3:E2	t
communalities		.374766		.336151	
difference			.038615 +.010499		3.678
Prefix-words differences in frequency with standard errors					
de-	E3:1H6	.0013617 + .0031487			0.432
	E3:E2	.0028535 + .0030525			0.935
dis-	E3:1H6	.0006781 + .0031463			0.216
	E3:E2	.0067807 + .0029074			2.332
en-	E3:1H6	.0041247 + .0029131			1.413
	E3:E2	.0072786 + .0028237			2.573
for-	E3:1H6	.0021132 + .0015280			1.386
	E3:E2	.0018179 + .0015875			1.145
pro-	E3:1H6	.0022675 + .0025792			0.878
	E3:E2	.0033154 + .0022712			1.460
un-	E3:1H6	.0011083 + .0027030			0.410
	E3:E2	.0001553 + .0029057			0.053
all six together	E3:1H6	.0020263 + .0053867			0.376
	E3:E2	.0093357 + .0053920			1.824
Compounds adjectival	E3:1H6	.0005759 + .0035780			0.161
	E3:E2	.0073958 + .0033769			2.190
other	E3:1H6	.0014504 + .0041085			0.353
	E3:E2	.0024399 + .0042723			0.571

Note: Summary of results of statistical calculations carried out on Hart's counts, instancing only *1H6* (Shakespeare?) and *E2* (Marlowe), in comparison with *Edward III*. The numbers of words per 100 lines of text are statistically significantly smaller in *1H6* than in *E3* (with *E2* far more different still); but this is the only point at which a statistically significant difference between *E3* and *1H6* is to be found. In addition to this, there are four other respects (underlined) where a statistically significant difference between *E3* and *E2* is to be found. Statistical significance is measured by the *t* test, i.e. ratio of observation to its standard error.

SUMMARY

Hart's work on Shakespeare's vocabulary in relation to the problem of *Edward III* can be briefly summarized and commented on.

1. His counts of the number of different lexical words in 37 Shakespeare plays can be made the basis of comparisons susceptible to statistical testing.

2. The number of different words per 100 lines of text varies very widely from 127 for *Macbeth* and *The Tempest* to 89 for *Richard III*. The general average is 102.

3. The differences between plays in this respect are highly significant statistically, but the reasons for them are unclear. Hart's speculation that there are differences in diversity of vocabulary between plays classed as comedies, tragedies and histories is shown to be unfounded. On the other hand there is a variation over time which is detectable between the plays arranged in putative date order, i.e. between a first phase ending with *King John*, a second phase from *Merchant of Venice* to *Othello*, and a final phase from *Timon* to *The Tempest*. Hart formed the impression that the number of different words per 100 lines distinguished Shakespeare's work from that of Marlowe and others; with 118 different words per 100 lines *Edward III* had a rich vocabulary. However, Hart's own counts show that some Marlowe plays equal or exceed some plays of Shakespeare.

4. The actual words used in the plays change over the course of time. Some go out of circulation while other new words are added. Accordingly the total of ever-used words grows consistently; and as not all words used once (or twice, or more) are ever used again, there is also a consistent growth in the number of rare words, i.e. those used only once or twice. The total effect of these two processes of adding never-used and dropping seldom-used words over the course of the playwright's production is to give such words a dating character, not in a precise but in a probabilistic sense. This quality can be used in chronological investigations, and has been so used, e.g. by the present writer.

5. Hart published his statistical study of *Edward III* in 1934. The first edition of R. A. Fisher's *Statistical Methods for Research Workers* was first published in 1925. It would have been of immense assistance to Hart, but it is hardly surprising that it never came his way. Hart was not able to apply tests of statistical significance to his counts; but in many instances he provides the actual results in such a form that we are able to do the testing for ourselves.

6. Hart's first important piece of evidence is the number of words held in common by a pair of plays. Together with the totals of different words contained in each member of the pair, we have a measure of the degree of verbal community between the two plays. Hart gives us the requisite numbers for fourteen plays arranged in seventeen pairs. The most closely akin pair, i.e. with the highest proportion of the words held in common, is the two parts of *Tamburlaine*, 42.7%. The most mutually remote pair is *Midsummer Night's Dream* and *The Tempest*, 26.5%. *Edward III* has high levels of community, from 38.5% to 37.5%, with all

three *Henry VI* plays, but statistically significantly lower degrees of community with all other pairings of this play (with *Richard II, John, 1 Tamburlaine, Edward II*).

7. Hart's next substantial piece of evidence relates to prefix words. He distinguished sixteen groups of prefix words, and he provides counts of their appearances in nine plays. It is shown that ten of the sixteen groups are uninformative, in that they show an insufficient degree of variation in frequency from play to play; and only six groups of prefix words, i.e. those beginning with *de-*, *dis-*, *en-*, *for-*, *pro-*, *un-*, provide statistically significant results. These go to show that there is very little difference ($0.50 > p > 0.30$) between *Edward III* and *1 Henry VI*, but large differences between *Edward III* and both *2 Henry VI* ($0.05 > p > 0.02$) and *3 Henry VI* ($p < 0.001$).

8. When all prefix words of the six named groups are taken together, *Edward III* remains very close to *1 Henry VI*, but now distinguishes itself sharply from the first and second parts of *Tamburlaine*.

9. From prefixes Hart passes on to suffixes; and he gives agglomerated counts for twelve adjectival forms, six noun forms and adverbs ending in -*ly*. No statistical information of value emerges, other than to distinguish *2 Tamburlaine* from other plays. It is quite possible that one or more of these forms taken separately might have provided a source of discrimination.

10. Hart's handling of compound words is also unsatisfactory.

11. In his concluding paragraphs Hart briefly examines the question whether a certain part of *Edward III* (he takes the second scene of Act I and the whole of Act II) could be by Shakespeare, with the rest of the play by another hand. While he finds differences between the one part and the other, they are not of a kind and degree to be decisive. The question, in effect, is left unanswered. His work on this important aspect of the problems offered by *Edward III* is too cursory to be helpful.

12. The total effect of Hart's work is to connect *Edward III* and *1 Henry VI* very closely in their vocabularies. There is no important point in which their vocabularies can be distinguished. In this respect there is nothing to show that they could not be by the same author.

6

Rare words and Shakespeare's chronology

INTRODUCTORY

About ten years ago the present writer began to take an interest in the possibility of applying statistical methods to some of the problems which confront students of Shakespeare. The work I could do on my own account, without the resources of computer technology, must be that for which the statistics of small samples would be the appropriate tools. I was reasonably familiar with these methods, having learned especially from the late Sir Ronald Fisher. This man of genius spent his life in devising and systematising statistical methods for research workers, especially in biology, and especially those methods which are simple to understand and can most universally be applied. In my past research work in medicine, psychiatry and genetics, Fisher was the giant whose strength I called in aid. I had great hopes that his methods might help to throw light where Shakespeare scholars themselves were in some doubt or disagreement.

My first effort was to examine the order in which Shakespeare wrote his Sonnets, distinguishing between the mode of address in second person singular and second person plural. It could readily be shown that this order was not a random one. I offered a note, presenting this (admittedly trivial) conclusion to *Notes and Queries*. The Editor, the late J. C. Maxwell, who replied to me returning my note, was kind enough to suggest I might continue in this line, but undertaking some more significant task.

Thus encouraged, I turned my attention to the problematic authorship of the poem *A Lover's Complaint*.[12] In the Cambridge edition of Shakespeare's poems, edited by J. C. Maxwell,[7] there is a glossary. It seemed that the glossary words distinguished themselves in a number of interesting ways, e.g. by being obsolete, or having a technical meaning or a meaning now forgotten, etc. The question arose whether these words were distributed fairly and randomly between each of the Shakespeare poems: *Venus and Adonis, The Rape of Lucrece, The Passionate Pilgrim, The Phoenix and the Turtle*, and *A Lover's Complaint*. Statistical testing showed that glossary words were significantly *rarer* in *The Passionate Pilgrim* than in the other poems, a finding readily compatible with the known fact that the greater part of that series of twenty items is known not to be by Shakespeare. The tests showed also that glossary words were significantly *more frequent* in *Complaint* than in *Venus* and *Lucrece*, which pair were statistically in good accord with one another. This finding was more difficult to explain. Kenneth Muir, writing in 1964[8] and again in 1973,[9] had not thought that the vocabulary of *Complaint* was exceptional for Shakespeare, nor that the parade of learned words was more obvious than in *Troilus and Cressida*.

Maxwell[7] records his own view that the poem was Shakespeare's, though one of little merit. He thought the vocabulary 'belongs to the Shakespeare of the 1600's, not the early 1590's, and the play to which it seems closest is *Troilus and Cressida*' (p. xxxv). Clearly this needed further investigation, and the next step would be an examination of the vocabulary relationships between Shakespeare's poems and plays.[12]

This idea had already been anticipated by MacD. P. Jackson,[5] who came to the firm conclusion that *A Lover's Complaint* was indeed Shakespearean. His arguments were based on a number of points: the number of new coinages in the poem; parallel phrases in the plays for several idiosyncratic expressions in *Complaint*; imagery of a Shakespearean type; and some other points of a more general and less precise kind. One argument advanced by Jackson was particularly relevant to my own approach. Using Bartlett's *Concordance* and Schmidt's *Lexicon*, he drew up a list of every word in the poem used elsewhere by Shakespeare only four or five times. The list provided 80 links in diction with the first nineteen works of Shakespeare and 202 with the later twenty works (omitting the Sonnets). Best represented were, in order, *Cymbeline, Hamlet, Troilus, Cariolanus, All's Well, Timon* and *Lear*.

My own work[12] was on similar lines, but more broadly based and controlled by statistical tests. Bartlett's *Concordance* was relied on. Not only *A Lover's Complaint* but also *Venus and Adonis, The Rape of Lucrece* and the Sonnets were examined. All lexical words (in modernized spelling as given in Bartlett) were listed which made a single or once-repeated appearance in one or two of the poems. Several tests were applied, which now do not need to be remembered. The most interesting was a tabulation (Table III, p. 161) of the numbers of appearances of catch words from *Venus, Lucrece*, Sonnets and *Complaint* in the 37 plays of Shakespeare, brought into relation with the number of different words in each play as enumerated by Alfred Hart. The four poems were associated with a different set of plays. The *Venus* words were in statistically significant excess in *Titus, Two Gentlemen* and *A Midsummer Night's Dream*. The *Lucrece* words were found in statistically significant excess in *1 Henry VI* and *2 Henry VI*, in *Richard III, Titus* and *Romeo*. Catch words from the Sonnets were linked with *Love's Labour's Lost* and *Henry V*. *A Love's Complaint* was linked with an altogether later series of plays: *Hamlet, Troilus, All's Well, Othello, Lear* and *Cymbeline*.

The conclusions which were thought to be justified by these results were, first, that the method of counting word links between poems and plays was sound. The results were not only statistically assured but also accorded well with existing informed opinion. Secondly, they provided weighty evidence that *A Lover's Complaint* was an authentic work of Shakespeare. One of the observations made while working on *Complaint* was that even quite commonplace and frequently used words were restricted to a range of plays and could carry a value for dating. The distribution of the appearances, when arranged by number in the plays in which they appeared, exhibited a clustering, of which the middle term might be early, or neutral, or late. The next table is an excerpt (from p. 163). 'Nevertheless', the article continued, 'it was found that the dating value of common words was less than that

	Word	Number of appearances	Median of distribution
'early' words	kindred	31	*R2*
	loose, adj.	38	*1H4/2H4*
	abroad	56	*2H4*
'late' words	undertake	57	*TN*
	satisfaction	32	*TN/Ham*
	carriage	27	*Ham*
	observe	47	*Ham*
	safe, adj.	102	*Ham*
	understand	123	*Ham*
	motive, n.	22	*Tro/AWW*
	quit	49	*AWW*
	minister, n.	40	*AWW/MM*
	charity	55	*MM*
	merely	25	*MM*
	extend	22	*Oth/Lr*
	crack, vb.	42	*Lr*
	diamond	21	*Tim*

of the more rarely used ones.' This conclusion has been specifically confirmed (see p. 89 below).

In the same number of *Notes and Queries* in which the above was published there was another communication.[14] Here I formulated the working hypothesis which has been the guiding principle of later work, including this book. After referring to Hart's counts of the number of different lexical words in Shakespeare's plays, I noted his view that Shakespeare's vocabulary not only changed over the course of time, but could be regarded as having grown with the writing of each new play. The following passage followed:

This assumes that a word once part of his vocabulary was never lost. However, some words at least, the 'peculiar' words in Hart's terminology, once used were never used again. While it is conceivable that Shakespeare had the whole of his 17,000 to 18,000 words available throughout, from start to finish, making the selection provoked by his theme, his characters and their setting, this seems unlikely – particularly in view of his neologisms, inventions and compound constructions. It is more probable that at any given time a part of his total vocabulary was more readily available than the rest; and that the change from play to play was a gradual transition, with a large measure of community between one play and the rest. This line of thought suggests that the degree of contemporaneity of two plays might be measured by the degree of community between their vocabularies.

This hypothesis was then used to check the placing of *The Merry Wives of Windsor*. This had been a matter of some differences of opinion. In the order of plays suggested by Sir E. K. Chambers the sequence runs *Twelfth Night, Hamlet, Wives, Troilus, All's Well*. The Cambridge editors, Quiller-Couch and Dover Wilson, preferred an earlier placing, about the time of *Henry V* and *Julius Caesr*. Hart placed it in the order *Much Ado, Henry V, Wives, Julius Caesar, As You Like It*. The Arden editor, H. J. Oliver,[10] in the 1971 edition, argued strongly in favour of the theory 'that *2 Henry IV* and *The Merry Wives* were being written at the same time – the composition of the former having been interrupted for the hasty writing of the latter' (p. lv).

To test these varying placements I took all the words in the glossary to the play in the Cambridge edition, which provided not more than forty citations in other plays in Bartlett's *Concordance*. These made a total of 1094. Assuming that the probability of a linking citation of a *Wives* glossary word in another play would, as a matter of random probability, be proportionate to the total number of different lexical words in that play, one could set the observed number against the expected number. The difference between the one and the other could be tested by the χ^2 test. It was found that only four plays contained a statistically significant excess of *Wives* glossary words, i.e. (showing the Observed as a percentage of the Expected number) *2 Henry VI* 135%, *1 Henry IV* 162%, *2 Henry IV* 174%, *Henry V* 141%. It was considered that these findings agreed very well with the hypothesis advanced by Mr Oliver:

If, following his [Oliver's] suggestion, we place *The Merry Wives* in the series *1 Henry IV*, *2 Henry IV*, *Wives*, *Much Ado*, *Henry V*, its four neighbours have a 40% excess of word links over expectation (χ^2 31.6), beyond the reach of chance except as an astronomical infinitesimal probability. On the other hand in the Chambers series *Twelfth Night*, *Hamlet*, *Wives*, *Troilus*, *All's Well*, links with the neighbours are in excess to only 6% (χ^2 0.5), which has a probability of 0.46, which one can attain with a single toss of a coin (p. 171).

On this experience one could feel reasonably well assured that Shakespeare's unusual words were marked by a time characteristic, not precise indeed but probabilistic in nature. The confidence I felt in this view justified a considerable extension of the basis for further studies. A card index was prepared, in the first instance on the basis of Bartlett's *Concordance*, but later checked, corrected and amplified by comparison with the Harvard *Concordance* of Marvin Spevack (one volume, 1973). Both these Concordances were in the main in modern spelling. Textual disagreements between the two were checked against the Cambridge editions of the plays (paperback, 1968), which were taken as authoritative. The card index included only and all lexical words found in two or more plays but with not more than ten citations. These were, then, the rarest but not the unique words. Classification followed the general principles of the *OED*, as has been mentioned previously (see p. 58). When at a later date a fresh search through the *Harvard Concordance* was made for links with *Edward III*, the aim in view changed. This now was to identify *all* lexical words linking with not 10 but now 12 canonical works, plays or poems, and even long entries in the *Concordance* were sifted for homonyms with rarer meanings. The new list was checked against the card index, with the result that the initial number of 5553 indexed words was found to be capable of being supplemented by 207 added words. This can be taken as an approximate estimate of the degree of incompleteness of the card index, i.e. a matter of about 4%. The word list prepared for *Edward III* was a new and independent effort, and does not concern us at the moment. There were, then, in all 5553 words in the card index, which are reported in Appendix 1. They are grouped into those linking two citations (1703), three citations (1092), four (753), five (591), six (409), seven (358), eight (272), nine (213), ten (162). These figures are fairly close to a geometric progression, descending by a constant ratio. As one can see from Fig. 6.1, in log form they close to a straight line. The first number, 1703, is well above the line, permitting the guess that if unique words were added at the hither end their number would be disproportionately higher still. The figure in fact suggests that it is related to the 'limp-flag-hanging-from-a-flag-pole' curve first discovered by Udny Yule, and referred to on pages 62 and 13.

The first task attempted with the aid of the card index was a contribution to the problem of dating *All's Well That Ends Well*. This was reported in *Notes and Queries* in 1977.[15] It had once been thought that Shakespeare's play *Love's Labour's Wonne*, mentioned by Francis Meres in 1598, had survived under another name, and could be most probably identified with *All's Well That Ends Well*. So Brigstocke,[2] in the edition of the play that he edited in 1904 (p. xi), took the view that critics were then almost unanimous in that opinion. In later years views changed. Professor Hunter,[4] the Arden editor of 1962, said (p. xix) that an early date, to bring *All's Well* into mention by Meres, was not acceptable to modern scholarship. However the question was thrown open again by the discovery, reported by T. W. Baldwin[1] in 1957, of a page from the account books of an Elizabethan bookseller showing that a play called 'loves labor won' was, in August 1603, to be had in print. It was set in a list with further Shakespearean and other plays (marchant of vennis, taming of a shrew, knak to know a knave, knak to know an honest man, loves labor lost, loves labor won). Baldwin argued that if *Love's Labour's Won* was included under another title in the Folio, it would be one of the fourteen classified as comedy. He then argued, by a series of progressive exclusions on a variety of grounds, that (if *Love's Labour's Won* had indeed survived) it was most likely to be either *All's Well* or, perhaps, *Measure for Measure*.*

The contemporaneity of the writing of *All's Well* with that of other plays of Shakespeare was, then, put in doubt. It seemed worth while to apply statistical tests of its vocabulary along the lines of previous work, for which the card index could be used. It was now possible to dispense with Hart's word counts for the plays when calculating Expected values; they were in any case notional estimates of the treasuries which could throw up links. We now had instead the actual numbers of words of the nine different categories for each of the plays, and it was between these words that links would be found. *All's Well* proved to be linked with *Troilus*, so:

The two- to six-words in the index provide a total of 23,502 citations, of which 594 are in *AWW* and 904 in *Tro*. The *AWW* words linked with a total of 972 citations in other plays. If *Tro* had had its fair share of these, i.e. 904/23,502 of the 972, that would have been 37.388. In fact 55 links were found, 144% of the chance value, statistically a highly significant excess.

* A strong case can also be made for *Much Ado*. Richard Proudfoot, personal communication, 1980.

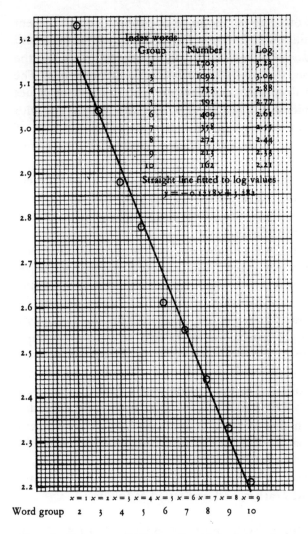

Index words		
Group	Number	Log
2	1703	3.23
3	1092	3.04
4	753	2.88
5	591	2.77
6	409	2.61
7	358	2.55
8	272	2.44
9	213	2.33
10	162	2.21

Straight line fitted to log values
$y = -0.13 x + 3.12$

Word group   2   3   4   5   6   7   8   9   10

Figure 6.1 Shakespeare: distribution of card index link words, by category

In fact, the rarer words (2 to 6 appearances) showed a statistically significant excess of links with only two plays, *Troilus* and *Measure for Measure*. Taking all words together, the most significant excess of links was with *MM* as before, but now not with *Troilus* but with *Othello*. The crucial finding was that the rare-word vocabulary of *All's Well* linked it with none of the early plays. Even with a hypothetical revision, some links with the early plays could be expected to survive if they had been present in the unrevised text. The fact that no such linking with early plays was found was a point in favour of Hunter's and against Baldwin's position.

Two further studies along these lines were reported in 1978.[16,17] The second of these was occasioned by an article by Miss Margaret Hotine,[3] '*Troylus and Cressida*: historical arguments for a 1608 date.' This led to a study of the connections in the card index between *Troilus* and other plays. *Troilus*, in Appendix 11 of the present book, shows statistically significant links with *Henry V*, *Hamlet*, *Othello* and *Macbeth*, most strongly with *Hamlet*. When Hart's counts were put aside and the card index data alone relied on, the constellation became a different one. The observed counts, of course, remained unchanged, but a new set of Expected values transformed their statistical significance. The links of *Troilus* with *Henry V* and with *Hamlet*, though still in excess of expectation, now dropped below the level of statistical significance. The links with *Othello* and *Macbeth* remained. But now links with two other relatively late plays emerged above the level of significance; and *Troilus* revealed itself as also linked with *All's Well* and *Timon*. The two different pictures are not wholly compatible. Nevertheless, on this evidence one might be tempted to postdate the writing of *Troilus* to a later position in the serial order than immediately after (or even before!) *Hamlet*.

The first of the two 1978 studies[16] was a double study of the rare words in *Timon of Athens* and *King Lear*. Chambers had placed *Timon* between *Coriolanus* and the last plays. J. C. Maxwell[6] thought it was earlier, and he agreed (p. xii) with Sir Walter Raleigh in thinking it antedated *Lear*, for which it might have been a preliminary sketch. The card index data showed a very strong association linking *Timon* with *Lear*, with observed links 185% of expectation in the two- to six-word groups, 171% with the commoner seven- to ten-word groups. Both of these figures were substantially bigger than *Timon*'s links with any other play. Turning to *Lear*, one found the complement and corollary. The two- to six-words linking with *Timon* were in a ratio of Observation to Expectation of 166%, the seven- to ten-words a ratio of 161%, both of them in higher proportion than with *Lear*'s links with any other play. It was considered that the Raleigh–Maxwell judgment had been fully supported.

The question now arose whether the linkages of these two plays with others gave any inkling which of the two was earlier, and was tested as follows:

Timon and *Lear* being put aside, as the plays under test, two further exclusions were made, namely of the first two acts of *Pericles* as only doubtfully Shakespeare's work and *Henry VIII* as a work of collaboration. The remaining plays were grouped by assumed chronological order into seven groups. To the plays in these groups the numbers 1 to 7 were assigned, corresponding to their assumed lateness. The numbers of links (a) of *Timon*, (b) of *Lear* with each of these groups, multiplied by the allotted 'weight', were summed, the sum of the products divided by the number of links, to arrive at a mean 'weight', or lateness coefficient, for each of the plays. Taking the whole of the 34 plays together, processed in this way, the mean 'weight' was 3.95. The average for *Timon* links was later, 4.14; and the mean for the *Lear* links was later still, 4.19. Both the *Timon* mean and the *Lear* mean differed from the average of all others to a statistically significant degree; they are, of course, late plays. But the difference between the *Timon* mean and the *Lear* mean was not a statistically significant one. After this demonstration the note ended:

We conclude that the word links support the view of those who consider that *Timon* was written at about the same time as *Lear*, or rather earlier; and it is a massive item of evidence against the Chambers view of *Timon* as a later play than *Coriolanus* (p. 149).

The method outlined above for calculating a 'lateness' coefficient led to a sustained attempt to apply it to the plays as a whole, an attempt that landed in the quicksands.

THE CARD INDEX

The result of these essays into Shakespearean chronology was thought to justify further work on Shakespeare's rare-word vocabulary. On advice, the author entered himself as a part-time postgraduate student at King's College, London. The plan agreed there was to use rare-word analysis in an area where it might prove appropriate, i.e. in a study of the problem play *The Reign of King Edward III*. The rare-word vocabulary of the play could be reviewed, and might or might not show links with known works of Shakespeare; and if yes, with Shakespeare works of a limited time range. An account of these efforts and their results will be given in the next chapter.

In the meantime further work was done on the card index words. The Computer Unit at King's College kindly carried out a programme to provide counts of all index words in all plays. The nine categories of words (two-words, three-words, etc.) were dealt with separately. Thus, beginning with the two-words, successive print-outs showed the number of such words in *2H6* which also appeared in *3H6*, in *1H6*, in *R3*, etc.; then the number of index words in *3H6* which also appeared in *2H6*, in *1H6*, in *R3*, etc. In short, for each category of word and for each play severally, there was a print-out showing its links with each and all of the other plays (and itself also). *Henry VIII* was included. Two parts of *Pericles*, Acts I and II on the one hand and Acts III–V on the other, were dealt with as separate plays; this was thought necessary because so many scholars are dubious about the authenticity of the first two acts. There were accordingly 38 tabulations for each of the word categories, or 342 tabulations altogether.

The work with rare words has justified itself by producing results which are meaningful, statistically significant and informative. The results have accorded with one or another school of scholarly opinion, lending weight to one or another side when questions of authorship or chronology were unsettled or in dispute. We must attempt now to demonstrate the logical validity of the hypothesis on which the work with rare words was based.

Even if the exact order in which Shakespeare wrote his plays is unknown, there is a wide measure of agreement among scholars about its general features; thus if two plays P and Q are taken at random, there will be general agreement that P was written earlier (or later, as the case may be). We arrange Shakespeare's plays in their order of composition, as near as may be, according to this general idea. The hypothesis now states that if a given rare word W appears in play P, its other appearances will not be distributed at random; there will be a greater chance of finding W again in plays near to P in time of composition than in those more remote. In other words, if W appears in half a dozen plays the intervals between these plays will be smaller than if the appearances of W were scattered at random.

If this is not so, and the chance of W appearing in another play (or again in P) is the same for all plays, disregarding for the time being such matters as the length of a play and the number of words it contains, then we can calculate the expected mean length of interval between appearances. We have n plays. If W appears in play 1, the chance that it appears again in play 1 is equal to the chance that it appears in play 2, in play 3, etc., up to the nth play. The intervals between these two appearances make an arithmetical progression, 0, 1, 2 ... $(n-1)$. The sum of the series is $n(n-1)/2$; and the expected mean length of interval will be one nth part of that, i.e. $(n-1)/2$. If we note the appearance of W somewhere in the middle of the series of n plays, then an equal distribution of its other appearances will make up two arithmetic progressions, one going back to the first play and the other going on to the nth. If W appears in the ith play, the two progressions sum to $i(i-1)/2$ and $(n-i+1)(n-i)/2$. Their mean value M will be $(i(i-1)+(n-i+1)(n-i))/2n$. Table 6.1 shows 36 of Shakespeare's plays in a putative order of composition mainly derived from Chambers. We substitute 36 for n in the above formula, and the ordinal number of the play for i. Thus for the first play, with $i=1$, $M=(1(0)+36 \times 35)/72=17.5$. For, say, $i=12$, $M=(12 \times 11+25 \times 24)/72=732/72=10.16$, or, as written in the table, 10.16r.

In Table 6.1 it can be seen that, in each of the plays, the index words occurring there are found in other plays on average at closer intervals than chance would predict. The numbers in column g nowhere attain the expected value of 1, though approaching it closely in the case of *Julius Caesar*. For the table as a whole, the mean interval between appearances of W is only 92% of what chance would dictate. There is some variation; the plays in the middle of the series show the phenomenon of contracted intervals to a lesser degree than plays at the two extremes. This may be because there is less scope for variation in the middle of the series.

In Table 6.2 all plays are taken together, and the classification is by word category. Very strikingly, there is a trend from the rarest words to the commonest. The rarest words show the greatest contraction of interval length, or, in other words, the greatest tendency to cluster. There are, of course, irregularities. But if we take the two-words and the three-words together, the mean length of interval is 85.8% of expectation; whereas if we take the nine-words and the ten-words together, the mean length of interval is 96.5% of expectation. The difference is a very large one. We can predict that the commoner the words we choose to track down through the course of the series of plays, the less useful they will be for purposes of dating. There is one reservation to be made here. As has been said, we have taken all plays as equivalent, and have supposed that, on a chance basis, the probability of finding a word W will be equal for plays P and Q. This will clearly not be true if P is the longer play with a greater store of lexical words. This does not affect the validity of our test. Differences between plays in the number of words they contain is an important disturbing factor which will tend to enlarge the random factor and to diminish the serial factor in the calculation of mean interval lengths. If the test survives this disturbance, we can be sure that the serial effect

Table 6.1. *Expected and Observed mean lengths of interval between two appearances of a rare word, in named play and in others*

a	b	c	d	e	f	g
1	2H6	17.500	2935	44881	15.2917	0.8738
2	3H6	16.55r	2358	32781	13.9020	0.8397
3	1H6	15.66r	2673	36658	13.7142	0.8754
4	R3	14.83r	2828	37523	13.2684	0.8945
5	Err	14.05r	1560	20444	13.1051	0.9324
6	Tit	13.33r	2209	25508	11.5473	0.8661
7	Shr	12.66r	2153	25138	11.6758	0.9218
8	TGV	12.05r	1424	15496	10.8820	0.9027
9	LLL	11.500	2410	25659	10.6469	0.9258
10	Rom	11.000	2410	24870	10.3195	0.9381
11	R2	10.55r	2263	22667	10.0163	0.9489
12	MND	10.16r	1810	17914	9.2171	0.9066
13	Jo	9.83r	2434	22857	9.3907	0.9550
14	MV	9.55r	1867	17323	9.2785	0.9710
15	1H4	9.33r	2568	22549	8.7808	0.9408
16	2H4	9.16r	2546	21621	8.4921	0.9264
17	Wiv	9.05r	1825	15062	8.2532	0.9114
18	Ado	9.000	1596	13393	8.3916	0.9324
19	H5	9.000	2987	26567	8.8942	0.9882
20	JC	9.05r	1476	13359	9.0508	0.9995
21	AYL	9.16r	2028	18042	8.8964	0.9705
22	TN	9.33r	1968	16595	8.4324	0.9033
23	Ham	9.55r	3687	32940	8.9341	0.9350
24	Tro	9.83r	3073	27969	9.1015	0.9256
25	AWW	10.16r	2199	20325	9.2428	0.9091
26	MM	10.55r	2174	20736	9.5382	0.9036
27	Oth	11.000	2396	24049	10.0371	0.9125
28	Lr	11.500	2743	28835	10.4951	0.9124
29	Mac	12.05r	2106	23540	11.1776	0.9272
30	Ant	12.66r	2314	26115	11.2857	0.8909
31	Cor	13.33r	2430	29240	12.0329	0.9025
32	Tim	14.05r	1785	23136	12.9613	0.9221
33	Per	14.83r	1961	28251	14.2610	0.9614
34	Cym	15.66r	2714	39048	14.3876	0.9183
35	WT	16.55r	2502	38501	15.3861	0.9295
36	Tmp	17.500	1990	30779	15.4668	0.8838
	Total	11.9907	82427	910371	11.0446	0.9211

Note: a: assumed order of composition. b: play. c: expected mean length of intervals between appearances of index word in named play and in other plays, if appearances are randomly distributed. d: total number of appearances of index words. e: total length of intervals between appearances. f: mean length of interval observed. g: ratio of observed to expected mean interval. The letter r after the last digit in column c indicates that that digit is a recurring one.

would show up still more sharply if we could eliminate or allow for the effect of play length. In other words, we might still find that the less uncommon words were useful chronological markers if we were able to make this adjustment.

In summary, the effect of our test is to show that there is a solid foundation for our working hypothesis, that rare words in Shakespeare can be used as chronological markers.

Table 6.2. *Expected and observed mean lengths of interval between two appearances of a rare word: classification by degree of rarity of word*

a	b	c	d	e	f
2	3272	33955	10.3774	11.9907	0.8655
3	6029	61751	10.2423	,,	.0.8542
4	7668	81292	10.6015	,,	0.8841
5	9739	105578	10.8407	,,	0.9041
6	10058	110766	11.0127	,,	0.9184
7	11661	127489	10.9329	,,	0.9118
8	11735	131823	11.2333	,,	0.9368
9	11433	132818	11.6171	,,	0.9688
10	10832	124899	11.5306	,,	0.9616
All	82427	910371	11.0446	,,	0.9211

Note: a: category of index word, i.e. appearing twice, three times, four times, etc.   b: total number of intervals between appearances in target play and in other plays.   c: total length of intervals.   d: mean length of intervals observed.   e: mean length of intervals expected, if appearances distributed at random.   f: ratio of observed to expected mean lengths.

INTERRELATIONSHIPS BETWEEN PLAYS

The work done on the card index words by the Computer Unit at King's College has been gratefully acknowledged. The computer made 12,996 independent counts and embodied them in 342 tables. Such a mass of material had to be condensed if any meaning was to be extracted. The nine categories of words were re-grouped into the rarest, those giving 2 to 6 links between play and play, and the less rare, giving 7 to 10 links. The first gave a total of 37,061 links, the second about 20% more, i.e. 44,759. Tables were then prepared for each of the 38 plays, showing its links with each of the others, for each of the two groups of index words, and for both groups taken together. These tables are shown in Appendix II. Apart from the links with other plays, in each table the play's links with itself are shown in small handwritten figures; but they do not enter into the next set of calculations. In all the tables Hart's count of the number of different lexical words in each play is entered at the extreme left.

The next step is to calculate whether the links connecting each pair of plays are less or more than the expected number, and if more, whether the excess is statistically significant. This involves relying on Hart's counts. This is best explained by an illustration.

In the first page of Appendix II, in which the links of *2 Henry VI* with other plays are considered, we have a total of 1287 links given by words in the 2–6 group. The total of Hart's counts for the other plays is 100,447. We take *3 Henry VI* as our example; Hart's count for the number of its words is 2790.

We would expect then that on a chance basis *3H6* would have 2790/100,447 parts of the total 1287 links. This would be 35.7475. The observed number of links from *2H6* to *3H6*, as shown in the table, is 83; and this is greater than 35.7475 by a factor of 2.32. Tested by χ^2 this is statistically highly significant. Accordingly all the three numbers entered, 83, 35.75 and 232, are underlined. Similar calculations and similar entries are made in the 7–10 group; and again, to cover the entire range from 2 to 10 link words. The probability 0.05 is taken as the upper limit for statistical significance throughout Appendix II (and also generally elsewhere); but such big departures from chance as a multiplication by 2.32 have probabilities at a vanishing point.

Proceeding in this way we end with 38 tables showing for each play (and separately for the first and second parts of *Pericles*) its links with all the other plays, with the statistically significant linkages distinguished by underlining. When turning over the pages of Appendix II, the reader is helped by these underlinings to appreciate the closer rare-word relationships between play and play, to detect trends and to be awakened to suggestions. We may make the following comments:

(1) There is obviously a strong tendency for plays to be most significantly connected with near neighbours in the chronological order from which we started. This is in line with the finding shown in Table 6.1 of an over-all contraction in interval length between plays connected by links. There we were dealing with all links; in the underlined relationships of Appendix II we are noticing only the statistically significant relationships. In Table 6.1 our observations were diluted by a random factor, in that play length and word content were ignored; in Appendix II we have taken the word content of plays into account, and the verbal relationships between plays – their verbal kinship, one might say – are emphasised. The existence of these kinships lies at the heart of our working hypothesis.

(2) These kinships tend to pull some of the plays together into a tight cluster. This is very strikingly so in the case of the early plays, *1 Henry VI*, *2 Henry VI*, *3 Henry VI*, *Richard III*, *Titus*, *Richard II*. Starting from each of these plays in turn, one finds it statistically significantly connected with each of the others, as shown by the + sign in the table overleaf. There is no other cluster so tight in the whole canon. It is to be noted that *The Comedy of Errors* is only tenuously connected with this cluster through a single line to *Richard III*. Other clusters are looser, notably *1 Henry IV*, *2 Henry IV*, *Wives* and *Henry V*. There are also pairs of plays bound together, such as *Hamlet* and *Troilus*, and *All's Well* and *Measure for Measure*. There are large differences between the plays, with kinships close or loose, strong or weak, narrow or extended. Early plays are necessarily mainly connected with later ones, and late plays with earlier. At the extremes, with the *Henry VI* plays and with *The Tempest* links are strong and many; in the middle of the canon they are fewer, looser and weaker. It seems probable that in early years the playwright employed a smaller vocabulary than later on, and that this could account for the closer early connections.

(3) Episodes of statistically significant linkage, if shown in the 2–6 group of index words, are also likely to appear in the 7–10 group, and vice versa; but there are many instances to the contrary. If we mark a statistically significant positive deviation (i.e.

	2H6	3H6	1H6	R3	Tit	R2
2 Henry VI		+	+	+	+	+
3 Henry VI	+		+	+	+	+
1 Henry VI	+	+		+	+	+
Richard III	+	+	+		+	+
Titus	+	+	+	+		+
Richard II	+	+	+	+	+	

excess of links) as + +, a positive deviation not reaching significance as +, and failure of linking to reach the chance value, the three possibilities in the 2–6 group combined with the same three possibilities in the 7–10 group give us the numbers in Table 6.3. The expected numbers in each cell are calculated from the marginal totals. Thus in the first cell, to the top and left, where + + is combined with + +, the expected number is the product of the marginal totals divided by the grand total, 1406. The differences between observed and expected numbers are so large that we may omit decimals; and the expected numbers, correct to the nearest whole number, are shown in brackets. Clearly, the 2 to 6 group links and the 7 to 10 group links are to some extent measuring the same tendency and are correlated. We can make a rough estimate of the degrees of correlation by writing + + = 2 and + = 1. The correlation coefficient at +0.410 is substantial. As the two estimates of linking have a good deal of dependence, it will be best to turn to the last three columns of the tables in Appendix II, where they are combined in a single estimate given by their sum.

(4) The fourth feature of these tables is not immediately obvious, but once observed is striking and enigmatic. This is that the links between plays are not symmetrical. If index words in play P can be found in significant excess in play Q, this does not imply that the same index words when looked at from the Q side will be found in significant excess in play P. Two facts conspire to produce this asymmetry. The two plays will be unequal in their length and word content, so that a number which in the smaller play is well over expectation in the larger play need not be so. Furthermore, if in P a word appears p times and q times in Q, the play P has q links with Q and Q has p links with P. These numbers, p and q, are often different.

Let us now condense the observations of the 38 tables of Appendix II into a single table (6.4). We can abandon the division of index words into 2 to 6 and 7 to 10 groups and concern ourselves only with their sum. We can also omit both *Pericles* Acts I and II and *Henry VIII* as collaborative or doubtfully Shakespeare. In our new table we enter only the ratios of observation to expectation where they are statistically significant (i.e. underlined). As the table is a large one, the ratios are restricted to their first two digits, rounded upwards or downwards to allow for the third omitted digit. For instance, in the *2 Henry VI* table of Appendix II the seven

Table 6.3. *Shakespeare: link words by category, correlation*

		Links with 7 to 10 group words			
Links with 2 to 6 group words: observed numbers (expected numbers in brackets)		+ +	+	o	Total
	+ +	52	64	20	136
		(12)	(51)	(73)	
	+	51	215	199	465
		(40)	(175)	(250)	
	o	18	251	536	805
		(69)	(304)	(432)	
Totals		121	530	755	1406

significant ratios are 193, 175, 145, 182, 128, 136, 143. We reduce these to 19, 18, 15, 18, 13, 14 and 14 respectively, and proceed in the same way with the other plays. We now have the material of Table 6.4. As will be seen, most of the table is blank, and there are a total of a mere 171 two-digit numbers to occupy the table's 1260 spaces. To help the eye, the order of the plays has been slightly rearranged, changing the chronology, though to no great extent. This has been done to bring closer together plays which on the vocabulary test seem to be related. The main difference from the order, derived from Chambers, which has been used elsewhere in this book, is that *Richard II* has been brought forward from 11th to 6th, *Titus* is placed before *Errors*, and *Two Gentlemen* before *Shrew*. The second part of *Pericles* is moved to one from last, before *Tempest*.

The asymmetry of the relationships between play and play now comes clearly to view. Looking at the total number of entries for each play in the sum column at the right-hand margin, we see that every play has at least some entries, varying in number from 2 to 8. If we look at the column totals in the bottom row we see that the number of entries in each column varies much more widely, from 15 as the maximum down to zero, exhibited by five plays. The plays are distributed quite differently in the two cases (see first table on p. 95). There seems to be no relation between the number of links a play has with other plays and the length of the play, apart from the fact that the last row shows four plays of low word content with the minimum number of links. In the case of the column totals there does seem to be a relationship between the average number of words in a play (Hart's count) and the number of links (see second small table). The wordy plays are mainly towards the head of the list; the shorter ones, with a smaller word treasury, come towards the bottom.

The fact that the two lists are so very different suggests that they differ in nature and meaning. Table 6.4 consists of two halves to either side of a diagonal running downwards from left to right. The diagonal is made up of the blank spaces where each play's links with itself have been omitted. To the right of the diagonal we have

Table 6.4. *Shakespeare plays: matrix of interconnections*

	16	26	36	R3	Tt	R2	Er	TG	Sh	LL	Ro	MD	Jo	MV	14	24	Wi	H5	Ad	AY	JC	TN	Ha	Tr	AW	MW	Ot	Tm	Lr	Mc	Cy	An	Co	WT	Pe	Tp	Sum
1H6		19	22	16	16	15	·	·	·	·	·	·	·	·	·	·	·	·	·	·	·	·	·	·	·	·	·	·	·	·	·	·	·	·	·	·	5
2H6	18		19	15	18	14	·	·	·	·	·	·	·	·	·	·	·	·	·	·	·	·	·	·	·	·	·	·	·	·	·	·	·	·	·	·	6
3H6	23	22		16	19	14	·	·	·	·	·	·	·	·	·	·	·	·	·	·	·	·	·	·	·	·	·	·	·	·	·	·	·	·	·	·	6
R3	15	15	17		14	14	·	·	·	·	·	·	·	·	·	·	·	·	·	·	·	·	·	·	·	·	·	·	·	·	·	·	·	·	·	·	5
Tit	15	20	19	20		13	·	·	14	·	·	·	13	·	·	·	·	·	·	·	·	·	·	·	·	·	·	·	·	·	·	·	·	·	·	·	7
R2	15	15	14	16	16		·	·	·	·	·	·	·	·	14	·	·	·	·	·	·	·	·	·	·	·	·	·	·	·	·	·	·	·	·	·	2
Err	·	·	·	·	·	·		14	14	14	·	·	·	·	·	·	·	·	·	·	·	·	·	·	·	·	·	·	·	·	·	·	·	·	·	·	4
TGV	14	·	13	16	16	·	14		16	13	·	13	14	·	·	·	·	·	·	16	·	13	·	·	·	·	·	·	·	·	·	·	·	·	·	·	5
Shr	·	13	16	15	17	·	14	16		13	·	13	13	·	·	·	·	·	13	13	·	·	·	·	·	·	·	·	·	·	·	·	·	·	·	·	6
LLL	·	·	·	13	14	15	14	16	13		·	13	13	·	·	·	·	·	·	14	·	·	·	·	·	·	·	·	·	·	·	·	·	·	·	·	5
Rom	·	·	13	14	15	·	13	·	·	·		·	·	·	·	·	·	·	·	·	·	·	·	·	·	·	·	·	·	·	·	·	·	·	14	·	4
MND	·	·	·	14	14	·	13	13	13	13	·		·	·	·	·	·	·	·	·	·	·	·	·	·	·	·	13	·	·	·	·	·	·	·	·	2
Jo	12	·	13	·	·	14	·	·	13	·	·	·		·	·	·	·	·	·	·	·	13	·	·	·	·	·	·	·	·	·	·	·	·	·	·	4
MV	·	·	·	15	·	13	·	·	·	·	·	·	·		·	·	·	·	·	·	·	·	·	·	·	·	·	·	·	·	·	·	·	·	·	·	3
1H4	·	·	·	14	·	13	·	·	·	·	·	·	·	16		·	16	15	·	·	·	·	·	·	·	·	·	·	·	·	·	·	·	·	·	·	4
2H4	·	·	·	13	·	·	·	·	·	·	·	·	·	16	16		16	15	13	·	·	·	·	·	·	·	·	·	·	·	·	·	·	·	·	·	5
WIv	12	13	·	·	·	·	·	·	·	·	·	·	·	·	·	·		14	·	·	·	·	·	·	·	·	·	·	·	·	·	·	·	·	·	·	6
H5	·	·	·	·	·	14	·	·	·	·	·	·	·	·	·	·	14		·	·	·	14	16	13	·	·	·	14	·	·	·	·	·	·	·	·	2
Ado	·	·	·	14	15	13	·	·	13	·	·	13	13	·	·	·	·	·		14	·	14	14	14	·	·	14	14	13	13	·	·	·	·	·	·	4
AYL	·	·	·	15	13	14	·	·	15	·	·	13	13	·	·	·	·	·	14		·	15	12	13	·	·	·	14	14	13	·	·	13	·	·	·	5
JC	·	·	13	·	·	·	·	·	·	·	·	·	·	·	·	·	·	·	·	·		·	·	13	13	·	·	·	·	·	·	·	·	·	·	·	4
TN	·	·	·	·	·	·	·	·	·	·	·	·	·	·	·	·	·	·	·	·	·		13	·	·	15	·	12	·	13	·	12	·	·	·	·	4
Ham	·	·	·	·	·	·	·	·	·	·	·	·	·	·	·	·	·	·	·	·	·	·		17	14	13	14	·	18	·	·	16	·	·	·	·	5
Tro	·	·	·	·	·	·	·	·	·	·	·	·	·	·	·	·	·	·	·	·	·	·	15		14	13	12	·	·	·	·	·	13	·	·	·	5
AWW	·	·	·	·	·	·	·	·	·	·	·	·	·	·	·	·	·	·	·	·	·	14	15	13		13	·	14	13	·	·	·	13	·	·	·	5
MM	·	13	·	·	·	·	·	·	·	·	·	·	·	·	·	·	·	·	·	·	·	13	15	14	13		·	14	14	13	·	16	13	13	·	·	6
Oth	·	·	·	·	·	·	·	·	·	·	·	·	·	·	·	·	·	·	·	·	·	·	17	14	14	·		·	13	13	·	13	13	13	·	·	5
Tim	·	·	·	·	·	·	·	·	·	·	·	·	·	·	·	·	·	·	·	·	·	15	14	13	13	14	·		18	·	·	·	·	·	·	·	6
Lr	·	·	·	·	·	·	·	·	·	·	·	·	13	·	·	·	·	·	·	·	14	15	15	·	·	·	14	·		14	·	·	·	·	13	·	6
Mac	13	·	·	·	·	·	·	·	·	·	·	·	·	·	·	·	·	·	·	·	·	15	13	13	·	·	14	13	13		13	12	13	·	14	13	5
Cym	·	·	·	·	·	·	·	·	·	·	·	·	·	·	·	·	·	·	·	·	·	13	13	13	13	·	13	·	13	13		14	13	·	14	16	6
Ant	·	·	·	·	·	·	·	·	·	·	·	·	·	·	·	·	·	·	·	·	·	·	·	·	·	·	14	·	·	·	14		13	13	·	·	6
Cor	14	·	·	·	·	·	·	·	·	·	·	·	·	·	·	·	·	·	·	·	·	·	·	·	·	·	·	·	·	·	14	13		·	·	·	5
WT	·	·	·	·	·	·	·	·	·	·	·	·	·	·	·	·	·	·	·	·	·	·	·	·	·	15	·	·	·	·	·	·	·		14	13	3
Per²	·	·	·	·	·	·	·	·	·	·	14	·	·	·	·	·	·	·	·	·	·	·	13	14	·	·	·	13	13	13	·	12	13	14		20	2
Tmp	·	·	·	·	·	·	·	·	·	·	·	·	·	·	·	·	·	·	·	·	·	·	·	·	·	·	·	·	·	13	14	13	13	15	20		8
Sum	7	8	5	10	9	8	–	–	10	6	2	4	1	–	5	3	10	–	3	–	1	15	14	4	3	3	1	8	5	6	2	5	5	3	4	4	171

For explanation see text, pp. 92–3.

No. of entries, rows		Plays	Av. no. words
8	1	*Tmp*	2562
7	2	*Tit, R2*	2706
6	7	*2H6, 3H6, LLL, AYL, Lr, Cym, Ant*	2998
5	13	*1H6, R3, Shr, Rom, MND, H5, Ado, Ham, Oth, Tim, Mac, Cor, MM*	2882
4	7	*TGV, Jo, 1H4, Wiv, TN, Tro, AWW*	2744
3	2	*2H4, WT*	3048
2	4	*Err, MV, JC, Per²*	2050

No. of entries, columns		Plays	Av. no. words
15	1	*Ham*	3882
14	1	*Tro*	3360
10	3	*R3, Shr, H5*	2948
9	1	*Tit*	2578
8	3	*2H6, R2, Lr*	3106
7	1	*1H6*	3014
6	2	*LLL, Cym*	3066
5	5	*3H6, 1H4, Mac, Cor, WT*	2913
4	3	*MND, AWW, Tmp*	2543
3	5	*2H4, AYL, MM, Oth, Per²*	2569
2	2	*Rom, Ant*	2960
1	4	*Jo, Wiv, TN, Tim*	2621
0	5	*Err, TGV, MV, Ado, JC*	2275

the links between P and Q where Q is later in chronological order. To the left are the links where Q is an earlier play than P. These are the more numerous, with 92 entries (sum 1332) as against 79 to the right (sum 1127). The suggestion arises that where a word links P with an earlier Q, Q is the source and P is the echo. On this basis, one would expect the earlier appearances to outnumber their echoes. To test this idea we can look at the cases where the number of appearances of a word in P greatly outnumbers the number of appearances in Q, say so many to one; if it proves that P is the earlier play of the two, it will tend to support the notion proposed. On pp. 96–7 is the list of all those cases where on one side there is only a single appearance, on the other side 3 or more.

There are 231 words in the card index with a 2:1 preponderance, lying respectively in 125 cases with the earlier play, in 106 cases with the later. This is not a statistically significant shift, and it would not be worth while to list these words. It seems, in fact, that the less the preponderance the less marked is the difference between earlier and later appearances. In terms of numbers of index words

Rare-word links between pairs of earlier and later plays

		earlier		later		
10-words	mouldy	2H4	9	Tro	1	
9-words	forfeiture	MV	8	Tim	1	
8-words	(none)					
7-words	fardel	Ham	1	WT	6	
	lanthorn	MND	6	2H4	1	61:16
	swaggerer	2H4	6	AYL	1	2: 1
6-words	disinherit	3H6	5	R3	1	
5-words	derision	MND	4	Tro	1	
	earldom	3H6	4	1H6	1	
	incestuous	Ham	4	Lr	1	
	intellect	LLL	4	R2	1	
	martyr, v	Tit	4	Rom	1	
	mountaineer	Cym	4	Tmp	1	
	ostler	1H4	4	Cor	1	
	plantain	LLL	4	Rom	1	
	sorrowful	Tit	4	Ant	1	
	toothache	Ado	4	Cym	1	41:14
	torch-bearer	Rom	1	MV	4	10: 1
4-words	a-field	1H6	1	Tro	3	
	agreement	Shr	3	1H4	1	
	apoplexy	2H4	3	Cor	1	
	apple-john	1H4	1	2H4	3	
	aspic	Oth	1	Ant	3	
	benefactor	MM	3	Tim	1	
	burgonet	2H6	3	Ant	1	
	bustle, v	R3	3	JC	1	
	butt,n (barrel)	Tro	1	Tmp	3	
	core, n	Ham	1	Tro	3	
	cuckoldly, a	Wiv	3	AYL	1	
	curiosity	Tim	1	Lr	3	
	desk	Err	3	Ham	1	
	disjoin	Jo	1	JC	3	
	elephant	JC	1	Tro	3	
	farthing	LLL	3	Jo	1	
	flier	Cor	3	Cym	1	
	galliard	TN	3	Cym	1	
	gelding	1H4	3	Wiv	1	
	guile	1H6	1	R3	3	
	hearth	Wiv	1	Cor	3	
	intelligent	Lr	3	WT	1	
	invade	H5	1	Lr	3	
	joiner	Rom	1	MND	3	
	justicer	Lr	3	Cym	1	
	leprosy	Tim	3	Ant	1	
	muffler	Wiv	3	H5	1	
	odorous	MND	3	Ado	1	
	opposer	AWW	1	Cor	3	
	pancake	AYL	3	AWW	1	
	permission	Jo	3	Oth	1	
	poetical	AYL	3	TN	1	
	probble	Wiv	3	H5	1	

	smite	Wiv 1	Ant 3	
	snare, v	2H6 3	Tmp 1	
4-words	spunge, n	MV 1	Ham 3	
contd.	storehouse	Mac 1	Cor 3	
	sundry	AYL 1	Mac 3	
	temperately	Ham 1	Cor 3	
	thwack	Cor 3	WT 1	
	traitorously	2H6 3	AWW 1	
	undaunted	1H6 3	Mac 1	31:13
	unsheathe	3H6 3	2H4 1	25:18

involved, the distinction between 'source' and 'echo', or between early and late, is nowhere statistically significant; but the differences become significant if we deal with them in terms of number of appearances. In the 5-words, with 4:1 outnumbering 1:4 by ten to one, or 41:14 in terms of appearances, the difference is a striking one. But if we were to include in the preponderances cases where the partition was 3:2 or 2:3, the effect would be less obvious. There is nothing to be wondered at if we find in some cases that an early word, picked up in a later play, then reverberates several times. Nevertheless, the fact that the preponderance is more usually the other way round falls in with our preconceptions of how the poet's mind is likely to work.

If we turn again to Table 6.4 there is another observation we can make. The numbers entered under '*Sum*' in the column to the extreme right vary between 2 and 8, but show no tendency to cluster. On the other hand the numbers entered in the bottom row against 'sum' not only vary very widely between 0 and 15, but also show phases or waves or clusters peaking at *R3* (10), *Shrew* (10), *Henry V* (10), *Hamlet–Troilus* (15–14), *Lear* (8) and perhaps, but faintly, at *Coriolanus–Winter's Tale* (5–5). In terms of our 'source' and 'echo' metaphor, these might be the plays which proved to be treasuries of rare words, paid out in driblets in other verbally less imaginative works. Could this suggestion be supported by contrasting these 'rich' plays with the verbally relatively impoverished ones, with only a 1 or a 0 to show for a link: *Errors, Two Gentlemen, John, Merchant of Venice, Wives, Much Ado, Julius Caesar, Twelfth Night, Timon*? Perhaps Shakespearean scholars might be willing to consider whether there is any merit in this suggestion.

The gaps or deficiencies in certain columns of Table 6.4 allow us to divide the 36 plays into six groups of six (see small table). The grouping is, of course, influenced by one of the standard chronologies, namely that of E. K. Chambers, from which it took its origin. This had to be modified to bring *Merry Wives* to the next place after *2 Henry IV*, following the suggestion of H. J. Oliver (p. iv)[10] with support from word-link counts,[14] and *Timon* into the next place to and preceding *Lear*, following the suggestion of J. C. Maxwell (p. xii)[6] which again was very strongly supported by statistical tests of word links by the present writer.[16] A further change has been necessitated by the demonstration, in the relevant table of Appendix II, that *Richard II* has very strong links, running in both directions, with all the earliest plays, the

Group	Plays						Total words (from Hart)
A	*1H6*	*2H6*	*3H6*	*R3*	*Tit*	*R2*	17,579
B	*Err*	*TGV*	*Shr*	*LLL*	*Rom*	*MND*	14,804
C	*Jo*	*MV*	*1H4*	*2H4*	*Wiv*	*H5*	17,319
D	*Ado*	*AYL*	*JC*	*TN*	*Ham*	*Tro*	16,968
E	*AWW*	*MM*	*Oth*	*Tim*	*Lr*	*Mac*	16,961
F	*Cym*	*Ant*	*Cor*	*WT*	*Per²*	*Tmp*	16,314

three *Henry VI* plays, *Titus* and *Richard III*. Yet one more change has been made, again on word-linkage data but this time not yet published, because the last three acts of *Pericles* have been found to be very strongly linked with *The Tempest*. Making all these modifications of the Chambers order has led me to abandon Chambers in favour of the Arden editors. Their order (together with those of Chambers and Harrison, kindly collated for me by Dr Ann P. Slater)* appears in Fig. 6.2.

For a long time I had great hopes that the tables of Appendix II could be synthesised into a single comprehensive ordering of the plays. I had the advice and help of the Computer Unit at King's College, University of London, and in particular of Miss Margaret Skinner. I proposed a technical method by which, starting from one order of the plays in chronological sequence, one could calculate an improved order. A repetition of the technique would lead, I hoped, to further improvement, so that by successive stages a final order would be arrived at asymptotically.

The technique would consist simply in assigning to each of the plays a weight corresponding to its place in the initial working sequence. For instance, weights of 0 to 5 could be given respectively to the groups A to F shown on p. 98. Each play would then be dealt with in turn. The links of the play P with all other plays, their number multiplied by their weights, would be summed and divided by the total number of P's links to calculate its mean weight. The value of the mean weight would then be an

---

* *New Arden chronology*. It is not possible to draw up a precise chronology from the separate editions of the New Arden series. Few plays can be assigned to a single year, and most editors prefer a tentative suggestion within several years confirmed by a play's firm terminal dates. Opinions about the relationships of neighbouring plays also differ from editor to editor. Furthermore, at the time of compilation, there were no New Arden editions of *Richard III*, *The Taming of the Shrew*, *Much Ado*, *Troilus and Cressida*, and *Hamlet*; for these plays Chambers's dating was adopted. Four minor adjustments should be made to the present order: in the opinion of the editors concerned, *Merry Wives* comes between *1* and *2 Henry IV*; *All's Well* precedes *Measure for Measure*; *Antony and Cleopatra* should probably precede *Timon*; and, according to Chambers, *Much Ado* should probably precede *Henry V*. This chronology was drawn up at an early stage of this study, when it was thought wisest to accept *King John*'s traditional and generally accepted dating between 1593–6, rather than E. A. J. Honigmann's arguments for the unusually early 1590–1. However, in the course of research a close correlation between the vocabularies of part A of *Edward III* and *King John* was discovered, supporting the early dating Honigmann prefers. J. Dover Wilson also argued for a 1590 dating for a postulated first draft of the play in his Cambridge edition (Cambridge University Press, 1936, pp. liv–lvii), and a similar dating was also proposed by P. Alexander: *Shakespeare's Life and Art* (London, 1939).

Chambers	Harrison	Arden edns.	Vocabulary rare-word order (approximated)	OED (Schäfer[17])	
2H6	1H6	Tit	Tit	LLL	1588
3H6	2H6	1H6	1H6	Tit	
1H6	3H6	2H6	2H6	Err	1590
R3	R3	3H6	3H6	MND	
Err	Tit	R3	R3	1H6	1591
Tit	LLL	TGV	R2	TGV	
Shr	TGV	Err	TGV	Rom	1592
TGV	Err	LLL	Err	2H6	1593
LLL	Shr	Shr	LLL	3H6	
Rom	Rom	Jo	Shr	R2	
R2	MND	R2	Jo	R3	1594
MND	R2	Rom	Rom	Jo	1595
Jo	Jo	MND	MND	1H4	1596
MV	MV	MV	MV	MV	
1H4	1H4	1H4	1H4	Shr	
2H4	2H4	2H4	2H4	2H4	1597
Ado	H5	Wiv	Wiv	Wiv	1598
H5	Ado	H5	H5	Ado	1599
JC	Wiv	Ado	Ado	H5	
AYL	AYL	AYL	AYL	AYL	1600
TN	JC	JC	JC	AWW	1601
Ham	Tro	Tro	Ham	JC	
Wiv	Ham	Ham	TN	TN	
Tro	TN	TN	MM	Ham	1602
AWW	MM	MM	AWW	MM	1603
MM	AWW	AWW	Tro	Oth	1604
Oth	Oth	Oth	Oth	Lr	1605
Lr	Lr	Lr	Tim	Mac	
Mac	Mac	Mac	Lr	Ant	1606
Ant	Tim	Tim	Mac	Tro	
Cor	Ant	Ant	Ant	Cor	1607
Tim	Cor	Per	Cor	Tim	
Per	Per	Cor	Cym	Per	1608
Cym	Cym	Cym	WT	Tmp	1610
WT	WT	WT	Per²	Cym	1611
Tmp	Tmp	Tmp	Tmp	WT	

Figure 6.2. Shakespeare's plays: chronological ordering by standard authorities and by rare word links (with best approximation to Arden editions)

estimate of the 'lateness' of P. Having estimates of the 'lateness' of all of the plays would lead to a new order. The new order would then be translated into a new lot of weights, and so lead to a further improvement of the ordinal sequence.

With what I now see was very remarkable generosity of spirit the arduous task was undertaken of writing what must have been a complex program. It was written and applied to the word counts already available from previous work by the computer. Unfortunately the first new order showed implausibilities, and when it was used to calculate a derived second order, this was not an improvement but chaotic. The logic of the approach was adequate, but it was not one which was appropriate to the nature of the material. Random errors of various kinds would have conspired to make the material statistically unstable, with errors compounding one another instead of smoothing each other out. The very considerable labours undertaken so kindly by Miss Skinner and her colleagues went unrewarded.

This unsuccessful experiment showed that the material of Appendix II could not be used as if it were self-sufficient. To try to use it as a single whole would be to overrate its precision and to make insufficient allowance for its probabilistic character. It was more useful as a complement and, perhaps, a corrective to arguments on an independent foundation. The order in which Shakespeare scholars arrange the chronological sequence of the plays is anchored to established historical facts. For the dates of composition the calendar years from, say, 1589 to 1611, provide in most cases a *terminus ad quem*; the *terminus a quo* is nearly always a much more difficult matter. Doubts and disagreements between scholars still exist, and arguments based on subjective considerations are by no means abandoned. It is in these grey areas where the light thrown by vocabulary studies, as I believe, can prove helpful. Figure 6.2 has been laid out with this in mind. The sequential order which can be synthesized from the arguments and judgments of the Arden editors has been adopted as the base on which the results of rare-word linkage work impose no more than four important modifications. These are the back-dating of two plays, *Richard II* and *Timon*, and the shifting forwards of *Troilus* and the three last acts of *Pericles*. These modifications are offered for consideration *secundum artem* by those concerned.

SUMMARY AND CONCLUSIONS

1. A brief autobiographical explanation is offered of how, in the years of his retirement, the present writer came into Shakespeare research. From the beginning this took the form of statistical work on Shakespeare's vocabulary.

2. Investigation of the vocabulary of *A Lover's Complaint* supported the views of those scholars who considered the poem an authentic work of Shakespeare written considerably later than his other poems. This positive result was an encouragement to continue cognate studies.

3. Words used by Shakespeare relatively rarely were found to cluster in a chronological list of his works, and therefore to link works which had been written at about the same period. The working hypothesis was formulated that 'the degree of contemporaneity of two plays might be measured by the degree of community between their vocabularies'.

4. Later studies, published in *Notes and Queries*, were concerned with the placing in a serial chronological order of *The Merry Wives of Windsor*, *All's Well That Ends Well*, *Troilus and Cressida*, *Timon of Athens*, *Lear*. These studies were fruitful in that they produced evidence relevant to incompletely settled problems of chronology.

5. A card index of Shakespeare's rare words was now built up, working first from Bartlett's and then from Spevack's *Concordance*. The plays covered 38 items, i.e. dividing *Pericles* into two parts, the first two and the last three acts, and including *Henry VIII* but not *Two Noble Kinsmen*. The 5553 words all appeared in more than one play, and so served to link plays with one another. They were grouped into those which occurred two, three, four, etc., up to ten times, making therefore nine separate groups.

6. Under advice, the author entered himself as a postgraduate student at King's College, London, with a view to further work under guidance. In consultation with

his Supervisor, Richard Proudfoot, it was decided to use rare-word analysis in a study of the anonymous play *The Reign of King Edward III* (1596).

7. The card index words were passed to the Computer Unit at King's College, which gave invaluable help in providing counts of all index words in all plays. The Unit made 12,996 independent counts and embodied them in 342 tables, retaining the classification of link words into nine separate groups.

8. It could be demonstrated that the index words are not distributed at random, but tend to cluster. On a rough calculation the mean interval between the two appearances of an index word, in two different plays, is less than (on average 92% of) what it would be in a random distribution. The rarest words come closest together. For instance the appearance of 2-link words are at 87% of their expected distance from one another, while 10-link words are at 96% of the expected distance.

9. A number of play-clusters were identified. The tightest and closest embraced the three *Henry VI* plays, *Titus*, *Richard III* and *Richard II*. Each of these plays was statistically significantly linked with each of the others, both forwards and backwards, i.e. by a total of 30 linkages. The statistical significance of a link was determined by comparing the number of links between play P and play Q with the number which would be expected in a random distribution taking into account Alfred Hart's enumerations of the numbers of different words in the plays.

10. Other clusters were looser. Links between plays were not infrequently asymmetrical in magnitude, P being more strongly linked to Q than Q to P. The causes of asymmetry and the meaning to be attached to it are discussed.

11. A computer program which the writer suggested, with a view to determining a 'least errors' chronological order, was tried out by the Computer Unit, but was found not to be feasible.

12. The writer's best effort at a total chronological order which would take account of the linkages, was, in effect, an acceptance of the serial order which can be extracted from the Arden editions of the plays. To this four modifications are proposed, back-dating *Richard II* and *Timon* by a few steps, and shifting forwards *Troilus* and *Pericles* to somewhat later places. The following is the serial order which is proposed for consideration: *Tit, 1H6, 2H6, 3H6, R3, R2, TGV, Err, LLL, Shr, Jo, Rom, MND, MV, 1H4, 2H4, Wiv, H5, Ado, AYL, JC, Ham, TN, MM, AWW, Tro, Oth, Tim, Lr, Mac, Ant, Cor, Cym, WT, Per, Tmp,*

7

The rare-word vocabulary of *King Edward III*

WHAT IS A 'WORD'?

The previous chapters have been concerned with the exploration of a writer's vocabulary in the search for idiosyncratic features which will distinguish his work from that of others. This can be looked on as a special instance in the vast field of enquiry concerned with the recognition of identities. Here success goes, as a rule, with the application of an advanced technology. Historically, we found two paradigms, on the one hand the Bertillon system of multiple measurements, on the other hand Galton's science of finger-prints. Bertillon relied on such characteristics as a man's stature, the breadth of his shoulders, the length of his nose, the colour of his skin. Identification by finger-prints relies on minute particularities in the skin of the fingers which need magnification to be counted and measured. The observations which Bertillon called for are full of meaning for us. They are the features by which we recognise our fellow man, which we define in a portrait, which in their unique combination enshrine his style and individuality. Finger-prints, on the other hand, with their almost countless and utterly precise points of reference, contain no intrinsic information, and tell us nothing whatever about the man who gave them – other than his identity. It is the finger-print system which has survived and flourished, and Bertillon's system which has become obsolete.

The lesson we learn is this. Observations which seem to have absolutely no content of information may be none the worse for that in a problem of identification. Dr Morton's reliance on filler words, on 'and', 'but' and 'the', on the commonest words of all, on the tip of everyone's pen, when combined and sorted, can be so firmly based as to justify remarkable conclusions, e.g. that it was unlikely to the point of being inconceivable that Helander was responsible for the letters of whose authorship he was accused. Nevertheless Dr Morton's primary data do not have the precision of finger-prints; they have to be transformed into statistics, and are probabilistic as a premiss for conclusions.

In this respect we are no worse off than he if we follow the leadership of Bertillon and choose as our objects, not the almost contentless filler words but the more meaty and interesting rare words. In pursuing rare words we are trying to approach an idea in the mind of our quarry. We hope, and we expect, that in his use of unusual words every writer will have his own predilections. It is the stem word which should really count for us. We might ask, 'How often does Shakespeare make use of the idea of "envy"? Or Marlowe? Or Fletcher, or Jonson?' But then we come up against the task of definition. 'Envy' is both noun and verb. These writers may well differ in the proportionality of the one use and the other. There is no help for it. We must define our terms, and nebulous ideas must be put into the straitjacket of words distinguished as parts of speech.

For statistical work no harm is done if the definition of an item of information is in some ways arbitrary. What is important is that the definition should be precise. Inclusion within the limits, or exclusion as beyond them, must not be subject to the possible bias of personal judgment. Rather than that, we might refer the decision to the toss of a coin, or have recourse to a table of random numbers. In what follows it is not claimed that our definition of a 'word' will be above criticism from grammarians or logicians or experts in linguistics. All that is required of it is that by it the student has it decided for him whether, in a given case, word W^1 and word W^2 are to be regarded as distinct, or as variants of one another and therefore equivalent. It would be a profitless exercise to distinguish, say, between the singular and the plural forms of nouns. We are not concerned with linguistic minutiae but with words as they correspond with concepts or ideas in the mind of the writer; and which are, perhaps, therefore characteristic of that writer as distinct from other writers (as a rule, of course, only in probabilistic terms, e.g. in the frequency of use), or characteristic of a writer more in phase P of his career than in phase Q.

The unfortunate consequence is that we cannot make direct use of our primary source of information, either the original text, or its bits and pieces as they are chopped up and arranged in alphabetical order in a Concordance. These 'concordance words' have to be digested and re-grouped in the semantically richer forms of words as they are recorded and defined in a dictionary: 'lexical words'. The dictionary has to be chosen (for this book it was the *Shorter Oxford English Dictionary – SOED*), and it then becomes the arbiter and supposedly infallible authority. My practice has already been made clear on an earlier page (p. 58), when the work of Alfred Hart was discussed. It is hoped that the following paraphrase will be sufficient now.

Any word is regarded as an independent entity if it has its own paragraph in *SOED*, or is entered in bold type under the heading of the catch word in question as a distinct formation. Homonyms which are different parts of speech are taken to be different words. Modifications of a stem word by inflection, declension, conjugation, etc., are not taken to constitute a difference. Verbal nouns and adjectives, e.g. those ending in *-ing*, are regarded as not distinct from the root verb. Words in the Dictionary which appear hyphenated are regarded as single distinct entities. A noun used attributively as an adjective is regarded as an adjective and therefore a different part of speech and an independent word in its own right. A verb used transitively or intransitively is regarded as two different words. These points of decision have been formulated as above with a view to making allowance for authorial style, originality, flexibility and even eccentricity in the use of words.

THE USE OF THE TEXT OF *THE REIGN OF KING EDWARD III*

The collection of words, coming under the above definition and omitting proper names, titles and other words with an initial capital (in modern orthography), was made from the Tudor Facsimile Text of *The Reign of King Edward III*, edited by John S. Farmer and issued in 1910. The original of the facsimile is said to have been in the

British Museum [C.34, g.1]. There the title page runs 'THE RAIGNE OF KING EDVVARD the third: As it hath bin sundrie times plaied about the Citie of London. LONDON, Printed for Cuthbert Burby. 1596.' On his modernized title page, Farmer states that the play was 'Written c. 1589 Date of first publication 1595 Reproduced in Facsimile 1910.' Farmer adds (next page):

the entry in the Stationers' Register [was] dated December 1st, 1595. From internal evidence it is clearly shown that the play was written early in 1589 and produced on the stage immediately. The question of authorship is debatable: scholars must therefore consult the opinion of critics. Many authorities hold that there are strong grounds for regarding this play as wholly or in part the work of Shakespeare in the early days of his dramatic activity.

There are 72 pages and title page. Acts and scenes are not marked as such, but are shown by a marginal 'exeunt' when the stage clears. This book follows standard editions of the play, i.e. that of R. L. Armstrong, for these divisions, as recorded in Appendix III, but does not rely on them for line-numbering. Instead of that, lines were numbered consecutively right through the play, including lines of stage directions, from line 1 'Enter King Edward...' to line 2600 'FINIS'.

The text was now read through, and a note was made of every word which seemed at all unusual. This word was then looked up in Spevack's one-volume *Concordance to Shakespeare*. If the total number of text citations of this word and its equivalents was twelve or less, the word was entered on a paper slip. The slips recorded:

1. The word as spelt in the printed text;
2. Its grammatical category as a part of speech; at times also its meaning;
3. The act, scene and line in which it appeared in the play;
4. The line in which it appeared in the sequence of continuous numeration;
5. The line numbers of its other (earlier or later) appearances;
6. Its serial number in the alphabetical list of link words;
7. The total number of its appearances (and of its equivalents) in those Shakespeare plays and poems which ranked for analysis;
8. The code names of the works in which it appeared and the number of its appearances there.

Exclusions

Certain works of the Shakespeare canon were excluded from the statistical analysis. This was because Hart did not provide a count of the total number of different lexical words in these works. This meant that they could not be used to provide denominators for probability fractions. The excluded works were *Two Noble Kinsmen* (TNK), *Sir Thomas More* (STM), *The Passionate Pilgrim* (PP), *A Lover's Complaint* (LC), *The Phoenix and the Turtle* (PhT). Hart provided counts for *Venus* and *Lucrece*, which have been used. But he merged the Sonnets in a single count with the other poems, which has been discarded. The writer made his own count on

Hart's principles of the number of different lexical words in the Sonnets with the help of Donow's *Concordance* to the sonnet sequences of Shakespeare and others.[1]

Difficulties, oversights and errors

For statistical purposes it was important to avoid the necessity of making personal and subjective judgments, since they must always carry the risk of an unconscious bias. The main precautions were twofold: on the one hand to rely on a single authority on Shakespeare's text (Spevack) to correspond with the single authority on the text of *Edward III* (the Tudor Facsimile edition); and on the other hand to confine the statistical units to single parts of speech. This latter safeguard is formulated on p. 103.

Nevertheless some difficulties remained. It might be necessary to read through long Concordance entries in more than one part of the volume to identify a homograph with an unusual and specific meaning (e.g. *sit* as a transitive verb, and *battle* in the sense specified as v² in the *SOED*). One is more than normally liable to an oversight when attention is minute and has to be prolonged. Moreover, a decision might have to be made whether or not to accept an editor's emendation. Sometimes it was not unambiguous what part of speech the function of a particular word was, in a particular context. More often a personal judgment had to be made whether two forms of a stem word were variants of one another, or distinct and different, such as: *arrogance* and *arrogancy*, *astonish* and *stonish*, *fortnight* and *vortnight*, *inconstant* and *unconstant*, *overbear* and *o'erbear*. Again, when the link citation was examined parsing difficulties might arise. It was impossible altogether to avoid second thoughts (highly objectionable when statistical objectivity is the aim).

In the end a list of 948 catch words was built up. They are reported in Appendices III and IV. Later on doubts arose about some of them, and supernumerary link citations were discovered in other cases; so that second thoughts in 8 cases ended in reducing the 948 words to 940. The excluded words, so marked in the Appendices, were: 336 *fraught*, 422 *inconstant*, 566 *overbear*, 600 *pitch*, 642 *quarter*, 658 *rebel*, 664 *recovery*, 780 *stronger*. It is the shorter list of 940 words which has been made the basis of the critical statistical tables, i.e. throughout this chapter, unless otherwise specifically noted.

It was important that the collection and classification of link words should be carried out accurately. But the statistical significance of the changes made in the final revision should not be rated too highly. Certainly it cannot be claimed that *all* the words linking *Edward III* with Shakespeare, within the limits described, are all correct and all that there are. One can be sure that some errors still remain. The revision by which 948 catch words suffered some changes in their link citations, and at the end were reduced from 948 to 940, meant that thereby there was approximately a 3% change in the link citations, in additions and eliminations. The improved accuracy will have probably meant some reduction, though a smaller one, in the error variance. It seems to the writer unlikely that even the most rigorous and scholarly of re-examinations would bring in more than another 3% of corrections. But when we come to the statistical tables, e.g. Tables 7.2 and 3, we shall find shifts of observation from expectation of a quite different order, greater by one or even two degrees of magnitude, with χ^2 values running into two and three figures for one degree of freedom. Against such massive departures from the expected, minutiae lose their weight.

LINKS BETWEEN *EDWARD III* AND WORKS OF SHAKESPEARE

The rare-word links between *Edward III* and the works of Shakespeare are the focus of interest of this investigation. They are listed in Appendices III and IV. The former shows the words in the order of their appearance in the play; and the second is an alphabetical key to the other. It is important to note that *every time* a given link word appears in the text, it appears also in the statistical analysis. The distribution of these appearances, classified by word class, is shown in Table 7.1. Not surprisingly, the higher the class of link word (i.e. the number of citations it finds in the works of Shakespeare), the more frequently it appears on average in *Edward III*. In other words, it is the link words appearing with exceptional frequency in *Edward III* that average the greatest numbers of links with Shakespeare works. These words have an influence on the statistical analysis proportionate to the number of times they appear in the text. Nevertheless, the rarer the link word (the lower its class) the more specific, and less scattered, its links are likely to be.

We now come to the central focus of interest of this investigation. Do the rare words extracted from *Edward III* link in a meaningful way with the works of Shakespeare? If the links were found to be distributed at random through Shakespeare's works, it would be a strong argument against his having had a substantial share in the authorship. If the distribution is uneven, then where is it mainly concentrated? For instance, with works of a certain stage in his development? If there is a concentration of links, does it apply to part A only (Act I scene ii, Act II and Act IV scene iv), or to part B (God save the mark!), or to both parts? Are there differences in link distribution between these parts? Is there evidence which could be of any value in discriminating between what is and what is not from Shakespeare's hand?

The distribution of the links with Shakespeare's works, recorded in Appendices III and IV, is shown in tables 7.2A and 2B, the former showing the links between Shakespeare and part A of *Edward III*, and the latter the links with part B. These tables report the main results of this book, and have to be described more exactly.

Table 7.2

Each part of the table is arranged in the same way. There are 18 columns grouped into 5 phalanxes. The first phalanx to the left has 2 columns showing the code name of the play or poem, plays to the top, poems at the foot. The order of the plays represents a

Table 7.1. *Distribution of link words, by class, with numbers of appearances in* Edward III

Word class	Numbers of appearances							Total words	Sum appearances	Av. A/W
	1	2	3	4	5	6	7			
0	79	10						89	99	1.11
1	108	7		1				116	126	1.09
2	90	10	2	1				103	120	1.17
3	74	5	2	1				82	94	1.15
4	72	4	1					77	83	1.08
5	67	15	3					85	106	1.25
6	63	10	3					76	92	1.21
7	54	9	2	1				66	82	1.24
8	38	14	5					57	81	1.42
9	52	5	1	1		1		60	75	1.25
10	33	2	1	3				39	52	1.33
11	34	10	1	1				46	61	1.33
12	29	8	2	3	1		1	44	75	1.70
Sums	793	109	23	12	1	1	1	940	1146	1.22

hypothetical chronological sequence. This is mainly based on the order which can be derived from the New Arden editions of Shakespeare's works, but modified to take account of the statistical work reported in Chapter 6, pp. 98–100. Next to the name of the play or poem is set Hart's count of the number of different lexical words it contains. In the case of the Sonnets the count made by the present writer is used. The sum of all these counts, 110,965, constitutes a denominator for the calculation of probability ratios.

The four succeeding phalanxes each consist in four columns. First comes the observational number, i.e. the number of appearances of *Edward III*'s link words in the play or poem in question. The first of these four phalanxes reports the number of appearances (links) given by all the words with from 1 to 6 appearances in Shakespeare; the second phalanx records the number of appearances of all words with 7 to 10 appearances; the next phalanx does the same for words with 11 or 12 appearances; and the last phalanx sums the observed numbers in the three preceding phalanxes. The arrangement is along the same lines as in Appendix II.

In each of these four phalanxes, next to the number of observed appearances comes the number to be expected on a chance basis, correct to the second place of decimals. The expected number is recorded in the table only where it is less than the observed number. This is done so that the reader's eye may see at a glance the places where there is some positive degree of linking between *Edward III* and Shakespeare. The expected number of links between a play or poem and *Edward III* is regarded as that fraction of all the links which is proportionate to the Hart count for that work. For instance, looking at Table 7.2A we see that there were in all 753 citations in

Table 7.2A. *Word links between* Edward III *part* A *and works of Shakespeare*

	Words	obs	exp	ratio	χ^2	obs	exp	ratio	χ^2	obs	exp	ratio	χ^2	obs	exp	ratio	χ^2
Tit	2578	24	17.49	157	ns	22	19.00	116	ns	2				48	45.70	105	ns
1H6	3014	34	20.45	166	9.0	30	22.22	135	ns	20	10.76	186	7.9	84	53.43	157	17.5
2H6	3146	22	21.35	103	ns	35	23.19	151	6.0	14	11.23	125	ns	71	55.77	127	4.2
3H6	2790	15				25	20.57	122	ns	14	9.96	141	ns	54	49.46	109	ns
R3	3218	39	21.04	179	12.0	36	23.72	152	6.4	15	11.48	131	ns	90	57.04	158	19.0
R2	2833	26	19.22	135	ns	26	20.88	125	ns	14	10.11	138	ns	66	50.22	131	5.0
TGV	2153	11				21	15.87	132	ns	8	7.68	104	ns	40	38.16	105	ns
Err	2037	12				18	15.02	120	ns	2				32			
LLL	2872	28	19.49	144	ns	30	21.17	142	ns	10				60	50.91	134	5.7
Shr	2463	16				21	18.16	116	ns	15	8.79	171	4.4	52	43.66	119	ns
Jo	2901	28	19.69	142	ns	41	21.39	192	18.0	6				75	51.42	146	10.8
Rom	2916	13				35	21.50	163	8.5	23	10.41	221	15.2	71	51.69	137	7.2
MND	2363	21	16.04	131	ns	23	17.42	132	ns	5				49	41.89	117	ns
MV	2571	8				18				5				31			
1H4	3028	15				21				14	10.81	130	ns	50			
2H4	3130	16				10				16	11.17	143	ns	42			
Wiv	2527	14				14				5				33			
H5	3162	31	21.46	144	4.2	28	23.31	120	ns	21	11.28	186	8.4	80	56.05	143	10.2
Ado	2396	18	16.26	111	ns	10				5				33			
AYL	2578	12				24	19.00	126	ns	10	9.20	109	ns	46	45.70	101	ns
JC	2218	9				21	16.35	128	ns	3				33			
Ham	3082	25				37	28.62	129	ns	13				75	68.81	109	ns
TN	2534	15				16				12	9.04	133	ns	43			
MM	2669	8				9				11	9.52	116	ns	28			
AWW	2705	23	18.36	125	ns	22	19.94	110	ns	7				52			
Tro	3360	23				18				10				51			
Oth	3015	17				12				5				34			
Tim	2521	11				7				5				23			
Lr	3339	15				22				15	11.92	126	ns	52			
Mac	2652	11				6				5				22			
Ant	3004	15				17				15	10.72	140	ns	47			
Cor	3130	12				12				9				33			
Cym	3260	19				17				12	11.63	103	ns	48			
WT	2965	21	20.12	105	ns	13				5				39			
Por	2442	12				15				8				35			
Tmp	2562	8				5				3				16			
H8	2659	14				12				9				35			
Ven	2096	18	14.22	127	ns	20	15.45	129	ns	8	7.48	107	ns	46	37.15	124	ns
Luc	2812	46	19.08	241	38.1	27	20.73	130	ns	9				82	49.85	164	20.7
Son	2464	28	16.72	167	5.2	22	18.16	121	ns	8				58	43.68	133	4.7
	110965	753				818				396				1967			

Note: For full explanation see pp. 106–9 of text. In each phalanx are listed observed links, expected links where less than observed, ratio and χ^2. Statistically significant deviations are underlined. Phalanxes show links with 1–6-link words, 7–10-link words, 11–12-link words, totals of all.

Shakespeare's works of link words in the 1 to 6 categories, and that 24 of them appeared in *Titus*. *Titus*'s expected share would be proportionate to its share of the total Shakespearean word count, i.e. 2578/110,965. This fraction of 753 is 17.49. The observed number, 24, is 137% of that expectation. But the shift is not statistically significant. $\chi^2 = (O-E)^2 E = (24-17.49)^2/17.49 = 2.42$, for which $0.20 > p > 0.10$.

It will have been gathered that these calculations are carried out only where an excess of links has been found. But where that is the case, the ratio O/E is entered next to the column of expected numbers. If the shift is large, and the value χ^2 is significant at the 0.05 level or better, its value is entered in the fourth column of the phalanx; and it and the preceding O/E ratio are *underlined*. If χ^2 does not reach statistical significance the letters ns (i.e. 'Not significant') are typed in.

Table 7.2B. *The same:* Edward III *part B*

Tit	2578	44	30.13	146	6.5	52	37.52	139	5.6	42	27.02	155	8.3	138	94.67	146	19.8
1H6	5014	112	35.23	318	167.3	92	43.87	210	52.8	52	31.59	165	13.2	256	110.60	231	190.8
2H6	3146	53	36.77	144	7.2	66	45.79	144	8.9	47	32.97	143	6.0	166	115.53	144	22.0
3H6	2790	78	32.61	240	63.2	70	40.61	172	21.3	68	29.24	233	51.4	216	102.46	211	125.8
R3	3218	49	37.61	130	ns	87	46.84	186	34.4	49	33.73	145	6.9	185	118.18	157	37.8
R2	2833	35	33.11	106	ns	46	41.23	112	ns	38	29.69	128	ns	119	104.04	114	ns
TGV	2153	24				23				11				58			
Err	2037	22				33				17				72			
LLL	2872	19				35				33	30.10	110	ns	87			
Shr	2463	36	28.79	125	ns	28				21				85			
Jo	2901	31				49	42.22	116	ns	26				106			
Rom	2916	28				42				34	30.56	111	ns	104			
MND	2363	29	27.62	105	ns	22				8				59			
MV	2571	28				31				27	26.95	100	ns	86			
1H4	3028	34				39				28				101			
2H4	3130	30				39				36	32.80	110	ns	105			
Wiv	2527	21				25				12				58			
H5	3162	47	36.96	127	ns	65	46.02	141	7.8	47	33.14	142	5.8	159	116.12	137	15.8
Ado	2396	19				25				18				59			
AYL	2578	19				27				20				66			
JC	2218	19				32				31	25.25	133	ns	82	81.45	101	ns
Ham	3082	45				48				24				117			
TN	2534	14				17				17				48			
MM	2669	16				37				17				70			
AWW	2705	23				23				24				70			
Tro	3360	35				31				46	35.22	131	ns	112			
Oth	3015	29				18				14				61			
Tim	2521	13				21				24				58			
Lr	3339	33				47				24				104			
Mac	2652	25				31				29	27.80	104	ns	85			
Ant	3004	30				58	43.72	133	4.7	31				119	110.32	108	ns
Cor	3130	27				42				30				99			
Cym	3260	32				55	47.45	116	ns	33				120	119.72	100	ns
WT	2965	32				35				22				89			
Per	2442	28				37	35.54	104	ns	29	25.59	113	ns	94	89.60	105	ns
Tmp	2562	17				34				23				74			
H8	2659	31				32				16				79			
Ven	2096	26	24.50	106	ns	29				22	21.97	100	ns	77	76.97	100	ns
Luc	2812	44	32.87	134	3.8	55	40.93	129	ns	42	29.47	143	5.3	139	103.27	135	12.4
Son	2464	23				39	35.86	109	ns	51	25.82	120	ns	93	90.49	103	ns
	110965	1297				1615				1163				4075			

Note: Same arrangements as in Table 7.2A, but now for part B of *Edward III*. For full explanation see pp. 106–9 of text.

The appearance (or non-appearance) of number in the second, third and fourth columns of each phalanx gives a general impression, taken in at a glance, of the rare-word vocabulary relationships between *Edward III* and Shakespeare's works. This is particularly sharpened where the underlining indicates statistical significance.

LINKS WITH PART A OF *EDWARD III*

It is part A of *Edward III* which is most generally attributed to Shakespeare. The total of rare-word links of this part with Shakespeare is shown in the last phalanx of Table 7.2A. In the order of the magnitude of the excess of observation over expectation the nine Shakespearean works with statistically significant linking with this part of the play are: *Lucrece* 164%, *Richard III* 158%, *1 Henry VI* 157%, *John* 146%, *Henry V* 143%, *Romeo* 137%, *Love's Labour's Lost* 134%, *Richard II* 131%

and *2 Henry VI* 127%. All the plays are relatively early ones, though not all of the earliest; and it is interesting that *Lucrece*, which came early in the poet's career, outranks all the plays. *Lucrece* and *Edward III* part A share some communities of sexual interest. *Richard III*, *1 Henry VI*, *Henry V* and *Romeo* all show significant positive linking in two out of the other three phalanxes; *Lucrece*, *John* and *2 Henry VI* in one other out of the three.

Nearly all the positive linking occurs with the first dozen works in Shakespeare's output – with some noteworthy exceptions. Links with *Titus*, though above expectation, are relatively weak; links with *Venus*, though more substantially above expectation, do not reach statistical significance; links with *Errors* are actually below expectation. The other exception to the general linking with early Shakespeare is the strong link with *Henry V*, which is near the middle of the chronological series. If we omit the Poems and *Henry VIII* (as only in part Shakespeare) we are left with the convenient number of 36 plays. These we can group into sixths, i.e. six sextets. Taken all together, they have 1746 links with *Edward III*, which are distributed through the six sextets in chronological order in steadily decreasing proportions: 24%, 19%, 16%, 15%, 13%, 12%. The earliest sixth of the series has about double the proportion of linking as the last.

We can proceed more exactly by taking the Hart counts into consideration, as in the next table, 7.3. This must be regarded as a demonstration of a logical relationship in the linking between part A of *Edward III* and Shakespeare's plays. This is a finding that has to be explained. The only plausible explanation is community, if not identity, of authorship. At least, the present writer can think of no other.

LINKS WITH PART B, AND A COMPARISON

Turning now to Table 7.2B, we see a picture which is striking in both its similarities and its differences. The most immediately obvious way in which this table differs from the previous one for part A is the concentration of very heavy linking to narrow bands. Most of the table is blank. In Table 7.2A there was a wider scatter. Yet the evidence in both tables relates *Edward III* with early Shakespeare, with *Henry V*, and with *Lucrece*. But now we see linking which is stronger and more consistent.

Taking the last phalanx, which sums the preceding three, we find the following shifts of observation from expectation, in order of magnitude: *1 Henry VI* 231%, *3 Henry VI* 211%, *Richard III* 157%, *Titus* 146%, *2 Henry VI* 144%, *Henry V* 137%, *Lucrece* 135%. Both *Henry V* and *Lucrece* show statistically significant positive shifts in three out of the four phalanxes (as also *Richard III*). But they are outshone by the four earliest plays of all, *Titus* and the three *Henry VI* plays, showing strong and statistically significant linking in all three of the independent counts, as well as in their sum. The three phalanxes of figures relating respectively to the 1–6-link words,

Table 7.3. *Distribution of links between part A of* Edward III *and Shakespeare's plays, chronologically grouped in sets of six*

Plays sextet	Word count (Hart)	Links		Ratio as %
		Observed	Expected	
Tit – R3	17579	413	304.09	136
TGV – Rom	15342	338	265.39	127
MND – H5	16781	285	290.28	98
Ado – MM	16277	258	281.57	92
AWW – Mac	17592	234	304.31	77
Ant – Tmp	17363	218	300.35	73
Sums	100934	1746	1745.99	

the 7–10 link words, and the 11–12 link words, are mutually independent of one another. The fact that they agree so well is impressive.

The play whose connection with part B of *Edward III* outranks all the others is *1 Henry VI*. Its links with that part are shown in each and all of the twelve categories of link words. Shown, in fact, with a degree of linking that diminishes as we pass from the very rarest words to the commoner ones. The same is true, though with an almost level gradient, of all the first five plays, *Titus* to *Richard III*, taken together (see small table overleaf).

The strength of the linking of part B of *Edward III* with *1 Henry VI* is phenomenal, falling below twice the expected value only with the commoner link words of categories 10 to 12. But the linking of all the first five plays of Shakespeare with part B of *Edward III* is just as steadily shown through all twelve categories of link words, and averages 177% of expectation. In fact the association of part B with works of the Shakespeare canon is even stronger and more striking than that of part A. It is more localised, and more specifically associated with the very earliest works (barring *Venus*). If part A is to be regarded as Shakespeare's work – as by vocabulary tests confirming the other evidence we must deem it – then, if we are to trust the vocabulary tests alone, *a fortiori* so part B must be also. Is there anything to be set against the conclusion that the whole play is Shakespeare's?

Before we can be quite comfortable with such a conclusion we must consider the statistical differences between the two parts. Part A has significant associations with several works of the second sextet, *Romeo, John, Shrew* and *Love's Labour's Lost*. Part B's links with these plays are only at an expected level, and in the case of the last two below it. A plausible explanation can be offered if we think that part A was by a later, more mature and more diversified Shakespeare than the Shakespeare of part B. Some of the vocabulary of the *Henry VI* plays and *Titus* has been left behind. The newer vocabularies of plays of the second sextet are more in his mind.

Nevertheless the difference between the two parts is more one of detail than one of large scale. Part A has more than the expected number of links with all the first

Link words	1	2	3	4	5	6	7	8	9	10	11	12
O/E%: *1H6*	466	344	230	280	334	329	218	213	230	174	171	153
Tit – R3	212	176	196	171	214	193	172	192	178	139	175	155

thirteen plays down to *Midsummer Night's Dream*, with the exception of *Errors*. Observed links number 800 against the expected 625.46, with a ratio O/E of 128%. In the case of part B the same thirteen plays yield 1651 links against the expected 1295.74. The ratio O/E, 127%, is practically identical.

The statistically significant association of both parts with *Henry V*, part B with 137% of expectation and part A with 143% of expectation, is a feature of close resemblance, and one of particular interest. It is worth while to glance at the words which constitute the links. In each part they may be roughly grouped into words of statecraft or of war, and words of a more general connotation:

Part A, statecraft and war: array, captive, carrion, crossbow, defiance, esquire, gallop, gimmal'd, martial, mightiness, passport, pike, progenitor, puissance, thrice-valiant, treasury, vassal (17);

Others: augment, babble, brief, closely, constraint, dazzle, defective, devout, fester, fluent, frosty, full-fraught, garnish, halfpenny, inconstant, inly, intellectual, jaw, lessen, meditate, mote, ordure, orisons, prevention, print, reduce, rider, rust, straight, succour, sunburnt, sweetness, task, tawny, thaw, turf, universe, unspotted, valley (39);

Part B, statecraft and war: admiral, array, arrayed, Baron, bullet, captive, carrion, conspiracy, coronet, crossbow, defiance, dub, embattled, encamp, enlarge, ensigns, esquire, famine, flower-de-luce, forage, fortify, gore, helmet, licence, lineal, majestical, martial, muster, navy, ordinance, passport, pedigree, pikes, pillage, puissant, retreat, squares, treasury, unfought, vaward, victuals (41);

Others: astonish, bit, bonnet, cheerfully, constraint, deface, desolation, diffuse, disdainful, disobey, drone, enclose, entrails, fig, flowering, girdle, gulf, honey-sweet, hoop, indirectly, maw, mickle, mould, neighbourhood, painful, paradise, pilfèr, print, proudly, ray, redoubted, refresh, robber, savour, solemnly, spouse, swift, swill, testament, threescore, unnecessary, valley, verify, vineyards, viper, watchful, wilfulness (47).

The balance is much more in favour of statecraft and war in part B than in part A, but this can be regarded as a natural consequence of the themes developed. The difference between the two parts is not statistically significant.

Another difference between part A and part B is the proportion of links with Shakespeare's poems. Part A has 186 out of 1967=9.46%; part B has 309 out of 4075 = 7.58%. The difference is statistically significant. Here again we are probably observing a thematic rather than a chronological effect.

THE DISTRIBUTION OF SHAKESPEARE'S RARE WORDS

In Chapter 6, p. 86, an important point emerged which we must now take into account. At an earlier stage we estimated the probability of a link word being found in play P or play Q as proportionate to the total number of different words in P and Q, numbers enumerated by Hart. On that basis *Troilus* showed statistically significant links with *Henry V*, *Hamlet*,. *Othello* and *Macbeth*. But as we are working with rare words, what we need, more strictly speaking, for comparative purposes is a count of the rare words, not of all the words, in the linked plays. When the card index totals for the various plays were substituted for Hart's numbers, *Troilus* was no longer significantly linked with *Henry V* and *Hamlet*; but, while remaining linked with *Othello* and *Macbeth*, it now showed in addition significant linkage with *All's Well* and with *Timon*. Its placing in the chronological order had shifted down a peg or two. The changes in emphasis occur because rare words are not distributed evenly among the plays. Some plays have more than the share one would expect, and others fewer. Both *Henry V* and *Hamlet* are plays with a disproportionate richness in rare words; so the probability that a catch word would be found in them is higher than one would estimate from the Hart counts. When that was allowed for, the connection between these plays and *Troilus* became non-significant.

We can make a good rough estimate of the number of rare words in a play by adding to the card index number (of words with 2 to 10 appearances) Hart's count of 'peculiar' (i.e. mainly unique) words. The sum of both gives us for every play a count of words appearing 1 to 10 times. These numbers are shown in Table 7.4, in which plays have been arranged in the order of their richness in rare words. *Hamlet* heads the list with 37.9% of its vocabulary being rare words; at the foot of the table come *Two Gentlemen* and *Caesar* with less than 21%. The range is a surprisingly large one.

Richness of vocabulary is a quality of the first importance in a creative work. And the capacity of a writer to express himself in a rich variety of language is a dominant characteristic of his style. We feel that the figures of Table 7.4 *must* be full of meaning. And yet their meaning is hard to see. The amount of variation from play to play is so large it cannot be random; and yet we are confronted by inexplicable oddities. The three *Henry VI* plays, for instance, which we think of as closely connected, are here widely separated, at the 9th, the 17th and the 28th places in the list.

The wildness of the variation is better seen when we arrange the plays in an (adjusted) Arden order, and display the figures of column 5 of Table 7.4 in a graph, fig. 7.1. The mean percentage of rare words for the 36 plays (omitting *Henry VIII*) is 29,460 in a total Hart count of 101,074 = 29.1; or, if we take an average of the percents shown in column 5, it is 28.8. Looking at the jagged peaks of the figure we can see no consistent trend. Percents above and below the average seem to follow one another haphazardly. Indeed, the lowest point, 20.5% in *Caesar*, occurs immediately next to the highest, 37.9% in *Hamlet*.

The statistical device of the 'cusum' has been used in a variety of industrial and other research laboratories to detect systematic changes when they are masked by random variation. We can use it here. Taking 28.8% as the mean of all our 36 observations, we accumulate, from the first observation to the last, the sum of

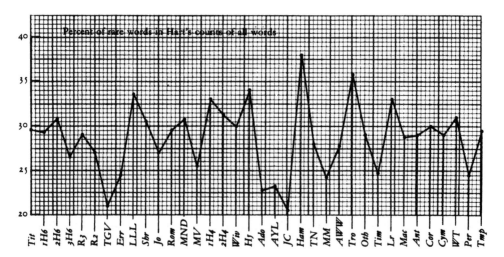

Figure 7.1. Shakespeare's plays: richness in rare words, by play order

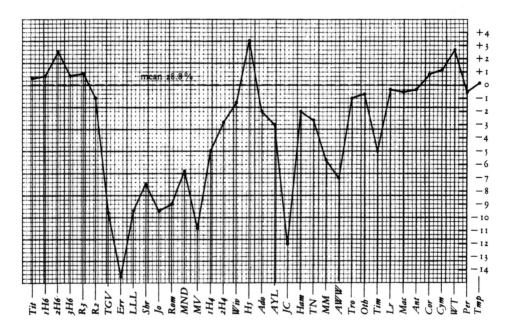

Figure 7.2. The same, converted into a cumulative sum ('cusum') curve. Curve shows accumulated summations of deviations from common mean

positive and negative deviations from the average, at each successive point. We start from zero, and inevitably return to zero at the end. The resulting graph is shown in Figure 7.2. Here at last we can see some signs of an explicable process of evolution. The earliest plays provide us with a small positive margin above the average. The curve, with *Two Gentlemen* and *Errors*, then plunges far into the

Table 7.4. *Shakespeare's plays: richness in rare words*

		1	2	3	4	5
1.	Hamlet	3882	396	1076	1472	37.9
2.	Troilus	3360	302	904	1206	35.9
3.	Henry V	3162	246	836	1082	34.2
4.	Love's Lab. Lost	2872	253	709	962	33.5
5.	Lear	3339	346	757	1103	33.0
6.	1 Henry IV	3028	269	730	999	33.0
7.	2 Henry IV	3130	245	744	989	31.6
8.	Winter's Tale	2965	219	699	918	31.0
9.	2 Henry VI	3146	157	815	972	30.9
10.	Mids. N. Dream	2363	160	568	728	30.8
11.	Shrew	2463	150	602	752	30.5
12.	Merry Wives	2527	229	532	761	30.1
13.	Coriolanus	3130	244	695	939	30.0
14.	Tempest	2562	202	555	757	29.5
15.	Titus	2578	114	643	757	29.4
16.	Romeo	2916	199	657	856	29.4
17.	1 Henry VI	3014	145	738	883	29.3
18.	Cymbeline	3260	219	731	950	29.1
19.	Othello	3015	222	654	876	29.1
20.	Antony	3004	233	638	871	29.0
21.	Richard III	3218	145	784	929	28.9
22.	Macbeth	2652	197	567	764	28.8
23.	As You Like It	2578	157	571	728	28.2
24.	Twelfth Night	2534	156	555	711	28.1
25.	All's Well	2705	159	594	753	27.8
26.	John	2901	140	643	783	27.0
27.	Richard II	2833	133	628	761	26.9
28.	3 Henry VI	2750	115	614	729	26.5
29.	Henry VIII	2659	127	553	680	25.6
30.	Merch of Venice	2571	115	535	650	25.3
31.	Timon	2521	138	486	624	24.8
32.	Pericles	2442	105	495	600	24.6
33.	Errors	2037	84	416	500	24.5
34.	Measure/Measure	2669	163	486	649	24.3
35.	Much Ado	2396	110	434	544	22.7
36.	Two Gentlemen	2153	74	373	447	20.8
37.	Julius Caesar	2218	70	385	455	20.5

Note: Columns: 1: Hart's count of different words in play. 2: Hart's count of 'peculiar' words. 3: Number of citations in card index. 4: Sum of numbers in columns 2 and 3. 5: Ratio, as percent, of numbers in column 4 to numbers in column 1.

negative. With the *Henry IV* plays it takes a sharp upward turn; turns down again with *Ado, As You Like It* and *Caesar*. But after that recovers, unsteadily, with *Hamlet* to reach thereafter the general average again.

The cusum curve cannot be explained on a basis of one single consistent state of verbal productivity, or inventiveness, or variety – let us say, one consistent state of mind. If that state of mind had been one and the same all through, the cusum curve would have approximated to an even level horizontal. If some single change had occurred over the course of a writing lifetime, then we would expect to see a simple curve, say that of a c laid on its side. If one change had been succeeded by its reversal, the curve would have been s-shaped. In Figure 7.2 we must suppose a greater degree of heterogeneity between the parts of the succession. It is unwise to speculate without a factual basis for speculation; and only with reservations can we advance a hypothesis where there is no outlook for confirmation or rebuttal. Nevertheless the following should be said. The suggestion that arises in the mind of a psychiatrist is that the 5 gradients, up-down-up-down-up, correspond with changes of mood in the mind of the writer. They are of some considerable duration. They are like tidal changes, and on them are superimposed the choppy waves of more ephemeral fluctuations.*

A SECOND TRIAL: RARE WORDS IN A RARE-WORD CONTEXT

We must now see what happens to the links between *Edward III* and works of the Shakespeare canon when we change our base from Hart's counts to the rare words of Table 7.4, column 4. We should get a sounder test, as these words are more nearly representative of the sample we are studying. The figures are set out in Table 7.5. Besides the elimination of Hart's counts, for which the rare-word counts are substituted in column 2, other changes are made. We have to omit the Poems and Sonnets, since we have no rare-word counts for them; and we take the opportunity of leaving out *Henry VIII*, as well, since it cannot provide us with any useful information. We cannot omit *Pericles*; but it is now necessary to conflate the two parts (Acts I and II, Acts III–V), and reconstitute the play as a single whole for statistical purposes. The material is now substantially smaller. Many of the 11- and 12-link catch words have been eliminated, since our comparisons will be with words of 1 to 10 appearances. But the biggest change is that instead of the total of 110,965 words available as a probability denominator in Table 7.2, we now have little more than a quarter of that number, 29,460. The effect of this will be to increase sampling errors, so that deviations of observation from expectation will have to be about twice as large in Table 7.5 as in Table 7.2 before statistical significance will be attained. The hope is that this disadvantage will be made good by the greater comparability in our standards of what is expected to set against what is observed.

What are the changes that we actually find? They are surprisingly unimpressive. Table 7.2A showed part A significantly linked with seven plays: *R3* 158%, *1H6* 157%, *Jo* 146%, *H5* 143%, *Rom* 137%, *LLL* 134% and *2H6* 127%. In our new tabulation we still have seven plays linked with *Edward III*; but now *2 Henry VI* has given place to *Richard II*; and *Love's Labour's Lost* has been replaced by *Two Gentlemen*. The new order, in percents, is *R3* 163, *Jo* 162, *1H6* 161, *TGV* 151, *R2* 146,

---

* Richard Proudfoot notes: 'External factors *must* include S's reading (e.g. vocab. from Montaigne, tr. Florio, in *Lr, Temp*, or from Chapman's *7 Books of the Iliad* in *T&C*)'. But we have downs as well as ups to account for.

Table 7.5. *Links of part A and part B of* Edward III *with named Shakespeare plays, using rare words only as base (see Table 7.4) and as counters. Words with 11–12 links excluded*

		part A				part B			
		O	E	O/E	χ^2	O	E	O/E	χ^2
Tit	757	48	44.86	107	ns	138	94.74	146	19.75
1H6	883	84	52.33	161	19.17	256	110.51	232	191.54
2H6	972	71	57.61	123	ns	166	121.65	136	16.17
3H6	729	54	43.21	125	ns	216	91.24	237	170.59
R3	929	90	55.06	163	22.17	185	116.27	159	40.63
R2	761	66	45.10	146	9.69	119	95.24	125	5.93
	5031	413	298.17	139	44.22	1080	629.64	172	322.13
TGV	447	40	26.43	151	6.97	58	55.94	104	ns
Err	500	32	29.63	108	ns	72	62.58	115	ns
LLL	962	68	57.01	119	ns	87	120.40		
Shr	752	52	44.57	117	ns	85	94.11		
Jo	783	75	46.41	162	17.61	106	97.99	108	ns
Rom	856	71	50.73	140	8.10	104	107.13		
	4300	338	254.85	131	27.13	512	538.16	95	
MND	728	49	43.15	114	ns	59	91.11		
MV	650	31	38.52			86	81.35	106	ns
1H4	999	50	59.21			101	125.03		
2H4	989	42	58.61			105	123.78		
Wiv	761	33	45.10			58	95.24		
H5	1082	80	64.13	125	3.93	159	135.42	117	4.11
	5209	285	308.72	92		568	651.92	87	
Ado	544	33	32.24	102	ns	59	68.08		
AYL	728	46	43.15	107	ns	66	91.11		
JC	455	33	26.97	122	ns	82	56.94	144	11.03
Ham	1472	75	87.24			117	184.22		
TN	711	43	42.14	102	ns	48	88.98		
MM	649	28	38.45			70	81.22		
	4559	258	270.20	95		442	570.57	77	
AWW	753	52	44.63	117	ns	70	94.24		
Tro	1206	51	71.48			112	150.93		
Oth	876	34	51.92			61	109.63		
Tim	624	23	36.98			58	78.10		
Lr	1103	52	65.37			104	138.04		
Mac	764	22	45.28			85	95.62		
	5326	234	315.65	74		490	666.56	74	
Ant	871	47	51.62			119	109.01	109	ns
Cor	939	33	55.65			99	117.52		
Cym	950	48	56.30			120	118.90	101	ns
WT	918	39	54.41			89	114.89		
Per	600	35	35.56			94	75.09	125	4.76
Tmp	757	16	44.86			74	94.74		
	5035	218	298.41	73		595	630.14	94	
	29460	1746	1746.00			3687	3686.99		

Rom 140 and *Hj* 125. That the linking with *Henry V* is now so much less marked, and that the linking with *LLL* has sunk below the level of statistical significance, are explained by the fact that both these plays are particularly rich in rare words. This has meant that the expected numbers of links are higher than could be estimated from Hart's counts, and the ratios O/E have been correspondingly reduced. Despite these changes in detail, the general picture has been little affected. Part A of *Edward III* has remained conspicuously linked with plays of the first and second sextet, as in Table 7.2. The 36 plays of Table 7.5 have been grouped into six sextets, with the observed and the expected numbers duly entered, together with the ratios O/E and χ^2. The association of *Edward III* with Shakespeare's plays all the way down to *Romeo* stands firm.

The change in expected numbers, following on the change of base, has also affected the linkings of part B. But this is in detail only, while leaving its massive connection with Shakespeare's first six plays more marked, if anything, than before. In Table 7.2B, the linkings of part B with Shakespeare's plays were, in percents and in order of magnitude, *1H6* 231, *3H6* 211, *R3* 157, *Tit* 146, *2H6* 144, *Hj* 137. Correspondingly now: *3H6* 237, *1H6* 232, *R3* 159, *Tit* 146, *2H6* 136, *R2* 125 link *all* the first six plays. *Henry V*, now reduced to 117, is still on the map; and we now find to our surprise that *Caesar*, at 144% of expectation, and *Pericles*, at 125%, have emerged into statistical significance. Both of these plays are poorly endowed with rare words, coming 37th and 32nd in this respect in the rank order of Table 7.4. This has the effect of magnifying the significance of the observed links with *Edward III*. If there are other reasons, they elude the perception of the present writer.

Grouping the 36 Shakespeare plays into six sextets smoothes out the differences from play to play, and brings out major differences between the larger scale stages of the writer's career. Part A of *Edward III* is strongly linked, both with the first six plays (139% of expectation), and with the second six plays (131%). The values of χ^2 for each of these deviations are far too large to be put down to chance. The findings are compatible with the hypothesis that Shakespeare was the author (in whole or in a large part) of part A. It would be difficult to reconcile this finding with any other authorship. As the balance of scholarly opinion is in favour of Shakespeare's authorship of this part of *Edward III*, and no other authorship has yet been seriously advanced, we might conclude that the scholars are right – at least until new as yet undiscovered facts appear, to surprise and disconcert us. But, if part A is Shakespeare's work, we can hardly avoid the conclusion that part B must be so as well. As is shown by table 7.5 and in Figure 7.3, this part of the play is even more strongly linked with the first six of Shakespeare's plays, and indeed exclusively linked with this part of the canon. These connections suggest that part B, if Shakespeare's work, is work of an earlier stage in his writing career than part A. The relative lack of merits of part B could then be plausibly explained as the consequence of lesser maturity and less understanding and control of his medium. If there is a difference in fertility of imagination, it could not be so plausibly accounted for.

To summarize the results of this part of the argument, we conclude that part A of

Table 7.6. *Distribution of links with Shakespeare: parts A and B of* Edward III *compared*

Word group	Observed links			Expected links			
	A	B	Total	A	B	Total	χ^2
1–6	753	1297	2050	667.39	1382.61	2050.00	16.28
7–10	818	1615	2433	792.07	1640.93	2433.00	1.26
11–12	396	1163	1559	507.54	1051.46	1559.00	36.34
1–12	1967	4075	6042	1967.00	4075.00	6042.00	53.88

Edward III, long attributed to Shakespeare, is indeed his work, but not in the very earliest stage of his career. The linkage score with *John* at 162% (cf. *R3* 163% and *1H6* 161%) is extraordinarily high. We conclude also that part B is also Shakespeare's, but the Shakespeare of an even earlier stage. Associations of this part with *Henry V*, *Caesar* and *Pericles* are probably thematic, anomalous or non-chronological for other and unknown causes.

DIRECT COMPARISON OF PART A AND PART B

As emerged in Chapter 1 of this book, scholars are divided on the question whether the two parts A and B of *Edward III* are by one author or are by different authors, whoever those authors be. We can now examine such statistical evidence on the question as we have been able to gather. We have already considered, at length, the data recorded in Tables 7.2, 7.3 and 7.5. We concluded that the statistically significant differences between the two parts were not incompatible with a common Shakespearean authorship, if it could be granted that part B was the earlier written of the two. We must now look for further differences.

Turning again to Table 7.2, we notice that the distribution of total link citations, provided respectively by the 1–6 group of link words, the 7–10 group, and the 11–12 group, is very different in the A table from what it is in the B table. The rarest words play a more prominent role in part A than they do in part B. This is shown in Table 7.6. There is a massive difference between the two parts; the probability that such a value of χ^2 could be reached by chance is negligible. Clearly, compared with part B, part A is much richer in quite rare words and relatively deficient in commoner words occurring 11 or 12 times. This suggests a maturer and more differentiated vocabulary; and it fits in with our finding (p. 112) that part A has stronger connections with the Poems than does part B.

The difference between the two parts in respect of the distribution of link citations is much less marked when we examine the distribution of the link words themselves. This is shown in Table 7.7. The total χ^2 of 13.92 for 12 degrees of freedom has a probability value 0.40 > p > 0.30. But if we look down the table we find rather high values of χ^2 at the two extremes. Part A has more than the expected number of link words in the 0 and 1 categories; part B has more than the expected

Table 7.7. *Distribution of link words, by individual word category: parts A and B compared*

Word category	Numbers observed			Numbers expected		χ^2
	A	B	Total	A	B	
0	42	57	99	34.99	64.01	2.17
1	53	73	126	44.53	81.47	2.49
2	42	78	120	42.41	77.59	0.00
3	33	61	94	33.42	60.78	0.00
4	28	55	83	29.33	53.67	0.09
5	39	67	106	37.46	68.54	0.09
6	34	58	92	32.51	59.49	0.11
7	31	51	82	28.98	53.02	0.22
8	28	53	81	28.63	52.37	0.02
9	26	49	75	26.51	48.49	0.02
10	15	37	52	18.38	33.62	0.96
11	12	49	61	21.56	39.44	6.56
12	22	53	75	26.51	48.49	1.19
Sum	405	741	1146	405.02	740.98	13.92

number in the 10 to 12 categories; while over the middle part of the range observations almost exactly match expectations. If we simplify Table 7.7 into three category groups only, 0–1, 2–9, and 10–12, the value of χ^2 is diminished very little, in fact only to 11.76, for which with 2 d.f. p is less than 0.005. On this basis we can say that, over the middle part of the range, the distribution of link words by word category is practically the same in the two parts, A and B, of *Edward III*. There is nothing in this to suggest that we are dealing with two different authors. On the other hand A exceeds B in its proportion of very rare words, and is exceeded in its proportion of the commonest words we have brought into our calculations. This difference does not have to be due to different identities of authorship, if we make an allowance for their chronology.

Our next test is to compare the links of part A and of part B with Shakespeare's plays, the one with the other directly. No account is taken of the theoretical expectations on which comparisons have been based till now. We assume only that the factors affecting the distribution of links will be the same for the two parts, A and B, *if the two parts are homogeneous with one another*. Part A has a total of 1746 links with the named Shakespeare plays; part B has 3687; together they have 5433. Our null hypothesis is that if both parts together have x links with play P, these links will be divided proportionately between the two parts, part A having $1746x/5433$ and part B $3687/5433$. The observations, shown in Table 7.8, test whether this is so.

As will be seen from the Table there are statistically significant differences between the two parts at twelve points. Links with part B are in marked excess in *1 Henry VI*, *3 Henry VI*, and again, at the end of Shakespeare's career, in *Macbeth* and *The Tempest*. The more numerous points where links with part A predominate are

Table 7.8. *Direct comparison of part A and part B links with Shakespeare*

Play	A	B	A+B	%A	in xs	χ²
Tit	48	138	186	26	B	3.42
1H6	84	256	340	25	B	8.61
2H6	71	166	237	30	B	.52
3H6	54	216	270	20	B	18.24
R3	90	185	275	33	A	.04
R2	66	119	185	36	A	1.06
				28	B	13.70
TGV	40	58	98	41	A	3.30
Err	32	72	104	31	B	.09
LLL	68	87	155	44	A	9.79
Shr	52	85	137	38	A	2.09
Jo	75	106	181	41	A	7.18
Rom	71	104	175	41	A	5.70
				40	A	22.68
MND	49	59	108	45	A	8.67
MV	31	86	117	26	B	1.71
1H4	50	101	151	33	A	.06
2H4	42	105	147	29	B	.86
Wiv	33	58	91	36	A	.71
H5	80	159	239	33	A	.19
				33	A	.63
Ado	33	59	92	36	A	.59
AYL	46	66	112	41	A	4.10
JC	33	82	115	29	B	.62
Ham	75	117	192	39	A	4.23
TN	43	48	91	47	A	9.55
MM	28	70	98	29	B	.57
				37	A	7.15
AWW	52	70	122	43	A	6.15
Tro	51	112	163	31	B	.06
Oth	34	61	95	36	A	.58
Tim	23	58	81	28	B	.52
Lr	52	104	156	33	A	.10
Mac	22	85	107	21	B	6.57
				32	A	.01
Ant	47	119	166	28	B	1.12
Cor	33	99	132	25	B	3.08
Cym	48	120	168	29	B	.97
WT	39	89	128	30	B	.16
Per	35	94	129	27	B	1.49
Tmp	16	74	90	18	B	8.50
				27	B	10.56
Sums	1746	3687	5433	32.137		

Note: χ² values underlined where there is significant preponderance of either.

Love's Labour's Lost, John, Romeo, Midsummer Night's Dream, As You Like It, Hamlet, Twelfth Night and *All's Well.* The table as a whole provides a χ^2 of 121.20 for 35 degrees of freedom. From Geigy's tables we read that for 35 d.f. the extreme value of $p = 0.0005$ corresponds to a χ^2 of merely 69.198. We may say, then, that for our distribution p, far less than 0.0005, can be taken as zero. It is not within the normal bounds of probability that part A and part B of *Edward III* have rare words from a single homogeneous distribution. However, this implies nothing about the causes of the heterogeneity.

Table 7.8 also shows the χ^2 values for each of the six sextets into which we have grouped Shakespeare's plays. The first sextet, *Tit* to *R3*, has a preferential association with part B (χ^2 13.70, p < 0.0005); the second sextet (*TGV* to *Rom*) has a preferential association with part A (χ^2 22.68, p < 0.0005). For the third sextet, χ^2 is only 0.63, (0.5 > p > 0.4); i.e. the two parts fit. The fourth sextet, (*Ado* to *MM*) again shows the preponderance of links with A (χ^2 7.15, 0.01 > p > 0.005). The fifth sextet, despite the B preponderance in *Macbeth*, shows the links with A and with B in balance. The last sextet, (*Ant* to *Tmp*) once again has a B preponderance (χ^2 10.56, 0.005 > p > 0.001). These seemingly haphazard variations can be regarded as another expression of the differences between parts A and B brought out in Figure 7.3.

We have attempted to explain the differences between parts A and B as due to the times at which they were written, by the one author. Is this adequate? A later time of writing for A seems to fit very well with the first five points on the A and B curves in the graph in Figure 7.3. But it seems very odd that part B, supposedly the earlier written, should have significantly more links than part A with Shakespeare's last six plays. How could this be explained?

Not easily, but perhaps so: when we look at the two curves in Figure 7.3 they seem to show a difference in pattern. The A curve has its peak in the first sextet, and therefore drops irregularly but almost steadily. At the second sextet it is still well above expectation (the broken 100% line). By the last sextet it has reached its lowest point. The links of part A with *Macbeth, Coriolanus* and *The Tempest* have sunk to very low levels (see Table 7.5). One might say that the evolutionary change shown by the whole A curve has a meaningful relationship with the general chronology of 36 plays. The same element of regularity, of a consistent evolutionary development, is not so easily seen in the B curve. It begins with an extremely high peak at the first sextet, but thereafter collapses. The numbers of links with the five sextets after the first could have been the result of merely random processes, from the look of the curve. It so happens that, when the B curve reaches the last sextet, it kicks up to a point actually a little higher than the one reached at the second sextet. The B curve does not show a special deficiency of links with *Macbeth* (49%), *Coriolanus* (59%) and *Tempest* (36%), as A does (see Table 7.5). When we are dealing with distributions we must not forget that an over-abundance at one point has to be balanced out by a deficiency elsewhere. The A/B difference in the last sextet seems to

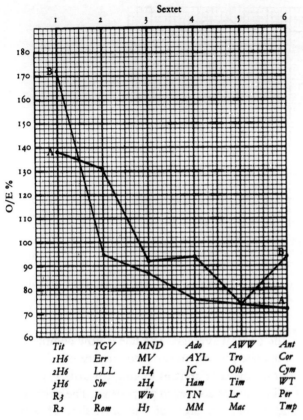

Figure 7.3. Ratio of observed to expected numbers of links with grouped plays. Part A and part B of *Edward III* separately

be more the consequence of a deficiency of A links at this point than of random variation in the number of B links.

The writer can suggest no other explanation, and one can think of none that seems plausible. However, if there were some special and particular cause for the reversal of the A/B balance in the last plays, it should show up if we follow that balance through from first to last. This is done in the cusum curve shown in Figure 7.4. We use the figures of the A column and of the A + B column in Table 7.8. To begin with we have *Titus*'s links, 48 with part A of *Edward III* and 138 with part B, total 186. The A proportion is then 48/186 = 25.8%. We then add the figures for *1 Henry VI*, 84 with part A out of a total of 340 for A + B. The accumulated sum is therefore 132 out of 526 = 25.1%. As the links for play after play are progressively added, the proportion of A links, out of all links, slowly changes. The proportion of A links, very low for the first plays, steadily rises to reach the general average for all plays, 32.137, shown in the graph by an interrupted level line, and then to exceed it, in a modest plateau. The line then slowly falls to reach, with the addition of the

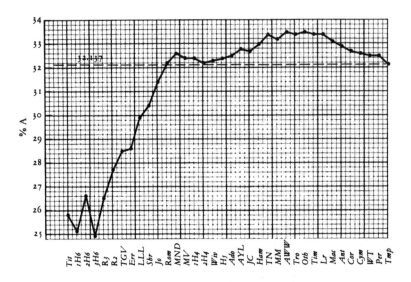

Figure 7.4 Cusum curve showing proportion (as percent) of A links out of all links, progressively accumulated from play to play. General average 32.137% A.

figures for *The Tempest* at the end, the general average. The tale is now complete. Clearly, the cusum curve has two opposite phases: an early dominance of B links, which is overtaken and balanced out by the later shift in linking towards A, itself equalised by the predominance of B links in the last seven plays or so. The curve is straightforwardly harmonious, and shows no sign of the incursion of any disturbing factor.

PROVISIONAL CONCLUSIONS

This concludes our examination of the rare-word vocabulary of *Edward III* in relation to the plays and poems of Shakespeare. It has shown that: (1) the rare-word vocabulary of *Edward III* has a very strong kinship with that of the early plays of Shakespeare, and would be compatible with authorship by Shakespeare; (2) there are statistically significant differences in vocabulary between part A (1.ii, II, IV.iv) and part B (the rest); (3) these differences do not conflict with Shakespeare's authorship of both parts; (4) but may be understood by supposing that part B was the earlier written.

On the basis of the statistical evidence presented so far it is not possible to go further and say the play probably was by Shakespeare. For that we would need comparative data gathered from other possible candidates. But the statistical evidence does fall in with, and support, the independent witness of scholars who have maintained that at least part of the play, namely part A, is Shakespeare's.

But on that basis, the statistical evidence does take us one step further. It shows that, if part A is Shakespeare's then part B, which is so much more closely linked with his earliest work, ought to be accepted as Shakespeare's too. The only effective argument to the contrary would have to bring evidence that someone else, other than Shakespeare, had a hand in the authorship. Alfred Hart seems to be the only scholar who has examined the possibilities of alternative authorship. He came to a negative conclusion. To pursue the matter statistically is not easy, owing to the lack of concordances for other Elizabethan playwrights. However, we do have Crawford's *Marlowe Concordance*; and the question whether the vocabulary of *Edward III* fits in with Marlowe's vocabulary will now be examined.

MARLOWE AND THE 948 LINK WORDS

If we are to compare the vocabularies of Marlowe and Shakespeare, we must have samples of approximately equal size. Crawford's Concordance covers the following works of Marlowe (together with other material):

Tragedy of Dido	1738 lines
Edward II	2674 „
Faustus (1616)	2161 „
Hero and Leander	832 „
Jew of Malta	2445 „
Massacre at Paris	1276 „
Fragment of „	35 „
Ovid's Elegies	2518 „
Passionate Shepherd	28 „
Tamburlaine I	2329 „
Tamburlaine II	2332 „
Total	18,368 „

To set against this sample we can take the following from Shakespeare's early works:

Titus Andronicus	2522 lines
1 Henry VI	2676 „
2 Henry VI	3069 „
3 Henry VI	2902 „
Richard III	3600 „
Venus and Adonis	1194 „
Rape of Lucrece	1855 „
Comedy of Errors	1753 „
Total	19,571 „

If we omit the *Comedy of Errors* our total for Shakespeare is 17,818 lines. Our first test makes use of this smaller number. Table 7.9 shows the links made by the 948 catch words in Appendices III and IV with the almost complete Marlowe sample above on the one hand, and with the limited Shakespeare sample on the other.

Table 7.9. *Links made by the catch words with Marlowe and Shakespeare*

Number of links	Shakespeare	Marlowe
0	357	427
1	240	215
2	152	102
3	89	68
4	55	31
5	30	27
6	13	27
7	7	13
8	2	5
9	1	10
10	2	4
11	—	3
12+	—	16
Sum	948	948

Note: Distribution of the numbers of links made by the catchwords in Appendices III and IV with a restricted Shakespeare sample and with Marlowe's works.

We can condense this table into the smaller table.

Links	Shakespeare	Marlowe	χ^2
0	357	427	6.26
1	240	215	1.38
2	152	102	9.84
3	89	68	2.80
4	55	31	6.70
5+	55	105	15.62
Sum	948	948	42.60

The distribution of the links is clearly quite different in the two cases. To begin with, Marlowe has a higher proportion of words with zero linkage, 45.0% as against Shakespeare's 37.7%, which gives a significant χ^2 on its own. Over the middle of the range Shakespeare has higher numbers of links than Marlowe. But at the far end there are a number of words which are common in Marlowe, but rare in Shakespeare. Shakespeare has only two words with as many as 10 links in the restricted sample we have used, 'regal' and 'ruthless'. This is a consequence of the fact that from the beginning the catch words of Appendices III and IV were restricted to rare words of no more than 12 occurrences. There has been no corresponding restriction of the total number of appearances permitted in Marlowe; so it can hardly be a matter for surprise if some words he has used frequently show up in our list. But the fact remains that a notable vocabulary difference between Shakespeare and Marlowe has been identified. The 23 catch words found in Marlowe with 10 or more occurrences are:

admiral, n	18
baron, n	16
batter, vb	13
captive, adj.	21
carcass, n	13
coach, n	13
dart, n	15
endless, adj.	10
ensign, n	10
gloomy, adj.	10
hover, vb	13
martial, adj.	24
midst, n	16
pitch, vb	11
resolute, adj.	21
retain, vb	11
shower, n	15
slender, adj.	15
treasury, n	17
veil, n	10
wealthy, adj.	16
whenas, conj.	11
wherewith, pr.	18

The different distributions of catch words in Shakespeare and Marlowe is assured by the very high value of $\chi^2 = 42.6$ with $p < < 0.0005$. Nevertheless it is somewhat surprising that no fewer than 55% of Shakespeare's rare words are to be found in Marlowe. We are reminded of Hart's comment that there was a large measure of community in the vocabularies of all the Elizabethan dramatists. The point is worth pursuing. Table 7.10 correlates the use made of the 948 catch words by Shakespeare and by Marlowe, grouping them into those not used, used once, or twice, or three times or more. It is clear that there is a marked degree of correlation between the two writers. In fact, this table yields a χ^2 of 120.07 for 9 degrees of freedom, with a probability value at vanishing point. If we use the table (somewhat artificially) for the calculation of a product–moment correlation coefficient, this works out as $+0.362$. This is a substantial degree of similarity, the kind of figure one might find in psychometric psychology if the two writers were a pair of brothers.

Nevertheless, as far as the link words can take us, they give a far better fit with early Shakespeare than with all-Marlowe.

Table 7.10. *Frequencies of occurrences of catch words, Marlowe and Shakespeare correlated*

In Shakespeare	In Marlowe				
	0	1	2	3 +	Total
0	222	68	33	34	357
1	107	58	28	47	240
2	55	40	18	39	152
3 +	43	49	23	84	199
Total	427	215	102	204	948

Note: Frequencies of occurrences of *E3*'s 948 catch words in 18,368 lines of Marlowe's works, and in 17,818 lines of Shakespeare's earliest works.

ONCE-ONLY NOUNS IN *EDWARD III*

There are 599 nouns in *Edward III* which appear there once and once only. They are listed in Appendix v, together with the number of their appearances in the three *Henry VI* plays on the one hand and the two *Tamburlaine* plays of Marlowe on the other. This distribution will be considered later.

As a preliminary we can consider the occurrences of these nouns in the 18,368 lines of Marlowe's works, detailed on p. 125, and in the 19,571 lines of Shakespeare's early works, detailed on the same page. Of these nouns 516 are suitable for inclusion in a correlation table, Table 7.9. Eighty-three words have been excluded from that table because their occurrences, 13 or more in either Marlowe or Shakespeare, would unbalance the distribution to a point where it would become less sensitive to analysis. These 83 excluded words, with the numbers of their appearances, first in Marlowe, then in Shakespeare, are as follows:–

act 5 17, babe 2 24, barons 16 1, birth 22 22, brain 19 8, brows 25 25, carcasses 13 0, circumstance 1 13, coach 13 1, conqueror 19 13, darts 15 4, debts 2 13, device 7 14, dinner 2 24, fiends 10 14, fleet 16 1, friar 38 2, goddess 18 2, governor 61 5, groans 2 18, grove 16 8, hair 50 29, haste 11 28, health 15 12, heat 17 14, heir 13 33, help 12 30, horns 25 9, hounds 3 14, humour 7 19, justice 6 36, labour 15 7, leg 25 15, leisure 1 15, limbs 16 15, maid 37 22, marriage 9 24, meat 19 8, misery 15 16, moon 19 8, morning 20 14, nature 31 32, naught 17 3, ocean 16 12, order 13 21, palace 12 15, passage 14 11, pearl 24 5, policy 19 16, prey 9 22, price 14 1, purpose 9 15, question 16 5, rain 3 15, regent 3 14, religion 17 2, robe 21 4, rocks 30 12, rose 9 25, sacrifice 14 2, sceptre 13 13, shadow 10 24, shoulders 16 15, sirrah 40 24, sleep 13 17, spear 17 6, speech 33 18, staff 6 13, streets 22 16, strife 3 20, temples 14 10, thief 19 15, tide 6 14, towers 24 47, traitor 55 45, truth 13 45, veins 15 8, wine 28 9, witch 2 18, work 25 11, wound 34 38, wrath 33 18, wretch 14 22

Table 7.11. *Appearances of 516 nouns from* Edward III *in Marlowe and Shakespeare, correlated*

Shakespeare	Marlowe													
Numbers of appearances	0	1	2	3	4	5	6	7	8	9	10	11	12	Total
0	92	26	11	4	6	1	1	—	—	1	—	—	—	142
1	52	21	14	10	3	4	3	3	1	1	—	—	—	112
2	15	12	10	7	4	3	4	3	—	3	1	—	1	63
3	9	8	13	4	7	—	2	2	—	—	1	1	2	49
4	12	6	11	2	5	4	—	3	2	—	2	—	1	48
5	1	5	2	4	6	1	1	1	—	2	—	—	—	23
6	1	3	1	4	1	1	—	—	—	1	—	—	1	13
7	4	—	1	1	4	3	2	2	1	1	—	—	—	19
8	1	3	2	3	—	1	1	—	3	—	—	2	—	16
9	—	3	1	3	1	—	1	1	—	—	—	1	—	11
10	—	—	1	—	1	—	1	1	1	1	1	—	1	8
11	—	—	—	1	—	2	—	—	1	1	1	—	1	7
12	—	—	—	—	—	3	1	—	—	1	—	—	—	5
Totals	187	87	67	43	38	23	17	16	9	12	6	4	7	516

Note: Numbers of appearances of 516 nouns from *Edward III* in 18,368 lines of Marlowe and 19,571 lines in early Shakespeare plays, correlated. For instance, 13 nouns appear 3 times in Shakespeare and twice in Marlowe. Statistical data: n = 516; S(x) (Shakespeare) = 1347; S(y) (Marlowe) = 1199; S(x²) = 7829; S(y²) = 6961; S(xy) = 5244. From which r = 2114/4243.3 = +0.498.

Taken on their own, the numbers of occurrences shown in this list provide a Marlowe–Shakespeare correlation of +0.097, which is not statistically significant. This suggests that the frequencies of use of common nouns do not show great resemblance between the two writers, in contrast with the less common nouns which show a different picture.

We are left with the 516 less common nouns: 374 of them (72%) appear, to a total of 1347 times, in the 19,571 lines of early Shakespeare; 329 (64%) appear, to a total of 1199 times, in 18,368 lines of Marlowe. The differences between the two writers, both in the proportion of words appearing, and in the numbers of their appearances, are small, and do not reach statistical significance. In these two respects, then, the nouns from *Edward III* could have been part of the vocabulary of either writer, with practically equal probability. In fact, the resemblances go deeper than that, as we shall learn from the correlation table, Table 7.11.

The table yields a correlation coefficient of 0.498. This is a quite remarkable degree of similarity in the way in which the two poets use the less common nouns. When the rare-word vocabularies of early Shakespeare and Marlowe have so much in common, we shall need a sensitive test to show which of the two is more closely related to *Edward III*. The distinction is more easily made with commoner words. In

Chapter 5, word counts by Alfred Hart provided the basis for two tests which successfully discriminated against Marlowe. One was a measure of the degree of community of vocabulary between plays taken in pairs (Tables 5.3 and 4). The other was based on the proportion of certain prefix words (Tables 5.8 and 9). In both these cases the material was representative of the total vocabularies of the plays investigated, and not restricted to the rare words. In both cases it was Marlowe's *Tamburlaine* plays that came nearest to *Edward III*. *Edward II*, which might have been expected to provide a kinship of vocabulary, was found to differ at a great number of points (Table 5.11). In the test which we now apply to the once-only nouns of *Edward III*, it is, accordingly, appropriate to take Marlowe's *Tamburlaine* plays for comparison with *Edward III*, on the same basis as we take the *Henry VI* plays of Shakespeare.

The vocabulary relationships of the five plays with *Edward III* are recorded in Appendix v. The statistical information is reproduced in Table 7.12. As is shown in the Appendix, the nouns have been grouped into those which do not appear at all in any of the five plays, those which appear once, twice, and so on. Very many of these nouns are included in the link words recorded in Appendices III and IV; these nouns have been distinguished by an asterisk. Table 7.12 follows this classification by showing the numbers of appearances of each of these categories of nouns, appearing once, twice, etc., in the successive rows of the table. Against the observed numbers of appearances are set the expected numbers, based on Hart's counts of the total numbers of different words in each of the five plays; then follows the ratio of observation to expectation as a percent, and that again by the corresponding value of χ^2. Where χ^2 surpasses the 0.05 chance probability, it is marked by underlining, as is also the ratio O/E. The numbers in the rows are cumulative, so that each row includes the observed occurrences in all the rows above it.

The answer that this table gives to our question is unequivocal. In all rows from 1 to 10 the appearances of *Edward III*'s nouns are significantly above expectation in the first part of *Henry VI*, and nowhere else. The other numbers attaining statistical significance, and marked by underlining, are all related to numbers of observations which fall *below* expectation. It is noteworthy, and perhaps surprising, that the numbers of links observed with *3 Henry VI* are consistently below expectation, and in the main to a statistically significant degree. This is a feature which could only have arisen because the vocabularies of all these five plays are related to one another, with many nouns held in common. From other counts, such as those shown in Tables 7.1 and 7.3, we know that the vocabularies of *Edward III* and *3 Henry VI* are closely related. If that kinship does not show up now, in Table 7.10, it is because in this particular test it is being compared with other close kin, and happens to show greater differences from *Edward III* than they do. If we look at the figures in the table under *2 Tam* we see that observation and expectation actually match one another. Nevertheless, it is the relationship of *Edward III* to *1 Henry VI* which is established in this table; and any particular relationship to either of the *Tamburlaine* plays is not supported.

Table 7.12. *Once-only nouns in* Edward III: *frequencies of appearances in the two Tamburlaine plays and the three Henry VI plays*

	N	1H6 (2908)				2H6 (3062)				3H6 (2740)				1Tam (2532)				2Tam (2418)				Tot. χ²
		O	E	O/E	χ²	O	E	O/E	χ²	O	E	O/E	χ²	O	E	O/E	χ²	O	E	O/E	χ²	
1	114	37	24.27	152	6.68	29	25.55	114	.47	16	22.87	70	2.06	12	21.13	57	3.94	20	20.18	99	.00	13.15
2	240	77	51.09	151	13.14	58	53.79	108	.33	38	48.14	79	2.14	27	44.49	61	6.88	40	42.48	94	.14	22.63
3	384	105	81.75	128	6.61	95	86.07	110	.93	64	77.02	83	2.20	56	71.18	79	3.24	64	67.97	94	.23	13.21
4	548	146	116.66	125	7.38	141	122.84	115	2.68	85	109.92	77	5.65	92	101.58	91	.90	84	97.00	87	1.74	18.35
5	653	171	139.01	123	7.36	164	146.38	112	2.12	104	130.98	79	5.56	108	121.04	89	1.40	106	115.59	92	.80	17.24
6	803	209	170.94	122	8.47	195	180.00	108	1.25	125	161.07	78	8.08	133	148.84	89	1.69	141	142.14	99	.01	19.50
7	915	238	194.78	122	9.59	220	205.11	107	1.08	133	183.54	72	13.92	158	169.60	93	.79	166	161.97	102	.10	25.48
8	1003	254	213.51	119	7.68	233	224.84	104	.30	150	201.19	75	13.02	181	185.91	97	.13	185	177.55	104	.31	21.44
9	1093	279	232.67	120	9.23	244	245.01	100	.00	165	219.24	75	13.42	193	202.59	95	.45	212	193.48	110	1.77	24.87
10	1193	293	253.96	115	6.00	266	267.43	99	.01	184	239.30	77	12.79	216	221.13	98	.12	234	211.18	105	.66	19.57
>10	630	124	134.12	92	.76	141	141.22	100	.00	117	126.37	93	.69	126	116.78	108	.73	122	111.52	109	.98	3.16

Note: All the nouns appearing once only in *Edward III* and their appearances in *1*, *2* and *3 Henry VI* and *1* and *2 Tamburlaine* have been recorded in Appendix v. The above table shows the distribution of these links, classified according to the total number of appearances (1, 2 … 10 or more) in the five target plays. Observed numbers (O) have been set against expected numbers (E) proportionate to the Hart counts of number of different words in each play (in brackets, at heads of columns). According to Hart, the number for *Edward III* is 2976. The first column shows the category of word giving 1 or more links with other plays. Numbers in rows are cumulative, each including all numbers in the rows above, except for the category >10, where the numbers are independent. N shows the total of appearances so far observed, all plays. O/E = ratio of observed to expected, as %. χ² is for 1 d.f. for plays singly, for 5 d.f. in total χ² column to the right. Underlining signifies statistical significance at the p <0.05 level or better.

Our attempt, then, to find a statistically significant link between *Edward III* and Marlowe has failed for a third time. In every case linking with Marlowe has fallen short of the linking with Shakespeare, when tested with the same test. The position we reached earlier in this chapter (p. 119) must now stand as a final conclusion. The rare-word vocabulary of *Edward III* is, in every respect we have tested, compatible with authorship by Shakespeare – more specifically, the author of the three *Henry VI* plays and *Richard III*. Moreover, this applies to the whole of *Edward III*, both part A and part B. Furthermore, we have come on no obtrusive points which would suggest authorship by any other dramatist.

SUMMARY AND CONCLUSIONS

1. A definition is given of what is a 'word' in the sense in which it will be used as a unit in the statistical data and their analysis.

2. From the Tudor Facsimile text of *The Reign of King Edward III*, 948 words, the catch words, have been singled out. They appear not more than twelve times in all, in 37 plays of Shakespare (including *Henry VIII*), in *Venus and Adonis, The Rape of Lucrece*, and the Sonnets. The catch words are subclassified into those that make 0, 1, 2 ... 12 appearances in these works. They are listed as they appear in line order in Appendix III, to which Appendix IV provides an alphabetical key. The words are designated as parts of speech by reference to the *Shorter Oxford English Dictionary* (*SOED*), and the numbers of their appearances in the 40 named works of Shakespeare are recorded. These are the data which are subjected to statistical analysis. Every time one of these words appears in the text it makes a fresh entry into the statistical counts. Some words appear as many as two, three or four times; and there are three words which appear respectively five, six and seven times.

3. For statistical purposes the play was divided into two parts: part A being Act I scene ii, Act II scenes i and ii, and Act IV scene iv. Part B is the remainder of the play. This division was made in deference to the great weight of scholarly opinion which regards these two parts as differing in respects of substantial literary quality, and therefore possibly (or even probably) of different authorship.

4. Links with certain Shakespearean works, though recorded in the Appendices, were not brought into the statistical analysis, for reasons stated. These were *Two Noble Kinsmen* (*TNK*), *Sir Thomas More* (*STM*), *The Passionate Pilgrim* (PP), *A Lover's Complaint* (*LC*), and *The Phoenix and the Turtle* (*PhT*).

5. An explanation is given of the difficulties which arose in the course of the preliminary work before statistical analysis, and of the occurrence of and the reasons for oversights and errors. Detected errors affected approximately 3% of all the link citations. It is considered that undetected errors, which must certainly exist, can hardly have had a larger effect. This margin of error is acceptable, as it is very small in proportion to the large systematic deviations of observed from expected numbers which are the essential findings.

6. The links (in terms of numbers of citations of rare words in the works of

Shakespeare) between *Edward III* and 40 plays and poems of Shakespeare are detailed in Tables 7.2A and 2B; the links themselves are made available in Appendices III and IV. In the tables the links are grouped into three groups: (1) those resulting from words with 1 to 6 links with Shakespeare; (2) those from words with 7 to 10 links; (3) those from words with 11 and 12 links. The summation of all these three groups is also entered.

7. In each of these groups observed numbers have been compared with expected ones. Expectations are based on Hart's counts of the numbers of different lexical words in each work. Where the observed exceeds the expected number, the latter also is entered in the table. Where the excess of observed over expected magnitude yields a statistically significant value of χ^2 (at $p < 0.05$), that value is entered, and the statistically significant linkage is distinguished by underlining.

8. On this basis it is found that part A of *Edward III* has a statistically significant excess (in the totals column) of link citations with nine of Shakespeare's works: *Lucrece* 164%, *Richard III* 158%, *1 Henry VI* 157%, *John* 146%, *Henry V* 143%, *Romeo* 137%, *Love's Labour's Lost* 134%, *Richard II* 131%, *2 Henry VI* 127%.

9. On the same basis it is found that part B has a statistically significant excess of links with seven of Shakespeare's works: *1 Henry VI* 231%, *3 Henry VI* 211%, *Richard III* 157%, *Titus* 146%, *2 Henry VI* 144%, *Henry V* 137%, *Lucrece* 135%. The connection with the earliest of Shakespeare's plays is a good deal stronger than was the case with part A, and more narrowly focused.

10. The suggestion arises that not only part A but also part B of *Edward III* could well be the work of Shakespeare. If so, it might be that the two parts were written not quite at the same time, and that part B dates from an earlier stage in his career. The links of part B with *1 Henry VI* and *3 Henry VI* are phenomenally high, more than double their expected values.

11. The distribution of rare words in Shakespeare is now considered. The words of the card index, described in Chapter 6 (p. 83), each with 2 to 10 appearances in the plays, were taken and distributed play by play. To them were added the numbers of 'peculiar words', as counted by Alfred Hart. This then gives us (with a reasonable latitude for error) the numbers of rare words with 1 to 10 appearances as they are distributed between the 37 plays (including *Henry VIII*), but excluding the Poems. The distribution, shown in Table 7.4, is most uneven, with some plays very much richer in rare words than others. At the head of the list comes *Hamlet* with 37.9% of its vocabulary in rare words; at the bottom are *Two Gentlemen* with 20.8% and *Julius Caesar* with 20.5%.

12. If we arrange the plays in a chronological order (modified from the chronology of the Arden editors, as shown in Chapter 7, Figure 2), the degree of 'richness' in rare words varies widely with abrupt ups and downs from play to play over the dramatist's writing career. When the figures are mapped in a 'cusum' (cumulative sum) curve, signs are found of phasic changes from stage to stage. One might speculate that these phases correspond with periodicity in the writer's basic mood.

13. The great difference between plays in their content of rare words should be allowed for in our statistics. Our primary observations are counts of rare words. When we are estimating the probability of a given rare word appearing in a particular play *P*, the chance of its appearance there will be proportionate to the number of rare words in *P*, and not to the total vocabulary of *P*, as enumerated by Hart. The latter has been the statistical base of our computations till now. But plainly it was a rather rough approximation to what should have been a more appropriate base.

14. We now correct our assessments, using the rare-word content of the plays as the basis on which expected numbers are to be calculated. Unfortunately, linkages with the poetical works have to be abandoned, as the numbers of their rare words are unknown. We also omit *Henry VIII*, as a collaborative work not very relevant to our problem now. We have, then, 36 plays, which we can group into six parts, or sextets. The distribution of links is now somewhat simplified, but changes remarkably little.

15. In the new arrangement, part A's links are reduced to seven plays: *R3* 163%, *Jo* 162%, *1H6* 161%, *TGV* 151%, *R2* 146%, *Rom* 140%, *H5* 125%. Part A has significantly raised linkage (139% of expectation) with the first sextet, and also with the second sextet (131%). Part B has a significant excess of links with each of the first six plays: *3H6* 237%, *1H6* 232%, *R3* 159%, *Tit* 146%, *2H6* 136%, *R2* 125%; with the first sextet as a whole, 172% of expectation. Part B is now also disclosed as having significant linkage with *JC* 144%, *Per* 125% and *H5* 117%. These last linkages are unexpected and anomalous.

16. The evidence is compatible with the view, held by a majority of scholars, that part A of *Edward III* was written by Shakespeare. But it goes farther in linking part B with the earliest plays of Shakespeare even more strongly than part A.

17. Direct comparisons of part A with part B are now made. Part A has a significantly higher proportion of the rarest link words. Part A also has a closer connection with the Poems. Grouping Shakespeare's plays into six sets of six, part A of *Edward III* has strong links with both the earliest and the second sextet; part B is linked only to the first sextet, but to that more strongly than is part A. Comparing part A and part B in terms of the proportion of all links that are with A, the ratio is to the advantage of B in *1H6, 3H6, Mac* and *Tmp*, to the advantage of A in *LLL, Jo, Rom, MND, AYL, Ham, TN* and *AWW*. All these differences are statistically significant. Together they amount to a statistically convincing demonstration of the heterogeneity of the two parts.

18. The differences do not have to imply a difference in the identity of the authorship; it is suggested that a difference in the date of authorship would be an acceptable provisional hypothesis. A cusum curve of change in the A/B proportionality shows a harmonious evolution from B preponderance to A preponderance and back again.

19. The point now arises whether we should consider any other dramatist than Shakespeare as the, or a, true author of *Edward III*. Materials are lacking for taking

any other playwright than Marlowe into consideration. Approximately equal samples are taken from Marlowe (18,368 lines) and the earliest Shakespeare works (17,818 lines, or with *Errors* 19,571 lines). The distribution of links between these works and the 948 catch words collected from *Edward III* are different in the two cases. Marlowe has a deficiency of links, many more words with zero links, more words with 5 links or more; the Shakespeare distribution is more even.

20. There is quite a high level of correlation ($r = +0.36$) between Marlowe and Shakespeare in respect of the number of links made with either by individual words. The two poets were using rare-word vocabularies which held many words in common.

21. A list was drawn up of the 599 nouns which appear in *Edward III* once and once only. In terms of their occurrences (0 to 12 times) in Marlowe's 18,368 lines and Shakespeare's 19,571 lines, there was once again a considerable measure of resemblance between the poets, with $r = +0.498$. Words which appeared more commonly, thirteen or more times in either writer, were used more differently by them, the numbers showing a negligible degree of correlation.

22. The 599 once-only nouns of *Edward III* were now used to relate it to a much more restricted group of plays: the three *Henry VI* plays of Shakespeare and the two *Tamburlaine* plays of Marlowe. These were the plays which, in studies presented earlier, seemed to have the closest relations with *Edward III*. In this restricted field it was only one play, *1 Henry VI*, which showed a consistant and statistically significant overplus of linkage with *Edward III* in comparison with all the others.

23. This evidence can be taken in conjunction with other evidence provided earlier (in Chapter 5). At all three points where it can be tested with statistical rigour, a theory of authorship by Marlowe fails to a statistically significant degree to compete with a theory of authorship by Shakespeare.

24. It is concluded that, as far as the rare-word vocabulary of *Edward III* goes, it is compatible with authorship by Shakespeare at an early stage in his dramatic career. Both part A and part B are regarded as his work, though probably written at different times.

The card indexed link words

A list of 5553 unusual words, occurring from two to ten times in more than one Shakespeare play, described and discussed in Chapter 6, to which is appended a list of a further 207 words, fulfilling the above criteria but missed on the first search and discovered later during the work on the vocabulary of *Edward III*.

Words appearing in part A of *Edward III* distinguished by heavy underlining. Words appearing in part B of *Edward III* but not in part A distinguished by light underlining. Words in the supplementary list are shown with line reference.

Two-Words: ABASE v, abet v, a-bleeding a, absolutely adv, abut v, abysm n, accommodation n, accoutrement n, accoutred ppl, accoutrement n, accumulate v, actual a, adage n, a-day adv, addiction n, addrest a, adjacent a, adjoin v, adjourn v, adjunct a, admonish v, admonishment n, admonition n, a-doing ppl, a-down-a adv, adulterous a, advantageous a, advisedly adv, aforesaid a, after-dinner n, after-love n, after-supper n, agitation n, agone adv, a-hungry a, ail v, alabaster n, a-land adv, alarumed ppl, alchemist n, alderman n, ale-wife n, alien n, allayment n, all-hale n, allicholy n, all-seeing a, alway adv, a-making ppl, amazedness n, amber a, ambiguity n, ambitiously adv, amort a, ancientry n, ant n, anthem n, antidote n, anvil n, anybody pr, apostle n, apricock n, aptness n, arbitrator n, arch a, archery n, arch-heretic n, arch-villain n, ardour n, armado n, arouse v, arrand/t a, arteries n, articulate v, aspen-leaf n, assailant n, ass-head n, astray adv, astronomer n, a-tilt adv, attaint a, attent a, attorney v, attractive a, auburn a, audacity n, audible a, augury n, austerely adv, avow v, aweless a, a-wooing ppl, axletree n, azured a, BABBLE n, back-door n, bae v, baker n, bang v, barbed a, bard n, bareness n, barricado n, baste v, battalion n, bawl v, bay [window] n, beach v, beadsman n, beagle n, beardless a, bear-herd n, bearing-cloth n, bear-whelp n, beck v, bedeck v, beginner n, begnaw v, behest n, bellows n, bell-wether n, bellyful n, belt n, benevolence n, berhyme v, besmirch v, besonian n, besort v, beteem v, bias a, big-swoln a, billet v, biscuit n, bitch n, bladed a, blameless a, blessedly adv, blindworm,n, bloodied ppl, bloodshed n, blood-sucker n, bloody-minded a, bloom n, bluster n, boar-spear n, bodement n, boldened ppl, boor n, border n, borough n, bottle-ale n, bottomless a, bounce n, bounce v, bounden a, bowstring n, boyish a, brabble n, braboler n, braggard n, breaker n, breast v, breese n, brock n, brick-wall n, bride-bed n, bridle n, brightly adv, brightness n, brine-pit n, brinish a, brink n, broad-spreading a, brood v, broth n, buck [laundry] n, buckle n, buckler n, bugle a, bullock n, burnished a, busily adv, butter v, butt-shaft n,

buxom a, buyer n, CACKLING ppl, calculate v, canker a,
cannoneer n, canopied v, cantle n, canvass v, caparison n,
cap-a-pe adv, cape [of land] n, cape [garment] n, capitulate v,
captainship n, carack n, carat n, carbonado n, carman r,
carnation [colour] n/a, carol n, carouse n, carp n, carver n,
casual a, casualty n, catechism n, caterwauling vn, catling n,
cautelous a, cavalier n, cavern n, cement n, censer n, chalk v,
chancellor n, chantry n, chapless a, chapmen n, charactery n,
charnel-house n, cheapen v, chestnut n, chevalier n, child-
like a, chill a, chimney-sweeper n, chimney-top n, chip v,
chorus n, chronicler n, circuit n, circumscribe v, circumspect a,
circumstantial a, circumvention n, clap n, clapper-claw v,
clasp n, cleanly adv. cleanly a, cloak-bag n, cloister v,
close-stool n, closure n, clouted ppl, coast v, cobble v,
cobweb n, cockerel n, cockle [shell fish] n, cockle [darnel] n,
cockney n, coffined ppl, cogitation n, cohere v, coinage n,
coldness n, collateral a, collied a, collop n, colossus n,
colt v, columbine n, combustion n, comedian n, comer n, comic a,
comma n, commencement n, commixture n, communication n,
community n, companionship n, compassionate a, competency n,
competent a, comprise v, compulsive a, computation n, concave a,
concert n, condign a, condolement n, confirmer n, conflicting
ppl, conformable a, confute v, conjectural a, conjointly adv,
conjunctive a, considerate a, consistory n, consolation n,
consonancy n, constitution n, consummation n, contemplative a,
contemptible a, contemptuous a, contentious a, continency n,
continuate a, contrariety n, contrarious a, contribution n,
controller n, conveniency n, conversion n, convertite n,
convict v, convocation n, cookery n, coop v, copulation n,
cereal n, cork n, coronation-day n, corrigible a, corrosive n,
corrupter n, cough n, council-board n, council-house n,
counterpoise n, countervail v, countess n, countrywoman n,
couplet n, courageously adv, courier n, court-gate n, covent n,
cover v, craftily adv, creaking ppl, creek n, crib n, crier n,
critical a, crossbow n, crow-keeper n, crum(b) n, cub n,
cuckold-maker n, cumber v, curd v, cureless a, curer n, curl n,
curtail v, curtain v, curtal a, curtle-axe n, customed ppl,
cut-throat n, DAINTILY adv, damage n, damp n, dancer n, dandle v
dapple v, dash n, dateless a, dawn n, deafness n, debatement n,
debile a, debitor n, deceivable a, deceiver n, decrepit a,
defacer n, defensible a, defensive a, defer v, deficient a,
degrade v, deject a, delectable a, deliberate v, deluge n,
delve v, demi-devil n, demon n, demonstration n, demurely adv,
denay v, deplore v, deracinate v, derivation n, dern a,
descant n, designment n, destitute a, destroyer n, detract v,
dewdrop n, dewlapped a, dialect n, digression n, dilatory a,
dilemma n, diminution n, diminutive a, diminutive n, ding-dong
int, dining-chamber n, dint n, dirge n, disadvantage n,
disannul v, discase v, disciplined ppl, discontinue v,
dismission n, discreetly adv, disembark v, disgestion n,
dishclout n, dishearten v, dishonestly adv, disjoint a,
disloyalty n, disparage v, dispensation n, displant v, disport v,
disprove v, disputation n, distrain v, distraught a,
distribution n, disturber n, divest v, divinely adv, dizzy a,
dock [plant] n, dollar n, dolt n, domineer v, double-dealer n,
down-trod v, draff n, drayman n, dreadfully adv, drench n,
drollery n, dropsy n, drowse v, dullard n, dull-eyed a,
dully adv, dumb v, dumbly adv, dungy a, dusty a, dutiful a,

dwelling-place n, dwindle v, EAVES n, ebony n, edged a, eel-skin n, effectless a, effuse v, egal a, egg-shell n, eglantine n, eighth a, elegies n, eleventh a, embalm v, emblem n, emphasis n, empoison v, emulate v, <u>enchantment n,</u> enchafed v, encircle v, encouragement n, endamage v, endanger v, endurance n, enginer n, enigma n, ennoble v, enrobe v, entomb v, envelop v, <u>epicure n,</u> equivocal a, equivocation n, erroneous a, estimable a <u>estranged</u> v, estridge n, etcetera n, eterne a, evade v, ever-burning a, evilly adv, excitement n, <u>execration n,</u> exempt v, exhort v, exhorcist n, expectancy n, exposure n, expulsion n, extinct a, extirp v, extortion n, exalt v, eyebrow n, eye-offending a, FABULOUS a, fadge v, faggot n, faintness n, falconer n, fallible a, fallow a, fallow n, falseness n, famously adv, fane n, fang v, fantastically adv, farm v, fashionable a, <u>fatherless a,</u> featly adv, felicity n, fell n, felony n, fence v, fencer n, fennel n, feodary n, fare n, fertility n, fet v, fetlock n, fetters n, fiddlestick n, fiend-like a, fiery-red a, fifty-five a, fire-eyed a, firework n, firmness n, firstling n, fitment n, fixure n, flame-coloured a, flamen n, flap-dragon n, flask n, fledge v, fleece v, flexible a, flexure n, flinch v, flood-gate n, floweret n, foal n, font n, foolhardy a, football n, footpath n, <u>forage v,</u> forcibly adv, forefinger n, foregone v, forehand a, forehand n, foreknowing v, foremost a, forenoon n, foreshow v, formally adv, formless a, fort n, forthright n, foster-nurse n, fracted v, franchise n, fraughtage n, freckled a, freshness n, frieze n, frightful a, fringe n, frog n, frugal a, fruitfully adv, frustrate a, fry v, <u>fugitive n,</u> <u>full-fraught a,</u> <u>fume v,</u> fundamental a, furbish v, furlong n, furnace n, furrow v, fustian a, fustian n, GABBLE v, gad n, gallimaufry n, gallop n, gallowglass n, gambol v, garbage n, garish a, garner n, <u>garrison n,</u> <u>garrisoned v,</u> garter v, geck n, gentility n, germen n, gest n, giant-like a, gib n, giddily adv, giglot a, gird n, gird v, gleek n, gleek v, <u>gloomy a,</u> glut v, glutton n, gnarl v, godliness n, goodwife n, gormandise v, gorgon n, gosling n, gossamers n, gouty a, gradation n, grapple n, grasp n, graze [scrape] v, great-bellied a, great-grandsire n, green-eyed a, greenly adv, griffon n, grime n, grimly adv, grisly a, grizzled a, grope v, grunt v, guardant n, guerdon n, guerdoned v, guileful a, gules a, gull v, gunner n, gust [taste] n, HABIT v, hailstone n, halcyon a, halfmoon n. halloing v, handfast n, <u>handful n,</u> handless a, handsaw n, harbourage n, hardiness n, <u>hare-brained a,</u> hare-lip n, harmonious a, harnessed v, harvest-home n, hatch [breeding] n, hatch v, hater n, hawthorn-bud n, hazel-nut n, healthy a, hearsed v, <u>heart-sick a,</u> hedge-corner n, heedless a, hell-pains n, hemmed v, hent v, heritage n, hermitage n, hey-day n, hilding a, <u>hindmost a,</u> hoar v, hoard n, hobgoblin n, hobnail n, hoise v, holland n, hollowly adv, home-bred a, honey v, honeysuckle n, hood n, hook v, horsemanship n, hot-blooded a, hour-glass n, householder n, housewifery n, howl n, huddle v, humanely adv, humidity n, hurly-burly n, hurricano n, hurry n, hurtle v, huswifery n, hyperbole n, hyperbolical a, ILL-BODING a, ill-disposed a, ill-taken a, illegitimate a, illumine v, imbrue v, impertinent a, impetuous a, implement n, imply v, importunacy n, imposthume n, improvident a, impugn v, inaccessible a, incaged v, incarnate a, inclusive a, inconsiderate a, incontinent a, inconvenience n, incorporate v,

incredulous a, incursion n, indebted a, indict v,
indifferency n, indigested a, indiscreet a, indiscretion n,
indistinct a, inexorable a, infallibly adv, infamous a,
inferior n, infix v, inflict v, infortunate a, ingraft v,
inhabitant n, inhibited v, inkhorn n, inkling n, inmost a,
inordinate a, inquisition n, inseparable a, insist v,
instalment n, instigate v, institute v, intellectual a,
intelligencer n, intemperance n, intemperate a, intention n,
interior a, intermingle v, interpose v, intestine a, intitle v,
intruder n, inventor n, invert v, investment n, inviolable a,
invocate v, inwards n, ivory a, JAUNCE v, jaundice n, jeer v,
jeweller n, jog v, jolt-head n, jordan n, journal a,
journeyman n, jovial a, jowl v, joyless a, joyous a,
judgement-day n, jurisdiction n, juror n, jury n, justly adv,
KENNEL n, kickshaw n, kiln-hole n, kitchen-wench n, knap v,
knotty a, knowingly adv, LABEL n, labourer n, laboursome a,
labyrinth n, lag v, lag-end n, by'r lakin int, lamkin n,
lamentably adv, landlord,n, languish n, lank a, lash n, latch
v, lated v, laud n, laud v, laudable a, leagued v, leaky a,
lean-faced a, leaven n, leaven v, lees n, leet n, leisurely
adv, lendings n, lewdly adv, lewdness n, lieger n, lien v,
lieutenancy/try n, lieve as, adv, lightning-flash n, lily-
livered a, lime v, lime-kiln n, limitation n, linen a,
linguist n, lining n, link [torch] n, livelihood n, loaf n.
local a, lodger n, logic n, loiter v, loiterer n, lone a,
loneliness n, 'lonely a, loop n, lording n, louse n, love-
letter n, love-sick a, love-suit n, lowing v, lown n, lucre n,
luke-warm a, lurch v, luscious a, lustihood n, lustrous a,
MAGNIFICO n, maidhood n, mail n, main n, main'd v, major a,
malign a, malkin n, malt-horse n, malt-worm n, mammel n,
manacle v, manager n, man-at-arms n, mandragora n, manfully adv,
mannered a, mannerly adv, many-coloured a, marigold n,
marjoram n, market-town n, marketable a, marriage-feast n,
marriage-vow n, martlet n, marvellously adv, masker n,
masque v, masterless a, masterly a, masterly adv, matchless a,
maul v, mazzard n, meadow n, measureless a, mechanical n,
meddler n, mediation n, medicinal a, meiny n, memorize v,
metaphor n, mete v, metheglin n, mi n, mid-day a,
midsummer a, midway n, milch a, mildew v, milkmaid n,
milksop n, miller n, milliner n, mindless a, mine v,
minnow n, mint [spice] n, mire v, miry a, miscall v,
mischievous a, misconstrue v, misdeed n, misdoubt n,
misinterpret v, missive n, mist n, mistempered a, misthink v,
mite n, moderately adv, module n, moist v, molest v, money-
bag n, monthly a, morris n, mossed v, mow v, muleter n,
multitudinous a, munch v, munition n, murky a, mustachio n,
mutability n, mutation n, mutine n, mutiner n, muzzle n,
NAPPING v, nasty a, neaf n, nectar n, negative a,
negotiate v, neighbourly a, nettle v, neutral a, new-
come a, new-delivered a, new-fallen a, new-fangled a, new-
healed a, nibbling v, nick n, nickname v, niggard a,
nighted a, nimble-footed a, nine-score a, nipple n, nit n,
noddle n, 'nointed v, noiseless a, noontide a, noontide n,
nosegay n, notify v, noun n, numberless a, nurture n,
nuthook n, nutshell n, OBLOQUY n, obscenely adv, obstinacy n,
occident n, occupy v, occurrence n, ode n, odoriferous a,
oeillade n, offensive a, olive a, operant a, operate v,
opportune a, opulent a, orbed a, ore n, organ-pipe n,

original a, orthography n, osier n, ousel n, outcast n,
outcry n, outswear v, outwear v, overeye v, overflow n,
overhang v, overlusty a, overmount v, overmuch adv,
overproud a, overroasted a, overset v, o'erworn a, oxlip n,
oyes n, NEAT'SLEATHER n, nick v, nightcap n, noble-minded a,
onward adv, outweigh v, overpower v, overpress v, PACKHORSE
n, packthread. n, paddock n, palate v, paleness n, palsy v,
paly a, pang v, pant n, pantaloon. n, paragon v, parcel v,
parishioner n, parricide n, participate v, participation n,
particle n, particularities n, particularly adv, partridge n,
passable a, pasty n, patchery n, pathway n, paunch n,
peaceable a, peaceably adv, peach-colour'd a, peas n, pease n,
peck n, pelf n, pencil n, penetrable a, pensioner n,
pensive a, pent-up v, perch n, perch v, perdurable a,
perfectness n, periwig n, pert a, pertinent a, pertly adv,
perturb v, pestiferous a, petition v, petitionary a, pewter.
n, phantasime n, pheese v, pibble n, pickaxe n, pight v,
pigmy n, pitcher n, pillory n, pills n, pinfold n, pint n,
pippin n, pitcher n, piteously adv, plain-dealing a,
planetary a, plank n, plaster v, playhouse n, plum n, plum-
tree n, plural a, point-blank adv, politely adv, pollute v,
pomegranate n, poop n, poor-john n, popularity n, porringer n,
portage n, portal n, portance n, positively adv, possessor n,
postscript n, potation n, potato n, potential a, potently adv,
pothecary n, pouch n, pout v, powder v, prattle n, prayer-
book n, precedence n, preceding v, predominate v,
preeminence n, prenominate v, presentation n, prest a,
priesthood n, priest-like a, primal a, primero n, primrose n,
principality n, priority n, pristine a, profitably adv,
profitless a, prognostication n, prolixity n, promise-breaker
n, prophetically adv, proposition n, propriety n, prose n,
prosperously adv, prostitute v, protract v, provident a,
provincial a, provocation n, prudence n, puddle n, puddled v,
pupil a, purgatory n, purify v, purple v, purr n, pursy a,
putrefy v, putter-on n, pyramis n, QUAGMIRE n, quail n,
questionless adv, quicksand n, quicksilver n, quiddity n,
quintessence n, quotidian n, RACKET n, radiance n, rankle v,
ransomeless a, rant v, rational a, ravening v, ravisher n,
real a, reasonless a, rebel a, recognizance n, recollect v,
redeliver v, re-edify v, reel [dance] n, register n, regreet n,
rehearsal n, reinforce v, reinforcement n, relapse n, reliques
n, remarkable a, remembrancer n, remotion n, renege v,
repentant a, reprieve v, resident a, respite v, restorative
n, resty a, retentive a, retinue n, retrograde a,
reverberate v, reverted v, riddance n, rift n, rift v,
rind n, ringlet n, rival a, robustious a, roe [fish] n,
roe [deer] n, rook n, rottenness n, rout v, row n, rudesby
n, rudiments n, runner n, rupture n, russet a, rye n,
SACKCLOTH n, sacriligious a, safeguard v, saffron a, saffron
n, salmon n, salt-water a, sampler n, sanctimonious a,
sapphire n, sarcenet a, savagery n, savory a, scaffold n,
scandalized v, scandalous a, scent n, scoff v, scornfully
adv, scowl v, screen n, scribbled v, scrip n, scrupulous a,
sea-coal a, seafaring a, sea-fight n, seamark n, sea-
monster n, secondary n, sectary n, seditious a, self-
slaughter n, se'nnight n, sensual a, sensuality n, sermon n,
sevenfold a/adv, seventy a, shackle v, shadowy a, shady a,
shallows n, shambles n, shamefaced a, shard n, sheen n,

sheer a, shipboard n, shivers n, shoal n, shoe n, shoe-
tie n, shoon n, short-winded a, shovel n, shreds n, shriek
n, shrilly adv, shrimp n, shrieve n, shrug v, significant n,
simp'ring v, similar n, sinfully adv, sinow n, siren n,
sir-reverence n, sithence adv/conj, situate a, situation n,
skein n, skirmish n, skirr v, slackness n, slash v, sleight n,
'slid int, slimy a, slings n, sliver v, smilingly adv,
slowness n, slubber v, slug n, sluice v, sluttery n, smart a,
smoothly adv, smoothness n, snail-pac'd a, sneaped v, snort v,
snowball n, snuff v, sobriety n, sort-hearted a, soldier-
like a, solicitor n, solitary a, somewhere adv, souse v,
southward adv, south-west a/adv, sparingly adv, spavin n,
speculative a, spendthrift n, spinner n, spleenful a,
splendor n, splinter n, splinter v, spousal n, sprawl v,
sprite v, squander v, squash n, squeal v, stable a,
stainless a, stanch v, starlight n, star-like a, statist n,
steely a, steep n, steer n, stem v, stew n, stews n,
stigmatic n, stomacher n, strait n, strengthless a, strictly
adv, strong-knit a, studient n, studious a, stupefy v,
subsidy n, subtilly adv, substitute v, subtlety n, suckle v,
sugar a, summary n, sunshine a, superficial a, supernatural
a, superscription n, superstition n, superstitiously adv,
supportance n, surcease v, surpass v, surplus n, surprise n,
surrender v, survivor n, suspire v, sustenance n, swabber n,
swath n, sweaty a, sweetmeats n, swift-winged a, swill v,
swimmer n, swinish a, sworder n, syrup n, TABLE-BOOK n,
taborines n, tacklings n, taffata a, taker n, talon n,
tameness n, tanner n, tap (out) v, taper-light n, tart a,
tartness n, tax n, teat n, tediously adv, tempest-tossed a,
tempestuous a, tenantless a, tenement n, tenfold a, tennis n,
tennis-balls n, terrestrial a, tester n, tetchy a, tetter n,
thanksgiving n, thaw n, thievery n, thinly adv, thrall v,
thrash v, thrasonical a, three-farthing n, three-foot a,
three-man a, three-piled a, thrice-gracious a, thrice-
valiant a, thrice-worthy a, throb v, throttle n,
throughfare n, thunderstone n, tike n, tilt-yard n, timber n,
timber'd a, time-pleaser n, tincture n, tine n, tiptoe adv,
tofore adv, tolerable a, toothpick n, topful a, tortoise n,
townsmen n, traffic v, trail v, transpose v, trappings n,
treatise n, tresses n, tribunal n, trident n, trinkets n,
triumpher n, trompery n, trot n, troubler n, trout n,
truckle-bed n, true-born a, truster n, tuck n, turncoat n,
turpitude n, twangling v, twentieth a, twine v, twink n,
ULCER n, umpire n, unbegot(ten) a, unbend v, unbid(den) a,
unbonnetted a, unbowed a, unbridled a, unburied a, uncapable
a, uncase v, uncaught v, uncharge v, unchecked a,
unconfirmed a, unconquered a, unconsidered a, unconstrained a,
uncouple v, uncouth a, underhand v, underprop v, undertaker n,
underwrite v, undeserver n, undeserving a, undivulged a,
undress v, unfilled a, unforced a, unfrequented a,
unfriended a, ungalled a, ungot(ten) a, unguided a, unhacked
a, unhaired a, unhandled a, unhappiness n, unhatched a,
unheedful a, unhoused a, unkennel v, unkiss v, unlaid a,
unloved a, unmanned a, unmannered a, unmask v, unmeasurable
a, unmeritable a, unmingled a, unmuzzle v, unnoted a,
unnumbered a, unpolished a, unpractised a, unpregnant a,
unprizable a, unquestioned a, unquietness n, unreal a,
unrespective a, unrevenged a, unroll v, unscarred a,

unschooled a, unshape v, unsolicited a, unsounded a, unstaid
a, unstanched a, unstate v, unsubstantial a, unsuitable a,
unsuspected a, unswear v, unswept a, untangle v, untender a,
untent v, unthrift n, untired a, untouched a, untoward a,
untrained a, untread v, untrod(den) a, untuneable a, untwine
v, unurged a, unused a, unvalued a, unwind v, unwished a,
unwittingly adv, unwonted a, unworthily adv, uprise n, upshot
n, upside (down) adv, upstart n, urgent a, useful a, usher
n, usually adv, usury n, VAINNESS n, valuation n, vanquisher
n, vendible a, vengeful a, venomously adv, venter v,
verdure n, vestment n, victual v, villain-like a, villainously
adv, viol n, volubility n, voluptuousness n, vowel n,
WAFTAGE n, waggish a, waiting-women n, wall-eyed a, wallow v,
warily adv, watchers n, waylay v, wedge n, wedge v, ween v,
weeping-ripe a, well-advised a, well-beseeming a, well-nigh
adv, well-seeming a, whatever pron/a, whelp v, whensoever
adv/conj, whereabout adv, wheresoever adv/conj, wherewithal
adv/n, whey-face n, whipstock n, white-bearded a, white-
livered a, whites n, wife-like a, wild-fowl n, wiles n,
willingness n, winch v, windmill n, windowed a, wind-shaked
(en) a, wisher n, woolly a, woosel n, wordly a, worldling n,
worshipper n, wrangler n, wreak v, wrongful a, YARELY adv,
yarn v, yearn v, yerk v, yesty a, yielder n, younker n,
ZANY n, zodiac n. (1703)

THREE-WORDS: ABBEY-WALL n, aoreast adv, abroach adv, absolve
v, abundant a, ace n, acorn n, activity n, adamant n,
addict(ed) a, addle a, adoration n, adulterate a, affectation
n, affiance n, affined a, agate n, allege v, allot v,
amazedly adv, amber n, amply adv, angerly adv, answerable a,
anticipate v, appeach v, appertinent a, arched a, armipotent
a, aroint v, array v, artist n, atonement n, attainder n,
attaint v, attract v, attraction n, auditor n, avised v,
await v, award v, a-work adv, accidental a, accidentally adv,
accite v, affability n, affy v, afire a, alias adv, altitude
n, amplify v, angle n, annoy n, apprehensive a, ardour n,
armory n, associate v, austerity n, awaken v, BACON n, badness
n, bail v, balk v, ballad-maker n, balm v, ban n, bankrupt
n, baptism n, barbarian n, bare(d.) v, barefaced a, barne n,
base-born a, bastinado n, bawdry n, bay [colour] a, beak
[of bird] n, bear-baiting n, bear-ward n, bechance v, bed
(ded) v, bedew v, bed-rid (bedred) a, bed-time n, beneficial
a, benefit v, bestial a, bestrow/bestrew v, bilbo n, bird-
bolt n, birthday n, bissom a, blackberry n, blameful a,
blasphemy n, bleach v, blear v, blessedness n, blink v,
blood-drinking a, bloodstained a, blossom v, blubber v,
bluntly adv, blur v, bluster v, bolt (fetter) v, bolt (sift)
v, bombard n, bombast n, bond-slave n, bookish a, borrower n,
botcher n, bots n, braves n, bray v, breather n, brewer n,
bribe v, briefness n, brimstone n, bringer n, broil v,
brother-in-law n, brotherly a, browse v, bruise n, bruit n,
brush (attack) n, brush v, buckler v, bud v, bum n, bunch n,
burgher n, buss v, butt (aim) n, butt v, buttock n, buzzard n,
CAITIFF a, caliver n, calmly adv, calumnious a, cambric n,
canary (dance) n, canary (wine) n, candy v, caparison v,
caper n, carbonado v, carnal a, carter n, carve v, castaway
n, catechize v, caudle n, causeless a, causer n, centaur n,
century n, cess(e) n, chalice n, chalky a, chamberlain n,
chambermaid n, chariot-wheel n, chastely adv, chattel n,

checker [chequer] v, cheveril n, child-bed n, childishness n, chime n, chine n, chops n, christen v, circumference n, cistern n, clamber v, claw n, clearness n, clepe v, clerkly adv, client n, clink v, clod n, clothier n, clotpoll n, clout [archery] n, cluster v, cockatrice n, cognizance n, coign n, colic n, collection n, collier n, comb v, combination n, commiseration n, comparative a, comply v, composure n, comrade n, concur v, condemnation n, condole v, congregate v, consequently adv, consort n, continually adv, controlment n, contumelious a, conversant a, cony n, copy v, coranto n, cormorant a, counter adv, countercheck n, countless a, covert n, coverture n, coy v, cozenage n, crabbed a, crabbed a, crab-tree n, cranny n, cream n, credence n, credent a, crest-fallen a, criminal a, crisp a, critic n, crowner n, crownet n, crupper n, cuff n, cuff v, cullion n, curd n, curfew n, custody n, cygnet n, DAD n, dainty n, daisy n, damm v, darkling a, darnel n, dastard a, deaf v, deafen v, death's-head n, deathsman, n, decease n, decide v, decision n, declension n, decorum n, dedication n, deep-mouthed a, defendant n, define v, defender n, defunct a, defuse v, delicious a, delude v, demerit n, demesnes n, demigod n, demure a, denier n, dependancy/ency n, dependant/ ent a, depute v, deserver n, devoutly adv, diffidence n, dimpled a, disarm v, discomfort v, disfurnish v, disgorge v, dismantle v, dismember v, disparagement n, dispraise n, disproportion v, disrobe v, dissembler n, dissever v, dissolute a, dissolutely adv, distain v, distinct a, distrust v, distrust n, divination n, dogged a, dominator n, dout v, drachma n, drybeat v, duck v, dunghill a, dye n, EAGERLY adv, ean v, easiness n, eater n, echo v, eclipse v, edifice n, eke adv, eld n, ell n, elm n, embolden v, emptiness n, enamel v, endue v, enfeeble v, englut v, engrave v, ensnare v, entangle v, entice v, equality n, erection n, ergo conj, espial n, essence n, essentially adv, evenly adv, ewer n, exaction n, excellency n, exigent n, exist v, exit n, expiration n, expressure n, extemporal a, extravagant a, eagerly adv, FACILITY/faint-hearted a, fair-faced a, falchion n, far-off a, farthingale n, fatherly a/adv, faultless a, faulty a, fay n, fearless a, feathered a, felon n, fence [defend] v, fervour n, fiction n, fiddler n, fierceness n, filial a, fillip v, finder n, fineness n, fire-brand n, fisher n, fist v, fitchew n, flash v, flaw v, fleet a, flush a, foggy a, fondness n, foot-cloth n, footman n, forcible a, forefather n, foremost adv, forerunner n, forethink v, forewarn v, forthcoming a, fortunately adv, foul-mouthed a, founder v, fount n, fraction n, franklin n, fraud n, fraught n, frequent v, frivolous a, fro adv, frontier n, fruit-tree n, frustrate v, furtherance n, furthermore conj, fusty a, GABERDINE n, gallantly adv, gambol n, gamesome a, gazer n, gender n, germane a, gibe v, gladness n, glassy a, glib a, glimpse n, goad v, goal n, goblet n, goddess-like a, gory a, grained v, grange n, grate n, gravel n, great-grandfather n, gree v, green- sickness n, grise/grize n, ground v, grovel v, grub n, gunpowder n, HALBERD n, halloo v, ham n, handiwork n, handle n, handsomely adv, hardiment n, harlotry n, harpy n, harrow v, harshly adv, harshness n, haught a, haunch n, hawthorn n, headpiece n, heady a, heartburn v, hearted v,

heath n, hedgehog n, heedfully adv, heifer n, hell-hound n,
helper n, helpless a, hemlock n, hempen a, herdsman n,
hereby adv, hinge n, holidame n, holily adv, hollowness n,
honey-sweet a, hoop v, horned a, hospitable a, housekeeper n,
house-keeping n, howbeit adv, howsomever adv, hoyday int,
hull v, hungerly a, hurly n, IDEA n, ignominious a,
illustrious a, impair v, impatiently adv, impawn v,
impeachment n, importunity n, impregnable a, impress n,
impressure n, impute v, incense n, incident a, incontinency n,
incontinent a, indent v, indirection n, indite v, induction n,
indulgence n, inestimable a, infernal a, infold v,
information n, infusion n, inkle n, inky a, innovation n,
inns [of court] n, insatiate a, insensible a, insert v,
insinuation n, inspiration n, instead of prep, insupportable
a, intendment n, interruption n, intimate v, intrude v,
inundation n, invulnerable a, inwardly adv, irk v, irksome a,
irreligious a, irregular a, irrevocable a, iteration n,
JELLY n, jet n, jig v, journey v, joyfully adv, jump adv,
KEEL n, ken n, ken v, kerchief n, kersey n, king(ed) v,
kinswoman n, kitchen n, knoll v, LA [music] n, lading n,
land-service n, lastly adv, lave v, lawfully adv, lawn n,
lazar n, lea n, leak v, leanness n, learnedly adv, lease v,
leash n, leavy/leafy a, leer n, leer v, leman n, lenten a,
leopard n, letter-patent n, leviathan n, liberality n,
library n, link [of chain] n, livelong a, loam n, loathing n,
loathly a, loathness n, loggerhead n, lowness n, lug v,
lunes n, lustily adv, MADAMS n, mad-brained a, madcap a,
maidenhood n, maidenly a, mail v, maintenance n, majestic a,
malapert a, malefactor n, maliciously adv, mane n, mannish a,
mantle v, manure v, marriage-bed n, marriage-day n, mart v,
masculine a, mason n, master v, mastership n, mattock n,
maugre prep, maze v, mechanic a, mechanical a, memorial n,
mental a, mention v, mercenary a, meritorious a, metre n,
mew [of cat] v, milky a, mill-stone n, minstrelsy n, mint
[of money] n, minx n, miraculous a, misbecome v. misleader n,
mislike v, mitigate v, mitigation n, molehill n, mongrel a,
mongrel n, monumental a, mope v, moralise v, mortally adv,
moss n, moth n, mourner n, mouse v, mover n, mow n,
muddied v, milberry n, mummy n, murmur n, murrain n,muzzle v,
NAG n, nameless a, nap n, narrowly adv, nave n, nay-word n,
neglection n, neigh n, neighbourhood n, new-married a,
newness n, newt n, niggard n, night-owl n, nill v,
nineteen a/n, nomination n, nonce n, nook n, northward a,
notebook n, notion n, nourishment n, novelty n, nowadays adv,
numb a, nutmeg n, OAR n, objection n, obscene a, observant a,
observer n, obstacle n, offal n, office(d) v, omnipotent a,
onset n, ordinary a, orient a, origin n, otherwhere adv,
out-dare v, out-stare v, outstrip v, oven n, overcast/o'er-
v, overgo,v, overleap v, overmaster v, overmatch v,
overpass v, overpay v, overspread v, oversway v, overswell v,
overturn v, overwatch v, overweigh v, PACIFY v, paddle v,
pagan a, pah int, pail n, pall v, palsy n, pamper v,
parings n, parlour n, passado n, passport n, patent n,
pathetical a, patroness n, pattern v, peacemaker n, peak v,
peascod n, peize v, pelican n, pelt v, pension n, pent-
house n, pepper v, perfectly adv, performer n, perpetually
adv, perpetuity n, perplexity n, persist v, personally adv,
perspective n, perverse a, pervert v, physic v, pia mater n,

pickle n, pinion v, pinnace n, pioner/eer n, pitchy a,
pitiless a, plain-dealing n, plaintiff n, plaint n, plaster n,
plate v, portentous/dous a, plausive a, plentifully adv,
plummet n, point-device/ise a, pollution n, pompous a, pop v,
pore v, porpentine n, portable a, positive a, posset n,
possibly adv, post-haste adv, post-horse n, potentate n,
pottle n, practicer n, prank v, predominance n, predicament
n, premeditate v, premises n, prescience n, prescript n,
privacy n, procession n, profanation n, professor n,
profitable a, progenitor n, prop v, property v, proportion v,
prowess n, psalms n, puttock n, puzzle v, pyramid(e) n,
QUALM n, quarrelsome a, quarry [hunting] n, queasy a, quickly
adv, quill n, RABBIT n, rack [clouds] n, rainbow n, rainy a,
ram v, ramp v, rankness n, rareness n, ratsbane n, razor n,
reakless a, rear n, recant v, reckless a, reclaim v, rectify
v, red-hot a, redouble v, reduce v, reechy a, refine v,
relics n, remorseless a, repast n, repeal n, repine v,
replenish v, replication n, represent v, repute n,
resemblance n, resistance n, resolutely adv, retention n,
retrait a, reverently adv, reverse v, revile v, riddling v,
ridge n, rigorous a, rivet n, rocky a, ruth n, ruthful a,
SABLE a, sagittary n, saint-like a, sapling n, satin n,
satire n, savageness n, scalp n, scarf v, sceptre(d) v,
school-days n, sciatica n, scimitar n, scion n, scold n,
scorpion n, scout v, screw v, scribe n, scutcheon n, scythe
n, seaman n, sea-sick a, seconded v, sedition n, seethe v,
seizure n, self-willed a, sententious a, sequestration n,
sere a, sessa int, severals n, sevennight n, shade v,
sharpen v, sharpness n, shear v, shelf n, shipboy n,
shipman n, shipwrack n, shove v, shrewdly adv, shrug n,
sightless a, signet n, sincere a, sincerely adv, single v,
silver v, sinowy/ewy a, skill(s) v, skilled a, skittish a,
sleek a, slink v, slop n, sluttish a, smart n, smith n,
smooth-faced a, smug a, snarl v, snip n, snore n, snow-
white a, sob n, solace n, soles n, solid a, sorceress n,
sorcery n, southern a, sow n, spangle v, specialty n,
spherical a, spinster n, spiteful a, sportive a, springe n,
spritely a, spruce a, spurn n, square a, squeak v, squier
n, squirrel n, stage v, staggers n, stalk n, stark a,
statesman n, stealer n, steep a, stench n, sterling a,
stern [of ship] n, stoutly adv, stow v, streak n, streak v,
stripling n, strumpet a, stubbornness n, student n,
subornation n, substantial a, successfully adv, successively
adv, successor n, sufficiently adv, summit n, sunny a,
sunset n, supporter n, suppose n, surmise v, surmount v
intr, surrender n, swoon v, sycamore n, TAFFATA n, talker n,
tamely adv, tar n, targe n, tarre v, tempter n, terribly
adv, tetchy a, thankings n, thankless a, theorie n,
thereabouts adv, thereat adv, thereunto adv, therewith adv,
thews n, thicken v, thievish a, thimble n, thinkings n,
thistle n, thrall n, thread v, thriftless a, tickle a,
tight a, tie v, tithe n, toast n, torrent n, torturer n,
tract n, tradesman n, tradition n, tragedian n, trap v,
travail v, treasonous a, treble [voice] n, tributary a,
triumphantly adv, true-bred a, true-hearted a, tub n, tuft n,
turbulant a, turkey-cock n, twist v, twopence n, type n,
tyrannize v, ULCEROUS a, umpeer a, unacquainted a, unbated a,
unbolt v, unbraced a, unburthen v, unbutton v, uncertainty n,

uncurrent a, under-bear v, undermine v, undiscovered a,
unfeigned a, unfeignedly adv, unfelt a, unfinished a, unfix
v, unfledged a, ungartered a, ungently adv, unguarded a,
unicorn n, university n, unlawfully adv, unlettered a,
unlikely a, unmake v, unnecessary a, unpaid a, unparalleled
unpruned a, unrelenting a, unreverend a, unreverent a,
unsanctified a, unseasonable a, unseasoned a, unsought a,
untuned a, untutored a, unwashed a, unwieldy a,
unwillingness n, unwise a, uprear v, urchin n, urinal n,
urine n, usurpation n, valure n, vane n, variation n, vast
n, vaulty a, vehemency n, venom a, verbal a, vestal a,
viceroy n, vie v, vigilance n, vigilant a, vilely adv,
vinegar n, viperous a, virginal a, visitor n, volley n,
voluble a, votarist n, voucher n, vouchsafe/vout- v, WAGGON
n, waggoner n, wand n, wanderer n, ward v, wares n,
warranty n, waspish a, water-drops n, water-fly n, weakly
adv, wean v, wearer n, weariness n, wearisome a,
weathercock n, well-appointed a, well-beloved a, well--
deserving a, well-spoken a, wend v, whatsomever pron,
whistle n, whoop int, wild-cat n, willow a, withstand v,
witless a, wittingly adv, wolvish a, womanly a, wood a.
woodbine n, woodman n, wool n, woollen a, worm-eaten a,
wreak n, wrist n, wronger n, YELL v, yoke-fellow n,
youngling n. (1092)

FOUR-WORDS: abatement n, abbot n, abortive a, abridge v,
abridgment n, abstinence n, absurd a, acquittance n,
adoption n, advertisement n, aery a, afar adv, affirm v,
affront v, a-field adv, afresh adv, aggravate v, agreement n,
alacrity n, alight v, alley n, almanac n, amendment n,
anatomy n, ancestry n, a-piece adv, apoplexy n, apple-john n,
approof n, arrest n, arrogant a, ascribe v, aspic n,
assuredly adv, atomy n, attaint n, attest v, austere a,
authentic a, awkward a, BAGPIPE n, ballet n, banns n,
barbarism n, bare-headed adv, barely adv, bargain v, basin n,
bath n, bawcock n, at bay adv, beldam(e) n, benefactor n,
benison n, bestir v, betime adv, bewail v, bile n, blackness
n, bladder n, blazon n, blazon v, blend/blent v, blindness
n, blister n, bloodily adv, bodily adv, bodkin n, booty n,
botch v, bowl v, brevity n, brimful a, brisk a, brittle a,
bruit v, bubble v, buck [animal] n, bucket n, buff n,
buffet n, burgonet n, bustle v, butler n, butt [barrel] n,
CALLAT/CALLET n, calumny n, cannibal n, captivate v, carpet
n, carrier n, cashier v, casque n, catalogue n, catastrophe
n, cattle n, certify v, chameleon n, changeable a, chaos n,
chaplain n, character v, cherry n, christian-like a,
chronicle v, cicatrice n, cinder n, cipher n, city-gate n,
civet n, clad v, clap v, claw v, cleanse v, clergy n,
clergyman n, clog v, cloister n, clutch v, college n,
comforter n, comment v, commerce n, commune v communicate v,
compromise n, compt n, congregation n, conserve v, consummate
v, continent a, contriver n, convent v, coney-catch v,
cordial a, core n, countermand n, covetousness n, cozener n,
crage v, cripple n, croak v, crotchet n, crouch v, cruelly
adv, crystal n, cuckoldly adv, cunningly adv, curate n,
curiosity n, curiously adv, DALE n, damsel n, dangerously
adv, dank a, daub v, dauntless a, debase v, debate n,
deboshed a, decipher v, decrease v, default n, deliberate a,
delivery n, demeanour n, denounce v, dependant/ent n, deprave

v, describe v, desist v, desk n, desperation n, destine v, determinate v, detraction n, digress v, diffuse v, dilate v, diminish v, disburse v, discomfit v, disgest v, dishonesty n, disjoin v, dismay n, dismount v, disobedient a, disobey v, disposing v, dissentious a, dissolution n, distaff n, distaste v, distressful a, dole [grief] n, dolphin n, donation n, dotard n, doubtfully adv, downy a, dreamer n, drizzle v, dross n, drunkenness n, dumb-show n, dwarf n, EARNESTNESS n, edify v, eel n, effectual a, effusion n, egregious a, eke v, elder [tree] n, elephant n, eloquent a, embassage n, embattle v, embowel v, endear v, endowment n, ensconce v, entitle v, equity n, erewhile adv, eruption n, especial a, esperance n, everlastingly adv, exalt v, exasperate v, excite v, exclaim n, executor n, exhalation n, exhibit v, expedience n, expend v, experiment n, expert a, extant a, exterior a, extract v, FABRIC n, fairness n, faithless a, familiarity n, familiarly adv, farmer n, farthing n, father-in-law n, favourer n, fealty n, festival a, festival n, feverous a, fife n, fighter n, fin n, fire-new a, flatly adv, flax n, fleer v, flier n, floor n, flowery a, foin v, foot-boy n, foppery n, forespent v, forgery n, forgetful a, fork n, fortress n, foully adv, fragrant a, fretful a, friend v, froth n, fruitless a, fry n, fuel n, fumble v, GAGE v, gale n, gallery n, galliard n, garlic n, garnish v, gauntlet n, gelding n, giant a, gin n, gipsy n, giver n, glare v, glorify v, glow-worm n, glue v, godden int, godhead n, godly a, goodnight n, good-year int, gorge n, gorge v, graff v, grandmother n, gratitude n, gratulate v, greediness n, gripe n, gule n, guise n, gum [resin] n, HABITATION n, half-faced a, harp n, hastily adv, hatch n, hearth n, heart-string n, heathen a, helpful a, heroical a, hight a, hoar a, holiday a, hood v, horn-mad a, hostility n, hotly adv, hulk n, ICICLE n, ignobly adv, ignominy/ignomy n, ill-favouredly adv, immure v, imp n, impartial a, impostor n, impotent a, impudence n, include v, incomparable a, incurable a, indictment n, industrious a, inevitable a, infirm a, ingredient n, inland a, inly a, instigation n, intelligent a, interchange n, interchange v, interchangeably adv, interlude n, intermission n, intrusion n, invade v, inveterate a, invocation n, ireful a, ivy n, iwis adv, JADE v, jangle v, joiner n, jointly adv, juggler n, justicer n, KENNEL n, kibe n, knack n, knead v, LADE(N) v, lamely adv, lance v, lapse v, lapwing n, largely adv, largess n, 'larum n, lash v, laurel n, leather a, lecher n, lecherous a, leprosy n, lesson v, licentious a, liegeman n, lifeless/liveless a, limbo n, litter v, lizard n, lobby n, lubber n, lull v, MACE n, madcap a, maim n, mainly adv, mandate n, mandrake n, mannerly a, marshal v, martyr n, mastiff n, maze n, meanly adv, meanwhile adv, medicinable a, medlar n, meekness n, mellow a, mellow v, mineral n, minority n, misconster v, miscreant n, misgive v, mishap n, misty a, misplace v, mixture n, mole n, momentary a, monastery n, muffler n, mutually adv, NAKEDNESS n, naturally adv, neat [cattle] n, niggardly a, nimbly adv, ODDLY adv, oily a, onion n, opposer n, oratory n, ostent n, ort n, outgo v, outlaw n, outright adv, outwardly adv, overjoy v, overnight adv, over-read v, overshade v, overshine v, overshoot v, PAINFULLY adv, pale-faced a, palfrey n, pancake n, pantler n, pap n,

parallel n, parallel v, parasite n, pard n, parish n,
parlous a, partaker n, partition n, patrimony n, pebble n,
pedigree n, perfidious a, permission n, personate v, pick-
purse n, pied a, pish int, pitifully adv, plainsong n,
platform n, plentiful a, plume v, poesy n, poise n,
ponderous a, pool n, position n, prabble n, prediction n,
prefix v, prentice n, preposterously adv, preserver n,
prim(e)rose n, privily adv, prompt a, properly adv,
prophetess n, prone a, propagate v, prorogue v, prosecute v,
prudent a, puling v, pump [shoe] n, punk n, purposely adv,
pursuivant n, poetical a, QUAFF v, quean n, RASHLY adv,
rave v, ravel out v, ravin n, rearward n, receptacle n,
recommend v, recorder n, recourse n, reflect v, refrain v,
register v, rein v, remission n, remit v, remorseful a,
rendezvous n, renowmed a, respective a, restitution n,
restless a, retail v, reveller n, reversion n, revolution n,
rhenish n, rheumatic a, riband n, ribbon n, rig v, rivet v,
rote n, rust n, SAINTED a, sally n, sanctimony n, sanguine
a, saw [saying] n, scabbard m, scamble v, scandal v,
scath(e) n, science n, scoff n, scraps n, scum n, sedge n,
self-love n, sender n, sensibly adv, separation n, sequence
n, sequester v, servitude n, severally adv, severity n,
shadow v, shamefully adv, shank n, shapeless a, sharply adv,
shears n, sheath n, sheep-cote n, shipwrack n, shiver v,
shortness n, shriek n, shrow n, shrud n, sibyl n, sieve n,
sift v, signory n, simple [drug] n, singularity n, sip v,
sixty a, skilless a, slavery n, slipper n, slut n, smack
[taste] n. smirch v, smite v, snap v, snare v, snatch n,
sneak v, soak v, sob v, sod(den) v, solace v, soothsayer n,
sorcerer n, sour v, specify v, spectator n, speculation n,
spell v, sportful a, spouse n, spout n, spray n, spring-
time n, sprinkle v, spunge n, spungy a, squadron n, stall
v, stand n, step-dame n, stockfish n, stope/stoup n, store-
house n, stormy a, strawberry n, stride v, stripe n,
struggle v, sty n, successive a, sufficiently adv, suffocate
v, suffrage n, sully v, sulphur n, sumptuous a, sunburn v,
sundry a, superfluity n, superstitious a, surname v, survey
n, swart a, swearer n, swiftness n, TATTLE v, teacher n,
tediousness n, teen n, temperately adv, temporize v,
temptation n, tendance n, test n, thatch v, thirst n,
thoroughly adv, throe n, thwack v, tinct n, tithe v, toast
v, tongueless a, topmast n, traitorously adv, trample v,
traverse v, trench v, tributary a, triple a, troublous a,
true-love a, trumpeter n, tumultuous a, tun n, twin a,
twin v, twins n, twit v, UNAPT a, unavoided a, unbuckle v,
unchaste a, unconstant a, undaunted a, undeserved a,
undoubted a, uneasy a, unfeeling a, unfirm a, unhandsome a,
unhappily adv, unheard a, unholy a, unknit v, unlearned a,
unlucky a, unmanly a, unmatchable a, unmatched a,
unreasonable a, unsafe a, unsavory a, unsay v, unshaked/n a,
unsheathe v, unskilful a, unspeak v, unstained a, untainted
a, unthankfulness n, unthrifty a, untrue a, untruth n,
unworthiness n, unyoke v, uproar n, VACANCY n, vagabond n,
vainglory n, valorous a, vassal a, venerable a, vestal n,
vicar n, victual n, videlicet adv, violation n, vital a,
vocation n, vomit v, WAITING-GENTLEWOMAN n, wan a, warble v,
wardrobe n, wassail n, watchman n, welfare n, well-a-day
int, westward adv, wheel v, whetstone n, whoso pron, wield

v, wizard n, working-day n, wormwood n, worry n, wreathe v,
(753)
FIVE-WORDS: adhere v, adjudge v, admiral n, adulteress n,
adventurous a, aery [of eagles] n, affable -, airy a, alarm
n, aleven a, allied a, allure v, anatomize v, anew adv,
annoyance n, annual a, antic n, antiquity n, antipodes n,
apish a, apology n, apothecary n, apparition n, appellant n,
artillery n, attention n, attentive a, audit n, augurer n,
avenge v, BARN n, baffle v, bat [mammal] n, beach n, beacon
n, beck n, beckon v, beer n, behove v, belch v, besmear v,
birthright v, bier n, blaspheme v, bleat v, blench v, blithe
a, bloodless a, boatswain n, bob v, bog n, boil n, bowls
[game] n, brainsick a, brawn n, bridle v, brim n, bristle
v, brothel n, brutish a, bug n, butchery n, button n,
CABLE n, canonize v, caruncle n, carelessly adv, carp v,
cates n, cavil v, celebration n, certes adv, chamber-door n,
chat v, chatter v, chew vclasp v, clearly adv, clog n,
comely a, comfortless a, comment n, complement n, complice
n, comprehend v, concealment n, conduit n, confederacy n,
consign v, conster v, consult v, consumption n, contradiction
n, conveniently adv, copper n, cordial n, cough v,
countenance v, counter n, courtezan n, covert a, coy a,
crawl v, crocodile n, crop n, crowd v, crust n, currish a,
curtsy n, curtsy v, cypress n, DAFF v, damask a, dastard n,
daunt v, defeat n, defective a, demean v, denote v,
deputation n, derision n, desperately adv, dexterity n,
difficulty n, dimensions n, disable v, discolour v,
discomfort n, displace v, dispossess v, distant a,
distemperature n, divert v, divine v, divulge v, doleful a,
dowager n, downward adv, dulness n, dumbness n, dwarfish a,
dwelling n, EARLDOM n, encamp v, encourage v, enkindle v,
enlargement n, enthral v, enthrone v, epithet n, espouse v,
estimate n, evasion n, exact v, exceedingly adv,
exclamation n, exhibition n, exposition n, expostulate v,
extempore adv, extent n, extol v, extraordinary a,
extremely adv, FAIRS n, fang n, fantastic a, favourable a,
feelingly adv, fee-simple n, fell v.a, fen n, fester v,
figure v, filch v, first-born a, fishermen n, flash n,
float v, flower-de-luce n, fob/fub v, foeman n, foison n,
foolishly adv, forgetfulness n, fornication n, fortitude n,
forwardness n, foulness n, fulness n, fulsome a, fume n,
fur(red) v, furniture n, future n, GARB n, gasp v, gaudy
a, gawds n, gentleman-like a, gibbet n, gibe n, gird
[encircle] v, girdle v, glimmer v, gloze v, godlike a,
gossip v, gotten v, gout n, graceless a, graciously adv,
graft v, greybeard n, gyves n, HABILIMENT n, haggard n, hairy
a, handkercherun, hammer v, handmaid n, harbinger n, hawk
[sport] v, hay [grass] n, headless a, hearse n, heedful a,
hoard v, hostile a, heraldry/dy n, hereabout(s) adv, hereof
adv, hest n, hilding v, hive [bee-] n, hoarse a, hobby-
horse n, hogshead n, homicide n, horseback, on adv, humble-
bee n, husks n, hypocrisy n, ICY a, idolatry n, ill-beseeming
a, illusion n, imitation n, immodest a, importance n,
importunate a, incapable a, incessant a, incestuous a,
inconstancy n, index n, indifferently adv, infallible a,
infidel n, infinitely adv, ingrate a, injunction n, injure v,
inside n, instal v, intellect n, interpretation n,
inter(ro)gatory n, interview n, invincible a, ire n, JAY n,

jet v, jig n, join(ed)-stool n, jointure n, jollity n,
judicious a, justle v, KNIGHTED v, KNIGHTLY a, LACE n, lap
v, lath n, lavish a, leathern a, leave-taking n, legacy n,
legitimate a, lively a, lively adv, loll v, 'long of prep,
looker-on n, lordly a, love-song n, lowliness n, luggage n,
lullaby n, lustful a, luxurious a, MAGICIAN n, maim v, maker
n, malcontent a/n, male n, manacle n, manned v, manor n,
mare n, margent n, marquess n, marrow n, martyr v, massy a,
material a, meagre a, melodious a, menace v, mickle a,
mightiness n, milk-white a, mill n, minstrel n, misbegot(ten)
a, miser n, modestly adv, motley a, motley n, mountaineer n,
mountebank n, mournful a, mutter v, NEARLY adv, new-born a,
night-gown n, noisome a, nonpareil n, novice n, nursery n,
O n, oats n, obstinate a, oostruction n, odour n, offering n,
olive n, orison n, ostler n, outstretch v, overpeer v,
overtop v, overture n, PALPABLE a, palmer n, paradox n,
partisan n, paste n, pave(i) v, paw n, peacock n, peal n,
pear n, pell-mell adv, pelting a, pendant n, penetrate v,
penitent n, perdie,'dy int, perfect v, perfit a, perpend v,
perturbation n, pester v, petitioner n, pill v, pillage n,
placket n, plantain n, politician n, pond n, poniard n,
poorly adv, porch n, portent n, possibility n, posy n,
precise a, predecessor n, predominant a, prescribe v,
presumptuous a, prettily adv, prime a, progeny n, prophetic
a, provender n, prune v, purblind a, QUART n, quillet n,
quirk n, quittance n, quiver v, quote v, RAG n, rake v,
ransack v, rapture n, rar(e)ity n, raught ppl, re [music] n,
reak v, reed n, refer v, reference n, refuge n, remiss a,
repulse n, reservation n, respite n, resume v, retirement n,
retort v, revoke v, revolve v, roll n, rood n, rudely adv,
rudeness n, rue n, ruff n, ruffle v, rugged a, runagate n,
SADDLE n, saddle v, safeguard n, sage a, sayings n, scab n,
scan v, schedule n, school v, screech-owl n, scripture n,
sear v, seel v, semblable a, seriously adv, serviceable a,
servitor n, seventeen a, shave v, shell n, shent ppl,
shepherdess n, shoot n, shrowd/ewd a, simile n, simpleness n,
singe v, singly adv, sink n, sisterhood n, slanderer n,
slaughterman n, slavish a, sleeper n, slime n, slough n,
slowly adv, smear v, smoky a, sop n, sorrowful a, span n,
spout v, stagger v, stall n, steeple n, stem n, sterile a,
stick n, stirrup n, stray n, strond n, stump n, subjection n,
succor v, sugar v, suppliant n, supposition n, supremacy n,
surgery n, suspicious a, sweeting n, TALLOW n, team n,
tell-tale n, tenderly adv, thicket n, thirst v, thirteen a,
threepence n, threshold n, thrice-noble a, thrifty a, thrill
v, tilt v, timely a, toll v, tool n, toothache n, topple
v, torch-bearer n, trade v, trader n, traduce v, tragical
a, trail n, transgress v, transparent a, trap n, treble v,
true-love n, trull n, trump n, truncheon n, tumult n,
twigs n, twinkle v, twofold a, UNACCUSTOMED a, unawares
adv, unbind v, unbruised a, unclean a, uncleanly a,
uncover v, undertaking n, unequal a, ungoverned a, union n,
unload v, unlock v, unmeet a, unprepared a, unprofitable a,
unseal v, unspeakable a, unspotted a, unsure a, untaught a,
unwelcome a, VACANT a, valiantly adv, validity n, varlot n,
varnish v, vasty a, vault v, vaward n, vehement a, veil n,
venomed a, venomous a, vent n, venturous a, verdict n,
vesture n, violently adv, venturously adv, visible a, void

v, votary n, WADE v, wall v, warder n, waver v, weaken v, whirlwind n, whiteness n, whoremaster n, whosoever pron, widower n, willfully adv, YEARLY a/adv, yellow n, ZEALOUS a.

(591)

SIX-WORDS: ABJURE v, abstract n, acceptance n, accomplished a, accustomed a, acquire v, across adv, active a, agony n, ambush n, anguish n, annoy v, antic a, appal v, appertain v, appliance n, aptly adv, aqua-vitae n, arbitrate v, arbitrament n, arch n, archer n, arithmetic n, armourer n, arrival n, arrogance n, assistant n, auspicious a, avail v, BABOON n, bane n, bashful a, basis n, bawdy-house n, bed-chamber n, beholder n, bellow v, benediction n, beset v, beweep v, blab v, blank a, blanket n, blaze n, bleak a, blister v, bolt [fetter] n, bonfire n, bonnet n, bout n, bracelet n, brach n, bran n, bribe n, bridal a, broker n, brooch n, brood n, bubole n, buffet v, bur/burr n, butterfly n, CANKER v, captivity n, carpenter n, cart n. caterpillar n, celerity n, challenger n, chap n, cheater n, chicken n, choice a, circle v, civility n, cliff n, clout n, coach n, coal-black a, combatant n, comet n, compact a, complot n, confiscate v, conjuration n, constantly adv, construe v, contradict v, cottage n, counterpoise v, covet v, cramp n, craven a, crystal a, curb n, customary a, customer n, cutpurse n, DAWNING n, dazzle v intr, deflower v, deformity n, dejected a, delightful a, desirous a, desolate a, determination n, detestable a, dialogue n, diligent a, dip v, discuss v, dishonourable a, disinherit v, dispose n, ditty n, doff v, dole [share] n, downfall n, drain v, dregs n, drone n, dulcet a, dump n, durance n, dusky a, dye v, EASTERN a, eclipse n, eighteen a, eminence n, eminent a, empery n, enamoured v, endow v, enforcement n, enfranchisement n, enroll v, entrap v, erst adv, evident a, exactly adv, examination n, excellently adv, excrement n, exhale v, external a, eyeless a, FA [music] n, fable n, factor n, familiar n, fee v, firmament n, fitly adv, fleece n, forbearance n, fordo v, forerun v, formerly adv, fraught v, GARDENER n, gasp n, ghastly a, glance n, god-a-mercy int, godfather n, graceful a, grasp v, grease n, greedy a, grievously adv, grossness n, grudge v, guardian n, HAMMER n, happily adv, hard-favoured a, hardness n, hardy a, harness n, harp v, haunt n, headlong adv, heir-apparent n, henceforward adv, hind [deer] n, hog n, homeward adv, honourably adv, hoodwink v, hoof n, hostage n, humane a, hymn n, IMMACULATE a, imperfect a, imperfection n, impiety n, impious a, incertain a, incision n, incite v, indue v, infectious a, inheritor n. insurrection n, intercession n, invent v, inventory n, islander n, JUICE n, KERNEL n, kick v, LACE v, lake n, lame v, lantern n, lease n, leather n, lesson n, lethargy n, levity n, libertine n, lid a, life-blood n, limit v, lisp v, litter n, log n, looking-glass n, lout n, lucky a, lump n, lunacy n, MANIFOLD a, marble n, merciless a, milk v, misprise v, misprision n, mishope(n/d) a, mistrust n, mocker n, moderate a, monarchy n, monk n, mote n, mow [cut down] v, mud n, mum a, NAMELY adv, necessaries n, needy a, nether a, nominate v, nonny int, OBSEQUIOUS a, officious, offspring n, ooze n, ounce [weight] n, outrageous a, o(v/')erblow(n) v, overreach/raught v, oyster

n, PAGAN n, palter v, paramour n, parch v, parish n,
passenger n, pat adv, penitence n, pent ppl, penury n,
piety n, pith n, plea n, plight v, poise v, popular a,
populous a, postern n, potency n, precedent n, precisely
adv, prescription n, preservation n, presumption n,
prevention n, privately adv, promontory n, prop n, prospect
n, prostrate a, providence n, pry v, puny a, purgation n,
QUAIL v, quaintly adv, quell v, quip n, quondam a,
RAVENOUS a, ray n, recall v, reflection n, reformation n,
rely v, renounce v, reprieve n, resort v, retreat n,
rhetoric n, righteous a, rip v, roam v, roughly adv,
ruinous a, runaway n, SALVATION n, sandy a, sauciness n,
scape n, score v, scout n, securely adv, sentinel n, shock
n, shrill a, shrine n, shrive v, sincerity n, sinister a,
skirts n, slack a, slack v, slaughter-house n, slide v.
slily adv, sloth n, smart v, snare n, snore v, sociable a,
solemnly adv, sorely adv, spin v, spiritual a, sprightly a,
square n, stag n, stalk v, stark adv, startle v, steer v,
stifle v, stir n, stride n, successful a, such-like a,
sunshine n, supplant v, supplication n, surveyor n, swarm v,
swerve v, synod n, TACKLE n, tangle v, tapestry n, tenant
n, testy a, thankfulness n, thunderbolt v, timorous a, top
v, tractable a, trudge v, turf n, UNABLE a, unadvised a,
unfurnished v, ungrateful a, unkindly adv, unloose v,
unpleasing a, unprovided a, unrest n, unsatisfied a,
unusual a, unwillingly adv, uplift(ed) v, upper a, usual a,
VALLEY n, variable a, vaunt v, veil v, venison n, void a,
vulture n, WARMTH n, weasel n, well-favoured a, whereas
conj, wholly adv, windy a, winnow v, worshipful a, wreath
n, YEW n.   (409)

SEVEN-WORDS: ache n, achievement n, acre n, adorn v,
adultery n, ally n, almighty a, amiable a anchor v,
artificial a, astonish v, athwart adv/prep, atone v,
attendance n, attire v, attribute n, audacious a, autumn n,
awry adv, BABBLE v, baleful a, banquet v, barber n,
barefoot adv, barge n, baron n, bay [dogs] v, beautify v,
beaver n, beetle n, behead v, blemish v, bonny a,
boundless a, bountiful a, bower n, bowl [cup] n, box [on
the ear] n, brake n, brandish v, bravery n, breeches n,
breeder n, brine n, brotherhood n, bulwark n, burden n,
butler n, CAGE n, canon [law] n, canopy n, carrion a,
caution n, ceremonious a, chant/chaunt v, cheat v,
childhood n, chough n, citadel n, cloud v, colt n, compact
n, compare n, compound n, concord n, confront v, conjoin
v, conjuror n, constraint n, contagion n, contaminate v,
convenience n, convoy n, corporal a, courtly a, cow n,
cowslip n, crab n, cricket n, DALLIANCE n, darken v,
darkly adv, darling n, daw n, deceitful a, deck n, deign
v, demonstrate v, despiteful a, devote v, digestion n,
direful a, dirty a, discharge n, disdain v, discredit v,
discreet a, disfigure v, dislike n, disorder v, dissuade v,
distinctly adv, distract a, ditch n, divine n, doctrine n,
doe n, doer n, dog n, dominion n, drench v, dub v,
EARTHQUAKE n, echo n, effeminate a, elsewhere adv, emboss
v, enact v, encompass v, endless a, engross v, ensign n,
envenom v, espy v, esquire n, eternity n, exact a,
example v, exchequer n, expel v, expound v, extenuate v,

extort v, eyesight n, FAMILY n, fardel n, farm n,
favourite n, fearfully adv, fence [art of] n, fence v,
fickle a, flat n, foresay v, forester n, fragment n,
freshly adv, GAINSAY v, galley n, gay a, geld v, gem n,
genius n, ghostly a, ginger n, goblin n, gore n, gore v,
grate v, grind v, grumble v, gun n, HAPLESS a, hard-
hearted a, haviour n, heart-blood n, hem int, herring n,
highway n, hoist v, honestly adv, hoop n, hoot v, hop v,
hopeless a, horribly adv, hover v, humbleness n, IDOL n,
ill-favoured a, imaginary a, imminent a, impossibility
n, imputation n, incest n, incorporate a, indirectly adv,
infringe v, inn n, innocency n, irons n, JACKANAPE n,
juggle v, juvenal n, KNAVISH a, LANTHORNE n, lard v,
lawless a, lecture n, legate n, liable a, limp v, link v,
lioness n, lot n, lottery n, lousy a, luxury n, MAGNANIMOUS
a, malignant a, marble a, mariner n, massacre n, mature a,
mead [meadow] n, meek a, melody n, merchandise r, mildly
adv, mildness n, misdoubt v, mix v, mortify v, moveable n,
multiply v, murmur v, musical a, mustard n, mutinous a,
mutiny v, NEGLIGENT a, ninth a, northern a, nostril n, nun
n, nut n, OBDURATE a, obligation, obsequies n, oftentimes
adv, operation n, oration n, orderly adv, overrule v,
PAINTER n, parchment n, pare v, parley v, partial a,
passionate a, pavilion n, peculiar a, peerless a, perplex
v, pertain v, pestilent a, pie n, pillar n, plod v,
portend v, portion n, portly a, posture n, preach v,
preposterous a, print v, privilege v, probation n,
prodigious a, prolong v, promotion n, protestation n,
prune/pruin n, puritan n, QUIETNESS n, RAIMENT n, rattle v,
raze v, recoil v, recreant n, refresh v, religiously adv,
relish n, remote a, repair n, replete a, reprehend v,
requital n, rigo(u)r n, robbery n, rosemary n, ruler n,
SACK v, sanctity n, scrape v, sconce n, sea-side n, sect
n, senate-house n, shameless a, shrewdly adv, singular a,
skilful a, soil v, source n, spade n, spoon n, spotless a,
stable n, station n, stature n, stony a, sulphurous a,
supreme a, swaggerer n, swiftly adv, sympathise v, TAINT n,
taunt n, tawny a, temporal a, testify v, thaw v, thirsty
a, thorny a, threescore a, throne n, totter v, tragic a,
transformation n, treasury n, treaty n, treble a, trim n,
trivial a, tug v, UNCLASP v, uneven a, unjustly adv,
unluckily adv, unpeople v, unquiet a, unsettle v,
unwilling a, VENGE v, vineyard n, violate v, viper n,
WAKEN v, wane v, wantonness n, ware a, wasp n, wasteful a,
weaver n, winner n, womanhood n, womanish a, wrongfully adv.
(358)

EIGHT-WORDS: ACCOMMODATE v, accomplish v, accord n, advocate
n, alteration n, angle v, animal n, appeal n, apron n,
argosy n, aright adv, arraign v, assay n, awful/aweful a,
BALANCE n, basilisk n, bastardy n, battlement n, bawdy a,
bearer n, befriend v, berry n, bewray v, blaze v, blemish
n, bourn n, butcher v, CALF'S-SKIN n, carcass n, card n,
career n, carefully adv, carouse v, carrion n, chaff n,
changeling n, chastisement n, chat n, childish a, chimney
n, chuck n, churl n, clime n, closely adv, codpiece n,
compulsion n, confuse v, congeal v, conjecture n, convince
v, coronet n, corporal n, courser n, courtship n, covenant
n, covetous a, creation n, credulous a, curl v, DART n,

death-bed n, declare v, deface v, deprive v, depth n,
devout a, disobedience n, dispense v, domestic a, doubly
adv, drawer n, drudge n, duck n, dug n, duly adv, EAGER
a, earnestly adv, earthy a, elect v, embark v, enclose v,
entire a, epilogue n, equally adv, erect v, exempt a,
expedient a, FACULTY n, feeder n, female a, fig n, firmly
adv, flay v, flea n, fleet v, foh int, foresee v,
forestall v, forked a, foster v, frank a, frosty a,
future a, GAMESTER n, gaol/jail n, gaze n, gentles n,
glide v, glister v, glitter v, gorgeous a, gramercy int,
grapple v, graze [cattle] v, HARMFUL a, hasten v,
hatches n, haven n, havoc n, hawk n, healthful a,
heavily adv, hedge v, hellish a, hen n, hereditary a,
heresy n, heretic n, hermit n, hitherward adv, hook n,
hurry v, IMPOSITION n, indenture n, indirect a, interior a,
inhuman a, injustice n, JAR n, jester n, jocund a, LASS n,
lenity n, lessen v, level n, lick v, lieu n, lighten v,
lightness n, lime v, lineal a, lineament n. liquid a,
loser n, lour/lower v, MAD v, magistrate n, majestical a,
male n, mate v, matron n, maw n, meditate v, method n,
mew [shut in] v, midst n, military a, mire n, moist a,
mole [birth-mark] n, moonlight n, morsel n, mule n, musty
a, NEAT a, neighbour a, neighbour by v, nerve n, new-made
a, OPENLY adv, ostentation n, over(o'er)board adv, over-
run v, PAINFUL a, parrot n, pedant n, phoenix n, pig n,
plebeians n, pledge v, plunge v, porridge n, powder n,
prank n, prattle v, precept n, prerogative n, prodigy n,
pudding n, puppy n, QUEST n, RADIANT a, rancor n, rapt
ppl, ratify v, reave/reft v, recompense v, recreant a,
recreation n, regiment n, remnant n, repentance n, resort
n, .revengeful a, rive v, roast v, royally adv, rub n,
rust v, SACRAMENT n, sallet n, salutation n, savo(u)r v,
separate v, sequent a, sergeant n, severe a, shuffle v,
smack v, snail n, snuff n, soften v, sojourn v,
solemnize v, somebody n, sot n, spaniel n, spear n, stint
v, straightway adv, strut v, suburbs n, summons n, supple
a, surmise n, TEMPERATE a, thankfully adv, thereupon adv,
throughout adv, thump v, timeless a, transgression n,
troublesome a, UNCIVIL a, ungracious a, unwholesome a,
uttermost a, VELVET a, velvet n, verge n, verify v, vial
n, viand n, WARP v, wheat n, whine v, wilderness n,
workman n, writer n. (272)

NINE-WORDS: ABODE n, abound v, accordingly adv, accuser n,
adopt v, adversity n, advertise v, amble v, appease v,
assign v, attorney n, augment v, aweary a, BAGGAGE n, bail
n, bark [of tree] n, basely adv, beadle n, bench n, betake
v, bias n, bitterly adv, bitterness n, blank n, board n,
bolt [missile] n, breadth n, CAKE n, caper v, celebrate v,
chariot n, charter n, cheerfully adv, cherub(im) n,
chivalry n, climate n, combat v, commendable a, commotion
n, compassion n, competitor n, confirmation n, conjunction
n, construction n, contention n, continuance n, conveyance
n, crow n, DEARTH n, deliverance n, detect v, diet v,
differ v, dignify v, discard v, disdainful a, disorder n,
dispute v, distemper n, doit n, dolour n, doubtless adv,
drab n, dungeon n, dunghill n, duteous a, EBB n, education
n, elf, elves n, enfranchise v, entirely adv, eyeball n,

eyne n, FETTER v, fifth a, finely adv, fist n, fitness n, fog n, fondly adv, forfeiture n, forfend v, forgiveness n, forgo v, fortnight n, foundation n, GESTURE n, giant n, glean v, gratify v, gratis adv, greasy a, grin v, groat n, guiltiness n, gulf n, gull n, HALFPENNY/CE n, hallow v, halter n, headstrong a, hearty a, hilt n, hitherto adv, hopeful a, hug v, hypocrite n, IGNOBLE a, implore v, important a, impression n, impudent a, inconstant a, induce v, industry n, infuse v, ingenious a, insolent a, intolerable a, JERKIN n, jolly a, KERN n, LEVEL a, 'long v, MAIN [ocean] n, manifest v, masque n, modern a, mould n, NICELY adv, nip v, OPPOSITION n, orphan n, o(v)ercharge v, PANT v, parle n, partake v, peck v, penn(yw)orth n, petticoat n, playfellow n, poetry n, prelate n, pretend v, principal n, provision n, puissance n, puissant a, QUIETLY adv, RACK v, rebuke v, redemption n, reform v, repetition n, residence n, robber n, SACRIFICE v, sale n, sauce v, savour n, servingman n, session n, seventh a, sexton n, shrift n, shroud v, sicken v, slightly adv, soldiership n, solely adv, square v, stealth n, stew v, strait a/adv, suborn n, sweeten v, TABOR n, target n, taunt v, tenor n, therewithal adv, threefold a/adv, thwart v, tinker n, trace v, traitorous a, trash n, travail n, trencher n, trot v, turtle n, tutor v, UNBORN a, unhallowed a, untie v, untimely adv, utterly adv, VALE n, vicious a, WAFT v, weave/woven v, wedlock n, wherewith pron, whirl v, wight n, wildness n, woodcock n, wooden a, wren n, wrest v, wretchedness n, (213)

TEN-WORDS: A-BED adv, abundance n, admittance n, advancement n, afore prep, alehouse n, amount v, anchor n, apparel v, BANDY v, batter v, bauble n, beggarly a, bewitch v, billow n, boil v, braggart n, brew v, budge v, bullet n, CABIN n, caitiff n, calendar n, cancel v, channel n, chapel n, chastise v, choleric a, circle n, cloy v, cog v, comedy n, commence v, commonweal n,

confessor n, conflict n, consideration n, contemn v, controversy n, conversation n, corpse n, courageous a, DART v, degenerate a, den n, denial n, different a, diligence n, dim a, din n, dinner-time n, dirt n, disaster n, dishonest a, dissension n, distinction n, dive v, divinity n, dotage n, draught n, EDICT n, embracement n, enow a/adv, environ v, expressly adv, FACTIOUS a, faintly adv, falcon n, flag n, flaw n, fling v, flinty a, formal a, fortify v, frankly adv, GALLOP v, gash n, gear n, generous a, 'gin, 'gan v, glow v, gnat n, gripe v, grudge n, HART n, helmet n, hind [boor] n, hip [anatomy] n, humanity n, huntsman n, IDIOT n, incur v, indignity n, influence n, iniquity n, insinuate v, inspire v, interpreter n, interrupt v, itch v, LICENSE n, lime n, MANIFEST a, martial a, meditation n, meteor n, mince v, mouldy a, muffle v, mutton n, NAVY n, ODIOUS a, ominous a, ordinary a, outrun v, overflow v, overween v, PACKET n, paragon n, patron n, pedlar n, penitent a, perdition n, persever v, plate n, probable a, publicly adv, pupil n, puppet n, purchase n, RACK [torture] n, rashness n, rebellious a, redress v, relation n, riotous a, roundly adv, SEQUEL n, sew v, shriek v, sleepy a, smock n, soar v, sola int, supper-time n, surly a, swan n, swinge v, swound v, TEMPERANCE n, <u>traffic n</u>, UNCERTAIN a, unfit a, unfortunate a, <u>utterance n</u>, VICTOR n, village n, <u>WESTERN</u> a, whale n, whelp n, wive v, YARE a, yawn v. (162)

In the foregoing list words which appear in Part A (Acts I,2; II; and IV,4) of <u>Edward III</u> are heavily underlined; words which appear in Part B (the rest of the play) are lightly underlined, if not also in Part A.   There are also many other words in <u>Edward III</u> which did not find their way into the above list, although they linked with 2 - 10 canonical plays.   This was partly due to differences in the principles by which the counts were made, but, more importantly, by the greater meticulousness with which differents parts of speech were distinguished, and with which long Concordance entries were scrutinised.   A list of these words, classified by their number of links, distinguishing Parts A and B of the play, and with line reference, is appended.

Part A. 2. 334 sere a, 342 vnder adv, 349 host v, 552 solace n, 638 combe n, 674 vomit n, 689 excommunicate v, 711 recantation n, 833 malcontent a, 1928 whole n, 2006 ingirt ppl, 2036 avail n, 3. 195 bubble n, 228 booty n, 318 contemplatiue a, 357 attracted v, 357 cherry a, 361 bricke n, 379 broad adv, 412 arber n, 449 layes n, 478 hollowes n, 610 clip v, 2063 proffer n, 4. 185 untuned a, 421 laments n, 550 consort n, 674 disgorged v, 935 winter a, 998 wedding a, 1993 submissiue a, 5. 198 reuerence v, 199 embassage n, 406 shadow v, 633 chaplaines n, 668 lesned v, 678 medicinable a, 907 choysest a, 988 verdict n, 1923 eie lesse a, 2016 capring v, 6. 532 sweetnes n, 535 disposse v, 830 via int, 1928 stronger adv, 2075 halfepenie n, 7. 184 scornefull a, 204 riders n, 275 hardie a, 433 abstract n, 747 heye n, 757 eye-sight n, 793 mote n, 1006 preuention n, 1940 streight a, 8. Citie a, 359 scarlet a, 444 passionat a, 739 housd v, 816 endles a, 9. 139 unseuill a, 202 neighbor a, 453 oreefe 474 voluntarie a, 623 Enacted v, 929 captiue a, 958 ouerbeare v, 1946 rounds v, 1985 Esquires n, 10. 205 rust v, 229 discry v, 330 Presageth v, 593 retaine v, 655 proferest v, 762 portion n, 914 lanthorne n, 1951 proudly adv,   (77)

Part B. 2. 63 entayld v, 1124 titely adv, 1379 pilfering v, 1430 luckles a, 1538 patronage v, 1541 saples a, 1650 intrencht v, 1654 often a, 1697 furtherance n, 2106 crauen a, 2119 metamorphosd v, 2185 safe conduct n, 2251 staruelings n, 2522 sere a, 2585 hereafter a, 3. 80 vnpolisht a, 116 scard v, 1055 malcontents n, 1504 impall v, 1514 lawrell a, 1528 deferd v, 1540 numb a, 1583 narrowly adv, 1640 regreet v, 1655 woodmans n, 1686 Pellican n, 1690 motto n, 2097 vnder a, 2187 presidents n, 2256 stoned v, 2344 Litter n, 4. 70 repossesse v, 1115 streaming v, 1119 Figuring v, 1171 cates n, 1223 lively adv, 1401 woluish a, 1468 bit n, 1493 intombed v, 1566 thousandfold adv, 1687 beak n, 2137 fraude n, 2201 beneath adv, 2204 hoopt v, 2220 fig int, 2255 elders n, 2488 ordynaunce n, 5. 6 Seignorie n, 83 fealty n, 98 droane n, 1053 flocke v, 1119 horned a, 1185 misgiues v, 1313 Shelter v, 1499 orderly adv, 1651 thicke adv, 2112 squares n, 2233 attainted v, 2355 assault v, 2409 reuerence v, 2479 diffusd v, 2523 hearse n, 2531 redoubted a, 2587 resolue n, 6. 146 footemen n, 1167 stir v, 1210 maymed v, 1214 aloft adv, 1287 flowring v, 2092 midnight a, 2276 brauerie n, 2486 trenches n, 2527 blaze v, 7. 82 arrogaunce n, 147 muster n, 148 elect v,

1090 hardie a, 1104 ouerweaning v, 1217 reeling v, 1316
tottering v, 1381 couenant n, 1399 foil v, 1600 snares n,
1610 sauor n, 1831 aduocate n, 2238 Rebell v, 2422 contradict
v, 8. 45 shewers n, 49 rakt v, 1049 soothing v, 1547
conspiratours n, 1563 betook v, 1651 battered v, 2083 husht v,
2085 Murmure v, 2092 tongue-tied a, 2095 coach n, 2372 seruile
a, 2491 deadly adv, 2498 fasten v, 2524 Citie a, 9. 98 lazy
a, 107 voluntarie a, 1125 plough v, 1133 Anchor n, 1179
Retreae n, 1319 guide n, 1436 Captiue a, 1757 deseased a,
1789 Esquire n, 2221 bandie v, 2299 louring v, 2491 darts n,
2496 chaind v, 10. 6 retayne v, 89 plumes n, 151 warie a,
1109 discribde v, 1224 compulsion n, 1306 midst n, 1345
poffered v, 1350 mould n, 1400 dym v, 1533 persaging v,
1643 gulphes n, 1871 paradise n, 2545 proudly adv, 2419
Northern a, 2484 descry v, 2492 slender a.   (130)

Interrelationships between Shakespeare's plays as revealed by the link words

Link words have been combined into two groups, those with 2 to 6 and those with 7 to 10 appearances. Expected numbers are proportionate to Hart's counts of the numbers of different (lexical) words in the plays (see pp. 90–1). Observations in statistically significant excess over their expectations are distinguished by underlining.

Enumeration of observed numbers by the Computer Unit, King's College, University of London.

Links with 2 HENRY VI

1	2	3	4	5	6	7	8	9	10	11
	2H6	55			65			110		
2790	3H6	83	35.75	232	71	43.97	161	154	79.72	193
3014	1H6	82	38.62	212	69	47.50	145	151	86.12	175
3218	R3	64	41.23	155	69	50.71	136	133	91.95	145
2037	Err	20	26.10		33	32.10	103	53	58.20	
2578	Tit	67	33.03	203	67	40.63	165	134	73.66	182
2463	Shr	42	31.56	134	48	38.82	124	90	70.37	128
2153	TGV	26	27.59		30	33.93		56	61.52	
2872	LLL	22	36.80		54	45.26	119	76	82.06	
2916	Rom	41	37.36	110	56	45.95	122	97	83.32	116
2833	R2	50	36.30	138	60	44.65	134	110	80.95	136
2363	MND	18	30.28		32	37.24		50	67.52	
2901	Jo	45	37.17	121	45	45.72		90	82.89	109
2571	MV	26	32.94		35	40.52		61	73.46	
3028	1H4	46	38.80	119	44	47.72		90	86.52	104
3130	2H4	46	40.10	115	38	49.33		84	89.43	
2527	Wiv	21	32.38		28	39.82		49	72.20	
2396	Ado	20	30.70		26	37.76		46	68.46	
3162	H5	66	40.51	163	63	49.83	126	129	90.35	143
2218	JC	23	28.42		34	34.95		57	63.37	
2578	AYL	22	33.03		37	40.63		59	73.66	
2534	TN	19	32.47		32	39.93		51	72.40	
3882	Ham	44	49.74		49	61.18		93	110.92	
3360	Tro	40	43.05		44	52.95		84	96.00	
2705	AWW	23	34.66		31	42.63		54	77.29	
2669	MM	21	34.20		41	42.06		62	76.26	
3015	Oth	24	38.63		41	47.52		65	86.15	
2521	Tim	21	32.30		31	39.73		52	72.03	
3339	Lr	31	42.78		51	52.62		82	95.40	
2652	Mac	38	33.98	112	37	41.79		75	75.77	
3004	Ant	26	38.49		34	47.34		60	85.83	
3130	Cor	28	40.10		31	49.33		59	89.43	
1049	Per[1]	10	13.44		18	16.63	109	28	29.97	
1393	Per[2]	14	17.85		23	21.95	105	37	39.80	
3260	Cym	31	41.77		50	51.38		81	93.15	
2965	WT	27	37.99		57	46.73	122	84	84.72	
2562	Tmp	27	32.83		25	40.38		52	73.20	
2659	H8	33	34.07		49	41.90	117	82	75.97	108
100447		1287	1287.00		1583	1582.99		2870	2870.02	

1. No. of different words in play (count by Hart). 2. Name of
play, abbreviated. 3. Two-six-fold link words: no. of links.
4. No. expected. 5. Ratio of observed to expected, as percent.
6. Seven-ten-fold link words, no. of links observed. 7. No. expected. 8. Ratio of observed to expected, as percent. 9. Total
two-ten-fold link words: no. of links observed. 10. No. expected.
11. Ratio of observed to expected, as percent.
Statistically significant positive deviations are underlined.

Links with 3 H E N R Y V I

1	2	3	4	5	6	7	8	9	10	11
3146	2H6	84	29.87	281	72	43.48	174	156	71.34	219
	3H6	48			40			94		
3014	1H6	81	28.61	283	77	39.74	194	158	68.35	231
3218	R3	52	30.55	170	67	42.43	158	119	72.98	163
2037	Err	20	19.34	103	28	26.86	104	48	46.19	104
2578	Tit	52	24.47	213	57	33.99	168	109	58.46	186
2463	Shr	24	23.38	103	52	32.47	160	76	55.86	136
2153	TGV	18	20.44		30	28.39	106	48	48.83	
2872	LLL	26	27.27		33	37.86		59	65.13	
2916	Rom	25	27.68		49	38.44	127	74	66.13	112
2833	R2	33	26.90	123	56	37.35	150	89	64.25	139
2363	MND	17	22.43		21	31.15		38	53.59	
2901	Jo	30	27.54	109	38	38.25		68	65.79	103
2571	MV	29	24.41	119	28	33.90		57	58.30	
3028	1H4	17	28.75		34	39.92		51	68.67	
3130	2H4	24	29.72		37	41.27		61	70.98	
2527	Wiv	13	23.99		18	33.32		31	57.31	
2396	Ado	15	22.75		16	31.59		31	54.34	
3162	H5	32	30.02	107	42	41.69	101	74	71.71	103
2218	JC	15	21.06		27	29.24		42	50.30	
2578	AYL	19	24.47		22	33.99		41	58.46	
2534	TN	12	24.06		20	33.41		32	57.47	
3882	Ham	37	36.85	100	42	51.18		79	88.04	
3360	Tro	22	31.90		42	44.30		64	76.20	
2705	AWW	19	25.68		28	35.66		47	61.34	
2669	MM	20	25.34		32	35.19		52	60.53	
3015	Oth	25	28.62		39	39.75		64	68.37	
2521	Tim	19	23.93		26	33.24		45	57.17	
3339	Lr	23	31.70		28	44.02		51	75.72	
2652	Mac	20	25.18		29	34.96		49	60.14	
3004	Ant	27	28.52		30	39.61		57	68.12	
3130	Cor	28	29.72		45	41.27	109	73	70.98	103
1049	Per[1]	6	9.96		17	13.83	123	23	23.79	
1393	Per[2]	2	13.22		20	18.37	109	22	31.59	
3260	Cym	16	30.95		40	42.98		56	73.93	
2965	WT	15	28.15		26	39.09		41	67.24	
2562	Tmp	16	24.32		27	33.78		43	58.10	
2659	H8	24	25.24		34	35.06		58	60.30	
100803		957	956.99		1329	1329.03		2286	2286.00	

1. No. of different words in play (count by Hart).   2. Name of play, abbreviated.   3. Two-six-fold link words: no. of links. 4. No. expected.   5. Ratio of observed to expected, as percent. 6. Seven-ten-fold link words, no. of links observed.   7. No. expected.   8. Ratio of observed to expected, as percent.   9. Total two-ten-fold link words: no. of links observed.   10. No. expected. 11. Ratio of observed to expected, as percent.
Statistically significant positive deviations are underlined.

Links with 1 HENRY VI

1	2	3	4	5	6	7	8	9	10	11
3146	2H6	85	37.32	228	73	44.85	163	158	82.17	192
2790	3H6	86	33.09	260	72	39.78	181	158	72.87	217
	1H6	52			54			100		
3218	R3	62	38.17	162	69	45.88	150	131	84.05	156
2037	Err	24	24.16		36	29.04	124	60	53.20	113
2578	Tit	48	30.58	157	59	36.76	161	107	67.33	159
2463	Shr	36	29.21	123	32	35.12		68	64.33	106
2153	TGV	32	25.54	125	21	30.70		53	56.23	
2872	LLL	33	34.07		32	40.95		65	75.01	
2916	Rom	34	34.59		39	41.57		73	76.16	
2833	R2	47	33.60	140	60	40.39	149	107	73.99	145
2363	MND	32	28.03	114	17	33.69		49	61.72	
2901	Jo	28	34.41		50	41.36	121	78	75.77	103
2571	MV	22	30.50		28	36.66		50	67.15	
3028	1H4	30	35.92		32	43.17		62	79.09	
3130	2H4	37	37.13		42	44.63		79	81.75	
2527	Wiv	17	29.97		18	36.03		35	66.00	
2396	Ado	22	28.42		23	34.16		45	62.58	
3162	H5	45	37.51	120	49	45.08	109	94	82.59	114
2218	JC	18	26.31		36	31.62	114	54	57.93	
2578	AYL	20	30.58		30	36.76		50	67.33	
2534	TN	15	30.06		22	36.13		37	66.18	
3882	Ham	35	46.05		61	55.35	110	96	101.39	
3360	Tro	47	39.85	118	60	47.91	125	107	87.76	122
2705	AWW	22	32.08		26	38.57		48	70.65	
2669	MM	17	31.66		41	38.05	108	58	69.71	
3015	Oth	25	35.76		39	42.99		64	78.75	
2521	Tim	21	29.90		25	35.94		46	65.85	
3339	Lr	31	39.60		42	47.61		73	87.21	
2652	Mac	25	31.46		38	37.81	101	63	69.27	
3004	Ant	22	35.63		44	42.83	103	66	78.46	
3130	Cor	32	37.13		40	44.63		72	81.75	
1049	Per[1]	18	12.44	145	9	14.96		27	27.40	
1393	Per[2]	8	16.52		12	19.86		20	36.38	
3260	Cym	36	38.67		42	46.48		78	85.15	
2965	WT	24	35.17		43	42.27	102	67	77.44	
2562	Tmp	17	30.39		39	36.53	107	56	66.92	
2659	H8	40	31.54	127	33	37.91		73	69.45	105
100579		1193	1193.02		1434	1434.03		2627	2626.97	

1. No. of different words in play (count by Hart). 2. Name of
play, abbreviated. 3. Two-six-fold link words: no. of links.
4. No. expected. 5. Ratio of observed to expected, as percent.
6. Seven-ten-fold link words, no. of links observed. 7. No. expected. 8. Ratio of observed to expected, as percent. 9. Total
two-ten-fold link words: no. of links observed. 10. No. expected.
11. Ratio of observed to expected, as percent.
Statistically significant positive deviations are underlined.

Links with R I C H A R D   I I I

1	2	3	4	5	6	7	8	9	10	11
3146	2H6	62	37.99	163	66	49.30	137	128	87.29	147
2790	3H6	55	33.69	163	74	43.72	169	129	77.41	167
3014	1H6	60	36.39	165	69	47.23	146	129	83.63	154
	R3	58			67			125		
2037	Err	26	24.60	106	37	31.92	116	63	56.52	111
2578	Tit	51	31.13	164	51	40.41	126	102	71.53	143
2463	Shr	31	29.74	104	35	38.60		66	68.34	
2153	TGV	31	26.00	119	31	33.74		62	59.74	104
2872	LLL	40	34.68	115	40	45.01		80	79.69	100
2916	Rom	33	35.21		53	45.70	116	86	80.91	106
2833	R2	52	34.21	152	56	44.40	126	108	78.60	137
2363	MND	28	28.53		28	37.03		56	65.56	
2901	Jo	41	35.03	117	57	45.46	125	98	80.49	122
2571	MV	33	31.04	106	32	40.29		65	71.33	
3028	1H4	30	36.56		42	47.45		72	84.01	
3130	2H4	34	37.79		43	49.05		77	86.84	
2527	Wiv	17	30.51		27	39.60		44	70.11	
2396	Ado	18	28.93		30	37.55		48	66.48	
3162	H5	46	38.18	120	60	49.55	122	106	87.73	121
2218	JC	21	26.78		36	34.76	104	57	61.54	
2578	AYL	31	31.13		37	40.40		68	71.53	
2534	TN	20	30.60		33	39.71		53	70.31	
3882	Ham	49	46.87	105	63	60.84	104	112	107.71	104
3360	Tro	40	40.57		37	52.66		77	93.23	
2705	AWW	28	32.66		41	42.39		69	75.05	
2669	MM	27	32.23		49	41.83	117	76	74.05	103
3015	Oth	28	36.41		53	47.25	112	81	83.65	
2521	Tim	24	30.44		27	39.51		51	69.95	
3339	Lr	34	40.32		41	52.33		75	92.64	
2652	Mac	26	32.02		28	41.56		54	73.58	
3004	Ant	23	36.27		53	47.08	113	76	83.35	
3130	Cor	24	37.79		35	49.05		59	86.84	
1049	Per¹	13	12.67	103	15	16.44		28	29.11	
1393	Per²	13	16.82		20	21.83		33	38.65	
3260	Cym	27	39.36		51	51.09		78	90.45	
2965	WT	28	35.80		50	46.47	108	78	82.27	
2562	Tmp	26	30.94		33	40.15		59	71.09	
2659	H8	42	32.11	131	40	41.67		82	73.78	111
100375		1212	1212.00		1573	1573.03		2785	2784.99	

1. No. of different words in play (count by Hart). 2. Name of play, abbreviated. 3. Two-six-fold link words: no. of links. 4. No. expected. 5. Ratio of observed to expected, as percent. 6. Seven-ten-fold link words, no. of links observed. 7. No. expected. 8. Ratio of observed to expected, as percent. 9. Total two-ten-fold link words: no. of links observed. 10. No. expected. 11. Ratio of observed to expected, as percent.
Statistically significant positive deviations are underlined.

Links with E R R O R S

1	2	3	4	5	6	7	8	9	10	11
3146	2H6	23	20.76	111	36	26.89	134	59	47.64	122
2790	3H6	18	18.41		29	23.85	122	47	42.25	111
3014	1H6	25	19.88	126	30	25.76	116	55	45.65	120
3218	R3	25	21.23	118	39	27.50	142	64	48.73	131
	Err	27			31			58		
2578	Tit	22	17.01	129	21	22.03		43	39.04	110
2463	Shr	20	16.25	123	32	21.05	152	52	37.30	139
2153	TGV	13	14.20		14	18.40		27	32.61	
2872	LLL	21	18.95	111	26	24.55	106	47	43.49	108
2916	Rom	27	19.24	140	29	24.92	116	56	44.16	127
2833	R2	10	18.69		23	24.21		33	42.90	
2363	MND	24	15.59	154	20	20.20		44	35.79	123
2901	Jo	25	19.14	131	30	24.79	121	55	43.93	125
2571	MV	14	16.96		20	21.97		34	38.94	
3028	1H4	28	19.98	140	17	25.88		45	45.86	
3130	2H4	24	20.65	116	25	26.75		49	47.40	103
2527	Wiv	25	16.67	150	17	21.60		42	38.27	110
2396	Ado	8	15.81		13	20.48		21	36.29	
3162	H5	20	20.86		28	27.03	104	48	47.89	100
2218	JC	8	14.63		18	18.96		26	33.59	
2578	AYL	14	17.01		20	22.03		34	39.04	
2534	TN	12	16.72		23	21.66	106	35	38.38	
3882	Ham	36	25.61	141	34	33.18	102	70	58.79	119
3360	Tro	20	22.17		37	28.72	129	57	50.89	112
2705	AWW	16	17.85		21	23.12		37	40.97	
2669	MM	14	17.61		24	22.81	105	38	40.42	
3015	Oth	16	19.89		21	25.77		37	45.66	
2521	Tim	11	16.63		25	21.55	116	36	38.18	
3339	Lr	26	22.03	118	24	28.54		50	50.57	
2652	Mac	16	17.50		18	22.67		34	40.16	
3004	Ant	11	19.82		20	25.68		31	45.49	
3130	Cor	16	20.65		25	26.75		41	47.40	
1049	Per[1]	8	6.92	116	5	8.97		13	15.89	
1393	Per[2]	8	9.19		12	11.91	101	20	21.10	
3260	Cym	21	21.51		28	27.86	100	49	49.37	
2965	WT	20	19.56	102	21	25.34		41	44.90	
2562	Tmp	11	16.90		21	21.90		32	38.80	
2659	H8	14	17.54		22	22.73		36	40.27	
101556		670	670.02		868	868.01		1538	1538.01	

1. No. of different words in play (count by Hart).   2. Name of play, abbreviated.   3. Two-six-fold link words: no. of links. 4. No. expected.   5. Ratio of observed to expected, as percent. 6. Seven-ten-fold link words, no. of links observed.   7. No. expected.   8. Ratio of observed to expected, as percent.   9. Total two-ten-fold link words: no. of links observed.   10. No. expected. 11. Ratio of observed to expected, as percent.
Statistically significant positive deviations are underlined.

Links with T I T U S

1	2	3	4	5	6	7	8	9	10	11
3146	2H6	66	30.71	215	67	36.19	185	133	66.90	199
2790	3H6	56	27.23	206	56	32.09	174	112	59.33	189
3014	1H6	47	29.42	160	48	34.67	138	95	64.09	148
3218	R3	48	31.41	153	56	37.02	151	104	68.43	152
2037	Err	22	19.88	111	22	23.43		44	43.32	102
	Tit	46			57			103		
2463	Shr	36	24.04	150	39	28.33	138	75	52.37	143
2153	TGV	22	21.02	105	28	24.77	113	50	45.78	109
2872	LLL	23	28.03		30	33.04		53	61.07	
2916	Rom	40	28.46	141	44	33.54	131	84	62.01	135
2833	R2	32	27.65	116	47	32.59	144	79	60.24	131
2363	MND	19	23.07		22	27.18		41	50.25	
2901	Jo	23	28.32		42	33.37	126	65	61.69	105
2571	MV	24	25.10		36	29.57	122	60	54.67	110
3028	1H4	24	29.56		25	34.83		49	64.39	
3130	2H4	22	30.55		26	36.01		48	66.56	
2527	Wiv	25	24.67	101	18	29.07		43	53.73	
2396	Ado	19	23.39		17	27.56		36	50.95	
3162	H5	32	30.86	104	36	36.37		68	67.24	101
2218	JC	14	21.65		30	25.51	118	44	47.16	
2578	AYL	22	25.16		34	29.65	115	56	54.82	102
2534	TN	17	24.73		21	29.15		38	53.88	
3882	Ham	30	37.89		38	44.66		68	82.55	
3360	Tro	33	32.80	101	36	38.65		69	71.45	
2705	AWW	15	26.40		23	31.12		38	57.52	
2669	MM	24	26.05		22	30.70		46	56.75	
3015	Oth	19	29.43		27	34.68		46	64.11	
2521	Tim	16	24.61		16	29.00		32	53.61	
3339	Lr	19	32.59		30	38.41		49	71.00	
2652	Mac	14	25.89		22	30.51		36	56.39	
3004	Ant	29	29.32		31	34.56		60	63.88	
3130	Cor	27	30.55		26	36.01		53	66.56	
1049	Per[1]	16	10.24	156	10	12.07		26	22.31	117
1393	Per[2]	11	13.60		14	16.02		25	29.62	
3260	Cym	32	31.82	101	43	37.50	115	75	69.32	108
2965	WT	32	28.94	111	31	34.11		63	63.05	
2562	Tmp	14	25.01		22	29.47		36	54.48	
2659	H8	22	25.95		27	30.59		49	56.54	
101015		986	986.00		1162	1162.01		2148	2148.02	

1. No. of different words in play (count by Hart).   2. Name of play, abbreviated.   3. Two-six-fold link words: no. of links.
4. No. expected.   5. Ratio of observed to expected, as percent.
6. Seven-ten-fold link words, no. of links observed.   7. No. expected.   8. Ratio of observed to expected, as percent.   9. Total two-ten-fold link words: no. of links observed.   10. No. expected.
11. Ratio of observed to expected, as percent.
Statistically significant positive deviations are underlined.

Links with S H R E W

1	2	3	4	5	6	7	8	9	10	11
3146	2H6	42	28.25	149	40	37.45	107	82	65.70	125
2790	3H6	23	25.05		50	33.22	151	73	58.27	125
3014	1H6	38	27.06	140	33	35.88		71	62.94	113
3218	R3	29	28.89	100	35	38.31		64	67.20	
2037	Err	19	18.29	104	31	24.25	128	50	42.54	118
2578	Tit	38	23.15	164	38	30.69	124	76	53.84	141
	Shr	35			54			89		
2153	TGV	22	19.33	114	28	25.63	109	50	44.96	111
2872	LLL	46	25.79	178	55	34.19	161	101	59.98	168
2916	Rom	29	26.18	111	35	34.72	101	64	60.90	105
2833	R2	17	25.44		36	33.73	107	53	59.16	
2363	MND	19	21.22		47	28.13	167	66	49.35	135
2901	Jo	23	26.05		32	34.54		55	60.58	
2571	MV	20	23.08		34	30.61	111	54	53.69	101
3028	1H4	49	27.19	180	31	36.05		80	63.24	127
3130	2H4	29	28.10	103	40	37.26	107	69	65.37	106
2527	Wiv	19	22.69		25	30.09		44	52.77	
2396	Ado	22	21.51	102	20	28.53		42	50.04	
3162	H5	23	28.39		43	37.65	114	66	66.04	
2218	JC	13	19.91		25	26.41		38	46.32	
2578	AYL	25	23.15	108	39	30.69	127	64	53.84	119
2534	TN	23	22.75	101	25	30.17		48	52.92	
3882	Ham	25	34.85		47	46.22	102	72	81.07	
3360	Tro	26	30.17		35	40.00		61	70.17	
2705	AWW	24	24.29		23	32.20		47	56.49	
2669	MM	17	23.96		20	31.78		37	55.74	
3015	Oth	22	27.07		29	35.89		51	62.97	
2521	Tim	23	22.63	102	25	30.01		48	52.65	
3339	Lr	34	29.98	113	40	39.75	|C|	74	69.73	107
2652	Mac	15	23.81		16	31.57		31	55.38	
3004	Ant	18	26.97		29	35.76		47	62.74	
3130	Cor	18	28.10		32	37.26		50	65.37	
1049	Per[1]	8	9.42		11	12.49		19	21.91	
1393	Per[2]	15	12.51	120	22	16.58	133	37	29.09	127
3260	Cym	25	29.27		38	38.81		63	68.08	
2965	WT	32	26.62	120	36	35.30	102	68	61.92	110
2562	Tmp	20	23.00		26	30.50		46	53.50	
2659	H8	18	23.87		33	31.66	104	51	55.53	

101130   908   907.99   1204 1203.98   2112 2111.99

1. No. of different words in play (count by Hart).   2. Name of
play, abbreviated.   3. Two-six-fold link words: no. of links.
4. No. expected.   5. Ratio of observed to expected, as percent.
6. Seven-ten-fold link words, no. of links observed.   7. No. expected.   8. Ratio of observed to expected, as percent.   9. Total
two-ten-fold link words: no. of links observed.   10. No. expected.
11. Ratio of observed to expected, as percent.
Statistically significant positive deviations are underlined.

Links with T W O G E N T L E M E N

1	2	3	4	5	6	7	8	9	10	11
3146	2H6	24	20.22	119	32	23.54	136	56	43.76	128
2790	3H6	18	17.93	100	32	20.88	153	50	38.81	129
3014	1H6	34	19.37	176	23	22.55	102	57	41.92	136
3218	R3	35	20.68	169	36	24.08	150	71	44.76	159
2037	Err	12	13.09		14	15.24		26	28.33	
2578	Tit	23	16.57	139	32	19.29	166	55	35.86	153
2463	Shr	21	15.83	133	33	18.43	179	54	34.26	158
	TGV	14			16			30		
2872	LLL	23	18.46	125	23	21.49	107	46	39.95	115
2916	Rom	22	18.74	117	27	21.82	124	49	40.56	121
2833	R2	25	18.21	137	24	21.20	113	49	39.41	124
2363	MND	20	15.19	132	18	17.68	102	38	32.87	116
2901	Jo	21	18.65	113	23	21.71	106	44	40.35	109
2571	MV	14	16.52		18	19.24		32	35.76	
3028	1H4	14	19.46		28	22.66	124	42	42.12	
3130	2H4	16	20.12		23	23.42		39	43.54	
2527	Wiv	22	16.24	135	15	18.91		37	35.15	105
2396	Ado	15	15.40		14	17.93		29	33.33	
3162	H5	19	20.32		19	23.66		38	43.98	
2218	JC	14	14.26		9	16.60		23	30.85	
2578	AYL	21	16.57	127	12	19.29		33	35.86	
2534	TN	16	16.29		12	18.96		28	35.25	
3882	Ham	23	24.95		28	29.05		51	54.00	
3360	Tro	20	21.60		15	25.14		35	46.74	
2705	AWW	11	17.39		19	20.24		30	37.63	
2669	MM	13	17.15		22	19.97	110	35	37.12	
3015	Oth	13	19.38		13	22.56		26	41.94	
2521	Tim	20	16.20	123	16	18.86		36	35.07	103
3339	Lr	18	21.46		27	24.98	108	45	46.44	
2652	Mac	12	17.05		18	19.84		30	36.89	
3004	Ant	9	19.31		20	22.48		29	41.78	
3130	Cor	19	20.12		15	23.42		34	43.54	
1049	Per[1]	3	6.74		6	7.85		9	14.59	
1393	Per[2]	6	8.95		15	10.42	144	21	19.38	108
3260	Cym	16	20.95		26	24.39	107	42	45.35	
2965	WT	20	19.06	105	22	22.18		42	41.24	102
2562	Tmp	11	16.47		12	19.17		23	35.64	
2659	H8	9	17.09		18	19.89		27	36.99	
101440		652	651.99		759	759.02		1411	1411.02	

1. No. of different words in play (count by Hart). 2. Name of play, abbreviated. 3. Two-six-fold link words: no. of links. 4. No. expected. 5. Ratio of observed to expected, as percent. 6. Seven-ten-fold link words, no. of links observed. 7. No. expected. 8. Ratio of observed to expected, as percent. 9. Total two-ten-fold link words: no. of links observed. 10. No. expected. 11. Ratio of observed to expected, as percent.
Statistically significant positive deviations are underlined.

Links with L O V E ' S   L A B O U R ' S   L O S T

1	2	3	4	5	6	7	8	9	10	11
3146	2H6	21	32.64		50	40.67	123	71	73.31	
2790	3H6	28	28.95		31	36.07		59	65.01	
3014	1H6	36	31.27	115	33	38.96		69	70.23	
3218	R3	42	33.39	126	40	41.60		82	74.99	109
2037	Err	21	21.13		25	26.33		46	47.47	
2578	Tit	24	26.75		34	33.33	102	58	60.07	
2463	Shr	44	25.55	172	47	31.84	148	91	57.39	159
2153	TGV	21	22.34		27	27.83		48	50.17	
	LLL	53			52			105		
2916	Rom	52	30.25	172	47	37.69	125	99	67.95	146
2833	R2	27	29.39		24	36.62		51	66.01	
2363	MND	33	24.52	135	40	30.55	131	73	55.06	133
2901	Jo	26	30.10		44	37.50	117	70	67.60	104
2571	MV	31	26.67	116	38	33.23	114	69	59.91	115
3028	1H4	35	31.42	111	43	39.14	110	78	70.56	111
3130	2H4	38	32.47	117	38	40.46		76	72.94	104
2527	Wiv	21	26.22		37	32.67	113	58	58.88	
2396	Ado	34	24.86	137	32	30.97	103	66	55.83	118
3162	H5	40	32.81	122	61	40.87	149	101	73.68	137
2218	JC	14	23.01		15	28.67		29	51.68	
2578	AYL	35	26.75	131	59	33.33	177	94	60.07	156
2534	TN	30	26.29	114	28	32.76		58	59.05	
3882	Ham	60	40.28	149	54	50.18	108	114	90.46	126
3360	Tro	47	34.86	135	44	43.43	101	91	78.29	116
2705	AWW	23	28.06		32	34.97		55	63.03	
2669	MM	22	27.69		33	34.50		55	62.19	
3015	Oth	22	31.28		32	38.97		54	70.26	
2521	Tim	18	26.16		19	32.59		37	58.74	
3339	Lr	24	34.64		42	43.16		66	77.81	
2652	Mac	12	27.52		24	34.28		36	61.80	
3004	Ant	14	31.17		37	38.83		51	70.00	
3130	Cor	21	32.47		24	40.46		45	72.94	
1049	Per[1]	7	10.88		15	13.56	111	22	24.44	
1393	Per[2]	10	14.45		18	18.01		28	32.46	
3260	Cym	26	33.82		38	42.14		64	75.96	
2965	WT	38	30.76	124	46	38.33	120	84	69.09	122
2562	Tmp	20	26.58		27	33.12		47	59.70	
2659	H8	28	27.59	101	24	34.37		52	61.96	
100721		1045	1044.99		1302	1301.99		2347	2346.99	

1. No. of different words in play (count by Hart). 2. Name of play, abbreviated. 3. Two-six-fold link words: no. of links. 4. No. expected. 5. Ratio of observed to expected, as percent. 6. Seven-ten-fold link words, no. of links observed. 7. No. expected. 8. Ratio of observed to expected, as percent. 9. Total two-ten-fold link words: no. of links observed. 10. No. expected. 11. Ratio of observed to expected, as percent.
Statistically significant positive deviations are underlined.

Links with R O M E O

1	2	3	4	5	6	7	8	9	10	11
3146	2H6	36	31.62	114	52	42.58	122	88	74.18	119
2790	3H6	25	28.04		42	37.74	111	67	65.79	102
3014	1H6	33	30.30	109	43	40.77	105	76	71.07	107
3218	R3	37	32.35	114	61	43.53	140	98	75.88	129
2037	Err	24	20.48	117	26	27.56		50	48.03	104
2578	Tit	46	25.91	178	38	34.88	109	84	60.79	138
2463	Shr	24	24.76		33	33.32		57	58.08	
2153	TGV	21	21.64		26	29.13		47	50.77	
2872	LLL	54	28.87	187	45	38.85	116	99	67.72	146
	Rom	46			44			40		
2833	R2	29	28.48	102	48	38.33	125	77	66.80	115
2363	MND	35	23.75	142	31.	31.97		66	55.72	118
2901	Jo	43	29.16	147	41	39.25	104	84	68.41	123
2571	MV	28	25.84	108	37	34.78	106	65	60.63	107
3028	1H4	43	30.44	141	51	40.96	125	94	71.40	132
3130	2H4	28	31.46		33	42.34		61	73.81	
2527	Wiv	25	25.40		23	34.19		48	59.59	
2396	Ado	23	24.08		24	32.41		47	56.50	
3162	H5	21	31.78		40	42.78		61	74.56	
2218	JC	17	22.30		30	30.01		47	52.30	
2578	AYL	29	25.91	112	49	34.88	140	78	60.79	128
2534	TN	22	25.47		25	34.28		47	59.75	
3882	Ham	45	39.02	115	47	52.52		92	91.54	101
3360	Tro	37	33.77	110	39	45.46		76	79.23	
2705	ANW	24	27.18		37	36.59	101	61	63.78	
2669	MM	20	26.83		34	36.11		54	62.94	
3015	Oth	27	30.31		32	40.79		59	71.09	
2521	Tim	12	25.34		41	34.11	120	53	59.45	
3339	Lr	30	33.56		47	45.17	104	77	78.73	
2652	Mac	22	26.66		32	35.88		54	62.54	
3004	Ant	14	30.20		35	40.64		49	70.84	
3130	Cor	20	31.46		36	42.34		56	73.81	
1049	Per[1]	9	10.54		14	14.19		23	24.74	
1393	Per[2]	11	14.00		23	18.85	122	34	32.85	104
3260	Cym	36	32.77	110	45	44.10	102	81	76.87	105
2965	WT	23	29.80		40	40.11		63	69.92	
2562	Tmp	22	25.75		25	34.66		47	60.41	
2659	H8	17	26.73		37	35.97	103	54	62.70	
100677		1012	1011.96		1362	1362.03		2374	2374.01	

1. No. of different words in play (count by Hart). 2. Name of play, abbreviated. 3. Two-six-fold link words: no. of links. 4. No. expected. 5. Ratio of observed to expected, as percent. 6. Seven-ten-fold link words, no. of links observed. 7. No. expected. 8. Ratio of observed to expected, as percent. 9. Total two-ten-fold link words: no. of links observed. 10. No. expected. 11. Ratio of observed to expected, as percent.
Statistically significant positive deviations are underlined.

Links with RICHARD II

1	2	3	4	5	6	7	8	9	10	11
3146	2H6	46	29.94	154	60	39.47	152	106	69.41	153
2790	3H6	36	26.55	136	51	35.00	146	87	61.55	141
3014	1H6	50	28.69	174	52	37.81	134	102	66.50	153
3218	R3	48	30.63	157	66	40.37	163	114	71.00	161
2037	Err	11	19.39		22	25.55		33	44.94	
2578	Tit	36	24.54	147	53	32.34	164	89	56.88	156
2463	Shr	17	23.44		38	30.90	123	55	54.34	101
2153	TGV	27	20.49	132	24	27.01		51	47.50	107
2872	LLL	30	27.33	110	26	36.03		56	63.36	
2916	Rom	28	27.75	101	45	36.58	123	73	64.33	113
	R2	34			58			92		
2363	MND	18	22.49		19	29.64		37	52.13	
2901	Jo	30	27.61	109	56	36.39	154	86	64.00	134
2571	MV	26	24.47	106	20	32.25		46	56.72	
3028	1H4	37	28.82	128	44	37.99	116	81	66.80	121
3130	2H4	41	29.79	138	34	39.26		75	69.06	109
2527	Wiv	18	24.05		8	31.70		26	55.75	
2396	Ado	14	22.80		17	30.06		31	52.86	
3162	H5	37	30.09	123	60	39.67	151	97	69.76	139
2218	JC	10	21.11		25	27.82		35	48.93	
2578	AYL	21	24.54		32	32.34		53	56.88	
2534	TN	18	24.12		17	31.79		35	55.91	
3882	Ham	39	36.95	106	46	48.70		85	85.65	
3360	Tro	40	31.98	125	42	42.15		82	74.13	111
2705	AWW	19	25.75		20	33.93		39	59.68	
2669	MM	20	25.40		22	33.48		42	58.88	
3015	Oth	19	28.70		29	37.82		48	66.52	
2521	Tim	18	23.99		18	31.63		36	55.62	
3339	Lr	30	31.78		42	41.89	100	72	73.67	
2652	Mac	28	25.24	111	31	33.27		59	58.51	101
3004	Ant	20	28.59		33	37.68		53	66.28	
3130	Cor	26	29.79		39	39.26		65	69.06	
1049	Per[1]	7	9.98		12	13.16		19	23.14	
1393	Per[2]	8	13.26		16	17.47		24	30.73	
3260	Cym	28	31.03		47	40.90	115	75	71.92	104
2965	WT	31	28.22	110	38	37.19	102	69	65.41	105
2562	Tmp	12	24.38		23	32.14		35	56.52	
2659	H8	15	25.31		37	33.36	111	52	58.66	
100760		959	958.99		1264	1264.00		2223	2222.99	

1. No. of different words in play (count by Hart). 2. Name of play, abbreviated. 3. Two-six-fold link words: no. of links. 4. No. expected. 5. Ratio of observed to expected, as percent. 6. Seven-ten-fold link words, no. of links observed. 7. No. expected. 8. Ratio of observed to expected, as percent. 9. Total two-ten-fold link words: no. of links observed. 10. No. expected. 11. Ratio of observed to expected, as percent.
Statistically significant positive deviations are underlined.

Links with M I D S U M M E R - N I G H T ' S   D R E A M

1	2	3	4	5	6	7	8	9	10	11
3146	2H6	19	26.29		29	28.41	102	48	54.70	
2790	3H6	16	23.32		20	25.19		36	48.51	
3014	1H6	30	25.19	119	23	27.21		53	52.40	101
3218	R3	25	26.89		33	29.06	114	58	55.95	104
2037	Err	24	17.02	141	20	18.39	109	44	35.42	124
2578	Tit	23	21.54	107	27	23.28	116	50	44.82	112
2463	Shr	18	20.58		32	22.24	144	50	42.82	117
2153	TGV	19	17.99	106	13	19.44		32	37.43	
2872	LLL	33	24.00	138	35	25.93	135	68	49.93	136
2916	Rom	31	24.37	127	31	26.33	118	62	50.70	122
2833	R2	16	23.68		21	25.58		37	49.25	
	MND	47			59			106		
2901	Jo	18	24.24		27	26.19	103	45	50.44	
2571	MV	20	21.49		27	23.21	116	47	44.70	105
3028	1H4	29	25.31	115	27	27.34		56	52.65	106
3130	2H4	30	26.16	115	21	28.26		51	54.42	
2527	Wiv	20	21.12		18	22.82		38	43.93	
2396	Ado	18	20.02		15	21.63		33	41.66	
3162	H5	36	26.43	136	34	28.55	119	70	54.98	127
2218	JC	7	18.54		19	20.03		26	38.56	
2578	AYL	33	21.54	153	30	23.28	129	63	44.82	141
2534	TN	16	21.18		24	22.88	105	40	44.06	
3882	Ham	46	32.44	142	36	35.05	103	82	67.49	121
3360	Tro	25	28.08		17	30.34		42	58.42	
2705	AWW	18	22.61		21	24.42		39	47.03	
2669	MM	16	22.31		15	24.10		31	46.40	
3015	Oth	19	25.20		14	27.22		33	52.42	
2521	Tim	16	21.07		16	22.76		32	43.83	
3339	Lr	32	27.90	115	41	30.15	136	73	58.05	126
2652	Mac	26	22.16	117	24	23.94	100	50	46.11	108
3004	Ant	25	25.11		37	27.12	136	62	52.23	119
3130	Cor	20	26.16		18	28.26		38	54.42	
1049	Per[1]	9	8.77	103	10	9.47	106	19	18.24	104
1393	Per[2]	12	11.64	103	22	12.58	175	34	24.22	140
3260	Cym	20	27.24		36	29.42	122	56	56.68	
2965	WT	29	24.78	117	28	26.77	105	57	51.55	111
2562	Tmp	23	21.41	107	26	23.13	112	49	44.54	110
2659	H8	29	22.22	131	27	24.01	112	56	46.23	121
101230		846	846.00		914	914.00		1760	1760.01	

1. No. of different words in play (count by Hart).   2. Name of play, abbreviated.   3. Two-six-fold link words: no. of links.
4. No. expected.   5. Ratio of observed to expected, as percent.
6. Seven-ten-fold link words, no. of links observed.   7. No. expected.   8. Ratio of observed to expected, as percent.   9. Total two-ten-fold link words: no. of links observed.   10. No. expected.
11. Ratio of observed to expected, as percent.
Statistically significant positive deviations are underlined.

Links with J O H N

1	2	3	4	5	6	7	8	9	10	11
3146	2H6	41	30.46	135	53	45.15	117	94	75.61	124
2790	3H6	28	27.02	104	43	40.04	107	71	67.05	106
3014	1H6	28	29.18		50	43.25	116	78	72.44	108
3218	R3	41	31.16	132	63	46.18	136	104	77.34	134
2037	Err	26	19.72	132	26	29.23		52	48.96	106
2578	Tit	22	24.96		42	37.00	114	64	61.96	103
2463	Shr	27	23.85	113	30	35.35		57	59.19	
2153	TGV	19	20.85		22	30.90		41	51.74	
2872	LLL	28	27.81	101	40	41.22		68	69.02	
2916	Rom	38	28.24	135	46	41.85	110	84	70.08	120
2833	R2	35	27.43	128	59	40.66	145	94	68.09	138
2363	MND	21	22.88		33	33.91		54	56.79	
	Jo	30			44			74		
2571	MV	26	24.89	104	37	36.90	100	63	61.79	102
3028	1H4	36	29.32	123	55	43.45	127	91	72.77	125
3130	2H4	40	30.31	132	51	44.92	114	91	75.23	121
2527	Wiv	19	24.47		24	36.26		43	60.73	
2396	Ado	27	23.20	116	30	34.38		57	57.58	
3162	H5	30	30.62		61	45.38	134	91	75.99	120
2218	JC	22	21.48	102	35	31.83	110	57	53.31	107
2578	AYL	25	24.96	100	35	37.00		60	61.96	
2534	TN	26	24.54	106	29	36.36		55	60.90	
3882	Ham	41	37.59	109	58	55.71	104	99	93.30	106
3360	Tro	40	32.53	123	46	48.22		86	80.75	107
2705	AWW	23	26.19		31	38.82		54	65.01	
2669	MM	24	25.84		31	38.30		55	64.15	
3015	Oth	20	29.19		30	43.27		50	72.46	
2521	Tim	21	24.41		27	36.18		48	60.59	
3339	Lr	28	32.33		40	47.92		68	80.25	
2652	Mac	31	25.68	121	36	38.06		67	63.74	105
3004	Ant	23	29.09		41	43.11		64	72.20	
3130	Cor	23	30.31		47	44.92	105	70	75.23	
1049	Per[1]	4	10.16		16	15.05	106	20	25.21	
1393	Per[2]	10	13.49		22	19.99	110	32	33.48	
3260	Cym	20	31.57		43	46.78		63	78.35	
2965	WT	20	28.71		40	42.55		60	71.26	
2562	Tmp	16	24.81		32	36.77		48	61.56	
2659	H8	26	25.75	101	41	38.16	107	67	63.91	105
100692		975	975.00		1445	1445.03		2420	2419.98	

1. No. of different words in play (count by Hart). 2. Name of play, abbreviated. 3. Two-six-fold link words: no. of links. 4. No. expected. 5. Ratio of observed to expected, as percent. 6. Seven-ten-fold link words, no. of links observed. 7. No. expected. 8. Ratio of observed to expected, as percent. 9. Total two-ten-fold link words: no. of links observed. 10. No. expected. 11. Ratio of observed to expected, as percent. Statistically significant positive deviations are underlined.

Links with M E R C H A N T   O F   V E N I C E

1	2	3	4	5	6	7	8	9	10	11
3146	2H6	26	25.44	102	37	31.48	118	63	56.93	111
2790	3H6	24	22.56	106	25	27.92		49	50.49	
3014	1H6	21	24.38		25	30.16		46	54.54	
3218	R3	27	26.03	104	33	32.20	102	60	58.23	103
2037	Err	14	16.47		20	20.39		34	36.86	
2578	Tit	25	20.85	120	44	25.80	171	69	46.65	148
2463	Shr	20	19.92	100	32	24.65	130	52	44.57	117
2153	TGV	15	17.41		19	21.55		34	38.96	
2872	LLL	28	23.23	121	29	28.74	101	57	51.97	110
2916	Rom	26	23.58	110	35	29.18	120	61	52.77	116
2833	R2	27	22.91	118	23	28.35		50	51.26	
2363	MND	22	19.11	115	28	23.65	118	50	42.76	117
2901	Jo	23	23.46		32	29.03	110	55	52.49	105
	MV	29			57			86		
3028	1H4	23	24.49		28	30.30		51	54.79	
3130	2H4	24	25.31		32	31.32	102	56	56.64	
2527	Wiv	14	20.44		12	25.29		26	45.73	
2396	Ado	14	19.38		15	23.98		29	43.36	
3162	H5	27	25.57		44	31.64	139	71	57.22	124
2218	JC	13	17.94		18	22.20		31	40.13	
2578	AYL	30	20.85	144	28	25.80	109	58	46.65	124
2534	TN	24	20.49	117	19	25.36		43	45.85	
3882	Ham	54	31.40	172	34	38.85		88	70.25	125
3360	Tro	29	27.17	107	45	33.63	134	74	60.80	122
2705	AWW	17	21.88		35	27.07	129	52	48.95	106
2669	MM	23	21.59	107	29	26.71	109	52	48.30	108
3015	Oth	24	24.38		35	30.17	116	59	54.56	108
2521	Tim	14	20.39		20	25.23		34	45.62	
3339	Lr	20	27.00		25	33.42		45	60.42	
2652	Mac	13	21.45		25	26.54		38	47.99	
3004	Ant	17	24.29		22	30.06		39	54.36	
3130	Cor	32	25.31	126	32	31.32	102	64	56.64	113
1049	Per¹	11	8.48	130	6	10.50		17	18.98	
1393	Per²	8	11.27		18	13.94	129	26	25.21	103
3260	Cym	25	26.36		25	32.63		50	58.99	
2965	WT	28	23.98	117	30	29.67	101	58	53.65	108
2562	Tmp	16	20.72		24	24.64		40	46.36	
2659	H8	19	21.50		28	26.61	105	47	48.11	
101022		817	816.99		1011	1011.00		1828	1828.04	

1. No. of different words in play (count by Hart).   2. Name of play, abbreviated.   3. Two-six-fold link words: no. of links. 4. No. expected.   5. Ratio of observed to expected, as percent. 6. Seven-ten-fold link words, no. of links observed.   7. No. expected.   8. Ratio of observed to expected, as percent.   9. Total two-ten-fold link words: no. of links observed.   10. No. expected. 11. Ratio of observed to expected, as percent.
Statistically significant positive deviations are underlined.

Links with 1 HENRY IV

1	2	3	4	5	6	7	8	9	10	11
3146	2H6	44	37.26	118	44	40.45	109	88	77.71	113
2790	3H6	18	33.04		35	35.87		53	68.91	
3014	1H6	31	35.70		40	38.75	103	71	74.45	
3218	R3	33	38.11		52	41.37	126	85	79.49	107
2037	Err	26	24.12	108	18	26.19		44	50.31	
2578	Tit	24	30.53		29	33.15		53	63.68	
2463	Shr	51	29.17	175	32	31.67	101	83	60.84	136
2153	TGV	13	25.50		22	27.68		35	53.18	
2872	LLL	32	34.01		42	36.93		74	70.94	104
2916	Rom	41	34.53	119	45	37.49	120	86	72.03	119
2833	R2	42	33.55	125	47	36.42	129	89	69.98	127
2363	MND	29	27.99	104	34	30.38	112	63	58.37	108
2901	Jo	34	34.36		46	37.30	123	80	71.66	112
2571	MV	26	30.45		28	33.06		54	63.50	
	1H4	46			50			96		
3130	2H4	65	37.07	175	58	40.24	144	123	77.31	159
2527	Wiv	29	29.93		44	32.49	135	73	62.42	117
2396	Ado	28	28.38		24	30.81		52	59.18	
3162	H5	56	37.45	150	55	40.65	135	111	78.10	142
2218	JC	20	26.27		16	28.52		36	54.79	
2578	AYL	35	30.53	115	34	33.15	103	69	63.68	108
2534	TN	25	30.01		28	32.58		53	62.59	
3882	Ham	53	45.97	115	49	49.91		102	95.89	106
3360	Tro	48	39.79	121	47	43.20	109	95	82.99	114
2705	AWW	25	32.04		26	34.78		51	66.81	
2669	MM	28	31.61		32	34.32		60	65.93	
3015	Oth	34	35.71		32	38.76		66	74.47	
2521	Tim	16	29.86		22	32.41		38	62.27	
3339	Lr	41	39.54	104	47	42.93	109	88	82.47	107
2652	Mac	32	31.41	102	22	34.10		54	65.51	
3004	Ant	28	35.58		30	38.62		58	74.20	
3130	Cor	41	37.07	111	35	40.24		76	77.31	
1049	Per[1]	9	12.42		20	13.49	148	29	25.91	112
1393	Per[2]	12	16.50		19	17.91	106	31	34.41	
3260	Cym	36	38.61		45	41.91	107	81	80.52	101
2965	WT	33	35.11		36	38.12		69	73.24	
2562	Tmp	30	30.34		29	32.94		59	63.28	
2659	H8	23	31.49		29	34.19		52	65.68	
100565		1191	1191.01		1293	1292.98		2484	2484.01	

1. No. of different words in play (count by Hart). 2. Name of play, abbreviated. 3. Two-six-fold link words: no. of links. 4. No. expected. 5. Ratio of observed to expected, as percent. 6. Seven-ten-fold link words, no. of links observed. 7. No. expected. 8. Ratio of observed to expected, as percent. 9. Total two-ten-fold link words: no. of links observed. 10. No. expected. 11. Ratio of observed to expected, as percent.
Statistically significant positive deviations are underlined.

Links with 2 H E N R Y I V

1	2	3	4	5	6	7	8	9	10	11
3146	2H6	45	36.01	125	34	42.09		79	78.10	101
2790	3H6	31	31.94		38	37.32	102	69	69.26	
3014	1H6	37	34.50	107	39	40.32		76	74.82	102
3218	R3	37	36.84	100	48	43.05	111	85	79.69	106
2037	Err	21	23.32		27	27.25		48	50.57	
2578	Tit	21	29.51		30	34.49		51	64.00	
2463	Shr	28	28.19		40	32.95	121	68	61.14	111
2153	TGV	16	24.65		23	28.80		39	53.45	
2872	LLL	42	32.88	128	39	38.42	102	81	71.30	114
2916	Rom	29	33.38		33	39.01		62	72.39	
2833	R2	43	32.43	133	40	37.90	106	83	70.33	118
2363	MND	29	27.05	107	25	31.61		54	58.66	
2901	Jo	37	33.21	111	48	38.81	124	85	72.02	118
2571	MV	24	29.43		37	34.39	108	61	63.83	
3028	1H4	59	34.66	170	52	40.51	128	111	75.17	148
	2H4	45			64			109		
2527	Wiv	45	28.93	156	38	33.81	112	83	62.73	132
2396	Ado	33	27.43	120	30	32.05		63	59.48	106
3162	H5	42	36.20	116	61	42.30	144	103	78.50	131
2218	JC	30	25.39	118	33	29.67	111	63	55.06	114
2578	AYL	30	29.51	102	29	34.49		59	64.00	
2534	TN	35	29.01	121	36	33.90	106	71	62.91	113
3882	Ham	43	44.44		62	51.93	119	105	96.37	109
3360	Tro	37	38.46		54	44.95	120	91	83.41	109
2705	AWW	30	30.96		31	36.19		61	67.15	
2669	MM	29	30.55		43	35.71	120	72	66.26	109
3015	Oth	27	34.51		38	49.33		65	74.85	
2521	Tim	18	28.86		26	33.73		44	62.58	
3339	Lr	35	38.22		27	44.67		62	82.89	
2652	Mac	28	30.36		26	35.48		54	65.84	
3004	Ant	24	34.39		42	40.19	105	66	74.57	
3130	Cor	34	35.83		38	41.87		72	'77.70	
1049	Per[1]	11	12.01		12	14.03		23	26.04	
1393	Per[2]	15	15.95		18	18.64		33	34.58	
3260	Cym	27	37.32		43	43.61		70	80.93	
2965	WT	33	33.94		35	39.67		68	73.61	
2562	Tmp	23	29.33		28	34.27		51	63.60	
2659	H8	22	30.44		41	35.57	115	63	66.01	
100463		1150	1150.14		1344	1343.98		2494	2494.00	

1. No. of different words in play (count by Hart).   2. Name of play, abbreviated.   3. Two-six-fold link words: no. of links. 4. No. expected.   5. Ratio of observed to expected, as percent. 6. Seven-ten-fold link words, no. of links observed.   7. No. expected.   8. Ratio of observed to expected, as percent.   9. Total two-ten-fold link words: no. of links observed.   10. No. expected. 11. Ratio of observed to expected, as percent. Statistically significant positive deviations are underlined.

Links with MERRY WIVES

1	2	3	4	5	6	7	8	9	10	11
3146	2H6	22	26.40		34	29.23	116	56	55.63	101
2790	3H6	15	23.41		20	25.92		35	49.33	
3014	1H6	18	25.29		19	28.00		37	53.29	
3218	R3	16	27.00		28	29.90		44	56.90	
2037	Err	22	17.09	129	16	18.93		38	36.02	105
2578	Tit	26	21.63	120	18	23.95		44	45.58	
2463	Shr	18	2o.67		23	22.88	101	41	43.55	
2153	TGV	21	18.06	116	14	20.00		35	38.07	
2872	LLL	23	24.10		37	26.68	139	60	50.78	118
2916	Rom	26	24.47	106	25	27.09		51	51.56	
2833	R2	20	23.77		8	26.32		28	50.09	
2363	MND	22	19.83	111	25	21.95	114	47	41.78	112
2901	Jo	18	24.34		21	26.95		39	51.29	
2571	MV	14	21.57		13	23.89		27	45.46	
3028	1H4	35	25.41	138	52	28.13	185	87	53.54	162
3130	2H4	48	26.26	183	43	29.08	148	91	55.34	164
	Wiv	54			31			65		
2396	Ado	23	20.10	114	29	22.26	130	52	42.36	123
3162	H5	28	26.53	106	42	29.38	143	70	55.91	125
2218	JC	16	18.61		15	20.61		31	39.22	
2578	AYL	34	21.63	157	23	23.95		57	45.58	125
2534	TN	24	21.26	113	31	23.54	132	55	44.80	123
3882	Ham	56	32.57	172	51	36.07	141	107	68.64	156
3360	Tro	44	28.19	156	38	31.22	122	82	59.41	138
2705	AWW	25	22.70	110	24	25.13		49	47.83	102
2669	MM	27	22.39	121	29	24.80	117	56	47.19	119
3015	Oth	25	25.30		26	28.01		51	53.31	
2521	Tim	20	21.15		22	23.42		42	44.58	
3339	Lr	30	28.02	107	23	31.02		53	·59.04	
2652	Mac	18	22.25		12	24.64		30	46.89	
3004	Ant	17	25.21		26	27.91		43	53.12	
3130	Cor	18	26.26		25	29.08		43	55.34	
1049	Per[1]	7	8.80		10	9.75	103	17	18.55	
1393	Per[2]	9	11.69		20	12.94	155	29	24.63	118
3260	Cym	19	27.35		34	30.29	112	53	57.64	
2965	WT	26	24.88	105	21	27.55		47	52.43	
2562	Tmp	6	21.50		22	23.80		28	45.30	
2659	H8	12	22.31		20	24.70		32	47.02	
101066		848	848.00		939	938.97		1787	1787.00	

1. No. of different words in play (count by Hart).   2. Name of play, abbreviated.   3. Two-six-fold link words: no. of links.
4. No. expected.   5. Ratio of observed to expected, as percent.
6. Seven-ten-fold link words, no. of links observed.   7. No. expected.   8. Ratio of observed to expected, as percent.   9. Total two-ten-fold link words: no. of links observed.   10. No. expected.
11. Ratio of observed to expected, as percent.
Statistically significant positive deviations are underlined.

Links with M U C H   A D O

1	2	3	4	5	6	7	8	9	10	11
3146	2H6	23	23.60		33	25.80	128	56	49.40	113
2790	3H6	15	20.93		19	22.88		34	43.81	
3014	1H6	23	22.61	102	22	24.72		45	47.33	
3218	R3	20	24.14		33	26.39	125	53	50.53	105
2037	Err	7	15.28		17	16.71	102	24	31.99	
2578	Tit	20	19.34	103	21	21.14		41	40.48	101
2463	Shr	25	18.47	135	18	20.20		43	38.67	111
2153	TGV	17	16.15	105	16	17.66		33	33.81	
2872	LLL	<u>32</u>	21.54	<u>149</u>	<u>34</u>	23.56	<u>144</u>	<u>66</u>	45.10	<u>146</u>
2916	Rom	24	21.87	110	20	23.92		44	45.79	
2833	R2	13	21.25		20	23.24		33	44.48	
2363	MND	23	17.72	130	14	19.38		37	37.10	
2901	Jo	26	21.76	119	26	23.79	109	52	45.55	114
2571	MV	15	19.28		16	21.09		31	40.37	
3028	1H4	29	22.71	128	28	24.84	113	57	47.55	120
3130	2H4	<u>37</u>	23.48	<u>158</u>	32	25.67	125	<u>69</u>	49.15	<u>140</u>
2527	Wiv	25	18.95	132	27	20.73	130	52	39.68	131
	Ado	21			21			42		
3162	H5	29	23.72	122	35	25.93	135	<u>64</u>	49.65	<u>129</u>
2218	JC	11	16.64		11	18.19		22	34.83	
2578	AYL	26	19.34	134	24	21.14	114	50	40.48	124
2534	TN	25	19.01	132	31	20.78	149	56	39.79	141
3882	Ham	35	29.12	120	47	31.84	148	82	60.96	135
3360	Tro	27	25.20	107	29	27.56	105	56	52.76	106
2705	AWW	21	20.29	103	24	22.19	108	45	42.47	106
2669	MM	14	20.02		28	21.89	128	42	41.91	100
3015	Oth	21	22.61		25	24.73	101	46	47.34	
2521	Tim	19	18.91	100	16	20.68		35	39.58	
3339	Lr	21	25.04		22	27.39		43	52.43	
2652	Mac	17	19.89		13	21.75		30	41.64	
3004	Ant	13	22.53		21	24.64		34	47.17	
3130	Cor	26	23.48	111	21	25.67		47	49.15	
1049	Per[1]	5	7.87		7	8.60		12	16.47	
1393	Per[2]	11	10.45	105	7	11.43		18	21.87	
3260	Cym	17	24.45		22	26.74		39	51.19	
2965	WT	18	22.24		23	24.32		41	46.56	
2562	Tmp	15	19.22		7	21.01		22	40.23	
2659	H8	14	19.94		21	21.81		35	41.75	
101197		759	759.05		830	830.01		1589	1589.02	

1. No. of different words in play (count by Hart).   2. Name of play, abbreviated.   3. Two-six-fold link words: no. of links.
4. No. expected.   5. Ratio of observed to expected, as percent.
6. Seven-ten-fold link words, no. of links observed.   7. No. expected.   8. Ratio of observed to expected, as percent.   9. Total two-ten-fold link words: no. of links observed.   10. No. expected.
11. Ratio of observed to expected, as percent.
Statistically significant positive deviations are underlined.

Links with H E N R Y V

1	2	3	4	5	6	7	8	9	10	11
3146	2H6	62	39.85	156	60	52.22	115	122	92.06	133
2790	3H6	32	35.34		38	46.31		70	81.65	
3014	1H6	46	38.17	121	62	50.03	124	108	88.20	122
3218	R3	48	40.76	118	58	53.41	109	106	94.17	113
2037	Err	21	25.80		31	33.81		52	59.61	
2578	Tit	35	32.65	107	37	42.79		72	75.44	
2463	Shr	23	31.19		39	40.88		62	72.08	
2153	TGV	19	27.27		22	35.74		41	63.01	
2872	LLL	46	36.36	127	67	47.67	141	113	84.05	134
2916	Rom	22	36.93		42	48.40		64	85.33	
2833	R2	36	35.88	100	60	47.02	128	96	82.90	116
2363	MND	36	29.93	120	34	39.22		70	69.15	101
2901	Jo	28	36.74		59	48.15	123	87	84.89	102
2571	MV	24	32.56		41	42.67		65	75.24	
3028	1H4	52	38.35	136	52	50.26	103	104	88.61	117
3130	2H4	44	39.64	111	52	51.95	100	96	91.60	105
2527	Wiv	29	32.01		44	41.94	105	73	73.95	
2396	Ado	26	30.35		35	39.77		61	70.12	
	H5	47			67			114		
2218	JC	19	28.09		34	36.82		53	64.91	
2578	AYL	35	32.65	107	39	42.79		74	75.44	
2534	TN	34	32.09	106	41	42.06		75	74.15	101
3882	Ham	60	49.17	122	78	64.44	121	138	113,60	121
3360	Tro	68	42.56	160	57	55.77	102	125	98.33	127
2705	AWW	29	34.26		44	44.90		73	79.16	
2669	MM	36	33.80	107	42	44.30		78	78.11	
3015	Oth	43	38.19	113	59	50.04	118	102	88.23	116
2521	Tim	20	31.93		28	41.84		48	73.77	
3339	Lr	41	42.29		44	55.42		85	97.71	
2652	Mac	22	33.59		45	44.02	102	67	77.61	
3004	Ant	32	38.05		41	49.86		73	87.91	
3130	Cor	35	39.64		52	51.95	100	87	91.60	
1049	Per[1]	11	13.29		16	17.41		27	30.70	
1393	Per[2]	22	17.64	125	25	23.12	108	47	40.76	115
3260	Cym	40	41.29		60	54.11	111	100	95.40	105
2965	WT	29	37.55		45	49.21		74	86.77	
2562	Tmp	38	32.45	117	37	42.53		75	74.97	100
2659	H8	29	33.68		47	44.14	106	76	77.87	
100431		1272	1271.99		1667	1666.97		2939	2939.00	

1. No. of different words in play (count by Hart).   2. Name of play, abbreviated.   3. Two-six-fold link words: no. of links.
4. No. expected.   5. Ratio of observed to expected, as percent.
6. Seven-ten-fold link words, no. of links observed.   7. No. expected.   8. Ratio of observed to expected, as percent.   9. Total two-ten-fold link words: no. of links observed.   10. No. expected.
11. Ratio of observed to expected, as percent.
Statistically significant positive deviations are underlined.

Links with J U L I U S   C A E S A R

1	2	3	4	5	6	7	8	9	10	11
3146	2H6	22	18.84	117	35	26.56	132	57	45.40	126
2790	3H6	14	16.71		30	23.56	127	44	40.26	109
3014	1H6	20	18.05	111	31	25.45	122	51	43.50	117
3218	R3	24	19.27	125	35	27.17	129	59	46.44	127
2037	Err	9	12.20		19	17.20	110	28	29.40	
2578	Tit	14	15.44		27	21.77	124	41	37.20	110
2463	Shr	13	14.75		26	20.80	125	39	35.54	110
2153	TGV	11	12.89		11	18.18		22	31.07	
2872	LLL	15	17.20		13	24.25		28	41.45	
2916	Rom	19	17.46	109	33	24.62	134	52	42.08	124
2833	R2	9	16.96		20	23.92		29	40.88	
2363	MND	7	14.15		19	19.95		26	34.10	
2901	Jo	20	17.37	115	32	24.50	131	52	41.87	124
2571	MV	14	15.39		21	21.71		35	37.10	
3028	1H4	20	18.13	110	18	25.57		38	43.70	
3130	2H4	<u>29</u>	18.74	<u>155</u>	27	26.43	102	56	45.17	124
2527	Wiv	15	15.13		12	21.34		27	36.47	
2396	Ado	11	14.35		10	20.23		21	34.58	
3162	H5	19	18.93	100	36	26.70	135	55	45.63	121
	JC	18			30			48		
2578	AYL	15	15.44		20	21.77		35	37.20	
2534	TN	13	15.17		21	21.40		34	36.57	
3882	Ham	<u>37</u>	<u>23.24</u>	<u>159</u>	36	32.78	110	<u>73</u>	<u>56.02</u>	<u>130</u>
3360	Tro	<u>35</u>	<u>20.12</u>	<u>174</u>	33	28.37	116	<u>68</u>	<u>48.49</u>	<u>140</u>
2705	AWW	12	16.20		23	22.84	101	35	39.04	
2669	MM	13	15.98		21	22.54		34	38.52	
3015	Oth	14	18.05		23	25.46		37	43.51	
2521	Tim	12	15.09		20	21.29		32	36.38	
3339	Lr	22	19.99	110	15	28.19		37	48.19	
2652	Mac	13	15.88		25	22.39	112	38	38.27	
3004	Ant	12	17.99		21	25.37		33	43.35	
3130	Cor	26	18.74	139	32	26.42	121	58	45.17	128
1049	Per[1]	4	6.28		9	8.86	102	13	15.14	
1393	Per[2]	4	8.34		14	11.76	119	18	20.10	
3260	Cym	18	19.52		30	27.53	109	48	47.05	102
2965	WT	16	17.75		23	25.04		39	42.79	
2562	Tmp	19	15.34	124	17	21.63		36	36.97	
2659	H8	17	15.92	107	18	22.45		35	38.37	
101375		607	607.00		856	856.01		1463	1462.97	

1. No. of different words in play (count by Hart).   2. Name of play, abbreviated.   3. Two-six-fold link words: no. of links.
4. No. expected.   5. Ratio of observed to expected, as percent.
6. Seven-ten-fold link words, no. of links observed.   7. No. expected.   8. Ratio of observed to expected, as percent.   9. Total two-ten-fold link words: no. of links observed.   10. No. expected.
11. Ratio of observed to expected, as percent.
Statistically significant positive deviations are underlined.

Links with A S Y O U L I K E I T

1	2	3	4	5	6	7	8	9	10	11
3146	2H6	22	28.19		36	33.60	107	58	61.79	
2790	3H6	22	25.00		22	29.80		44	54.80	
3014	1H6	20	27.00		34	32.19	106	54	59.20	
3218	R3	34	28.83	118	45	34.37	131	.79	63.20	125
2037	Err	15	18.25		18	21.76		33	40.01	
2578	Tit	23	23.10		28	27.54	102	51	50.63	101
2463	Shr	23	22.06	104	45	26.31	171	68	48.37	141
2153	TGV	22	19.29	114	13	23.00		35	42.29	
2872	LLL	39	25.73	152	43	30.68	140	82	56.41	145
2916	Rom	28	26.12	107	48	31.15	154	76	57.27	133
2833	R2	17	25.38		36	30.26	119	53	55.64	
2363	MND	32	21.17	151	31	25.24	123	63	46.41	136
2901	Jo	25	25.99		32	30.99	103	57	56.98	100
2571	MV	30	23.03	130	27	27.46		57	50.50	113
3028	1H4	33	27.13	122	30	32.34		63	59.47	106
3130	2H4	27	28.04		36	33.43	108	63	61.48	102
2527	Wiv	35	22.64	155	26	26.99		61	49.63	123
2396	Ado	24	21.47	112	20	25.59		44	47.06	
3162	H5	34	28.33	120	46	33.78	136	80	62.10	129
2218	JC	15	19.87		21	23.69		36	43.56	
	AYL	45			42			87		
2534	TN	29	22.70	128	25	27.07		54	49.77	108
3882	Ham	36	34.78	104	37	41.47		73	76.24	
3360	Tro	31	30.10	103	30	35.89		61	65.99	
2705	AWW	27	24.23	111	31	28.89	107	58	53.13	109
2669	MM	22	23.91		27	28.51		49	52.42	
3015	Oth	18	27.01		32	32.20		50	59.22	
2521	Tim	19	22.59		22	26.93		41	49.51	
3339	Lr	30	29.91	100	31	35.67		61	65.58	
2652	Mac	19	23.78		19	28.33		38	52.09	
3004	Ant	21	26.91		39	32.09	122	60	59.00	102
3130	Cor	19	28.04		20	33.43		39	61.48	
1049	Per[1]	6	9.40		5	11.20		11	20.60	
1393	Per[2]	7	12.48		12	14.88		19	27.36	
3260	Cym	25	29.21		38	34.82	109	63	64.03	
2965	WT	33	26.56	124	29	31.67		62	58.23	106
2562	Tmp	25	22.95	109	20	27.37		45	50.32	
2659	H8	18	23.82		25	28.40		43	52.22	
101015		905	905.00		1079	1078.99		1984	1983.99	

1. No. of different words in play (count by Hart).   2. Name of play, abbreviated.   3. Two-six-fold link words: no. of links. 4. No. expected.   5. Ratio of observed to expected, as percent. 6. Seven-ten-fold link words, no. of links observed.   7. No. expected.   8. Ratio of observed to expected, as percent.   9. Total two-ten-fold link words: no. of links observed.   10. No. expected. 11. Ratio of observed to expected, as percent.
Statistically significant positive deviations are underlined.

Links with T W E L F T H   N I G H T

1	2	3	4	5	6	7	8	9	10	11
3146	2H6	18	28.17		32	32.34		50	60.52	
2790	3H6	13	24.98		16	28.68		29	53.67	
3014	1H6	15	26.99		26	30.99		41	57.98	
3218	R3	22	28.82		33	33.08		55	61.90	
2037	Err	13	18.24		21	20.94	100	34	39.18	
2578	Tit	19	23.09		23	26.50		42	49.59	
2463	Shr	26	22.06	118	31	25.32	122	57	47.38	120
2153	TGV	18	19.28		13	22.14		31	41.42	
2872	LLL	30	25.72	117	30	29.53	102	60	55.25	109
2916	Rom	24	26.11		26	29.98		50	56.09	
2833	R2	17	25.37		14	29.13		31	54.50	
2363	MND	18	21.16		31	24.29	128	49	45.46	108
2901	Jo	27	25.98	104	29	29.83		56	55.80	100
2571	MV	23	23.02		22	26.43		45	49.46	
3028	1H4	23	27.12		30	31.13		53	58.25	
3130	2H4	30	28.03	107	37	32.18	115	67	60.21	111
2527	Wiv	24	22.63	106	26	25.98	100	50	48.61	103
2396	Ado	25	21.46	116	26	24.63	106	51	46.09	111
3162	H5	36	28.32	127	40	32.51	123	76	60.83	125
2218	JC	14	19.86		23	22.80	101	37	42.67	
2578	AYL	33	23.09	143	19	26.50		52	49.59	105
	TN	11			30			52		
3882	Ham	58	34.76	167	51	39.91	128	109	74.68	146
3360	Tro	46	30.09	153	39	34.54	113	85	64.63	132
2705	AWW	28	24.22	116	31	27.81	111	59	52.03	113
2669	MM	22	23.90		37	27.44	135	59	51.24	115
3015	Oth	38	27.00	141	31	31.00	100	69	58.00	119
2521	Tim	16	22.58		18	25.92		34	48.49	
3339	Lr	42	29.90	140	45	34.33	131	87	64.23	135
2652	Mac	23	23.75		25	27.27		48	51.01	
3004	Ant	11	26.90		39	30.88	126	50	57.79	
3130	Cor	35	28.03	125	27	32.18		62	60.21	103
1049	Per[1]	5	9.39		8	10.78		13	20.18	
1393	Per[2]	11	12.47		15	14.32	105	26	26.80	
3260	Cym	36	29.19	123	45	33.52	134	81	62.71	129
2965	WT	35	26.55	132	32	30.48	105	67	57.04	117
2562	Tmp	13	22.94		28	26.34	106	41	49.28	
2659	H8	18	23.81		20	27.34		38	51.15	
101059		905	904.98		1039	1039.01		1944	1944.02	

1. No. of different words in play (count by Hart).   2. Name of
play, abbreviated.   3. Two-six-fold link words: no. of links.
4. No. expected.   5. Ratio of observed to expected, as percent.
6. Seven-ten-fold link words, no. of links observed.   7. No. expected.   8. Ratio of observed to expected, as percent.   9. Total
two-ten-fold link words: no. of links observed.   10. No. expected.
11. Ratio of observed to expected, as percent.
Statistically significant positive deviations are underlined.

Links with H A M L E T

1	2	3	4	5	6	7	8	9	10	11
3146	2H6	41	55.40		51	59.69		92	115.10	
2790	3H6	34	49.13		46	52.94		80	102.07	
3014	1H6	35	53.08		61	57.19	107	96	110.27	
3218	R3	55	56.67		66	61.06	108	121	117.73	103
2037	Err	39	35.87	109	39	38.65	101	78	74.53	105
2578	Tit	27	45.40		39	48.92		66	94.32	
2463	Shr	23	43.38		52	46.74	111	75	90.11	
2153	TGV	25	37.92		27	40.85		52	78.77	
2872	LLL	61	50.58	121	53	54.50		114	105.07	108
2916	Rom	48	51.35		44	55.33		92	106.68	
2833	R2	41	49.89		52	53.76		93	103.65	
2363	MND	48	41.61	115	39	44.84		87	86.45	101
2901	Jo	44	51.09		61	55.05	111	105	106.14	
2571	MV	52	45.28	115	34	48.78		86	94.06	
3028	1H4	56	53.33	105	46	57.46		102	110.78	
3130	2H4	43	55.12		62	59.39	104	105	114.51	
2527	Wiv	56	44.50	126	47	47.95		103	92.45	111
2396	Ado	34	42.20		46	45.46	101	80	87.66	
3162	H5	59	55.69	106	80	60.00	133	139	115.68	120
2218	JC	34	39.06		33	42.09		67	81.15	
2578	AYL	38	45.40		35	48.92		73	94.32	
2534	TN	56	44.63	125	47	48.08		103	92.71	111
	Ham	59			60			119		
3360	Tro	87	59.17	147	82	63.76	129	169	122.93	137
2705	AWW	47	47.64		53	51.33	103	100	98.96	101
2669	MM	57	47.00	121	52	50.64	103	109	97.65	112
3015	Oth	81	53.10	153	68	57.21	119	149	110.31	135
2521	Tim	56	44.40	126	49	47.84	102	105	92.23	114
3339	Lr	76	58.80	129	89	63.36	140	165	122.16	135
2652	Mac	63	46.70	135	57	50.32	113	120	97.03	124
3004	Ant	58	52.90	110	56	57.00		114	109.90	104
3130	Cor	51	55.12		56	59.39		107	114.51	
1049	Per[1]	12	18.47		20	19.90	101	32	38.38	
1393	Per[2]	24	24.53		31	26.43	117	55	50.96	108
3260	Cym	63	57.41	110	74	61.85	120	137	119.27	115
2965	WT	57	52.22	109	57	56.26	101	114	108.48	105
2562	Tmp	37	45.12		45	48.61		82	93.73	
2659	H8	38	46.83		43	50.45		81	97.28	
99711		1756	1755.99		1892	1892.00		3648	3647.99	

1. No. of different words in play (count by Hart). 2. Name of play, abbreviated. 3. Two-six-fold link words: no. of links. 4. No. expected. 5. Ratio of observed to expected, as percent. 6. Seven-ten-fold link words, no. of links observed. 7. No. expected. 8. Ratio of observed to expected, as percent. 9. Total two-ten-fold link words: no. of links observed. 10. No. expected. 11. Ratio of observed to expected, as percent.
Statistically significant positive deviations are underlined.

Links with T R O I L U S

1	2	3	4	5	6	7	8	9	10	11
3146	2H6	45	46.61		45	48.27		90	94.88	
2790	3H6	25	41.34		44	42.81	103	69	84.15	
3014	1H6	42	44.65		47	46.25	102	89	90.90	
3218	R3	42	47.68		38	49.38		80	97.05	
2037	Err	18	30.18		29	31.26		47	61.44	
2578	Tit	34	38.19		42	39.65	106	76	77.75	
2463	Shr	30	36.49		42	37.79	111	72	74.28	
2153	TGV	22	31.90		19	33.04		41	64.93	
2872	LLL	46	42.55	108	45	44.07	102	91	86.62	105
2916	Rom	38	43.20		42	44.74		80	87.95	
2833	R2	44	41.97	105	44	43.47	101	88	85.44	103
2363	MND	29	35.01		16	36.26		45	71.27	
2901	Jo	42	42.98		46	44.51	103	88	87.49	101
2571	MV	29	38.09		49	39.45	124	78	77.54	101
3028	1H4	50	44.86	111	48	46.46	103	98	91.32	107
3130	2H4	39	46.37		66	48.03	137	105	94.40	111
2527	Wiv	39	37.44	104	45	38.77	116	84	76.21	110
2396	Ado	24	35.50		23	36.76		47	72.26	
3162	H5	65	46.85	139	54	48.52	111	119	95.37	125
2218	JC	31	32.86		35	34.03	103	66	66.89	
2578	AYL	33	38.19		27	39.56		60	77.75	
2534	TN	44	37.54	117	36	38.88		80	76.42	105
3882	Ham	82	57.51	143	79	59.57	133	161	117.08	138
	Tro	62			55			117		
2705	AWW	50	40.08	125	49	41.51	118	99	81.58	121
2669	MM	49	39.54	124	33	40.95		82	80.50	102
3015	Oth	47	44.67	105	64	46.26	138	111	90.93	122
2521	Tim	41	37.35	110	39	38.68	101	80	76.03	105
3339	Lr	58	49.47	120	52	51.23	102	110	100.70	109
2652	Mac	60	39.29	153	40	40.69		100	79.98	125
3004	Ant	53	44.51	119	48	46.09	104	101	90.60	111
3130	Cor	53	46.37	114	43	48.03		96	94.40	102
1049	Per[1]	12	15.54		14	16.10		26	31.64	
1393	Per[2]	11	20.64		22	21.37	103	33	42.01	
3260	Cym	57	48.30	118	45	50.02		102	98.32	104
2965	WT	35	43.93		44	45.50		79	89.42	
2562	Tmp	39	37.96	103	44	39.31	112	83	77.27	107
2659	H8	27	39.39		40	40.80		67	80.19	
100233		1485	1485.00		1538	1537.98		3023	3022.96	

1. No. of different words in play (count by Hart).   2. Name of play, abbreviated.   3. Two-six-fold link words: no. of links. 4. No. expected.   5. Ratio of observed to expected, as percent. 6. Seven-ten-fold link words, no. of links observed.   7. No. expected.   8. Ratio of observed to expected, as percent.   9. Total two-ten-fold link words: no. of links observed.   10. No. expected. 11. Ratio of observed to expected, as percent.
Statistically significant positive deviations are underlined.

Links with A L L ' S W E L L

1	2	3	4	5	6	7	8	9	10	11
3146	2H6	28	30.37		35	38.11		63	68.48	
2790	3H6	20	26.94		28	33.79		48	60.73	
3014	1H6	25	29.10		30	36.51		55	65.60	
3218	R3	31	31.07		48	38.98	123	79	70.05	113
2037	Err	17	19.67		22	24.67		39	44.34	
2578	Tit	15	24.89		28	31.23		43	56.11	
2463	Shr	22	23.78		26	29.83		48	53.61	
2153	TGV	11	20.79		17	26.08		28	46.86	
2872	LLL	26	27.73		34	34.79		60	62.51	
2916	Rom	22	28.15		33	35.32		55	63.47	
2833	R2	19	27.35		27	34.31		46	61.67	
2363	MND	20	22.81		19	28.62		39	51.43	
2901	Jo	25	28.01		30	35.14		55	63.15	
2571	MV	18	24.82		35	31.14	112	53	55.96	
3028	1H4	28	29.23		26	36.68		54	65.91	
3130	2H4	32	30.22	106	32	37.91		64	68.13	
2527	Wiv	27	24.40	111	26	30.61		53	55.00	
2396	Ado	23	23.13		22	29.02		45	52.15	
3162	H5	29	30.53		43	38.30	112	72	68.83	105
2218	JC	12	21.41		20	26.87		32	48.28	
2578	AYL	30	24.89	121	34	31.23	109	64	56.11	114
2534	TN	30	24.46	123	32	30.69	104	62	55.16	112
3882	Ham	47	37.48	125	50	47.02	106	97	84.50	115
3360	Tro	<u>55</u>	<u>32.44 170</u>		46	40.70	113	<u>101</u>	<u>73.14 138</u>	
	AWW	21			39			**		
2669	MM	37	25.77	144	51	32.33	158	88	58.10	151
3015	Oth	31	29.11	106	57	36.52	156	88	65.63	134
2521	Tim	25	24.34	103	39	30.54	128	64	54.87	117
3339	Lr	33	32.24	102	37	40.44		70	72.68	
2652	Mac	23	25.60		29	32.12		52	57.73	
3004	Ant	32	29.00	110	35	36.39		67	65.39	102
3130	Cor	36	30.22	119	47	37.91	124	83	68.13	122
1049	Per[1]	12	10.13	118	17	12.71	134	29	22.83	127
1393	Per[2]	10	13.45		18	16.87	107	28	30.32	
3260	Cym	37	31.47	118	48	39.49	124	85	70.96	120
2965	WT	33	28.62	115	41	35.91	114	74	64.54	115
2562	Tmp	29	24.73	117	27	31.03		56	55.77	100
2659	H8	24	25.67		33	32.21	102	57	57.88	
100888		974	974.02		1222	1222.02		2196	2196.01	

1. No. of different words in play (count by Hart). 2. Name of play, abbreviated. 3. Two-six-fold link words: no. of links. 4. No. expected. 5. Ratio of observed to expected, as percent. 6. Seven-ten-fold link words, no. of links observed. 7. No. expected. 8. Ratio of observed to expected, as percent. 9. Total two-ten-fold link words: no. of links observed. 10. No. expected. 11. Ratio of observed to expected, as percent.
Statistically significant positive deviations are underlined.

Links with M E A S U R E   F O R   M E A S U R E

1	2	3	4	5	6	7	8	9	10	11
3146	2H6	22	29.83		43	37.84	114	65	67.67	
2790	3H6	20	26.46		31	33.56		51	60.02	
3014	1H6	19	28.58		34	36.25		53	64.83	
3218	R3	27	30.51		43	38.71	111	70	69.22	101
2037	Err	13	19.32		22	24.50		35	43.82	
2578	Tit	26	24.45	106	30	31.01		56	55.46	101
2463	Shr	19	23.36		24	29.63		43	52.98	
2153	TGV	13	20.42		26	25.90	100	39	46.31	
2872	LLL	19	27.23		35	34.55	101	54	61.78	
2916	Rom	18	27.65		37	35.08	105	55	62.73	
2833	R2	21	26.86		26	34.08		47	60.94	
2363	MND	17	22.41		21	28.42		38	50.83	
2901	Jo	27	27.51		27	34.90		54	62.40	
2571	MV	24	24.38		28	30.93		52	55.31	
3028	1H4	29	28.71	101	28	36.42		57	65.14	
3130	2H4	35	29.68	118	38	37.65	101	73	67.33	108
2527	Wiv	22	23.96		27	30.40		49	54.36	
2396	Ado	13	22.72		27	28.82		40	51.54	
3162	H5	36	29.98	120	41	38.04	108	77	68.02	113
2218	JC	13	21.03		19	26.68		32	47.71	
2578	AYL	23	24.45		24	31.01		47	55.46	
2534	TN	23	24.03		29	30.48		52	54.51	
3882	Ham	56	36.81	152	56	46.70	120	112	83.51	134
3360	Tro	55	31.86	173	35	40.42		90	72.28	125
2705	AWW	39	25.65	152	47	32.54	144	86	58.19	148
	MM	11			45			67		
3015	Oth	31	28.59	108	45	36.27	124	76	64.86	117
2521	Tim	25	23.91	105	24	30.32		49	54.23	
3339	Lr	40	31.66	126	49	40.16	122	89	71.83	124
2652	Mac	28	25.15	111	36	31.90	113	64	57.05	112
3004	Ant	28	28.49		36	36.13		64	64.62	
3130	Cor	31	29.68	104	29	37.65		60	67.33	
1049	Per[1]	5	9.95		11	12.62		16	22.57	
1393	Per[2]	7	13.21		13	16.76		20	29.97	
3260	Cym	38	30.91	123	48	39.21	122	86	70.13	123
2965	WT	48	28.12	171	51	35.67	143	99	63.78	155
2562	Tmp	15	24.29		33	30.82	107	48	55.11	
2659	H8	32	25.21	127	41	31.98	128	73	57.20	
00924		957	957.02		1214	1214.01		2171	2171.03	

1. No. of different words in play (count by Hart).   2. Name of play, abbreviated.   3. Two-six-fold link words: no. of links.
4. No. expected.   5. Ratio of observed to expected, as percent.
6. Seven-ten-fold link words, no. of links observed.   7. No. expected.   8. Ratio of observed to expected, as percent.   9. Total two-ten-fold link words: no. of links observed.   10. No. expected.
11. Ratio of observed to expected, as percent.
Statistically significant positive deviations are underlined.

Links with OTHELLO

1	2	3	4	5	6	7	8	9	10	11
3146	2H6	26	31.87		42	43.01		68	74.88	
2790	3H6	24	28.27		43	38.14	113	67	66.41	101
3014	1H6	27	30.54		37	41.20		64	71.74	
3218	R3	29	32.60		58	43.99	132	87	76.60	114
2037	Err	18	20.64		24	27.85		42	48.49	
2578	Tit	19	26.12		34	35.24		53	61.36	
2463	Shr	24	24.95		31	33.67		55	58.63	
2153	TGV	13	21.81		14	29.43		27	51.25	
2872	LLL	26	29.10		32	39.26		58	68.36	
2916	Rom	26	29.54		35	39.86		61	69.41	
2833	R2	19	28.70		34	38.73		53	67.43	
2363	MND	18	23.94		14	32.30		32	56.25	
2901	Jo	23	29.39		29	39.66		52	69.05	
2571	MV	24	26.05		40	35.15	114	64	61.20	105
3028	1H4	34	30.68	111	37	41.40		71	72.07	
3130	2H4	29	31.71		44	42.79	103	73	74.50	
2527	Wiv	25	25.60		26	34.55		51	60.15	
2396	Ado	21	24.27		25	32.76		46	57.03	
3162	H5	42	32.04	131	52	43.23	120	94	75.26	125
2218	JC	16	22.47		25	30.32		41	52.79	
2578	AYL	21	26.12		34	35.24		55	61.36	
2534	TN	39	25.67	152	30	34.64		69	60.32	114
3882	Ham	83	39.33	211	73	53.07	138	156	92.40	169
3360	Tro	50	34.04	147	61	45.93	133	111	79.98	139
2705	AWW	32	27.41	117	55	36.98	149	87	64.39	135
2669	MM	31	27.04	115	50	36.49	137	81	63.53	127
	Oth	27			35			61		
2521	Tim	29	25.54	114	29	34.46		58	60.01	
3339	Lr	29	33.83		50	45.65	110	79	79.48	
2652	Mac	36	26.87	134	32	36.26		68	63.12	108
3004	Ant	38	30.43	125	43	41.07	105	81	71.50	113
3130	Cor	33	31.71	104	42	42.79		75	74.50	101
1049	Per[1]	4	10.63		16	14.34	112	20	24.97	
1393	Per[2]	10	14.11		16	19.04		26	33.16	
3260	Cym	24	33.03		56	44.57	126	80	77.60	103
2965	WT	34	30.04	113	42	40.53	104	76	70.57	108
2562	Tmp	20	25.96		33	35.03		53	60.98	
2659	H8	23	26.94		37	36.35	102	60	63.29	
100578		1019	1018.99		1375	1374.98		2394	2394.02	

1. No. of different words in play (count by Hart). 2. Name of play, abbreviated. 3. Two-six-fold link words: no. of links. 4. No. expected. 5. Ratio of observed to expected, as percent. 6. Seven-ten-fold link words, no. of links observed. 7. No. expected. 8. Ratio of observed to expected, as percent. 9. Total two-ten-fold link words: no. of links observed. 10. No. expected. 11. Ratio of observed to expected, as percent.
Statistically significant positive deviations are underlined.

Links with T I M O N

1	2	3	4	5	6	7	8	9	10	11
3146	2H6	23	25.03		34	30.47	112	57	55.50	103
2790	3H6	17	22.19		29	27.02	107	46	49.22	
3014	1H6	22	23.98		27	29.19		49	53.17	
3218	R3	26	25.60	102	23	31.17		49	56.77	
2037	Err	12	16.20		22	19.73	112	34	35.93	
2578	Tit	18	20.51		16	24.97		34	45.48	
2463	Shr	27	19.59	138	27	23.86	113	54	43.45	124
2153	TGV	19	17.13	111	16	20.85		35	37.98	
2872	LLL	19	22.85		19	27.82		38	50.66	
2916	Rom	13	23.20		40	28.24	142	53	51.44	103
2833	R2	17	22.54		23	27.44		40	49.98	
2363	MND	17	18.80		14	22.89		31	41.69	
2901	Jo	21	23.08		26	28.10		47	51.18	
2571	MV	15	20.45		24	24.90		39	45.30	
3028	1H4	15	24.09		22	29.33		37	53.42	
3130	2H4	16	24.90		34	30.32	112	50	55.22	
2527	Wiv	19	20.10		20	24.48		39	44.58	
2396	Ado	18	19.06		17	23.21		35	42.27	
3162	H5	22	25.15		29	30.63		51	55.78	
2218	JC	11	17.64		17	21.48		28	39.13	
2578	AYL	20	20.51		19	24.97		39	45.48	
2534	TN	16	20.16		16	24.54		32	44.70	
3882	Ham	54	30.88	175	51	37.60	136	105	68.48	153
3360	Tro	43	26.73	161	41	32.55	126	84	59.27	142
2705	AWW	23	21.52	107	39	26.20	149	62	47.72	130
2669	MM	26	21.23	122	24	25.85		50	47.08	106
3015	Oth	29	23.98	121	28	29.20		57	53.18	107
	Tim	1*			27			45		
3339	Lr	50	26.56	188	53	32.34	164	103	58.90	175
2652	Mac	17	21.10		25	25.69		42	46.78	
3004	Ant	22	23.90		34	29.10	117	56	52.99	106
3130	Cor	27	24.90	108	43	30.32	142	70	55.22	127
1049	Per[1]	7	8.34		4	10.16		11	18.51	
1393	Per[2]	16	11.08	144	16	13.49	119	32	24.57	138
3260	Cym	29	25.93	112	31	31.58		60	57.51	104
2965	WT	22	23.59		23	28.72		45	52.31	
2562	Tmp	19	20.38		27	24.82	109	46	45.20	102
2659	H8	17	21.15		26	25.76	101	43	46.91	
101072		804	804.03		979	978.99		1783	178 3.01	

1. No. of different words in play (count by Hart).   2. Name of play, abbreviated.   3. Two-six-fold link words: no. of links. 4. No. expected.   5. Ratio of observed to expected, as percent. 6. Seven-ten-fold link words, no. of links observed.   7. No. expected.   8. Ratio of observed to expected, as percent.   9. Total two-ten-fold link words: no. of links observed.   10. No. expected. 11. Ratio of observed to expected, as percent.
Statistically significant positive deviations are underlined.

Links with L E A R

1	2	3	4	5	6	7	8	9	10	11
3146	2H6	31	39.35		49	46.19	106	80	85.54	
2790	3H6	22	34.90		28	40.96		50	75.86	
3014	1H6	34	37.70		39	44.25		73	81.95	
3218	R3	38	40.25		41	47.25		79	87.50	
2037	Err	27	25.48	106	23	29.91		50	55.39	
2578	Tit	20	32.25		29	37.85		49	70.10	
2463	Shr	36	30.81	117	49	36.16	136	85	66.97	127
2153	TGV	18	26.93		23	31.61		41	58.54	
2872	LLL	24	35.92		40	42.17		64	78.09	
2916	Rom	30	36.47		47	42.81	110	77	79.29	
2833	R2	29	35.44		48	41.60	115	77	77.03	
2363	MND	37	29.56	125	40	34.70	115	77	64.25	120
2901	Jo	25	36.29		39	42.59		64	78.88	
2571	MV	20	32.16		29	37.75		49	69.91	
3028	1H4	37	37.87		48	44.46	108	85	82.33	103
3130	2H4	35	39.15		34	45.96		69	85.11	
2527	Wiv	28	31.61		25	37.10		53	68.71	
2396	Ado	22	29.97		22	35.18		44	65.15	
3162	H5	44	39.55	111	46	46.43		90	85.98	105
2218	JC	20	27.74		18	32.57		38	60.31	
2578	AYL	35	32.25	109	40	37.85	106	75	70.10	107
2534	TN	43	31.70	136	42	37.21	113	85	68.90	123
3882	Ham	77	48.56	159	83	57.00	146	160	105.56	152
3360	Tro	64	42.03	152	55	49.33	111	119	91.36	130
2705	AWW	33	33.83		45	39.72	113	78	73.55	106
2669	MM	40	33.38	120	42	39.19	107	82	72.57	113
3015	Oth	26	37.71		52	44.27	117	78	81.98	
2521	Tim	45	31.53	143	49	37.02	132	94	68.55	137
	Lr	48			46			94		
2652	Mac	51	33.17	154	33	38.94		84	72.11	116
3004	Ant	28	37.57		47	44.11	107	75	81.68	
3130	Cor	36	39.15		46	45.96	100	82	85.11	
1049	Per[1]	12	13.12		5	15.40		17	28.52	
1393	Per[2]	14	17.42		23	20.45	112	37	37.88	
3260	Cym	55	40.78	135	59	47.87	123	114	88.64	129
2965	WT	46	37.09	124	55	43.53	126	101	80.62	125
2562	Tmp	40	32.05	125	39	37.62	104	79	69.66	113
2659	H8	32	33.26		40	39.04	102	72	72.30	
100254		1254	1254.00		1472	1472.01		2726	2725.98	

1. No. of different words in play (count by Hart).   2. Name of play, abbreviated.   3. Two-six-fold link words: no. of links.
4. No. expected.   5. Ratio of observed to expected, as percent.
6. Seven-ten-fold link words, no. of links observed.   7. No. expected.   8. Ratio of observed to expected, as percent.   9. Total two-ten-fold link words: no. of links observed.   10. No. expected.
11. Ratio of observed to expected, as percent.
Statistically significant positive deviations are underlined.

Links with M A C B E T H

1	2	3	4	5	6	7	8	9	10	11
3146	2H6	39	30.70	127	41	35.09	117	80	65.79	122
2790	3H6	22	27.23		32	31.12	103	54	58.35	
3014	1H6	26	29.41		40	33.62	119	66	63.03	105
3218	R3	28	31.40		35	35.90		63	67.30	
2037	Err	16	19.88		23	22.72	101	39	42.60	
2578	Tit	14	25.16		22	28.76		36	53.91	
2463	Shr	16	24.03		18	27.47		34	51.51	
2153	TGV	13	21.01		20	24.02		33	45.03	
2872	LLL	12	28.03		25	32.04		37	60.06	
2916	Rom	27	28.45		33	32.53	101	60	60.98	
2833	R2	28	27.64	101	28	31.60		56	59.25	
2363	MND	28	23.06	121	36	26.36	137	64	49.42	130
2901	Jo	31	28.31	110	39	32.36	121	70	60.67	115
2571	MV	14	25.09		24	28.68		38	53.77	
3028	1H4	33	29.55	112	23	33.78		56	63.33	
3130	2H4	28	30.54		29	34.92		57	65.46	
2527	Wiv	20	24.66		15	28.19		35	52.85	
2396	Ado	15	23.38		14	26.73		29	50.11	
3162	H5	24	30.86		47	35.27	133	71	66.13	107
2218	JC	14	21.64		25	24.74	101	39	46.39	
2578	AYL	19	25.16		23	28.76		42	53.91	
2534	TN	23	24.73		24	28.27		47	52.99	
3882	Ham	61	37.88	161	62	43.30	143	123	81.19	151
3360	Tro	62	32.79	189	42	37.48	112	104	70.27	148
2705	AWW	23	26.40		33	30.17	109	56	56.57	
2669	MM	25	26.04		36	29.77	121	61	55.82	109
3015	Oth	35	29.42	119	29	33,63		64	63.05	102
2521	Tim	18	24.60		25	28.12		43	52.72	
3339	Lr	62	32.58	190	36	37.25		98	69.83	140
	Mac	23			25			48		
3004	Ant	36	29.31	123	37	33.51	110	73	62.82	116
3130	Cor	34	30.54	111	36	34.92	103	70	65.46	107
1049	Per[1]	6	10.24		5	11.70		11	21.94	
1393	Per[2]	7	13.59		19	15.54	122	26	29.13	
3260	Cym	45	31.81	141	46	36.37	126	91	68.18	133
2965	WT	31	28.93	107	39	33.07	118	70	62.01	113
2562	Tmp	28	25.00	112	34	28.58	119	62	53.58	116
2659	H8	22	25.95		31	29.66	105	53	55.61	
100941		985	985.00		1126	1126.00		2111	2111.02	

1. No. of different words in play (count by Hart).   2. Name of
play, abbreviated.   3. Two-six-fold link words: no. of links.
4. No. expected.   5. Ratio of observed to expected, as percent.
6. Seven-ten-fold link words, no. of links observed.   7. No. expected.   8. Ratio of observed to expected, as percent.   9. Total
two-ten-fold link words: no. of links observed.   10. No. expected.
11. Ratio of observed to expected, as percent.
Statistically significant positive deviations are underlined.

Links with A N T O N Y

1	2	3	4	5	6	7	8	9	10	11
3146	2H6	28	28.77		32	43.04		60	71.81	
2790	3H6	25	25.52		31	38.17		56	63.68	
3014	1H6	24	27.57		43	41.23	104	67	68.80	
3218	R3	24	29.43		49	44.02	111	73	73.45	
2037	Err	12	18.63		16	27.86		28	46.50	
2578	Tit	29	23.58	123	37	35.27	105	66	58.84	112
2463	Shr	19	22.53		31	33.69		50	56.22	
2153	TGV	10	19.69		17	29.45		27	49.14	
2872	LLL	13	26.27		40	39.29	102	53	65.56	
2916	Rom	15	26.67		34	39.89		49	66.56	
2833	R2	21	25.91		42	38.75	108	63	64.66	
2363	MND	26	21.61	120	36	32.32	111	62	53.94	115
2901	Jo	24	26.53		34	39.68		58	66.22	
2571	MV	16	23.51		25	35.17		41	58.68	
3028	1H4	29	27.69	105	28	41.42		57	69.12	
3130	2H4	28	28.63		45	42.82	105	73	71.44	102
2527	Wiv	15	23.11		24	34.57		39	57.68	
2396	Ado	14	21.91		22	32.78		36	54.69	
3162	H5	32	28.92	111	38	43.25		70	72.17	
2218	JC	11	20.29		21	30.34		32	50.63	
2578	AYL	20	23.58		41	35.27	116	61	58.84	104
2534	TN	10	23.18		28	34.66		38	57.84	
3882	Ham	57	35.51	161	56	53.10	105	113	88.61	128
3360	Tro	50	30.73	163	50	45.96	109	100	76.69	130
2705	AWW	33	24.74	133	40	37.00	108	73	61.74	118
2669	MM	25	24.41	102	30	36.51		55	60.92	
3015	Oth	37	27.58	134	45	41.24	109	82	68.82	119
2521	Tim	23	23.66		37	34.39	107	60	57.54	104
3339	Lr	26	30.54		53	45.68	116	79	76.21	104
2652	Mac	37	24.26	153	39	36.28	107	76	60.53	126
	Ant	31			45			76		
3130	Cor	33	28.63	115	59	42.82	138	92	71.44	129
1049	Per[1]	9	9.59		17	14.35	118	26	23.94	109
1393	Per[2]	16	12.74	126	26	19.06	136	42	31.80	132
3260	Cym	41	29.82	137	64	44.59	144	105	74.41	141
2965	WT	39	27.12	144	43	40.56	106	82	67.68	121
2562	Tmp	34	23.43	145	60	35.05	171	94	58.48	161
2659	H8	15	24.32		43	36.37	118	58	60.69	
100589		920	920.01		1376	1376.00		2296	2295.97	

1. No. of different words in play (count by Hart).   2. Name of play, abbreviated.   3. Two-six-fold link words: no. of links. 4. No. expected.   5. Ratio of observed to expected.
6. Seven-ten-fold link words, no. of links observed.   7. No. expected.   8. Ratio of observed to expected, as percent.   9. Total two-ten-fold link words: no. of links observed.   10. No. expected.
11. Ratio of observed to expected, as percent.
Statistically significant positive deviations are underlined.

Links with C O R I O L A N U S

1	2	3	4	5	6	7	8	9	10	11
3146	2H6	30	34.20		29	41.12		59	75.31	
2790	3H6	26	30.33		47	36.46	129	73	66.79	109
3014	1H6	33	32.76	101	47	39.39	119	80	72.15	111
3218	R3	24	34.98		30	42.06		54	77.04	
2037	Err	20	22.14		26	26.62		46	48.76	
2578	Tit	30	28.02	107	27	33.69		57	61.72	
2463	Shr	20	26.77		36	32.19	112	56	58.96	
2153	TGV	18	23.40		12	28.14		30	51.54	
2872	LLL	20	31.22		25	37.54		45	68.75	
2916	Rom	21	31.70		34	38.11		55	69.81	
2833	R2	26	30.79		41	37.03	111	67	67.82	
2363	MND	19	25.69		22	30.88		41	56.57	
2901	Jo	24	31.53		40	37.91	106	64	69.45	
2571	MV	29	27.95	104	27	33.60		56	61.55	
3028	1H4	42	32.91	128	36	39.57		78	72.49	108
3130	2H4	36	34.02	106	36	40.91		72	74.93	
2527	Wiv	17	27.47		27	33.03		44	60.49	
2396	Ado	27	26.04	104	20	31.31		47	57.36	
3162	H5	33	34.37		48	41.33	116	81	75.70	107
2218	JC	28	24.11	116	34	28.99	117	62	53.10	117
2578	AYL	20	28.02		19	33.69		39	61.72	
2534	TN	35	27.54	127	31	33.12		66	60.66	109
3882	Ham	50	42.20	118	53	50.74	104	103	92.93	111
3360	Tro	55	36.52	151	49	43.91	112	104	80.44	129
2705	AWW	36	29.40	122	47	35.35	133	83	64.76	128
2669	MM	30	29.01	103	30	34.88		60	63.89	
3015	Oth	35	32.77	107	41	39,40	104	76	72.18	105
2521	Tim	25	27.40		43	32.95	131	68	60.35	113
3339	Lr	36	36.29		44	43.64	101	80	79.93	100
2652	Mac	33	28.83	114	42	34.66	121	75	63.49	118
3004	Ant	36	32.65	110	58	39.26	148	94	71.91	131
	Cor	43			46			89		
1049	Per[1]	7	11.40		17	13.71	124	24	25.11	
1393	Per[2]	16	15.14	106	18	18.21		34	33.35	102
3260	Cym	52	35.44	147	58	42.61	136	110	78.04	141
2965	WT	47	32.23	146	42	38.75	108	89	70.98	125
2562	Tmp	26	27.85		43	33.48	128	69	61.33	113
2659	H8	30	28.90	104	34	34.75		64	63.65	101
100463		1092	1091.99		1313	1312.99		2405	2405.01	

1. No. of different words in play (count by Hart). 2. Name of play, abbreviated. 3. Two-six-fold link words: no. of links. 4. No. expected. 5. Ratio of observed to expected, as percent. 6. Seven-ten-fold link words, no. of links observed. 7. No. expected. 8. Ratio of observed to expected, as percent. 9. Total two-ten-fold link words: no. of links observed. 10. No. expected. 11. Ratio of observed to expected, as percent.
Statistically significant positive deviations are underlined.

Links with P E R I C L E S (acts 1 and 2)

1	2	3	4	5	6	7	8	9	10	11
3146	2H6	8	9.11		20	14.02	143	28	23.13	121
2790	3H6	6	8.08		19	12.43	153	25	20.51	122
3014	1H6	19	8.73	218	9	13.43		28	22.16	126
3218	R3	12	9.32	129	14	14.34		26	23.66	110
2037	Err	8	5.90	136	7	9.08		15	14.98	100
2578	Tit	15	7.47	201	13	11.49	113	28	18.96	148
2463	Shr	9	7.13	126	12	10.98	109	21	18.11	116
2153	TGV	2	6.24		6	9.60		8	15.83	
2872	LLL	5	8.32		16	12.80	125	21	21.12	
2916	Rom	11	8.45	130	14	13.00	108	25	21.44	117
2833	R2	6	8.21		14	12.63	111	20	20.83	
2363	MND	9	6.84	132	10	10.53		19	17.37	109
2901	Jo	4	8.40		15	12.93	116	19	21.33	
2571	MV	12	7.45	161	7	11.46		19	18.90	101
3028	1H4	8	8.77		24	13.49	178	32	22.26	144
3130	2H4	11	9.07	121	17	13.95	122	28	23.01	122
2527	Wiv	7	7.32		11	11.26		18	18.58	
2396	Ado	4	6.94		10	10.68		14	17.62	
3162	H5	10	9.16	109	13	14.09		23	23.25	
2218	JC	3	6.42		10	9.88	101	13	16.31	
2578	AYL	5	7.47		6	11.49		11	18.96	
2534	TN	5	7.34		6	11.29		11	18.63	
3882	Ham	12	11.24	107	16	17.30		28	28.54	
3360	Tro	13	9.73	134	16	14.97	107	29	24.71	117
2705	AWW	12	7.83	153	15	12.06	124	27	19.89	136
2669	MM	5	7.73		7	11.89		12	19.62	
3015	Oth	5	8.73		18	13.44	134	23	22.17	104
2521	Tim	7	7.30		4	11.24		11	18.54	
3339	Lr	12	9.67	124	4	14.88		16	24.55	
2652	Mac	6	7.68		6	11.82		12	19.50	
3004	Ant	9	8.70	103	22	13.39	164	31	22.09	140
3130	Cor	9	9.07		19	13.95	136	28	23.01	122
	Per[1]	:			11			19		
1393	Per[2]	8	4.03	199	8	6.21	129	16	10.24	156
3260	Cym	5	9.44		23	14.53	158	28	23.97	117
2965	WT	6	8.59		13	13.21		19	21.80	
2562	Tmp	2	7.42		5	11.42		7	18.84	
2659	H8	7	7.70		8	11.85		15	19.55	
02544		297	297.00		457	457.01		754	753.97	

1. No. of different words in play (count by Hart).   2. Name of play, abbreviated.   3. Two-six-fold link words: no. of links. 4. No. expected.   5. Ratio of observed to expected, as percent. 6. Seven-ten-fold link words, no. of links observed.   7. No. expected.   8. Ratio of observed to expected, as percent.   9. Total two-ten-fold link words: no. of links observed.   10. No. expected. 11. Ratio of observed to expected, as percent. Statistically significant positive deviations are underlined.

Links with P E R I C L E S (acts 3 to 5)

1	2	3	4	5	6	7	8	9	10	11
3146	2H6	15	13.61	110	24	24.20		39	37.80	103
2790	3H6	2	12.07		19	21.46		21	33.52	
3014	1H6	9	13.04		13	23.18		22	36.22	
3218	R3	13	13.92		16	24.75		29	38.67	
2037	Err	8	8.81		11	15.67		19	24.48	
2578	Tit	13	11.15	117	20	19.83	101	33	30.98	107
2463	Shr	15	10.65	141	26	18.94	137	_41_	_29.59_	_139_
2153	TGV	7	9.31		16	16.56		23	25.87	
2872	LLL	11	12.42		22	22.09		33	34.51	
2916	Rom	13	12.61	103	29	22.43	129	42	35.04	120
2833	R2	8	12.25		22	21.79	101	30	34.04	
2363	MND	13	10.22	127	25	18.17	138	38	28.39	134
2901	Jo	10	12.55		25	22.31	112	35	34.86	100
2571	MV	9	11.12		21	19.77	106	30	30.89	
3028	1H4	18	13.10	137	23	23.29		41	36.38	113
3130	2H4	15	13.54	111	17	24.07		32	37.61	
2527	Wiv	9	10.93		17	19.43		26	30.36	
2396	Ado	11	10.36	106	6	18.43		17	28.79	
3162	H5	_22_	_13.68_	_161_	25	24.32	103	47	37.99	124
2218	JC	4	9.59		15	17.06		19	26.65	
2578	AYL	7	11.15		12	19.83		19	30.98	
2534	TN	13	10.96	119	19	19.49		32	30.45	105
3882	Ham	_26_	_16.79_	_155_	33	29.86	111	59	46.64	127
3360	Tro	11	14.53		24	25.84		35	40.37	
2705	AWW	10	11.70		25	20.80	120	35	32.50	108
2669	MM	7	11.54		12	20.53		19	32.07	
3015	Oth	11	13.04		15	23.19		26	36.23	
2521	Tim	16	10.90	147	16	19.39		32	30.29	106
3339	Lr	15	14.44	104	29	25.68	113	44	40.12	110
2652	Mac	8	11.47		24	20.40	118	32	31.87	100
3004	Ant	16	12.99	123	28	23.10	121	44	36.10	122
3130	Cor	16	13.54	118	21	24.07		37	37.61	
1049	Per^1	8	4.54	176	9	8.07	112	17	12.60	135
	Per^2	5			17			22		
3260	Cym	16	14.10	113	27	25.07	108	43	39.17	110
2965	WT	14	12.82	109	_34_	_22.80_	_149_	_48_	_35.63_	_135_
2562	Tmp	16	11.08	144	_46_	_19.70_	_234_	_62_	_30.78_	_201_
2659	H8	7	11.50		20	20.45		27	31.95	
102200		442	442.02		786	786.02		1228	1228.00	

1. No. of different words in play (count by Hart).   2. Name of play, abbreviated.   3. Two-six-fold link words: no. of links.
4. No. expected.   5. Ratio of observed to expected, as percent.
6. Seven-ten-fold link words, no. of links observed.   7. No. expected.   8. Ratio of observed to expected, as percent.   9. Total two-ten-fold link words: no. of links observed.   10. No. expected.
11. Ratio of observed to expected, as percent.
Statistically significant positive deviations are underlined.

Links with C Y M B E L I N E

1	2	3	4	5	6	7	8	9	10	11
3146	2H6	32	36.97		55	48.32	114	87	85.29	102
2790	3H6	18	32.78		40	42.85		58	75.64	
3014	1H6	36	35.42	102	40	46.29		76	81.71	
3218	R3	25	37.81		50	49.42	101	75	87.24	
2037	Err	21	23.94		30	31.29		51	55.22	
2578	Tit	32	30.29	106	37	39.60		69	69.89	
2463	Shr	22	28.94		34	37.83		56	66.77	
2153	TGV	13	25.30		23	33.07		36	58.37	
2872	LLL	25	33.75		41	44.11		66	77.86	
2916	Rom	38	34.27	111	44	44.79		82	79.05	104
2833	R2	26	33.29		43	43.51		69	76.80	
2363	MND	19	27.77		32	36.29		51	64.06	
2901	Jo	20	34.09		36	44.56		56	78.65	
2571	MV	25	30.21		27	39.49		52	69.70	
3028	1H4	36	35.58	101	44	46.51		80	82.09	
3130	2H4	30	36.78		46	48.07		76	84.85	
2527	Wiv	22	29.69		36	38.81		58	68.51	
2396	Ado	20	28.16		19	36.80		39	64.95	
3162	H5	45	37.16	121	55	48.56	113	100	85.72	117
2218	JC	19	26.06		33	34.07		52	60.13	
2578	AYL	25	30.29		36	39.60		61	69.89	
2534	TN	36	29.78	121	40	38.92	103	76	68.70	111
3882	Ham	67	45.62	147	69	59.62	116	136	105.24	129
3360	Tro	61	39.48	155	48	51.61		109	91.09	120
2705	AWW	36	31.79	113	49	41.55	118	85	73.33	116
2669	MM	34	31.36	108	45	40.99	110	79	72.36	109
3015	Oth	25	35.43		52	46.31	112	77	81.74	
2521	Tim	28	29.62		34	38.72		62	68.34	
3339	Lr	55	39.24	140	61	51.28	119	116	90.52	128
2652	Mac	42	31.16	135	49	40.73	120	91	71.89	127
3004	Ant	43	35.30	122	55	46.14	119	98	81.44	120
3130	Cor	52	36.78	141	52	48.07	108	104	84.85	123
1049	Per[1]	5	12.33		24	16.11	149	29	28.44	102
1393	Per[2]	17	16.37	104	26	21.39	122	43	37.76	114
	Cym	37			50			87		
2965	WT	50	34.84	144	51	45.54	112	101	80.38	126
2562	Tmp	47	30.11	156	42	39.35	107	89	69.46	128
2659	H8	32	31.25	102	43	40.84	105	75	72.08	104
100333		1179	1179.01		1541	1541.01		2720	2720.01	

1. No. of different words in play (count by Hart).   2. Name of play, abbreviated.   3. Two-six-fold link words: no. of links.
4. No. expected.   5. Ratio of observed to expected, as percent.
6. Seven-ten-fold link words, no. of links observed.   7. No. expected.   8. Ratio of observed to expected, as percent.   9. Total two-ten-fold link words: no. of links observed.   10. No. expected.
11. Ratio of observed to expected, as percent.
Statistically significant positive deviations are underlined.

Links with W I N T E R ' S   T A L E

1	2	3	4	5	6	7	8	9	10	11
3146	2H6	23	34.73		62	42.96	144	85	77.69	109
2790	3H6	15	30.80		29	38.10		44	68.90	
3014	1H6	27	33.28		42	41.15	102	69	74.43	
3218	R3	28	35.53		46	43.94	105	74	79.47	
2037	Err	21	22.49		19	27.81		40	50.30	
2578	Tit	30	28.46	105	28	35.20		58	63.66	
2463	Shr	30	27.19	110	32	33.63		62	60.82	102
2153	TGV	19	23.77		25	29.40		44	53.17	
2872	LLL	36	31.71	114	42	39.22	107	78	70.92	110
2916	Rom	24	32.19		47	39.82	118	71	72.01	
2833	R2	28	31.28		39	38.68	101	67	69.96	
2363	MND	29	26.09	111	29	32.26		58	58.35	
2901	Jo	19	32.03		31	39.61		50	71.64	
2571	MV	25	28.39		33	35.11		58	63.49	
3028	1H4	37	33.43	111	36	41.35		73	74.78	
3130	2H4	35	34.56	101	34	42.74		69	77.30	
2527	Wiv	26	27.90		23	34.50		49	62.40	
2396	Ado	18	26.45		21	32.72		39	59.17	
3162	H5	31	34.91		47	43.17	109	78	78.09	
2218	JC	16	24.49		25	30.29		41	54.77	
2578	AYL	37	28.46	130	30	35.20		67	63.66	105
2534	TN	36	27.98	129	35	34.60	101	71	62.58	113
3882	Ham	59	42.86	138	54	53.01	102	113	95.87	118
3360	Tro	37	37.10		42	45.88		79	82.97	
2705	AWW	34	29.86	114	42	36.93	114	76	66.80	114
2669	MM	45	29.47	153	51	36.44	149	96	65.91	146
3015	Oth	30	33.29		41	41.17		71	74.46	
2521	Tim	26	27.83		27	34.42		53	62.26	
3339	Lr	46	36.86	125	52	45.59	114	98	82.46	119
2652	Mac	32	29.28	109	39	36.21	108	71	65.49	108
3004	Ant	37	33.17	112	39	41.02		76	74.18	102
3130	Cor	49	34.56	142	41	42.74		90	77.30	116
1049	Per¹	6	11.58		14	14.32		20	25.90	
1393	Per²	15	15.40		34	19.02	179	49	34.40	142
3260	Cym	47	35.99	131	48	44.51	108	95	80.51	118
	WT	34			57			9?		
2562	Tmp	32	28.29	113	47	34.98	134	79	63.27	125
2659	H8	26	29.36		48	36.31	132	74	65.66	113
100628		1111	1111.02		1374	1374.01		2485	2485.00	

1. No. of different words in play (count by Hart).   2. Name of
play, abbreviated.   3. Two-six-fold link words: no. of links.
4. No. expected.   5. Ratio of observed to expected, as percent.
6. Seven-ten-fold link words, no. of links observed.   7. No. expected.   8. Ratio of observed to expected, as percent.   9. Total
two-ten-fold link words: no. of links observed.   10. No. expected.
11. Ratio of observed to expected, as percent.
Statistically significant positive deviations are underlined.

Links with T E M P E S T

1	2	3	4	5	6	7	8	9	10	11
3146	2H6	26	24.48	106	26	36.59		52	61.06	
2790	3H6	18	21.71		28	32.45		46	54.15	
3014	1H6	16	23.45		46	35.05	131	62	58.50	106
3218	R3	25	25.04		33	37.43		58	62.46	
2037	Err	14	15.85		22	23.69		36	39.54	
2578	Tit	10	20.06		22	29.98		32	50.04	
2463	Shr	20	19.16	104	27	28.64		47	47.81	
2153	TGV	11	16.75		13	25.04		24	41.79	
2872	LLL	14	22.34		29	33.40		43	55.75	
2916	Rom	23	22.69	101	23	33.91		46	56.60	
2833	R2	10	22.04		25	32.95		35	54.99	
2363	MND	21	18.38	114	35	27.48	127	56	45.87	122
2901	Jo	17	22.57		34	33.74	101	51	56.31	
2571	MV	17	20.00		30	29.90	100	47	49.90	
3028	1H4	26	23.56	110	32	35.22		58	58.77	
3130	2H4	22	24.35		30	36.40		52	60.75	
2527	Wiv	5	19.66		22	29.39		27	49.05	
2396	Ado	14	18.64		7	27.87		21	46.51	
3162	H5	37	24.60	150	36	36.77		73	61.37	119
2218	JC	18	17.26	104	20	25.80		38	43.05	
2578	AYL	24	20.06	120	20	29.98		44	50.04	
2534	TN	12	19.71		24	29.47		36	49.18	
3882	Ham	38	30.20	126	41	45.15		79	75.35	105
3360	Tro	38	26.14	145	50	39.08	128	88	65.22	135
2705	AWW	28	21.04	133	26	31.46		54	52.50	103
2669	MM	14	20.76		32	31.04	103	46	51.80	
3015	Oth	20	23.46		38	35.06	108	58	58.52	
2521	Tim	18	19.61		33	29.32	113	51	48.93	104
3339	Lr	34	25.98	131	47	38.83	121	81	64.81	125
2652	Mac	28	20.63	136	40	30.84	130	68	51.48	132
3004	Ant	29	23.37	124	53	34.94	152	82	58.31	141
3130	Cor	29	24.35	119	51	36.40	140	80	60.75	132
1049	Per[1]	2	8.16		5	12.20		7	20.36	
1393	Per[2]	12	10.84	111	43	16.20	265	55	27.04	203
3260	Cym	45	25.36	177	48	37.91	127	93	63.28	147
2965	WT	31	23.07	134	55	34.48	160	86	57.55	149
	Tmp	48			30			78		
2659	H8	20	20.69		29	30.92		49	51.61	

.01031　　　786 786.02　　　1175 1174.99　　　1961 1961.00

1. No. of different words in play (count by Hart).   2. Name of play, abbreviated.   3. Two-six-fold link words: no. of links. 4. No. expected.   5. Ratio of observed to expected, as percent. 6. Seven-ten-fold link words, no. of links observed.   7. No. expected.   8. Ratio of observed to expected, as percent.   9. Total two-ten-fold link words: no. of links observed.   10. No. expected. 11. Ratio of observed to expected, as percent. Statistically significant positive deviations are underlined.

Links with H E N R Y   V I I I

1	2	3	4	5	6	7	8	9	10	11
3146	2H6	29	26.31	110	42	38.81	108	71	65.11	109
2790	3H6	23	23.33		38	34.41	110	61	57.74	106
3014	1H6	38	25.20	151	36	37.18		74	62.38	119
3218	R3	37	26.91	137	47	39.69	118	84	66.60	126
2037	Err	17	17.03		29	25.13	115	46	42.16	109
2578	Tit	26	21.56	121	34	31.80	107	60	53.36	112
2463	Shr	17	20.60		30	30.38		47	51.02	
2153	TGV	9	18.00		16	26.56		25	44.56	
2872	LLL	26	24.02	108	24	35.43		50	59.44	
2916	Rom	15	24.38		36	35.97	100	51	60.35	
2833	R2	15	23.69		41	34.97	117	56	58.63	
2363	MND	29	19.76	147	31	29.15	106	60	48.91	123
2901	Jo	25	24.26	103	43	35.78	120	68	60.04	113
2571	MV	17	21.50		33	31.71	104	50	53.21	
3028	1H4	25	25.32		27	37.35		52	62.67	
3130	2H4	18	26.17		41	38.61	106	59	64.78	
2527	Wiv	12	21.13		19	31.17		31	52.30	
2396	Ado	14	20.04		19	29.55		33	49.59	
3162	H5	29	26.44	110	55	39.00	141	84	65.44	128
2218	JC	16	18.55		21	27.36		37	45.91	
2578	ATL	23	21.56	107	32	31.80	101	55	53.36	103
2534	TN	18	21.19		21	31.26		39	52.45	
3882	Ham	39	32.46	120	48	47.88	100	87	80.34	108
3360	Tro	29	28.10	103	49	41.44	118	78	69.54	112
2705	AWW	23	22.62	102	35	33.37	105	58	55.98	104
2669	MM	35	22.32	157	40	32.92	122	75	55.24	136
3015	Oth	24	25.21		33	37.19		57	62.40	
2521	Tim	17	21.08		23	31.10		40	52.18	
3339	Lr	32	27.92	115	36	41.19		68	69.11	
2652	Mac	22	22.18		31	32.71		53	54.89	
3004	Ant	19	25.12		48	37.05	130	67	62.17	108
3130	Cor	30	26.17	115	32	38.61		62	64.78	
1049	Per[1]	8	8.77		9	12.94		17	21.71	
1393	Per[2]	7	11.65		21	17.18	122	28	28.83	
3260	Cym	34	27.26	125	42	40.21	104	76	67.47	113
2965	WT	24	24.79		55	36.57	150	79	61.37	129
2562	Tmp	23	21.42	107	28	31.60		51	53.02	
	H8	37			32			59		
100934		844	844.02		1245	1245.00		2089	2089.04	

1. No. of different words in play (count by Hart). 2. Name of play, abbreviated. 3. Two-six-fold link words: no. of links. 4. No. expected. 5. Ratio of observed to expected, as percent. 6. Seven-ten-fold link words, no. of links observed. 7. No. expected. 8. Ratio of observed to expected, as percent. 9. Total two-ten-fold link words: no. of links observed. 10. No. expected. 11. Ratio of observed to expected, as percent.
Statistically significant positive deviations are underlined.

The 940 (948) words, linking *Edward III* with the works of Shakespeare, in the order of their appearance

This shows the results of a search through the text of *Edward III* in an attempt to find all the (lexical) words in the play, which appear to a total of not more than 12 times in the 37 plays of Shakespeare (including *Henry VIII*), in *Venus and Adonis*, *The Rape of Lucrece*, and the Sonnets. The extent to which the attempt may be thought to have succeeded is discussed in the paragraphs headed 'Difficulties, Oversights and Errors' in pp. 105–6 of the text.

For the definition of a 'lexical word', as understood in this thesis, see p. 103 of the text. The list of words (link words or catch words) has been drawn up by reference to Spevack's one-volume *Concordance to Shakespeare*. The numbers of the appearances of the words in the 40 works of Shakespeare specified are the raw material of the statistical analyses shown in Chapter 7. Appearances of these words in other works covered by Spevack's *Concordance* (*Two Noble Kinsmen*, *The Passionate Pilgrim*, *A Lover's Complaint*, *The Phoenix and the Turtle*, *Sir Thomas More*) are shown in this Appendix enclosed in brackets. They were not used in the statistical analyses, nor did they qualify to restrict the total number of appearances permitted per word.

Appendix III groups the appearances of words into the play's acts and scenes, as shown in modern editions. In the Tudor Facsimile edition, on which the work of the present study was done, these divisions are made apparent by the stage direction of 'exeunt' when the stage clears. Acts and scenes have not been used for the numeration of lines of verse or stage direction of the facsimile edition. Instead a continuous numeration, line by line, from the first 'Enter . . .' to the final 'FINIS', was used.

In successive lines the Appendix shows:

1. The line number (in cntinuous numeration) in which the link word appears in *Edward III*;

2. The identifying number of this word in the alphabetical list, Appendix IV;

3. The word, as printed in the text;

4. In brackets, equivalents as found in the concordance; if the sole equivalent in the concordance is identical with the word as printed in the *E3* text, the brackets are closed so (), without an inclusion; if there is no equivalent in the concordance, no entry is made; such words are also identified by a zero at the end of the line;

5. The code names (not underlined) of Shakespeare's works where the word or its equivalent is found, with the total number of times it appears there;

6. The total number (0–12) of its appearances in Shakespeare's works, as used for

the statistical analysis, i.e. not counting the works of Shakespeare enclosed in brackets, *TNK, PP, LC, PhT, STM.*

NB. The following words, with line number, were excluded from the main statistical analyses: 352 inconstant, 746 recouerie, 956 ouerbeare, 1123 quartred, 1144 pitch, 1244 quartering, 1495 pitched, 1801 pitch, 1928 stronger, 1942 Quartred, 2238 Rebell, 2387 quartering. For an explanation, see the paragraphs on 'Difficulties, Oversights and Errors', pp. 105–6 of the text.

Act 1 scene 1

```
    6 693 retayne (retain, retain'd, retaining, retains) 1H6 Err²ₐRom Joh
Ham Lr.2 Tmp H8 (TNK.2)                                                    19
    6 720 Seigniorie (seigniory, seignery, signiory, signories) R2.2 2H4
Oth Tmp                                                                     5
    8 582 pedegree (pedigree) 3H6.2 1H6 H5                                  4
   10 788 successefully (successfully) Tit Shr AYL                          3
   11 672 regall (regal) 2H6 3H6.7 1H6 R2.2 Tro                            12
   12 482 loynes (loins) 3H6 R3 Rom Ado JC Ham Tro MM Lr.2 Cor Cym         12
   17 331 fragrant () Tit.2 MND Wiv Son                                     5
   19 429 inheritor (inheritor, inheritors) R3 LLL 2H4 Ham Tro Per⁺ Son     7
   20 650 rancor (rancor, rancor's, rancors) 2H6.2 R3.2 Rom R2 Ado Mac      8
   20 659 rebellious () 2H6 1H6.2 Rom R2 AYL Ham.2 Mac.2 (TNK)             10
   21 477 lynage                                                            0
   26 681 repleat (replete) 2H6 3H6 1H6.3 LLL AWW Son.2                     9
   28 495 male (male, males) 3H6.2 Err 2H4 Mac (TNK)                        5
   30 929 Wherewith () 2H6 3H6 1H6.2 TGV LLL R2 Joh Mac Son (PP)           10
   30 279 exclude (excludes) Err                                           1
   32 230 dusty () Tro Mac (TNK)                                            2
   32 92 brittile (brittle) R3 R2.2 1H4 (PP.2)                              4
   38 460 lauish (lavish) 1H6 1H4 2H4 MM Mac                                5
   39 478 lyneal (lineal) 1H6 R3.2 R2 Joh.2 2H4 H5                          8
   39 921 watch men (watchman, watchmen) 1H6 Ado Ham Ant Son               5
   40 423 in directly (indirectly) R3 Joh MV.2 1H4 H5 MM Son               8
   43 657 rebate () MM                                                      1
   45 737 shewers (shower, showers) 3H6 Tit Shr Ham Ant.2 Cor H8 Ven Son  10
   47 906 vigor () Err Tit LLL R2 Joh Ham Tro.2 MM Cym Tmp Ven (TNK)       12
   48 254 engendred (engender, engenders, engend'red, engend'ring) 3H6
1H6.2 Shr LLL MV JC AYL Tro Oth Tim Ant                                   12
   49 397 heeretofore                                                       0
   49 649 rakt (rack, rack'd) 2H6.2 LLL MV TN MM.2 Tmp                      8
   63 262 entayld (entail) 3H6.2                                            2
   68 473 liegeman (liegeman, liegemen) 1H6 1H4 Ham WT                      4
   70 683 repossesse (repossess) 3H6.4                                      4
   74 257 inioynd (enjoin, enjoin'd, enjoineth) TGV.2 LLL Rom MV Ado AWW
Per² WT.2 Tmp                                                              11
   78 724 seruilely (servilely) Ven                                         1
   80 873 vnpolisht (unpolish'd, unpolished) 2H6 Shr LLL                    3
   81 910 visard (vizard, vizards) LLL.7 1H4.3 Wiv Mac                     12
   82 35 arrogannce (arrogance)          R3 Shr Tro.2 AWW H8                6
   83 294 fealty () 2H6 Tit TGV R2 Cym                                      5
   87 223 Dominions (dominion, dominions) R2 Jo Ham Lr Cym WT H8           7
   88 368 grudging (grudg'd, grudge, grudging) 1H6.2 R3 Ado JC Lr          6
   89 608 plumes (plume, plumes) 1H6 LLL Jo H5 TN Tro AWW MM Cor Tmp Ven  11
   90 935 wildernes (wilderness) 2H6 Tit.2 TGV R2 MV 2H4 MM Luc            9
   92 185 defyaunce (defiance) Rom R2 Jo 1H4.2 2H4 H5.3 JC Tro MM (TNK)    12
```

```
 93 185 Defiance () Rom R2 Jo 1H4.2 2H4 H5.3 JC Tro MM (TNK)      12
 93 660 rebound                                                    0
 97 716 scurrylous (scurrilous) WT                                 1
 98 465 lazy () 3H6 Rom MND H5 AYL Tro.2 H8.2 Ven (TNK)           10
 98 226 droane (drone, drones) 2H6 MV H5 Per².2                    5
 99 770 stelth (stealth) Err Rom MND.2 TN MM Tim Lr.2 Son         10
104 594 peecemeale                                                 0
106 800 surrender () R2 H8                                         2
107 911 voluntarie (voluntary) Jo.3 MV JC AYL Tro Oth Cym          9
109 673 Regenerate () R2                                           1
109 909 viper (viper, vipers) R2 H5 Tro.2 Oth Cor Per¹            7
110 329 fostred (foster, foster'd, fostered, fosters, fost'ring)
Tit TGV LLL R2 Jo Per² per⁺ Cym                                    8
110 424 infancy () 2H6 1H6 R3 TGV LLL Wiv Tro.3 WT Tmp            11
111 148 conspiracy () R2.2 Wiv H5 JC.3 Lr WT Tmp.2               11
113 732 sharpnes (sharpness) AWW Lr Ant (TNK)                     3
114 300 Feruent                                                    0
115 818 thornie                                                    0
116 540 nightingale (nightingale, nightingale's, nightingales)
Shr.2 TGV.2 Rom.3 MND MV TN Lr Ant (PP TNK)                       12
116 711 scard (scarr'd) R3 Tit Cor Oth                             4
119 304 finall                                                     0
129 215 disseuered (dissever, dissever'd) Jo AWW WT                3
133 443 inuasion (invasion) Jo Luc                                 2
133 85 bordering (bordered) Lr                                     1
135 66 beguirt                                                     0
136 248 inclosd (enclos'd, enclose, enclosed, encloses, enclo-
seth, enclosing) 2H6 1H6 R3 H5 JC.2 Cym WT Luc.2 Son (LC PhT TNK)11
142 415 Ignoble () 2H6.2 3H6 1H6.2 R3.2 WT Tmp                     9
144 749 snailie                                                    0
146 319 footemen (footman, footmen) Tit Ant WT.4                   6
147 532 muster (muster, musters) 1H4 2H4.2 H5.2 Lr Ant             7
147 497 men at armes (man-at-arms, men-at-arms) LLL 2H4            2
148 736 shire () H8                                                1
148 236 elect (elect, elected) 1H6 Tit R2 Tro MM Con Cym           7
151 919 warie (wary) 1H6.2 Rom JC Ham.2 MM Oth.2 WT Son           11
151 137 comence (commenc'd, commence, commences, commenced,
commencing) 2H6 1H6 1H4 2H4.3 Ado Tim Mac Per² Son (PhT)          11
154 292 Father in Law (father-in-law) R3.2 H8.2                    4
156 16 allies (allies, ally) R3.4 Rom 1H4 AYL                      7
159 451 ioyntly (jointly) 2H6 Ham Mac Lr. Luc.2                    6
161 685 repulse                                                    0
161 839 trayterous (traitorous, trait'rous) 2H6 1H6 Tit.4 Ham
Lr Cor                                                             9
162 687 resolute () 2H6.2 3H6.2 1H6.2 R3 LLL AYL TN MM Mac        12
165 889 ure                                                        0
167 847 tumult (tumult, tumults) 3H6 1H6.2 Jo 2H4 Luc              6
174 117 cheerefully (cheerfully) 1H6 R3.3 Shr H5.2 Ham.2 (TNK) 9
```

Act 1 scene 2

```
179 789 souccour (succor, succors) 2H6 1H6.3 R2 1H4 H5 AYL
Per¹ H8.3                                                         12
181 731 sharpely (sharply) TN AWW Cym Tmp Ven                      5
182 898 vehement () R3 Jo MV MM Oth Luc                            6
184 713 scornefull (scornful) Shr MND Wiv AWW.2 Lr Cym Ven Luc
(TNK.2)                                                            9
185 883 vntuned (untun'd, untune) Err R2 Tro Lr Luc                5
```

```
186  56 barbarisme (barbarism) LLL R2 Tro WT                          4
188 191 deride (derides) Lr                                           1
189 854 vnseuill (              uncivil) 2H6 TGV.2 R2 TN.4
189 450 giggs (jig) LLL Ado.2 TN Ham (TNK)                            5
190  88 bray (bray, bray'd, braying) Jo Ham TN                        3
191  78 bleake (bleak) Jo AYL AWW Tim Lr Per³                         6
191 340 fruitlesse (fruitless) MND.2 TN Mac Ven                       5
194 128 closely () R3.2 Shr LLL Rom Jo H5 Ham                         8
195  51 babble () TGV H5 TN                                           3
198 695 reuerence (reverenc'd reverence) 1H6.2 MV Per² Cym            5
198 265 intirely (entirely) LLL MV Ado AWW MM Oth.2 Lr Ant            9
199 238 embassage (ambassage, embassage) R3 LLL R2 Ado.2 Son          6
202 537 neighbor () LLL Rom R2 2H4 AYL Ham    Tim Cym Ven             9
202 590 persist (persist, persisted, persists) Tro AWW Ant            3
203 231 eager () 3H6.2 1H6 R2.3 Ham.2 Luc.2 Son                      11
2C4  83 bonny () 2H6 R3 Shr.2 Ado AYL Ham (TNK)                       7
204 696 riders (rider, rider's, riders) LLL.2 R2.2 H5 AYL Cym Ven.3
Son (LC TNK.3)                                                       11
205 701 rust (rust, rusted) 2H6 3H6 LLL Rom   . H5 AWW Oth Cor Per²   9
206 748 snaffles (snaffle) Ant                                        1
207 354 Gymould (gimmal'd) H5                                         1
207 490 mayle (mail) Tro                                              1
208 364 grayned (grained) Err Ham Cor (LC)                            3
208  39 ash () Cor                                                    1
209 939 wise () Per⁵ (PP)                                             1
209 122 Citie (city) R3 Tit Rom Jo Tim Cor.3                          8
210 100 buttond (button'd) Err                                        1
210 809 tawny () 1H6 Tit LLL MND H5 Ant Tmp                           7
210 467 leatherne (leathern, leathren) MND 2H4 AYL.2 Ven              5
210  68 belts (belt) 2H4 Mac  (PP)                                    2
211 930 whinyards                                                     0
217   5 acceptable () Son                                             1
224 471 liable () LLL Jo.3 JC.2 Per⁴ (TNK)                            7
228  84 booty () 3H6 Tit 1H4                                          3
228 402 hitherward (hitherward, hitherwards) 2H6 3H6 Jo 1H4.2 Lr Cor
Per¹                                                                  8
229 194 discry (descry, descried) 1H6 R3 Shr LLL Rom Oth Lr Ant
Per¹ Per⁵ Luc                                                        11
230 669 reflicting (reflect, reflecting, reflects) R3 Tit Cym WT
Ven Luc                                                               6
231 602 plate (plate, plates) Shr Rom R2.2 2H4.2 Tim Ant.2 Cym H8    11
231 595 pickes (pike, pikes) 3H6 1H6 2H4 Ado H5.2 Cor.2 Cym.2 Tmp
Ven                                                                  12
232 759 speedely (speedily) 3H6 1H4.3 AWW.2 MM.2 Lr.2 Cym H8  (TNK)  12
234 401 hindmost ()    Tro Son                                        2
235 209 Dislodge (dislodg'd) Cor                                      1
235 209 dislodge Cor                                                  1
236 703 saddle () R3 R2.2 2H4 Lr                                      5
236  83 bonny  2H6 R3 Shr.2 Ado AYL Ham                               7
250  83 bonnie (bonny) 2H6 R3 Shr.2 Ado AYL Ham                       7
251 440 intollerable (intolerable) 2H6.2 1H6 Tit Shr   1H4 Wiv.2      8
258 288 facelesse.                                                    0
259 542 North-east (northeast) R2                                     1
268 366 gratulate () R3 Tit MM Tim                                    4
273 856 vncupple (uncouple) Tit MND Ven                               3
275 381 hardie (hardiest, hardy) 3H6   R3.2 TN Ham Mac  (TNK.3)       6
280 793 sullied (sullied, sully) 1H6 1H4 Wiv WT Son (TNK)             5
280 567 ouercast (overcast) MND (o'ercast) R3 Jo                      3
```

```
285 247 enchantment () TN WT                                                    2
287 180 declyne                                                                 0
299 347 gallop (gallop, galloping, gallops) 2H6 Tit LLL Rom.3 H5
AYL.2 Mac (TNK)                                                                10
306 539 niggard (niggard, niggarding) JC Son (TNK)                              2
313 684 repulse () 1H6 TGV Cor Cym Tmp                                          5
316 176 day stars                                                               0
318 153 Contemplatiue (contemplative) LLL AYL TN  (TNK)                         3
323 552 Oratorie (oratory) 1H6 R3.2 Tit Luc.2                                   6
327 431 inner                                                                   0
330 620 Presageth (presage, presages, presageth, presaging) 3H6.2
1H6 MV.2 JC Lr Ant.2 Rom                                                       10
330 430 inly ()          H5 Tmp                                                 2
330 65 beautified (beautified, beautify) 2H6 Tit TGV Rom Ham.2 Per⁵Luc 8
332 557 Ore () Ham AWW                                                          2
333 857 vndect (undeck) R2                                                      1
333 805 tapestrie (tapestries, tapestry) Err Shr 2H4 Ado Oth Cym               6
334 721 sere () Err MM                                                          2
334 864 vnfertill                                                               0
334 340 fructles (fruitless) MND.2 TN Mac Ven                                   5
335 885 vpper (upper) R3 TGV JC Cor WT H8                                       6
335 848 turfe (turf) LLL MND H5 AYL Ham Cym                                     6
336 578 party colloured (parti-color'd) MV                                      1
337 190 Delue (delve, delves) Ham Cym Son                                       3
338 556 ordure () H5                                                            1
342 859 vnder (under) MV ("seal'd under") AWW ("kept under")                    2
342 348 garnisht (garnish, garnish'd, garnished) LLL Jo MV H5                   4
349 408 host () Err AWW                                                         2
```

Act 2 scene 1

```
351 890 vtterance (utterance, utt'rance) Tit R2 Jo JC.2     Cor
WT Ham                                                                          8
                                                                               ex.
352 422 inconstant () Rom.3 MND H5.2 AYL TN WT Son.2
353 648 racke (racking) 3H6                                                     1
357 46 Attracted (attract, attracts) 2H6 1H4 TN                                3
357 118 cherie (cherry) R3 MND.2 (TNK)                                         3
359 712 scarlet () 1H6.2 Shr Rom R2 1H4 Tim H8 Luc Son                        10
360 559 oryent (orient) 2H4 Son                                                2
361 90 bricke (brick, bricks) 2H6 MM                                           2
361 159 Corrall (coral) Tmp Son                                                2
365 416 immodest () 1H6 TGV 2H4 Ado WT Ven                                     6
366 891 wale (vail, vail'd, vailed, vailing) 1H6 R3 Shr LLL MV 2H4
Ham MM Cor Per² Per⁴ Ven                                                      12
377 314 fluent () H5                                                           1
379 93 broad () 1H6 Tit Ham                                                    3
380 273 epithites (epithets) LLL.3 Ado Oth  (epithite, epithites)             5
385 185 defiance Rom R2 Jo 1H4.2 2H4 H5.3 JC Tro MM (TNK)                      12
388 913 wakened (waken, waken'd, wakened) 3H6 R3 Rom.2 Tro Oth Cym
Son                                                                             8
389 65 beautified 2H6 Tit TGV Rom Ham.2 Per⁵ Luc                               8
390 318 foolishness () Err                                                      1
393 338 frosty () 2H6 Tit.2 R2 1H4 H5.2 AYL Ven                                9
400 119 Chesse                                                                 0
401 510 meditate (meditate, meditates, meditating) 1H6 R3 JC.2 H5 TN
AWW H8                                                                          8
403 609 poetrie (poetry) Tit Shr.2 LLL MV 1H4 AYL.3 (PP)                       9
404 591 perswasiue                                                             0
406 728 shadow (shadow, shadowed, shadowing) Tit Jo MV Oth Mac Ven Luc 7
```

```
406 899 vaile (veil) 3H6 R3 Wiv H5 TN Ven Son                          7
406 463 lawne (lawn, lawns) Oth WT.2 Ven Luc.2                         6
412  30 arber (arbor, arbors) 2H4 Ado JC (TNK)                         3
413 163 counsel house (council-house) 2H6 R3                           2
413 102 cabynet (cabinet) Ven Luc                                      2
414 157 conuenticle (conventicles) 2H6                                 1
415 203 disburdning (disburdened) R2                                   1
416 445 inuocate (invocate) 1H6 R3 Son                                 3
420 250 encouch                                                        0
421 456 laments (lament, laments) 1H6 Tit.2 R2 Luc                     5
423 309 flynt (flint) R2 R3 2H4                                        3

427 142 concordant () (PhT)                                            0
428  43 attendance () 2H6 R3 Shr TN Tim Lr H8 (TNK)                    7
432 758 sots (TNK)                                                     0
433   3 abstract () R3 Jo Wiv Ham AWW Ant.2                            7
433  91 breefe (brief) MND Jo 1H4    AWW.2    Ant                      6
438 751 soare                                                          0
439 158 conuicted (convict, convicted) R3 Jo                           2
443 152 contemplat (contemplate) 3H6                                   1
444 579 passionat (passionate) 2H6 R3     TGV LLL MND Jo Ham           7
445 391 hart sicke (heart-sick) Rom Cym                                2
445 457 languishment () Tit Luc.2                                      3
449 464 layes (lay, lays)     Ham Per.5 Son.3                          5
452 686 requisit (requisite) WT                                        1
454 320 footstoole (footstool) 3H6                                     1
456 516 mightines (mightiness) Tit Shr H5.2 H8                         5
458 540 nightingale  Shr.2 TGV.2 Rom.3 MND MV TN Lr Ant               12
460 795 sunburnt (sunburn'd, sunburning, sunburnt) Ado H5 Tro Tmp      4
461 540 nightingale  Shr.2 TGV.2 Rom.3 MND MV TN Lr Ant               12
462 540 nightingale  Shr.2 TGV.2 Rom.3 MND MV TN Lr Ant               12
462  10 adulterate () R3 Err Ham Luc Son (LC)                          5
463 708 satyrical (satirical) Ham                                      1
466 739 silke wormes                                                   0
466 850 twist () Cor                                                   1
468  20 amber () LLL Ham WT (LC)                                       3
471 670 reflection () JC.2 Tro Mac Cym.2                               6
471 660 rebound                                                        0
473 193 descant () R3 TGV                                              2
474 911 voluntarie (voluntary) Jo.3 MV JC AYL Tro Oth Cym              9
478 403 hollowes (hollow, hollows) Tit Rom Lr Ven                      4
479 609 poetrie (poetry) Tit Shr.2 LLL MV 1H4 AYL.3                    9
487 502 massie (massy) Ado Ham Tro.2 Tmp                               5
488 626 print (print, printed, printing) 2H6.2 Tit Wiv Ado H5 WT Son   8
490 862 vnended                                                        0
493 574 palpable () R3 1H4 Ham Oth Mac                                 5
499 871 vnmaskt (unmask) Ham MM Luc.2                                  4
499 564 outshine (out-shining) R2                                      1
504 651 ransack (ransack, ransack'd, ransacking) Jo Wiv Tro.2 WT Luc   6
506 525 moone                                                          0
507 476 likened (lik'ned) 3H6                                          1
508 761 splendour (splendor) Rom Jo Luc Son                            4
509 243 emulats (emulate) Wiv                                          1
510 605 plenteous () 2H6 R3 AYL MM Oth Tim.3 Lr Mac H8                11
511 812 thaw (thaw, thaw'd, thawing, thaws) Shr TGV MV H5 JC Ham Tim
Ven Luc (TNK.2)                                                        9
513 177 dazle (dazzle, dazzled, dazzleth, dazzling) 3H6 1H6 Tit TGV
LLL H5 Ven Luc                                                        8
513 352 gazers (gazer, gazers) 2H6 3H6 Per² Ven Son                    5
```

```
  514  29 application (applications) AWW                                    1
  517 487 louinglie (lovingly) Tit                                         1
  517 331 fragrant  Tit.2 MND Wiv Son                                      5
  518 526 moonelight (moonlight) MND                                       1
  530 418 emured (immur'd, immure, immured) R3 LLL.2 MV Ven Son            6
  530 150 constraint ().Jo.2 H5 AWW.3 Per³                                 7
  532 802 sweetnes (sweetness) 1H4 H5 Tro MM Lr Per³ Ven Son.2             9
  534 550 opposite (opposite, opposites) 2H6 R3 2H4 TN.2 Ham.2 MM Lr.2
Ant Cor                                                                   12
  538 840 treasurer () Ant                                                 1
  540 306 flankars                                                         0
  540 763 squadrons (squadron, squadrons) 1H6 JC Oth Ant                   4
  541 183 defectiue (defective) H5 Ham AWW Oth Cor                         5
  543 823 thrice gracious (thrice-gracious) R2 1H4                         2
  544 442 intrusion () Err.2 Rom Wiv                                       4
  550 361 gloomy () 1H6 Tit Luc                                           3
  550 147 consort () 2H6 TGV.2 Lr                                          4
  552 752 solace () 2H6 Cor (PP.2)                                         2
  555 822 thrice gentle (thrice-gentle) Oth                                1
  572 821 thrice dread                                                     0
  574 197 deuout (devout) R3 LLL Rom Jo H5 TN Tro Oth                      8
  580  47 augment (augment, augmented, augmenting) 2H6 3H6 Rom H5
JC AYL Mac Ant H8 Luc                                                     10
  585 214 disposse (dispossess, dispossess'd, dispossessing)
Jo.3 TN MM Tim                                                            6
  586 753 souldered (solder) Ant                                           1
  588 797 sunshine () 3H6.2 LLL 2H4 AWW Lr Ven                             7
  590 437 intellectual () Err H5                                           2
  593 693 retaine  1H6 Err.2 Rom Jo Ham Lr.2 Tmp H8 (TNK.2)               10
  594  88 bower (bower, bow'r, bow'rs) MND.3 1H4 Ado TN Cor Son            8
  595 878 vnspotted (unspotted) 2H6 1H6 H5 Per¹ H8 Luc  (TNK)             6
  610 126 clip (clip, clipt) LLL Lr Per⁵  (TNK)                            3
  615 908 violating (violate, violated, violates) LLL R2.2 AYL
Ant Cym Tmp Luc.2                                                         9
  618 629 progenitour (progenitors) 1H6.2 H5 Luc                           4
  619 869 vniuerse (universe) H5 Son                                       2
  623 244 enacted (enact, enacted, enacts) 1H6.3 R3     MV Ham.2
Tmp Luc                                                                    9.
  624 427 infringe (infring'd, infringe, infringed) 3H6 R3 Err
LLL.2 MM Cor Luc                                                          8
  633 115 chaplaines (chaplain, chaplains) 3H6 R3 H8.3                     5
  634  65 beautifie  2H6 Tit TGV Rom Ham.2 Per⁵ Luc                       8
  638 135 combe (comb) 2H4 Cym                                            2
  640 453 vice (juice) MND.3 Wiv Ham Ant Ven                              7
  641  48 austere () LLL TN AWW Tim                                        4
  642 369 gardion (guardian, guardians) Jo Ado Tro.2 Lr Mac               6
  654 171 comber (cumber) JC Tim                                          2
  655 911 voluntary  Jo.3 MV JC AYL Tro Oth Cym                           9
  655 628 proferest (proffer, proffer'd, proffered, proffers)
1H6.2 R3.2 R2 Jo 1H4.2    Cym  (PP)                                       9
  658 830 tip (tip, tipp'd, tips) Rom Ado.2                               3
  659 583 peise (peize, peized) R3 Jo MV                                  3
  662 460 lauish  1H6 1H4 2H4 MM Mac                                      5
  663 116 carectred (character, character'd) 2H6 TGV AYL Ham
Luc Son.2                                                                 7
  666 174 cyncke (cynic) JC                                               1
  668 469 lesned (lessen, lessen'd, lessens) Ado H5 Cym.2 H8              5
  674 653 rash () Oth                                                     1
```

```
674 208 disgorged (disgorge, disgorges) 2H4 AYL Tro Per³        4
674 912 vomit () 2H4 Oth                                        2
675 394 helples (helpless) R3. Err.2 Ven Luc.3                  7
678 509 medicinable (med'cinable, medicinable) Ado Tro.2 Oth Cym  5
680 894 vantage                                                 0
682 879 answere (unswear) Jo Oth  (excl. "unsworn" MM)          2
689 280 excommunicat (excommunicate) Jo.2                       2
703 196 detestable () Tit Rom.2 Jo Tim WT                       6
709 414 idoll (idol) TGV.2    TN Ham Tro.2 Ven Son              8
711 662 recantation () AWW.2                                    2
712 617 preacht (preach, preach'd, preaches, preaching) 1H6 Err
Jo TN Ham Lr Per⁴ (LC.2)                                        7
725 238 embassage  R3 LLL R2 Ado.2 Son                          6
730 363 gracelesse (graceless) 2H6 1H6 Shr.2 Jo Luc             6
735 252 indammagement (endamagement) Jo                         1
738 45 atturnie (attorney, attorneys) 1H6 R3.3 Err R2 AYL AWW
H8 Ven                                                          10
739 409 housd (hous'd, house) Err.4 Rom Lr Per² Cym             8
746 664 recouerie (recoveries, recovery) 2H6 3H6 Err.2 Wiv Ham.2
Tro AWW.2 Per⁵.2                                         ex.
747 386 heye (hay) 3H6 MND.3 Lr Mac WT (TNK)                    7
748 217 distaine (distain, distains) R3 Tro Per⁴ Luc            4
751 521 misdoo                                                  0
752 448 jawes (jaw, jaws) 2H6 Rom MND Jo 1H4 H5 Ham.2 Tro Ant
Son TN                                                          12
753 322 forragement                                             0
754 895 vassell (vassal) LLL R2 1H4 H5 Luc Son                  6
757 287 eie-sight (eyesight) LLL.3 Rom.2 1H4 Lr                 7
759 411 hugie                                                   0
759 896 vastures                                                0
760 549 operation (operation, operations) Rom 2H4 Wiv Tro
Lr Ant.2                                                        7
761 520 misdeeds (misdeed, misdeeds) 3H6 R3 Luc.2               4
762 615 portion (potion, potion's, potions) Rom.2 MND 1H4 2H4.2
Wiv Ham Per¹ WT Son.2                                           12
763 792 sugred (sugar) Ham                                      1
763 186 delitious (delicious) Tit Shr Ant Luc                   4
767 28 Apparraled (apparel, apparell'd, apparelled) 2H6 1H6
Err.2 Shr.2 LLL.2 Ado Per¹                                      10
769 73 beseege                                                  0
771 271 inuierd (environ, environ'd, environed) 3H6.3 1H6 R3
Tit TGV Rom 2H4 Per²                                            10
774 710 scandalous () MM WT                                     2
774 755 soliciter (solicitor) LLL Oth                           2
776 249 encompassed (encompass'd, encompassed, encompasseth)
3H6.2 1H6.2 R3 Wiv JC Luc (TNK)                                 8
777 468 leprous () Ham (TNK)                                    1
778 270 inuennometh (envenom, envenom'd, envenomed, envenoms)
2H6 Jo JC AYL Ham.3                                             7
778 229 Dug (dug, dugs) 2H6 R3 Rom.3 R2 AYL Ham Ven             9
779 580 pasport (passport) H5 AWW Per³                          3
782 104 cannon (canon, canons) LLL Jo Ham AWW Tim Cor.2 (TNK)   7
782 621 prescribes (prescrib'd, prescribe) R2 Wiv Tim Lr.2      5
786 363 gracelesse  2H6 1H6 Shr.2 Jo Luc                        6
788 877 vnsaie (unsay, unsay't) R2 MND 1H4 H8                   4
790 610 polluted (pollute, polluted) 1H6 Tro Luc.3              5
793 875 vnreputed                                               0
793 527 mote (mote, motes) LLL.2 MND Jo H5 Ham Per⁴ Luc         8
```

796 109 carrion (carrion, carrions) Rom MV 2H4 Wiv H5 JC Ham MM   8
798 14 agreuate (aggravate) R2 MND 2H4 Wiv Son   5
801 786 subbornation (subornation) 2H6.2 1H4 Luc   4
802 831 tissue () Ant   1
807 475 lightning () Tit Cym   2
808 301 fester (fester, fest'red, fest'ring) 1H6 Rom R2 H5
Cor Son   6
810 842 treble () Tit 2H4 Ham.2 MM.2 Mac Ven (TNK)   8
810 550 opposite 2H6 R3 2H4 TN.2 Ham.2 MM Lr.2 Ant Cor   12
816 253 endles (endless) 1H6 TGV R2.2 Jo Tro AWW H8 Luc Son (TNK.I) 10

Act 2 scene 2

819 825 thrice noble (thrice-noble, thrice-nobler) 2H6 Tit Shr
R2 Ant   5
821 328 fortnight () R3 Rom MND MV 1H4 2H4 Wiv Lr$_{1}^{2}$ Cor (vortnight)
823 7 accordingly () 1H6 Jo 1H4 Ado AWW MM Ant.2 Cym   9
824 32 aray (array) 2H6 3H6 1H6 Shr.2 Rom.2 H5 AYL.2 Lr Ven   12
828 474 leiuetenant generall   0
829 223 dominions R2 Jo Ham Lr Cym WT H8   7
830 902 via () 3H6 LLL.2 Wiv   4
833 493 malcontent (malecontent) 3H6.2   2
835 439 interrupt (interrupt, interrupted, interruptest,
interrupts) 3H6 Shr LLL.2 Rom Jo Tro Cor Per^5 Tmp Luc   11
838 861 Vndoubtedly (undoubtedly) H8   1
852 845 trudge () R3 Err Rom.2 Wiv.2   6
859 4 aboundant (abundant) R2.2   Son   3
861 420 imperator () LLL   1
871 734 shipskin (sheep-skins) Ham   1
872 577 parchment () R2   1
876 667 reduce () R3.2 H5 (TNK)   3
879 227 drummer () 3H6   1
881 854 vnciuill (uncivil) 2H6 TGV.2 R2 TN.4   8
882 689 resounds   0
885 587 penytrable (penetrable) R3 Ham Luc   3
888 931 wherle (whirl, whirl'd, whirling, whirls) 1H6 R3 Tit.2
              whirled
LLL Jo.2 Ham Tro   9
888 38 artyllerie (artillery) 1H6.2 Shr Jo 1H4   5
893 177 dazles 3H6 1H6 Tit TGV LLL H5 Ven Luc   8
897 826 thrice valiant (thrice-valiant) Tit H5   2
900 523 Modeld   0
901 815 theeuish (thievish) Rom AYL AWW Luc.2 Son.2   7
903 237 elsewhere () 3H6 Err.2 Shr R2 1H4 Cor Son.3   10
904 127 cloke (cloak) Luc   1
907 121 choysest (choice, choicest) Shr LLL JC Ham H8.2 1H6 Lr1 9
910 187 delineate   0
912 940 wistely (wistly)   Ven Luc (PP)
913 278 euidence (evidence, evidences) 2H6 R3.2 Ado Ham AWW
Lr Ant Cym WT H8 Luc   12
914 458 lanthorne (lanthorn, lanthorns) 2H6 Rom MND.5 2H4
Wiv Ado   10
916 922 wauering (waver, wavering, wav'ring) 1H6 R2 MV 2H4 TN
(LC)   5
919 503 master (master'd) Cym Ven (masters) TGV AYL H5   5
924 801 sweete   0
929 106 captiue (captive) 3H6.2 R3 Tit H5 JC Tro.2 Ant Luc Son
(TNK) AWW   12
935 938 winter () 2H6 AYL Tim   Luc (PP 2)   4
938 870 vnlawfull (unlawful) 1H6 R3.2 Err AWW.2 MM Oth.2
Ant WT   11

```
    939 675 register (register, registers) Wiv Ant Luc Son (LC)        4
    939 652 rarieties (rarieties, rariety, rarities, rarity) AWW
Tim Lr Tmp.2 Son (PhT)                                                 6
    940 467 Letherne  MND 2H4 AYL.2 Ven                                5
    943 697 ryot (rioting) Ant                                        1
    945 603 plaiefellow (playfellow, playfellows) 2H6 R3 MND Ant
Per¹ Cym WT.2 H8 (TNK)                                                9
    947 546 obiection (objections) 2H6 1H6 H8                          3
    953 253 endles  1H6 TGV R2.2 Jo Tro AWW H8 Luc Son               10
    955 884 vnwillingnes (unwillingness) R3.2 R2                       3
    957 516 mightines  Tit Shr H5.2 H8                                 5
    958 566 ouerbeare (overbear, overbears, overborne) 1H6.3 Tit
MND.2 Jo Ado H5                                                     ex.
    961 470 lets () Luc (TNK) H5                                       2
    967 824 thrice loning                                             0
    971 551 opposition (opposition, oppositions) LLL Rom 1H4.2
Ham.2 Oth Cym.2                                                       9
    979 64 Beardles (beardless) Jo 1H4                                2
    984 389 hart bloods (heart-blood) 2H6 3H6 1H6 R2.3 Tro            7
    987 278 euidence  2H6 R3.2 Ado Ham AWW Lr Ant Cym WT H8 Luc      12
    988 900 verdict () 1H6.2 R3 Cor H8 Son (LC)                       6
    990 768 Starre-chamber                                            0
    991 726 Sessions (session, sessions) MM Oth.2 Lr WT.4 H8 Son
(PhT)                                                                10
    993 687 resolute  2H6.2 3H6.2 1H6.2 R3 LLL AYL TN MM Mac         12
    994 687 Resolute  2H6.2 3H6.2 1H6.2 R3 LLL AYL TN MM Mac         12
    994 216 dissolude (dissolute) R2.2 Wiv                            3
    998 924 wedding () 1H6 Shr.2 Rom (TNK)                            4
   1006 624 preuention (prevention, preventions) 2H6 R2 H5.2 JC.2
Tro                                                                  7
   1009 867 vnholie (unholy) TGV Ham Cor Per⁴                        4
   1011 733 sharpe poynted (sharp-pointed) R3                        1
   1021 651 ransackt  Jo Wiv Tro.2 WT Luc                            6
   1021 841 treasurie (treasuries, treasury) 2H6.2 Tit R2 H5 Lr WT  7
   1021 807 taskt (task, task'd tasking) LLL.2 R2 1H4.3 Wiv H5.2
Oth Cor Son                                                         12
   1029 918 Warden                                                   0
   1031 714 Scoure (scour, scour'd, scoured) 2H6 TGV.2 1H4 2H4
Wiv.2 H5 Mac Per² WT (TNK)                                          11
   1036 233 esterne (eastern) Rom R2 MND.2 Tro Ant Luc              7
   1037 500 Marshall (martial) 1H6.3 Rom 2H4 H5 AYL TN Ham Cym Luc 11


Act 3 scene 1

   1043 Nauie (navy, navy's) R3.2 2H4 H5 Ant.5 H8                   10
   1045 246 incampe (encamp, encamp'd) 3H6 Tit Rom 1H4 H5 (LC)      5
   1048 500 marshiall  1H6.3 Rom 2H4 H5 AYL TN Ham Cym Luc          11
   1048 344 furniture () 2H6 Shr 1H4 AWW H8                          5
   1049 872 vnnecessary (unnecessary) H5 Lr.2                        3
   1049 757 soothing (sooth'd, soothe, soothing, sooth'st) 3H6
R3 Err Jo Lr Cor.3 Ven                                              9
   1051 94 bruted (bruit, bruited) 1H6 2H4 Ham Mac                  4
   1051 111 certenty (certainties, certainty) MV 2H4 Ham AWW.3
MM Cor Cym.2 WT                                                     11
   1052 326 fortified (fortified, fortifies, fortify) 3H6 1H6.2
Jo 2H4 H5 TN Ham Mac Cym Son.2 (LC)                                 12
   1053 311 flocke (flock) 3H6 R3 2H4.2 AYL                         5
```

1055 494 malcontents (malcontent, malecontent, malecontents)
TGV LLL Wiv Ven   4
  1056 80 Bloodthirsty (blood-thirsty) 1H6   1
  1056 718 seditious () 2H6 Err   2
  1057 760 Spend thrifts (spendthrift, spendthrift's) Ham Tmp   2
  1058 19 alteration () 1H6 2H4 Oth Tim Lr Cor WT.2 Son   9
  1061 754 sollemnly (solemnly) R3 R2 MND 1H4 H5 H8   6
  1062 397 heeretofore   0
  1064 23 anchredge (anchorage) Tit   1
  1066 693 retaynd 1H6 Err.2 Rom Jo Ham Lr.2 Tmp H8   10
  1067 272 Epicures (epicure, epicures) Mac Ant   2
  1068 339 frothy () Ven   1
  1069 804 swill (swill'd, swills) R3 H5   2
  1070 14 aggruate R2 MND 2H4 Wiv Son   5
  1070 446 ire () 3H6 1H6 Err R2 Per² (TNK)   5
  1071 146 conioynes (conjoin, conjoin'd, conjoins) 1H6 R3 MND
2H4 Ado.2 Ham   7
  1072 767 stalls (stall, stall'd, stalled, stalling) R3 AYL AWW
Ant Ven (PP)   5
  1075 222 drum stricke (domestic) R3 JC Oth Tim Lr Mac Ant Cym 8
  1078 144 confederates (confederate, confederates) 2H6 1H6 R3
Err.2 Tit.3 2H4 Tmp   10
  1086 538 neighborhood () H5.2 Tim   3
  1090 381 hardie (hardiest, hardy) 3H6.2 R3.2 TN Ham Mac (TNK.3) 7
  1091 725 seruitors (servitor, servitors) 3H6 1H6 R3 Tit Oth Luc 6
  1095 606 plentiful () Err 1H4 Ham Cym (STM)   4
  1096 841 Treasory 2H6.2 Tit R2 H5 Lr WT   7
  1097 382 hare braind (hare-brain'd) 1H6 1H4   2
  1098 842 trebble Tit 2H4 Ham.2 MM.2 Mac Ven   8
  1100 635 puissant () 2H6 3H6.3 R3 H5.2 JC   8
  1101 384 Hauen (haven, havens) 3H6 Shr R2 Ant Per¹ Cym.3   8
  1103 816 thirst (thirst, thirsts) 3H6 Shr . Cor   3
  1104 571 ouerweaning (overween, overweening) 2H6 R3 Tit TGV
R2 2H4 TN (o'erween, o'erweening, o'erweens) 2H6 3H6 WT   10
  1107 27 a peeces (a-pieces) H8 (TNK)   1
  1109 194 discribde 1H6 R3 Shr LLL Rom Oth Lr Ant Per¹ Per⁵ Luc 11
  1110 920 watchfull (watchful) R3.3 TGV Jo.2 2H4 H5 JC Tro Mac 11
  1111 31 Armado (armado, armadoes) Err Jo   2
  1112 454 ken (ken, kenn'd, kenst) 2H6 Wiv Tro (TNK.2)   3
  1113 599 pines (pine, pines) 2H6 R2 MV Tro Ant.2 Cym WT Tmp.3
Luc   12
  1115 779 streaming (stream, stream'd, streaming) Rom R2 JC
AWW Luc   5
  1115 260 Ensignes (ensign, ensigns) 1H6 Tit Rom R2 JC.2 Cym Ven 8
  1116 507 meddow (meadows) Tit LLL Son   3
  1116 796 sundry () AYL Mac.3 Luc (TNK)   5
  1117 9 Adornes (adorn, adorn'd, adorned, adorning, adorns) 1H6
R3 Tit R2 Ant Per¹ WT Luc   8
  1118 492 Maiesticall (majestical) 1H6 R3 LLL.2 H5.2 Ham.2   8
  1119 303 Figuring (figure, figured, figures, figuring) 3H6 2H4.2
MM (PP) (LC) MND   5
  1119 407 horned (horning, horned) Tit MND.2 Oth Ant   5
  1120 833 top gallant (top-gallant) Rom   1
  1120 8 Admirall (admiral) 3H6 R3 1H4 H5 Ant   5
  1121 379 handmaides (handmaid, handmaids) 1H6 Tit TN Cym H8 Luc 6
  1122 868 vnite (unite, united) 2H6 1H6 R3.2 Jo 2H4.2 Wiv Ham
Cym H8   11
  1123 642 quartred (quarter, quarter'd, quartered, quartering)

```
1H6 R3 Jo.2 Wiv JC.2 Ham Ant Cor Cym H8                              ex.
  1123 275 equally () R3 1H4 Ado AYL MM Lr Ant Cym Ven (TNK.2)        9
  1124 828 titely (tightly) Wiv.2                                     2
  1124 346 gale (gale, gales) 3H6 Shr Lr Tmp                          4
  1125 607 plough (plough, plough'd, ploughed, plough'st) Tit R2
Tro Tim Ant.2 Cor.2 Per⁴ (TNK)                                       9
  1125 402 hitherward  2H6 3H6 Jo 1H4.2 Lr Cor Per¹                   8
  1126 308 Flewer de Luce (flower-de-luce, flower-de-luces,
flow'r-de-luce) 2H6 1H6.2 H5 WT                                      5
  1130 534 Nauy  R3.2 2H4 H5 Ant.5 H8                                10
  1132 715 scouts (scout, scouts) 3H6.3 1H6.2 LLL                     6
  1133 22 Anchor (anchor, anchor's, anchors) 3H6.2 R3 Tit Wiv
Ham Per⁵ WT.2                                                        9
  1136 506 mawe (maw, maws) Err Rom Jo H5 MM Tim Mac.2 Ven            9
  1139 145 conflict (conflict, conflicts) 2H6 3H6.2 Tit LLL Ado
Tim Lr.2 Mac Ven                                                    11
  1144 600 pitch (pitch, pitch'd, pitched) 3H6.2 1H6.3 R3 Shr
LLL MM Tim Tmp Ven                                                 ex.
  1152 141 concept                                                    0
  1155 582 pedegree  3H6.2 1H6 H5                                     4
  1159 143 Conduit (conduit, conduits) Err Tit Rom Cor WT Luc         6
  1160 777 stragling (straggling) Tim Luc                             2
  1160 888 vpstarts (upstart) 1H6                                     1
  1162 679 repast () Shr LLL Cym                                      3
  1163 773 sternly                                                    0
  1166 947 younglings (youngling, younglings) Tit ₂Shr    (PP)        3
  1167 772 Stir (steer, steer'd, steering, steers) 2H6 Oth Ant.2
Cym H8                                                              6
  1168 794 sulphur                                                    0
  1170 234 eckoing (echo, echo'st) Tit Shr Oth                        3
  1170 103 Cannon shot (cannon-shot) 1H6                              1
  1171 110 cates () 1H6 Err 1H4 Per²                                  4
  1175 282 exalations (exhalation, exhalations) Jo 1H4 JC H8          4
  1176 475 lightning () Tit Cym                                       2
  1178 650 rancor (rancor, rancor's, rancors) 2H6.2 R3.2 Rom R2
Ado Mac                                                             8
  1178 400 high swolne (high-swoll'n) R3                              1
  1179 694 Retreae (retrait, retreat) 2H6 3H6 1H6 1H4 2H4.2 H5
AYL AWW                                                             9
  1185 522 misgiues (misgive, misgives, misgiving) 3H6 Rom Wiv
JC Oth (TNK)                                                        5
  1188 204 discomfiture () 1H6                                        1
  1192 534 Nauies  R3.2 2H4 H5 Ant.5 H8                              10
  1193 682 reporter () Ant                                            1
  1196 146 conioynd  1H6 R3 MND 2H4 Ado.2 Ham                         7
  1196 8 Admirall  3H6 R3 1H4 H5 Ant                                  5
  1197 8 Admirall  3H6 R3 1H4 H5 Ant                                  5
  1199 232 earnest peny                                               0
  1201 747 smoky () 1H4.2 2H4 AWW Cym Luc                             6
  1203 361 gloomy  1H6 Tit Luc                                        3
  1204 248 inclose  2H6 1H6 R3 H5 JC.2 Cym WT Luc.2 Son              11
  1205 656 reft (reave, reaves, reft, refts) 2H6 R3 Err.2 Ado
AWW Per² Cym Ven.2                                                 10
  1210 779 streaming  Rom R2 JC AWW Luc                               5
  1210 362 gore () 1H6 MND H5.2 Ham Tim Mac Ven                       8
  1210 491 maymed (maim, maim'd, maimed, main'd) 2H6 Shr Ham
Oth.2 H8 (TNK) (LC)                                                6
  1211 372 gushing (gush) Luc                                         1
```

```
1211 524 moysture (moisture) 3H6 Ven.2 (LC)                        3
1212 166 cranny                                                    0
1212 124 cleftures                                                 0
1212 827 through shot                                              0
1212 601 planks () Jo Ant                                          2
1213 215 disseuered ` Jo AWW WT                                    3
1214 17 aloft () 2H6.2 Tit.3 Cym Luc Son                           8
1215 932 wherle winde (whirlwind, whirlwinds) Shr TGV Ham Tim
Lr Luc                                                             6
1217 668 reeling (reel, reeleth, reeling, reels) R3 Rom Ant Cor
Cym Tmp H8 (TNK₂)Son                                               8
1218 835 tottering (totter'd, tottered, tottering, totters,
tott'ring) 1H6 R3 R2 Jo AWW Per³ Tmp Son.2 (TNK)                   9
1218 702 ruthlesse (ruthless) 2H6 3H6.5 1H6 R3 Tit.2 MM (PP)      11
1223 481 liuely () Shr TGV Tim WT (PP)                             4
1223 593 pictured (pictur'd) Cym Son                               2
1224 140 compulsion () Jo.2 MV 1H4.4 Tro AWW Lr                   10
1227 83 bonnier  2H6 R3 Shr.2 Ado AYL Ham                          7
1229 315 foemens (foeman, foeman's, foemen, foemen's) 3H6.2 1H6
Tit 2H4                                                            5
1232 881 vntimly (untimely) 3H6.2 R3.2 Rom.2 Mac Ham Lr (TNK,PP)   9
```

Act 3 scene 2

```
1242 641 quarter                                                   0
1243 52 baggage () Err Shr Rom.2 Wiv AYL Per4.2 WT                 9
1244 641 Quarter                                                   0
1244 642 quartering (quarter, quarter'd, quartered, quartering)
1H6 R3 Jo.2 Wiv JC.2 Ham Ant.Cor Cym H8                           ℓX
1247 534 Nauy  R3.2 2H4 H5 Ant.5 H8                               10
1255 365 Grashopper (grasshopper) Rom                              1
1256 518 mirthfull (mirthful) 3H6                                  1
1256 452 iollitie (jollity) Err MND.2 Cym WT Son                   6
1258 541 nipt (nip, nipp'd, nipping, nips) 2H6 Tit Shr LLL.2
Ham MM Per5 H8                                                     9
1267 784 subiugate                                                 0
1273 377 handfull (handful) LLL MND                                2
1281 927 When as ()                                                0
1282 308 fluerdeluce  2H6 1H6.2 H5 WT                              5
1283 791 such like (such-like) R3 Err Ham Tro Tim Tmp Ven.2 (PP)   8
1283 798 surmises (surmise, surmises) R3 Tit 2H4.2 Oth Mac Cym
WT Luc.2                                                          10
1287 313 flowring (flower'd, flow'red, flowring) 2H6 1H6 Tit
Rom.2 H5                                                           6
1288 1 abandoned (abandon, abandon'd, abandoned) 3H6 Tit Shr
AYL.4 TN Tro AWW Oth Tim                                          12
1288 284 expulsd (expuls'd) 1H6                                    1
1289 651 ransackt  Jo Wiv Tro.2 WT Luc                            6
1292 876 vnrestrained (unrestrained) R2                            1
1292 385 hauock (havoc) Jo.2 1H4 Ado JC TN Ham Cor (TNK)          8
1297 161 Corne fieldes (cornfield) AYL                            1
1297 907 vineyards (vineyard, vineyards) H5.2 MM.3 Tmp.2          7
1297 565 ouen (oven, oven's) Tit Tro Per³ Ven                    4
1298 466 leaking (leak, leak'd) 1H4 2H4 Tim                       3
1300 428 inhabitants () 2H4 Mac                                   2
1301 545 numberles (numberless) Tim H8                            2
1301 595 pikes  3H6 1H6 2H4 Ado H5.2 Cor.2 Cym.2 Tmp Ven         12
1303 837 tragicke (tragic) 2H6 3H6 R3 Err Tit 2H4 Oth (PhT,LC)    7
1305 853 vnbridled (unbridled) Tro AWW                           2
```

APPENDIX III

```
1306 515 midst () 3H6 R3 Err Shr MND Mac Ant.2 Cor.2 Luc       11
1306 360 glittering (glittering, glitt'ring) R2.2 MND Jo 1H4.2
Tim Per⁴ Luc                                                     9
1307 218 distant () MND Ham MM Per² Per³ (LC)                    5
1308 195 desolation () 2H6 R3 LLL.2 Jo H5.2 AYL Ant Per¹ Cym    11
1310 373 habitation () MND MV 2H4 MM Son                         5
1313 735 Shelter () R3 R2 1H4.2 Wiv Ven                          6
1316 835 tottering  1H6 R3 R2 Jo AWW Per³ Tmp Son.2             9
```

Act 3 scene 3

```
1319 370 guide (guide, guides) 2H6 Rom 2H4 AWW MM Oth Tim
Lr Ant Luc                                                      10
1320 730 shalow (shallows) MV JC                                 2
1326 259 inlarge (enlarg'd, enlarge, enlargeth) 1H6 1H4 2H4
Wiv H5.2 JC TN Ham Tro Ant Son                                  12
1337 34 arriuall (arrival) 1H6 Err Shr R2 1H4 WT                 6
1338 788 successfullie  Tit Shr AYL                              3
1343 756 sollitarines                                            0
1343 630 progresse (progress) Jo                                 1
1345 628 poffered  1H6.2 R3.2 R2 Jo 1H4.2 . . Cym                9
1347 547 obstinate () 1H6 Ado Ham Cor H8                         5
1348 241 imbracement (embracement, embracements) R3 Err Tit
Shr Tro Cor Per¹ Cym WT H8 Ven.2                                12
1350 529 mould (?)                                     Cor       1

1351 206 disdainfull (disdainful) Shr MND.2 H5 AYL Ado.2 Ant H8  9
1352 742 skittish () TN Tro.2                                    3
1352 880 vntamed                                                 0
1352 134 coult (colt, colts) LLL R2 MND MV.2 Tmp H8 Ven          8
1363 32 araie  2H6 3H6 1H6 Shr.2 Rom.2 H5 AYL.2 Lr Ven          12
1369 251 incroach (encroaching) 2H6                              1
1371 787 subuert (subverta) 1H6                                  1
1373 36 arrogant () 2H6 1H6 Tim Cym                              4
1373 442 intrusion  Err.2 Rom Wiv                                4
1374 341 fugitiue (fugitive) 1H6 Ant                             2
1375 815 theeuish  Rom AYL AWW Luc.2 Son.2                       7
1375 535 needie (needy) 2H6 Err Rom.3 Per Son                    7
1379 596 pilfering (pilfering, pilf'rings) H5 Lr                 2
1380 435 insomuch () AYL                                         1
1380 427 infringed  3H6 R3 Err LLL.2 MM Cor Luc                  8
1381 165 couenant (covenant, covenants) 1H6.2 Shr R2 Cym.3       7
1384 425 inferior () 3H6 1H6.2 Shr R2 Jo Oth Cor Son             9
1385 816 thirst  3H6 Shr    Cor                                  3
1390 589 persecute (persecuted) AWW                              1
1391 145 conflict  2H6 3H6.2 Tit LLL Ado Tim Lr.2 Mac Ven       11
1393 597 pillage () 2H6 1H6 Tit H5.2 Luc                         6
1393 498 manfully () Tit TGV                                     2
1394 943 wormwood () LLL Rom.2 Ham Luc                           5
1395 705 sallutation (salutation, salutations) R3 LLL Rom 1H4
JC AYL Lr Mac Son                                               9
1395 404 hony sweete (honey-sweet) H5 Tro.2                      3
1397 708 satiricall  Ham                                         1
1398 808 tants (taunt, taunts) 3H6.2 1H6 R3 Wiv Ant Cor          7
1399 317 foile (foil, foil'd) 3H6 AYL.3 Tro Cor Cym Ven Son (PP) 9
1400 200 dym (dim, dimm'd, dimming) 2H6.3 3H6 1H6 R3.2 Tit R2
MV Luc Son                                                      12
1401 941 woluish (wolvish, woolvish) Rom MV Lr Cor               4
1402 746 slylie (slily) 2H6 3H6.3 R3 Cor                         6
```

210

```
1402 433 insinuate (insinuate, insinuateth, insinuating) 1H6
R3.2 Tit LLL R2 AYL Oth Cor WT Ven                                    11
1403  37 artifitiall (artificial) 3H6 Rom MND Tim.2 Mac Per³           7
1404 904 vitious (vicious) 1H6 Err Ham Oth Tim Lr.2 Cym H8             9
1408 829 timerous (timorous) 3H6 1H6.2 R3 AWW Oth Ven.2 (TNK)          8
1409 536 negligent () 1H6 LLL Tro Ant.2 WT.2                          7
1410 743 slacke (slack) 2H6 1H6 R3 Shr Lr Perᴹ (PP)                   6
1413 717 securelie (securely) Tit R2.2 Jo Wiv Tro Luc                 7
1416 741 skirmish () 1H6                                              1
1416 597 pillage  2H6 1H6 Tit H5.2 Luc                                6
1419 444 inuectiues (invectives) 3H6                                  1
1420 281 execrations () 2H6 Tro                                       2
1422 678 remorseles (remorseless) 2H6 3H6 Ham Luc                     4
1425 416 immodest  1H6 TGV 2H4 Ado WT Ven                             6
1426 710 scandalous  MM WT                                            2
1427 623 pretended (pretend, pretended, pretending) 3H6 1H6.2
Tit TGV MM Mac Cym.2 Luc (TNK)                                        10
1430 489 luclles (luckless) 3H6.2                                     2
1434 738 sickles (sickle, sickle's) Son.2                             2
1435 258 inkindled (enkindle, enkindled) Jo JC Tro Lr Mac             5
1437  59 basely () 1H6 Tit.4 R2.2 1H4 Ant Ven Luc.2 (TNK)             12
1438 114 Champion (champaign) Luc                                     1
1438 613 poole (pool) Lr Cym Tmp.2                                    4
1439 631 prospect () 2H6 Jo Ado TN Oth Mac                            6
1439 744 slaughter house (slaughter-house) 2H6.2 3H6 R3.2
Jo Luc                                                                7
1442 267 entrailes (entrails) 3H6 R3,2 Tit.2 Wiv H5 JC.2
Mac Tmp                                                               11
1443 817 thirstie (thirsty) 3H6 Shr LLL 1H4 JC MM Per³ Ven            8
1446 421 impotent () LLL                                              1
1447 846 true borne (true-born) 1H6 R2                                2
1449 256 ingraud (engrav'd, engrave, engraven) 1H6 R3 TGV Luc         4
1451 774 stiffe (stiff) 2H6 Err Rom.2 R2 1H4 Lr Ant Cor.2
Cym H8                                                                12
1451 417 immouable                                                   0
1452 932 whirlewind  Shr TGV Ham Tim Lr Luc                          6
1455 477 linage                                                       0
1457 149 conspiratours (conspirator, conspirators) 1H6 Tit
R2 JC.5 Luc                                                           9
1458 846 true borne  1H6 R2                                           2
1461 865 vnfought (unfought) H5                                       1
1466 324 forrener (foreigners) Jo                                     1
1467 125 clemencie (clemency) Ham                                     1
1468  76 byt (bit, bits) Shr H5 MM H8 Ven                             5
1470 264 inthrone (enthron'd, enthroned) MV Tro Ant.2 H8 (TNK)        5
1472 173 Curtall (curtail'd) R3                                       1
1476 341 fugitiues  1H6 Ant                                          2
1477  67 belly god                                                   0
1478 917 wantonnes (wantonness) LLL Jo 1H4 Wiv.2 Ham Tro Son          8
1481 120 chines (chine, chines) 2H6 Shr H8                            3
1482 225 downie (downy) 1H6 2H4 Mac Ant                               4
1482 295 featherbedds (feather-bed) MV                                1
1483 692 resty () Tro Cym Son                                         3
1483 774 stiffe 2H6 Err Rom.2 R2 1H4 Lr Ant Cor.2 Cym H8              12
1484 569 ouerridden (overrode) 2H4                                    1
1486 106 Captiue  3H6.2 R3 Tit H5 JC Tro.2 Ant Luc Son AWW            12
1492 710 scandalous  MM WT                                            2
1493 266 intombed (entomb, entomb'd, entombed, entombs) Tro
Tim Mac Cor Luc.3 Son                                                 8
```

```
1495 600 pitched  3H6.2 1H6.3 R3 Shr LLL MM Tim Tmp Ven        ex.¯
1496 501 Martialists (martialist) (TNK)                           0
1497 228 dub (dub, dubb'd) 3H6 R3 Jo 2H4 H5.2 TN                  7
1497 851 tipe (type, types) 3H6 R3 H8 Luc                        4
1499 554 orderly () Shr.2 R2 MV Ham                              5
1500  44 attirement                                              0
1504 419 impall (empale, impale, impaled) 3H6.2 Tro             3
1505 874 vnrelenting (unrelenting) 3H6 1H6 Tit                  3
1506 914 wald (wall, wall'd, walled) 1H6.2 LLL AYL Lr Cym R2   7
1506 505 matchlesse (matchless) LLL Tro (TNK)                   2
1506 327 fortitude () 1H6 Oth Mac Tmp H8                       5
1511 393 helmet (helmet, helmets) 3H6 R3 R2.2 Jo H5.3 Tro Ant 10
1512 929 Wherewith () 2H6 3H6 1H6.2 TGV LLL R2 Jo Mac Son      10
1512 299 fenst (fenc'd, fence, fencing) 3H6.2 MV 2H4 Wiv AYL
TN Ham Tim Per¹ Per⁴ Luc                                        12
1514   9 adornd 1H6 R3 Tit R2 Ant Per¹ WT Luc                   8
1514 459 lawrell (laurel) 3H6 Tit Ant                          3
1518  89 brasen (brazen) 2H6.2 3H6.2 LLL R2 Jo 1H4 Ham Tro Ant 11
1520 626 print  2H6.2 Tit Wiv Ado H5 WT Son                     8
1523 806 target (target, targets) 3H6 1H4 Ham Ant.2 Cor Per¹
Per² H8                                                         9
1525  41 astonish (astonish. astonish'd, astonished)
         2H6 1H6.2 H5 JC    AWW    Luc Son                      8
1526 508 meger (meagre) 2H6 Rom Jo.2 MV Ven (TNK)              6
1528 184 deferd (defer, deferr'd) 2H6 1H6 R3                   3
1531  24 animates                                             0
1533 620 persaging  3H6.2 1H6 Rom MV.2 JC Lr Ant.2            10
1535 927 When as                                              0
1538 581 patronage () 1H6.2                                   2
1538 293 fatherles (fatherless) R3 Mac                        2
1540 544 numb () 1H6 R3 Tit                                   3
1541 707 saples (sapless) 1H6.2                               2
1544 897 vowarde (vaward) 1H6 MND 2H4 H5 Cor                  5
1545 199 dignifie (dignified, dignifies, dignify) TGV.2 Rom
2H4 AWW Cor Per⁴ Cym Luc Son.2 Tro                            12
1548 496 manage () Rom R2.2 Jo MV 1H4 AYL Tro Per⁴ Tmp H8
(TNK) (LC)                                                     11
1550 655 rereward (rearward) 1H6 Rom 2H4 Ado Son               5
1551 554 orderly  Shr.2 R2 MV Ham                             5
1551  32 ray  2H6 3H6 1H6 Shr.2 Rom.2 H5 AYL.2 Lr Ven        12
```

Act 3 scene 4

```
1558 349 garrison (garrison, garrisons) 2H6 1H6              2
1560 368 Grudging  1H6.2 R3 Ado JC Lr                        6
1561 323 forefront                                           0
1563  74 betook (betake, betakes, betook) 2H6 Rom TN.2 AWW
Per¹ Per² WT Luc.2 (TNK) (PP) LLL                            11
1565 129 clustering (clust'ring) 1H6 Tmp.2                    3
1566 819 thousandfold () 3H6.2 Tro H8                        4
1567 380 haplesse (hapless) 2H6 3H6.2 1H6 Err TGV.2 Luc      8
```

Act 3 scene 5

```
1574 224 dooming (doom, doom'd) R3.2 Err Tit.2 Rom R2 Jo Ham
Cor Cym (TNK)                                                11
1574 634 prouidence (providence) JC Ham.2 Tro Tmp.2          6
1575 432 inscrutable () TGV                                  1
1583 533 narrowly () Shr Ado Per⁴                           3
```

```
  1583  72 beset () Shr TGV.2 MV Ado TN Luc                          7
  1590 790 succour (succor) 2H6 3H6.3 Tit (PP)                       5
  1591 249 incompast  3H6.2 1H6.2 R3 Wiv JC Luc                      8
  1600 750 snares (snare, snares) 2H6.  1H6 Tim Mac Ant Luc          7
  1600 242 Emmets                                                    0
  1602 263 Intangled (entangled, entangles) Ant.2 Cor (TNK)          3
  1603 333 Frantiquely (franticly) Tit Ven                           2
  1603 944 wouen (weav'd, weave, weaves, weaving, woven) 2H6 MND
MV.2 TN Lr Per⁴.2 H8 Luc (TNK)                                      10
  1606 790 succour  2H6 3H6.3 Tit                                    5
  1607 553 ordaynd (ordain, ordain'd, ordained, ordaining) 2H6
3H6.2 1H6.3 Tit Shr Rom Jo Wiv Cym (TNK)                            12
  1610 709 sauor (savor, savoring, savors) LLL H5.2 TN.2 Per⁴ WT     7
  1613 936 wilfulnes (willfulness) H5 Son                            2
  1625 106 captiue  3H6.2 R3 Tit H5 JC Tro.2 Ant Luc Son AWW        12
  1630 694 retreat  2H6 3H6 1H6 1H4 2H4.2 H5 AYL AWW                 9
  1640 676 regreet () R2.3                                           3
  1640 392 harty (hearty) 1H6 TGV 2H4 Wiv MM Lr Mac Ant Tmp (TNK)    9
  1642 573 paynefull (painful) Shr LLL Ado H5 MM Cor Per³ Tmp
Luc Son                                                             10
  1643 371 gulphes (gulf, gulfs) 3H6 R3 Err H5.2 Ham Oth Mac
Cor.2 Luc                                                          11
  1643 771 steely () 3H6 AWW                                         2
  1644 335 fraught () Tit TN Oth                                     3
  1647 305 first fruit (first-fruits) WT                             1
  1650 269 intrencht (entrench'd, intrench'd) 1H6 AWW                2
  1651 814 thicke (thick) MV Ant Cym H8 Tmp Luc.2 (TNK.3)            7
  1651  60 battered (batter, batter'd, battering, batters) Err
Jo Tro.2 Mac Ant Cym Tmp Luc.3                                     11
  1652  25 Anuell (anvil) Jo Cor                                     2
  1652 612 ponderous () Ham MM Lr WT                                 4
  1652 358 glaues                                                    0
  1653 499 marble () 3H6 Err Ham MM Oth Cym.2 Luc                    8
  1653 860 vnderprop (underprop) R2 Jo Luc                           3
  1654 548 often () AYL Cym                                          2
  1655 155 continuall                                                0
  1655 942 Wood-mans (woodman) Wiv MM Cym Luc                        4
  1656 257 enioynd (enjoin, enjoin'd, enjoineth) TGV.2 LLL Rom
MV Ado AWW Per² WT.2 TMP                                           11
  1656 297 fell (fell, fell'd) 2H6 R2 Tim.2 Lr (TNK) (fells)3 H6     6
  1657 289 faulter (falter, falt'ring) R2 Luc                        2
  1658 948 zealous () R3 LLL Jo.2 AWW Son                            6
  1666  54 bane () 2H6 Tit Tro MM Mac Cym Ven                        7
  1671 145 conflict  2H6 3H6.2 Tit LLL Ado Tim Lr.2 Mac Ven         11
  1672  57 Barons (baron, barons) 2H6 MV 1H4 H5.3 H8                 7
  1676 917 wantonesse (wantonness) LLL Jo 1H4 Wiv.2 Ham Tro Son      8
  1677 486 loue sicke (love-sick) Tit Ant Ven.2                      4
  1677 132 cockney () TN Lr                                          2
  1682  66 begyrt                                                    0
  1682 383 hauen                                                     0
  1683 887 vpshot (upshoot, upshot) LLL TN Ham                       3
  1684 940 wistlie  R2 Ven Luc                                       3
  1686 584 Pellican (pelican) R2 Ham                                 2
  1687  63 beak (beak, beaks) 2H6 Lr Cym Tmp Ven Luc (TNK)           6
  1690 528 motto () Per².3                                           3
```

Act 4 scene 1

```
  1695 643 quietly () 3H6 1H6.2 Tit Shr Ham Tim.2 Per4 Ven          10
```

```
1697 345 furtherance () 1H6 Per²                                    2
1699 162 Coronet (coronet, coronets) 1H6.2 MND H5 JC Lr Tmp H8      8
1703 223 Dominions  R2 Jo Ham Lr Cym WT H8                          7
1704 800 surrendred  R2 H8                                          2
1707 112 certified (certified, certifies, certify) 1H6.2 R3 MV      4
1714 332 Francks                                                    0
1715 693 retayne  1H6 Err.2 Rom Jo Ham Lr.2 Tmp H8                 10
1715 106 captiue  3H6.2 R3 Tit H5 JC Tro.2 Ant Luc Son AWW         12
1718 580 pasport  H5 AWW Per³                                       3
1720 663 recourse () R3 TGV Wiv Tro                                 4
1724 783 students (student, students) LLL.2 Ham                     3
1734 863 vnfàynedly (unfeignedly) R3 Jo AWW (TNK)                   3
```

Act 4 scene 2

```
1738 628 profered  1H6.2 R3.2 R2 Jo 1H4.2      Cym                  9
1740 269 intrench  1H6 AWW                                          2
1741 905 vituals (victual, victuals) TGV Ado H5 Cym (TNK)           4
1742 790 succour  2H6 3H6.3 Tit                                     5
1743 290 Famine () 2H6.2 1H6 Rom 2H4 H5 Mac.2 Ant.2 Cym Son        12
1743 136 combate (combat, combated, combating) 2H6 3H6 1H6
LLL R2 Wiv Ado Ham Ant (TNK.2)                                      9
1752 359 glyding (glide, glided, glides, glideth, gliding)
2H6 Tit TGV Rom MND JC AYL Cym Ven                                  9
1756 428 inhabitants  2H4 Mac                                       2
1757 207 deseased (diseas'd, disease, diseased) 1H4 2H4.2 Ham
Tim Mac Cor Cym WT Son.2                                           11
1760 905 victuals  TGV Ado H5 Cym                                   4
1765 628 proffered  1H6.2 R3.2 R2 Jo 1H4.2      Cym                 9
17.0 905 victuals  TGV Ado H5 Cym                                   4
1771 26 a peece (a-piece) 1H4 Wiv Ham AWW                           4
1773 307 fresh (flesh, flesh'd, fleshes) 1H6 R3 Jo 1H4 2H4.2
H5.2 TN AWW Lr                                                     11
1774 782 stubbornnes (stubbornness) AYL Ham Oth                     3
1774 592 peruerse (perverse) 1H6.2 Rom Ven                          4
1778 903 vicegerent () LLL                                          1
1784 573 painefull  Shr LLL Ado H5 MM Cor Per³ Tmp Luc Son         10
1789 276 Esquire (esquire, esquires) 2H6.2 2H4.2 Wiv.2 H5.3         9
1791 799 surrender () LLL Ham Lr                                    3
1793 367 greouously (grievously) TGV Jo Wiv.2 JC Oth               6
1794 637 Pursueaunt (pursuivant, pursuivants) 2H6 1H6 R3 H8         4
1801 600 pitch  3H6.2 1H6.3 R3 Shr LLL MM Tim Tmp Ven         ex.
1801 706 sandy () 2H6.2 1H6 Tit MV Tro                             6
1803 98 Burgesses                                                  0
1804 181 decreed (decree, decreed, decrees) Err Tit Rom R2
1H4 Ado AYL TN Tro Cor Per¹ Per²                                  12
1809 236 elect  1H6 Tit R2 Tro MM Cor Cym                          7
1811 125 Clemencie  Ham                                            1
1815 923 welthiest (wealthy, wealthiest) 2H6.2 3H6 Shr.2 MV.3
AWW Oth Tim.2 (TNK)                                               12
1816 479 linnen (linen) Shr Mac                                    2
1817 376 halter (halter, halters) 2H6 Tit MV.2 1H4.2 Oth Lr.2       9
1818 632 prostrate () 2H6 1H6 Err Rom 2H4 JC                       6
1820 504 masterships (mastership) TGV MV Cor                       3
1824 185 defiance  Rom R2 Jo 1H4.2 2H4 H5.3 JC Tro MM             12
1825 661 recall (recall, recall'd) 2H6 1H6 Err TGV Per³ WT Luc     7
```

Act 4 scene 3

```
1831 13 aduocate (advocate, advocate's) R3 Err Cym WT.4 Tmp
Son (TNK)                                                          9
```

```
1838 138 comixt (commix, commix'd) Cym (LC)                           1
1839 710 scandalous  MM WT                                            2
1840 441 intricate () Err                                             1
1840 546 obiections  2H6 1H6 H8                                       3
1844 580 pasport  H5 AWW Per³                                         3
1848 330 fowlers (fowler) MND                                         1
1848 355 gin (gin, gins) 2H6 3H6 TN Mac                               4
1849 261 insnard (ensnar'd, ensnare, ensnareth) R3 Oth.2 Luc.2        5
1851 371 gulfe  3H6 R3 Err H5.2 Ham Oth Mac Cor.2 Luc                11
1854 908 violate  LLL R2.2 AYL Ant Cym Tmp Luc.2                      9
1858 886 vprightly                                                    0
1860 165 couenant  1H6.2 Shr R2 Cym.3                                 7
1861 462 lawlesse (lawless) R3 Tit TGV 2H4 Ham.2 MM                   7
1866 461 lawfully () MV AWW Per² (TNK)                                3
1869 427 infringe  3H6 R3 Err LLL.2 MM Cor Luc.2                      8
1871 575 paradise () Err LLL.2 Rom.2 MND H5 AWW MM Tmp (PP,LC)       10
1873 277 eternally () MND (TNK)                                       1
1874 184 deferd  2H6 1H6 R3                                           3
1876 928 wheretofore                                                  0
1880 580 pasport  H5 AWW Per³                                         3
1885 268 intrapt (entrap, entrapp'd) 1H6 MV.2 1H4 AYL Per²            6
1890 820 threescore () 3H6 1H4.2 Ado H5 Ham Mac Son                   8
1893 562 outragious (outrageous) 1H6.2 Err Tit MV Ham Luc             7
1895 399 Hermyt (ermite, hermit, hermits', hermits) 1H6 Tit
LLL MV 2H4 TN Tro Mac                                                 8
1896 296 fethered (feather'd, feathered, feath'red) 1H4 Oth
Per⁵ Ven Luc Son (PhT)                                                6
1897 310 flint stones                                                 0
1897 62 battell'ray                                                   0
1899 380 haples  2H6 3H6.2 1H6 Err TGV.2 Luc                          8
1904 62 battaileray                                                   0
1909 321 forrage (forage) Jo H5 Ven                                   3
1911 337 fryuolous (frivolous) 3H6 1H6 Shr                           3
1912 261 insnard  R3 Oth.2 Luc.2                                      5
```

Act 4 scene 4

```
1919 215 disseuered  Jo AWW WT                                        3
1923 15 all ending (all-ending) R3                                    1
1923 286 eie lesse (eyeless) Rom Tim Lr.3                             5
1924 283 expedient () 2H6 R3 R2 Jo.3 Ado AWW                          8
1926 893 vallie (valley, valleys) Tit MND H5 Cym WT.2 (PP)            6
1927 894 vantagd                                                      0
1928 780 stronger () 3H6.2 Ado Ham.3                               ex
1928 61 battaild (battle)                                             0
1928 933 whole () 1H6 Jo Luc.2 Son                                   5
1931 602 plate  Shr Rom R2.2 2H4.2 Tim Ant.2 Cym H8                 11
1932 640 quarrie (quarries) Oth                                      1
1933 18 Aloft () Jo                                                   1
1933 55 bannarets (bannerets) AWW                                     1
1934 585 pendants                                                    0
1934 680 replenisht (replenish, replenish'd, replenished)
R3 LLL WT Luc                                                         4
1934 170 cuff () 1H6 Shr TN                                           3
1935 351 gaudinesse                                                   0
1936 781 struggles (struggle, struggles, struggling) 2H6 3H6
Jo Ham Ven.3                                                          7
1938 131 Coting                                                       0
1938 32 arraie  2H6 3H6 1H6 Shr.2 Rom.2 H5 AYL.2 Lr Ven             12
```

```
    1939 595 pikes   3H6 1H6 2H4 Ado H5.2 Cor.2 Cym.2 Tmp Ven        12
    1940 778 Streight (straight, straightest) Shr Rom 1H4.2 H5
Per³ Cym Ven Son (TNK)                                                9
    1940 585 pendant ()                                               0
    1941 395 heraldry (heraldry, heraldy) MND Ham.2 AWW Oth Luc       6
    1942 642 Quartred  1H6 R3 Jo.2 Wiv JC.2 Ham Ant Cor Cym H8        ₤×
    1942 796 sundy  AYL Mac.3 Luc                                     5
    1945 374 halfe Moone (half-moon) 1H4.2 WT                         3
    1946 699 rounds (round, rounded, rounding, rounds) R3 R2 MND
Jo Tro AWW WT.2 Tmp (PP) (TNK)                                        9
    1947 169 Crosbowes (cross-bow, cross-bows) 3H6 H5                 2
    1949 893 valleie  Tit MND H5 Cym WT.2                             6
    1951 633 proudly () 1H6.2 R3 R2 Jo 2H4 Ado H5 Tro.2 Son          11
    1951 700 royalized (royalize) R3                                  1
    1955 576 parcelling (parcel, parcell'd) R3 Ant                    2
    1957 377 handful  LLL MND                                         2
    1964 763 squadrons  1H6 JC Oth Ant                                4
    1964 674 regements (regiment, regiments) R3.4 Jo AWW.2 Ant
(TNK)                                                                 8
    1977 635 puissant  2H6 3H6.3 R3 H5.2 JC                           8
    1979 274 equalitie (equalities, equality) Jo Lr Ant               3
    1985 276 Esquires  2H6.2 2H4.2 Wiv.2 H5.3                         9
    1991 628 profered  1H6.2 R3.2 R2 Jo 1H4.2      Cym                9
    1993 785 submissiue (submissive) 1H6.2 Shr LLL                    4
    1993 560 orizons (orisons) 3H6 Rom H5 Ham Cym                     5
    1995 604 plea () LLL Jo MV.4 Luc Son.3 (TNK)                     10
    1998 99 burgonet () 2H6.3 Ant                                     4
    2001 185 defiance  Rom R2 Jo 1H4.2 2H4 H5.3 JC Tro MM            12
    2006 255 ingirt (engirt, engirts) 2H6.2 Ven Luc.2                 5
    2007 449 iennet (gennets, jennet) Oth Ven                         2
    2009 813 therewithall (therewithal) Err TGV.2 LLL Rom MM Lr
Mac Cym                                                               9
    2012 740 sit                                                      0
    2016 105 capring (caper, caper'd, capers) 2H6 R3 LLL 2H4 Wiv TN   6
    2022 342 full fraught (full-fraught) TGV H5                       2
    2024 510ₗ1H6 R3 JC.2 H5 TN AWW H8ʼmeditate                        8
    2029 852 vnaduised (unadvis'd, unadvised) Tit TGV Rom Jo.3 Luc    7
    2032 285 extemporall (extemporal) 1H6 LLL.2                       3
    2033 139 common place                                            0
    2034 12 aduersitie (adversities, adversity, adversity's) 3H6
1H6 Err.2 TGV Rom AYL Tro Oth (TNK)                                   9
    2036 49 auaile (avail, avails) AWW.2                              2
    2039 164 courtly () 2H6 AYL Tro.2 AWW Tim Cym                     7
    2043 517 milke white (milk-white) 2H6 Tit TGV MND Tim (PP)        5
    2046 325 forepast (fore-past) AWW                                 1
    2047 811 texted                                                   0
    2055 96 bud (bud, budded, budding) Shr 1H4 H8 Ven Luc Son         6
    2055 719 seed (seeded) Tro Luc                                    2
    2063 627 proffer () 1H6.2 Per² (PP) AWW                           4
    2066 434 lotterie (lottery, lott'ry) MV.2 JC Tro.2 AWW Ant        7
    2069 413 idiot (idiot, idiots) Err Tit Jo MV Wiv TN Tro.2 Mac
Cym Luc                                                              11
    2075 375 halfepenie (halfpence, halfpenny) LLL.2 Ado H5 AYL
Ham                                                                   6
```

Act 4 scene 5

```
    2081 182 defast (defac'd, deface, defaced, defacing) 2H6.2 1H6.2
R3.2 MV H5 Luc Son.2 (PP)                                            11
```

```
2083 412 husht (hush, hush'd, hushes) R2 Jo 2H4 Ado TN Oth
Cor Tmp Ven Son                                                      10
2085 531 Murmure (murmur, murmur'd, murmuring, murmur'st)
Jo 1H4 AYL Oth Lr Ant Tmp                                             7
2092 832 tongue-tied () 3H6 1H6 R3,2 MND JC Tro WT Son.4             12
2092 514 midnight () Jo Ham Mac Ant Cor Tmp                           6
2094 611 pompeous (pompous) R2 AYL Per³                               3
2095 130 coach (coach, coaches) Tit LLL.2 MV Wiv.3 Ham                8
2097 858 vnder () Cor Tim Lr (TNK) Son                                4
2098 855 vncomfortable (uncomfortable) Rom                            1
2099 561 outcrie (outcries, outcry) Rom MV Luc                        3
2102 620 presage  3H6.2 1H6 Rom MV.2 JC Lr Ant.2                     10
2106 167 crauen (craven) 1H6 Ham                                      2
2108 353 gastly (ghastly) 2H6                                         1
2108 626 printed  2H6.2 Tit Wiv Ado H5 WT Son                         8
2111 168 croke (croak, croaking, croaks) Ham Tro Lr Mac               4
2111 410 houer (hover, hover'd, hovering, hovers) R3.2 Tit Jo
Ham Mac WT Luc (LC)                                                   8
2112 844 triangles                                                    0
2112 160 cornerd                                                      0
2112 764 squares (square, squares) H5 Lr Ant.2 WT (TNK)               5
2113 239 imbatteled (embattailed, embattle, embattled) Jo Wiv
H5 Ant                                                                4
2114 316 fog (fog, fogs) Tit MND.2 TN Lr.2 Mac Cor Cym                9
2115 312 flower (floor) MND MV Cym.2                                  4
2119 512 metamorphosd (metamorphos'd) TGV.2 (TNK)                     2
2120 79 Bloudlesse (bloodless) 2H6 R3 Tit TN Tro Ven Luc (LC)         7
2123 390 harten (hearten, heartens) 3H6 Luc                           2
2126 378 handie worke (handiwork) R3 Jo JC                            3
2127 625 praie (prey, prey'd, preyed, preys) R3 Tit.2 R2 Jo
1H4 Ado AYL Ham MM Oth Ant                                           12
2127 109 carrion  Rom MV 2H4 Wiv H5 JC Ham MM                         8
2129 654 rauenous (ravenous) 2H6 1H6 Tit.2 R2 MV (STM)                6
2131 108 carcases (carcass, carcasses) MND Jo MV JC Cor Cym.2
Tmp (LC)                                                              8
2133 410 houer  R3.2 Tit Jo Ham Mac WT Luc                            8
2137 334 fraude (fraud) 3H6 1H6 TGV Ado Ven Luc                       6
2143 249 incompast  3H6.2 1H6.2 R3 Wiv JC Luc                         8
2153 172 currant (current) R3.4 R2.2 1H4.4 2H4 H8                     12
2160 116 Carectred  2H6 TGV AYL Ham Luc Son.2                         7
2162 765 stable () TN Jo                                              2
2162 900 verdict  1H6.2 R3 Cor H8 Son                                 6
2167 212 disobey (disobey, disobeys) 1H6 R3 H5 Tmp                    4
2174 472 lisence (licence) 2H6 2H4 H5.2 AYL TN Ham MM.2 Ant          10
2175 150 constraint  Jo.2 H5 AWW.3 Per³                               7
2178 356 girdle (girdle, girdles) LLL MND 1H4 2H4.2 Ado H5 Ham
Tim Lr Cym                                                           11
2179 369 gardion  Jo Ado Tro.2 Lr Mac                                 6
2185 704 safe conduct (safe-conduct) Tro.2                            2
2187 618 presidents (precedent) R3 MV WT (LC)                         3
2196 926 westward () Rom 1H4 Ham WT                                   4
2198 834 toplesse (topless) Tro                                       1
2199 50 azure () Cym Tmp                                              2
2201 892 () 2H6 Err Tit.2 Tro Oth Ant Cym H8 (LC) (vale,vales)        9
2201 70 beneath () MV Ham Tro Lr                                      4
2204 405 Hoopt (hoop, hoop'd, hooping) H5 AYL Cor WT                  4
2210 97 bullets (bullet, bullet's, bullets) 1H6 LLL.2 2H4.3
Jo.2 Ado H5 Ven (PP)                                                 11
```

Act 4 scene 6

    2216 219 distract () 2H6 Err Tit JC TN Ham Lr (LC)   7
    2217 646 quiuers (quiver) Ado (TNK)   1
    2217 729 shafts (shaft, shafts) Tit. Rom MND MV 2H4 Wiv TN Tro
Lr Mac Per²   11

    2220 302 fig (fico, fig, figo) 2H6 Wiv H5.2 Oth   5
    2220 296 feathered 1H4 Oth Per⁵ Ven Luc Son   6
    2220 729 shafts Tit Rom MND MV 2H4 Wiv TN Tro Lr Mac Per²   11
    2221 296 feathered 1H4 Oth Per⁵ Ven Luc Son   6
    2221 53 bandie (bandy, bandying) 3H6 1H6 Tit Shr Rom.2 AYL Lr.2 10
    2222 133 coil (coil, coil's) Err Tit TGV Rom MND Jo Ado.2 Ham
AWW Tim Tmp (TNK)   12
    2223 563 outscolde (outscold) Jo   1
    2226 946 Ew (yew) Tit   R2 TN Mac   4

Act 4 scene 7

    2231 220 distraught () R3 Rom   2
    2231 803 swift () 1H6 Tit.3 LLL MV H5 Ham Tro Cym.3   12
    2232 101 buzd (buzz, buzz'd, buzzing) 2H6 3H6.2 Tit.2 R2 MV
2H4 JC H8.2   11
    2232 210 dismaie (dismay) MV.2 Ham Tmp   4
    2233 202 disaduantaᵹo (disadvantage) 2H4 Cor   2
    2234 11 abiect (abject) 2H6.3 1H6 Err Shr MV 2H4 Tro.2 H8   11
    2236 661 recalling 2H6 1H6 Err TGV Per³ WT Luc   7
    2238 658 Rebell (rebel, rebell'd, rebelling) 1H6 R2 MV Ant Cor
Cym H8   ex.
    2238 42 attainted (attaint, attainted) 2H6 1H6.3 LLL Son (PP)   6
    2243 205 discouragement   0
    2251 769 staruelings (starveling) 1H4.2   2
    2252 635 puisant 2H6 3H6.3 R3 H5.2 JC   8
    2253 33 Araid (array, array'd, arrayed) H5 MM Lr Son   4
    2253 299 fenst 3H6.2 MV 2H4 Wiv AYL TN Ham Tim Per¹ Per⁴ Luc 12
    2253 6 accomplements   0
    2254 647 quait (quoit) 2H4   1
    2255 235 elders () Shr JC Cor.2   4
    2256 776 stoned (ston'd, stone) Oth WT.2 Luc   4
    2258 192 derisiom () MND.4 Tro   5
    2259 81 blurt (blurted) Per⁴   1
    2262 849 twentith () MV Ham   2
    2263 639 quaile (quail, quailing) 3H6 MND 1H4 AYL Ant Cym   6
    2264 377 handfull LLL MND   2
    2264 11 aduerse (adverse) 1H6 R3.2 Err R2 Jo.2 Ado TN AWW MM
Son   12

Act 4 scene 8

    2276 87 brauerie (bravery) JC AYL Ham MM Oth Cym (TNK)   6

Act 4 scene 9

    2284 250 Ensignes 1H6 Tit Rom R2 JC.2 Cym Ver   8
    2284 106 captiue 3H6.2 R3 Tit H5 JC Tro.2 Ant Luc Son AWW   12
    2287 125 clemencie Ham   1
    2295 357 giuer (giver, givers) TGV Ham Tro Tim (TNK)   4
    2298 901 verefied (verified, verify) 3H6 1H6.2 Jo Ado H5 Cor H8 8
    2299 435 louring (low'r, low'r'd, low'reth, low'ring, low'rs,
low'r'st) 2H6 R3.2 Err Rom.2 R2.2 Ant Ven.2 Son   12
    2301 205 discouragement   0

```
2306 245 enamored (enamor'd, enamored) Rom MND.2 1H4 2H4 Ado      6
2308 483 lopt (lop, lopp'd) 2H6 3H6 1H6 Tit.2 R2 1H4 Per'
Cym.3 H8                                                          12
2309 69 bemoning (bemoan'd) 3H6                                    1
2310 455 knell () MV AWW Tim Mac.3 Cor WT Tmp H8.2 Luc (PP)       12
2314 106 captyue  3H6.2 R3 Tit H5 JC Tro.2 Ant Luc Son AWW        12
2315 691 restoritiue                                              0
2317 213 dispence (dispense, dispenses) 2H6 1H6 Err LLL Wiv
MM.2 Tim Luc.3 Son                                               12
2319 934 wholie (wholly) LLL Wiv Tro.2 Ant Cym                    6
2321 107 captiuitie (captivity) 2H6 3H6 1H6 JC Oth Mac (TNK.2)    6
2325 937 willingnes (willingness) 2H6 3H6                         2
2326 151 consummation () Ham Cym (TNK)                            2
2329 762 spouse () Err Shr H5 Lr (TNK)                            4
2338 71 bequeath                                                  0
2338 810 testament () 1H6 R2 H5.2 JC.2 AYL.2 AWW Tim Per⁴ Luc     12
2344 430 Litter () 1H6 Jo Lr                                      3
2345 633 proudly  1H6.2 R3 R2 Jo 2H4 Ado H5 Tro.2 Son            11


Act 5 scene 1

2351 572 pacifie (pacified, pacify) 1H4 2H4 TN                    3
2355 40 assault (assault, assaulted, assaults) Jo Oth Lr Cor
Tmp                                                               5
2356 169 deluded (deluded, deluding) 1H6 Shr Oth                  3
2359 154 Contemptuous () 2H6 Jo                                   2
2365 690 respit (respite) 1H6 R3 MM H8.2                          5
2366 937 willingnes 2H6 3H6                                       2
2372 723 seruile (servile) 2H6 1H6 Tit.2 R2 JC MM Lr Ven.2 Luc   11
2373 298 fellonious (felonious) 2H6                               1
2373 698 robbers (robber, robber's, robbers) 3H6.2 R2 H5 JC
Tro Tim Lr Cym                                                    9
2375 727 seuerity (severity) 1H6 Rom MM Cor                       4
2376 568 ouerreach (overreach) Shr (o'er-*) Tit Err Wiv Ham.2     6
2377 925 western () 3H6 R3.2 TGV MND.2 Jo AYL MM Mac             10
2379 558 Orient () R3 MND Ant Ven (PP)                            4
2379 636 purple () 1H4                                            1
2381 614 portion () 1H6 Shr AYL MM Lr WT H8 (TNK)                 7
2382 165 couenant  1H6.2 Shr R2 Cym.3                             7
2387 642 quartering  1H6 R3 Jo.2 Wiv JC.2 Ham Ant Cor Cym H8 ex.
2390 766 stablish () 1H6                                          1
2398 644 quietnes (quietness) 3H6 1H6 MV Tro Ant.2 Cor            7
2400 435 insomuch  AYL                                            1
2401 503 master  Cym Ven TGV AYL H5                               5
2402 201 dynt (dint) 2H4 JC Ven                                   3
2404 125 clemencie  Ham                                          1
2409 695 reuerence  1H6.2 MV Per² Cym                             5
2411 361 glomy  1H6 Tit Luc                                       3
2411 570 orespent                                                 0
2412 350 garrison (garrison'd) Ham Cym                            2
2416 622 presumtious (presumptuous) 2H6 3H6 1H6.2 AWW             5
2416 276 Esquire  2H6.2 2H4.2 Wiv.2 H5.3                          9
2419 543 Northern (northen, northern, northren) 2H6 3H6.2 Tit
LLL R2.2 1H4 JC WT Luc                                           11
2419 276 Esquire  2H6.2 2H4.2 Wiv.2 H5.3                          9
2420 434 insolent () 2H6    Tro.2 Oth Lr Cor.2 Tmp                8
2421 547 obstinate  1H6 Ado Ham Cor H8                            5
```

    * (o'erraught, o'erreach, o'erreaches, o'erreaching)

2422 156 contradict (contradict, contradicted, contradicts) 2H6
Rom Jo Lr Mac WT H8 Luc   8
  2423 211 disobedience () 1H6 MND 1H4 Wiv AWW Cor Cym WT   8
  2427 619 preheminence (pre-eminence) Err Lr   2
  2430 891 vale 1H6 R3 Shr LLL MV 2H4 Ham MM Cor Per² Per⁴ Ven   12
  2430 82 bonnet () R2 MV H5 AYL Ham Cor Ven.3   9
  2431 335 fraught Tit TN Oth   3
  2432 923 wealthie 2H6.2 3H6 Shr.2 MV.3 AWW Oth Tim.2   12
  2433 800 surrendred R2 H8   2
  2437 695 reuerence 1H6.2 MV Per² Cym   5
  2444 663 recourse R3 TGV Wiv Tro   4
  2445 677 relation (relation, relations) MV Tro Mac.2 Per⁵ Cym
WT.3 Tmp   10
  2453 162 Coronet 1H6.2 MND H5 JC Lr Tmp H8   8
  2458 838 tragicall (tragical) 1H6 R3 MND.3   5
  2459 221 dolefull (doleful, dolefull'st) Rom Jo 2H4 WT.2 Luc
(PP.3)   6
  2461 72 beset Shr TGV.2 MV Ado TN Luc   7
  2463 722 seruiceable (serviceable) Shr TGV TN Lr Cym   5
  2464 704 safe conduct Tro.2   2
  2468 231 eager 3H6.2 1H6 R2.3 Ham.2 Luc.2 Son   11
  2472 188 deliuerance (deliverance) 3H6 MV 2H4 AWW.2 MM.2 Cym
H8 (TNK)   9
  2477 645 quittance () 1H6   1
  2479 198 diffusd (defus'd, defuse, diffused, diffusest) R3
Wiv H5 Lr Tmp   5
  2479 915 wan () Err Tit 1H4   3
  2484 194 descry (descried, descry) 1H6 R3 Shr LLL Rom Oth Lr
Ant Per¹ Per⁵ Luc   11
  2485 893 vallie Tit MND H5 Cym WT.2   6
  2486 843 trenches () 1H6 Tit 1H4 Cor.3 Son   7
  2487 58 Barricados (barricado, barricadoes) TN WT   2
  2488 814 thicke MV Ant Cym H8 Tmp Luc.3   8
  2488 240 imbost (emboss'd, embossed) Shr 1H4 AYL AWW Tim Lr
Ant (TNK)   7
  2488 89 brasen 2H6.2 3H6.2 LLL R2 Jo 1H4 Ham Tro Ant   11
  2488 555 ordynaunce (ordinance, ord'nance) 1H6 Shr H5 Ham   4
  2490 595 pikes 3H6 1H6 2H4 Ado H5.2 Cor.2 Cym.2 Tmp Ven   12
  2490 638 quadrant   0
  2490 939 wise Per⁵ (PP)   1
  2491 169 Crosbowes 3H6 H5   2
  2491 178 deadly () 3H6 R3.2   Ado AWW Tro Cor   7
  2491 175 darts (dart, darts) 2H6.2 JC MM Oth Ant Cor Per¹ Cym
Ven.2 (TNK)   11
  2492 515 midst 3H6 R3 Err Shr MND Mac Ant.2 Cor.2 Luc   11
  2492 745 slender (slender, slenderer) Shr.3 TGV LLL 2H4.2
AYL Ham Tim   10
  2493 406 horison (horizon) 3H6   1
  2494 95 bubble (bubble, bubbles) R3 1H4 AYL Ham AWW Mac   6
  2495 387 Hasle (hazel) Rom   1
  2495 916 wand (wand, wands) 2H6 TGV MV   3
  2495 21 amidst () Tro   1
  2495 599 Pynes 2H6 R2 MV Tro Ant.2 Cym WT Tmp.3 Luc   12
  2496 118 chaind (chain, chain'd, chained, chains) 2H6 3H6 1H6
Err TGV Rom Ant Cor Tmp Luc   10
  2498 291 fasten (fasten, fasten'd, fastened, fastens) Err JC
MM Oth Lr Cym WT Ven AWW   9
  2499 455 knell MV AWW Tim Mac.3 Cor WT Tmp H8.2 Luc   12

```
2502 123 clangor () 3H6                                              1
2505 441 intricate  Err                                             1
2507 616 pouder (powder) Tit Rom.3 Jo 1H4.2 Ant                     8
2507 345 fuming (fume, fumes, fuming) Shr Ant Luc                   3
2518 866 vnheard of                                                 0
2521 530 mourners (mourner, mourners) R3.2 Rom Ven Luc Son.2
(PhT)                                                               7
2522 721 sere   ErrMM                                               2
2523 598 pillers (pillar, pillars) 2H6 3H6 MV Tro Ant Tmp H8
(TNK.2)                                                             7
2523 388 hearse () 1H6 R3 2H4 JC Per⁴                               5
2524 529 mould                                  Cor                 1
2524 122 Citie  R3 Tit Rom Jo Tim Cor.3                             8
2525 455 knell   MV AWW Tim Mac.3 Cor WT Tmp H8.2 Luc              12
2527 77 blaze (blaze, blazed, blazing) 3H6.2 Rom JC Ham AWW
Ven Luc Err Tim      blaz'd                                        10
2528 75 bewaile (bewail, bewailed, bewailing, bewails) 2H6
MND Cor H8 Son                                                     5
2528 179 decease (decease, decesse) 2H6 3H6 1H6     Son.2          5
2531 666 redoubted () 1H6 R3 R2 MV H5                              5
2532 725 seruitor  3H6 1H6 R3 Tit Oth Luc                         6
2535 488 lowly () AWW H8                                           2
2535 775 stirop (stirrup, stirrups) 2H6 Shr.2 Tim Cor             5
2537 106 captiue  3H6.2 R3 Tit H5 JC Tro.2 Ant Luc Son           11
2545 588 perplext (perplex, perplex'd, perplexed) 1H6 Jo.2
Oth Cym.3 Ven Luc                                                 9
2549 945 wreath (wreath, wreaths) 3H6 R3 JC Lr Per².2 Luc
(TNK.3)                                                           7
2550 513 mickle () 2H6 1H6 Err Rom H5 (TNK) (PP)                 5
2552 436 Install (install'd, installed, installs) 3H6.2
1H6.2 H8 (STM)                                                   5
2553 398 heerewithall                                            0
2559 882 vntoucht (untouch'd) R3 JC                              2
2562 881 vntimely  3H6.2 R3.2 Rom.2 Mac Ham Lr                   9
2563 447 irreuocable (irrevocable) 2H6 3H6 AYL                   3
2571 519 misconster (misconster, misconsters, misconst'red)
1H6 R3 MV AYL    (misconstrued) 1H4 JC                           6
2581 145 conflicts  2H6 3H6.2 Tit LLL Ado Tim Lr.2 Mac Ven      11
2582 511 menaces () Lr                                           1
2582 628 proffered  1H6.2 R3.2 R2 Jo 1H4.2       Cym            9
2584 665 redoubled () R2 1H4 Mac Ven                            4
2585 396 hereafter () 1H6 R3                                    2
2586 573 painfull Shr LLL Ado H5 MM Cor Per³ Tmp Luc Son       10
2586 836 traffike (traffic, traffic's) 1H6 Err Shr Rom TN
Tim.3 WT Tmp Son                                               11
2587 426 inflamd (inflam'd, inflame, inflaming) 1H6 Jo.2
2H4 JC Tro Oth Lr Per¹ Per² Per⁴ (TNK) (LC)                   11
2587 688 resolue (resolve) 3H6 1H6 Shr.2 Rom                   5
2590 446 ire  3H6 1H6 Err R2 Per²                              5
2593 438 intercession () 1H6 TGV Rom Cor.2 H8 (TNK)            6
2593 573 painfull  Shr LLL Ado H5 MM Cor Per³ Tmp Luc Son     10
2594 671 refresh (refresh, refresh'd, refreshing) Shr H5 JC
Per⁵ WT Tmp.2 (TNK)(PP)                                        7
2596 383 hauen                                                 0
```

Add (omitted in error):
```
2385 181 decreed  Err Tit Rom R2 1H4 Ado AYL TN Tro Cor Per¹
Per²                                                          12
```

Alphabetical key to Appendix III with further data

This Appendix is an alphabetical key, or index, to Appendix III.

It shows:

1. The serial number of the word from '1 ABANDON' to '948 ZEALOUS';

2. The lexical word in the form in which it is entered in the *Shorter Oxford English Dictionary*, 3rd edition, 1969. Words which are not found in the *Dictionary* are marked with an asterisk (*);

3. The classification of the word as a part of speech, together with the figure or letter or combination of both used in the *Dictionary* to classify the meaning. An effort was made to match dictionary meaning with the meaning read from the text of the play;

4. The number(s) of the line(s) in the text (continuous order) where the word appears;

5. The word as it appears in the text;

6. The number of links, as citations, in Shakespeare's works as embodied in Spevack's *Concordance*. Appearances in works excluded from the statistical analysis are not counted here. If the word does not appear at all in Shakespeare's named works, a zero is entered.

7. On occasions in which either Armstrong or Crawford has changed the reading in a way which might have affected the statistics, their readings, marked A or C, are inserted in brackets. The writer has also entered comments of his own on the words: 235 elders, 728 shadow, 731 sharpely, 772 Stir, 774 stiffe, 858 vnder.

Eight words in this appendix have been excluded from the main statistical analyses in Chapter 7, and are marked 'ex'. This is because they may not have qualified according to the criteria set out in p. 103 of the text, e.g. because of an ambiguity of meaning or grammatical classification, or the doubtful acceptability of spelling, or the possibility that there are more than the maximum permitted 12 links with Shakespeare's named works.

These words are: 336 fraught, 422 inconstant, 566 overbear, 600 pitch, 642 quarter, 655 rebel, 664 recovery, 780 stronger.

 1 ABANDON, v.4   1288 abandoned   12
 2 ABJECT, a.2   2234 abiect   11
 4 ABUNDANT, a   859 aboundant (A:"heart's abundance")   3
 3 ABSTRACT, n.B.1   433 abstract   7
 5 ACCEPTABLE, a   217 acceptable   1
 6 ACCOMPLEMENT, n   2253 accomplements   0
 7 ACCORDINGLY, adv   823 accordingly   9
 8 ADMIRAL, n.5   1120 Admirall, 1196 Admirall,   1197 Admirall   5
 9 ADORN, v.1   1117 Adornes, 1514 adornd   8
10 ADULTERATE, a.1   462 adulterate   5
11 ADVERSE, a.1   2264 aduerse   12
12 ADVERSITY, n.2   2034 aduersitie   9
13 ADVOCATE, n.1   1831 aduocate   9
14 AGGRAVATE, v.2   798 agreuate, 1070 aggrauate   5
*15 ALL-ENDING, a   1923 all ending   1
16 ALLY, n.III.3   156 allies   7
17 ALOFT, adv.3   1214 aloft   8
18 ALOFT, prep.5   1933 aloft   1
19 ALTERATION, n.2   1058 alteration   9
20 AMBER, n.3   468 amber   3
21 AMIDST, prep.B.2   2495 amidst   1
22 ANCHOR, n.1   1133 anchor   9
23 ANCHORAGE, n.3   1064 anchredge   1
24 ANIMATE, v.4   1531 animates   0
25 ANVIL, n.1   1652 Anuell   2
26 APIECE, adv   1771 a peece   4
27 A-PIECES, adv   1107 a peeces   1
28 APPAREL, v.3   767 Apparaled   10
29 APPLICATION, n.5   514 application   1
30 ARBOUR, n.4   412 arber   3
31 ARMADO, n.1   1111 Armado   2
32 ARRAY, n.1   824 aray, 1363 araie, 1551 ray, 1938 arraie   12
33 ARRAY, v.1   2253 araid   4
34 ARRIVAL, n.1   1337 arriuall   6
35 ARROGANCE, n   82 arrogannce   6
36 ARROGANT, a.1   1373 arrogant   4
37 ARTIFICIAL, a, A.I.3   1403 artifitiall   7
38 ARTILLERY, n.3   888 artyllerie   5
39 ASH, n'.2   208 ash   1

40 ASSAULT, v.1   2355 assault   5

41 ASTONISH, v.2   1525 astonish   5

42 ATTAINT, v.6   2238 attainted   6

43 ATTENDANCE, n.1   428 attendance   7

44 ATTIREMENT, n   1500 attirement   0

46 ATTRACT, v.3   357 attracted   3

45 ATTORNEY, n.4   738 atturnie   10

47 AUGMENT, v.2   580 augment   10

48 AUSTERE, a.3   641 austere   4

49 AVAIL, n.2   2036 auaile   2

50 AZURE, a.B.2   2199 a$_z$ure   2

51 BABBLE, n.2   195 babble   3

52 BAGGAGE, n.1   1243 baggage   9

53 BANDY, v.1   2221 bandie   10

54 BANE, n.1   1666 bane   7

55 BANNERETTE, n   1933 bannarets   1

56 BARBARISM, n.2   186 barbarisme   4

57 BARON, n.1   1672 Barons   7

58 BARRICADO, n.1   2487 Barricados   2

59 BASELY, adv.3   1437 basely   12

60 BATTER, v.1   1651 battered   11

61 BATTLE, v²   1928 battaild   0

*62 BATTLE-ARRAY, n   1897 Battell'ray, 1904 battaileray   0

63 BEAK, n.1   1687 beak   6

64 BEARDLESS, a   979 Beardles   2

65 BEAUTIFY, v   330 beautified, 389 beautified, 634 beautifie   8

66 BEGIRD, v.3   135 begirt, 1682 begyrt   0

67 BELLY-GOD, n   1477 belly god   0

68 BELT, n.1   210 belts   2

69 BEMOAN, v   2309 bemoning   1

70 BENEATH, adv.A.1   2201 beneath   4

71 BEQUEATH, n.2   2338 bequeath   0

72 BESET, v.2   1583 beset, 2461 beset   7

*73 BESIEGE, n   769 beseege   0

74 BETAKE, v.2   1563 betook   11

75 BEWAIL, v.1   2528 bewaile   5

76 BIT, n¹.5   1468 byt   5

77 BLAZE, v².1   2527 blaze   10

78 BLEAK, a.3   191 bleake   6

79 BLOODLESS, a   2120 Bloudlesse   7

80 BLOODTHIRSTY, a   1056 Bloodthirsty   1

81 BLURT, v.2 (cited in S.O.E.D.)   2259 blurt   1

82 BONNET, n.1a   2430 bonnet   9

83 BONNY, a.2a   204 bonny,   236 bonny,   250 bonnie,   1227 bonnier   7

84 BOOTY, n.1a   228 Booty   3

85 BORDER, v.4   133 bordering   1

86 BOWER, n.2   594 bower   8

87 BRAVERY, n.3   2276 brauerie   6

88 BRAY, v¹.2b   190 bray   3

89 BRAZEN, a.1   1518 brasen ,   2488 brasen   11

90 BRICK, n.1   361 bricke   2

91 BRIEF, n.5   433 breefe   6

92 BRITTLE, a.1   32 brittile   4

93 BROAD, adv.C3   379 broad   3

94 BRUIT, v.1   1051 bruted   4

95 BUBBLE, n.2   2494 bubble   6

96 BUD, v.a   2055 bud   6

97 BULLET, n.2   2210 bullets   11

98 BURGESS, n.2   1803 Burgesses   0

99 BURGONET, n.b   1998 burgonet   4

100 BUTTONED, ppl. a   210 buttoned   1

101 BUZZ, v.5   2232 buzd   11

102 CABINET, n.II.1   413 cabynet   2

103 CANNON-SHOT, n.1   1170 Cannon shot   1

104 CANON, n¹.1   782 cannon   7

105 CAPER, v¹   2016 capring   6

106 CAPTIVE, a.1; a.3; a.1; a.1; a.3; a.1; a.3   929 captiue, 1486   12
          captiue, 1625 Captiue,   1715 captiue,   2284 captiue,
          2314 captyue,   2537 captiue

107 CAPTIVITY, n.1   2321 captiuitie   6

108 CARCASS, n.1   2131 carcases   8

109 CARRION, n.A.2; A.1   796 carrion,   2127 carrion   8
110 CATE, n   1171 cates   4

111 CERTAINTY, n.2   1051 certenty   11

112 CERTIFY, v.1   1707 certified   4

113 CHAIN, v.2   2496 chaind   10

114 CHAMPAIGN, CHAMPIAN, CHAMPION, a(=A.n³.attrib)   1438 Champion   1

115 CHAPLAIN, n.2   633 chaplaines   5

116 CHARACTER, v.1; v.1   663 carectred,   2160 Carectred   7

```
117 CHEERFULLY, adv (of a.1)    174 cheerefully                      9
118 CHERRY, a.5    357 cherie                                        3
119 CHESS, n.1    400 Chesse                                         0
120 CHINE, n.3    1481 chines                                        3
121 CHOICE, a.1    907 choysest                                      3
122 CITY, a (=n.6.attrib)    209 Citie,  2524 Citie                  8
123 CLANGOR, n    2502 clangor                                       1
*124 CLEFTURE, n    1212 cleftures                                   0
125 CLEMENCY, n.1    1467 clemencie, 1811 clemencie, 2287 clem-      1
            encie, 2404 clemencie
126 CLIP, v².1    610 clip                                           3
127 CLOAK, v.2    904 cloke                                          1
128 CLOSELY, adv.2    194 closely                                    8
129 CLUSTER, v.2    1565 clustering                                  3
130 COACH, n.1    2095 coach                                         8
131 COAT, v.2    1938 coting                                         0
132 COCKNEY, n.A.3    1677 clckney                                   2
133 COIL, n.1.3    2222 coile                                        12
134 COLT, n¹.1    1352 coult                                         8
135 COMB, n¹.6    638 combe                                          2
136 COMBAT, v.1    1743 combata                                      9
137 COMMENCE, v.1    151 comence                                     11
138 COMMIX, v    1838 comixt                                         1
139 COMMONPLACE, n.A.3    2033 common place                          0
140 COMPULSION, n    1224 compulsion                                 10
141 CONCEPT, (=CONCEIT, n.3)    1152 concept                         0
142 CONCORDANT, a    427 concordant                                  0
143 CONDUIT, n.2    1159 Conduit                                     6
144 CONFEDERATE, n.B.1    1078 confederates                          10
145 CONFLICT, n.1; n.1; n.1    1139 conflict, 1391 conflict,         11
            1671 conflict,  2581 conflicts
146 CONJOIN, v.3; v.3    1071 conioynes,  1196 conioynd              7
147 CONSORT, n.1    550 consort                                      4
148 CONSPIRACY, n.2    111 conspiracy                                11
149 CONSPIRATOR, n    1457 conspiratours                             9
150 CONSTRAINT, n.2; n.1    530 constraint,  2175 constraint         7
151 CONSUMMATION, n.2    2326 consummation                           2
152 CONTEMPLATE, v.5    443 contemplat                               1
153 CONTEMPLATIVE, a, A.1    318 Contemplatiue                       3
154 CONTEMPTUOUS, a.2    2359 Contemptuous                           2
```

*155 CONTINUAL, adv (continual, a.1, adverbially)   0
            1655 continuall

156 CONTRADICT, v.3   2422 contradict   8

157 CONVENTICLE, n.4   414 conuenticle   1

158 CONVICT, v.1   439 conuicted   2

159 CORAL, n.1a   361 Corrall   2

160 CORNER, v.1   2112 cornerd   0

*161 CORN-FIELD, n   1297 Corne fieldes (A: cornfields;   1
            C: corn-fields)

162 CORONET, n.1   1699 Coronet, 2453 Coronet   8

*163 COUNCIL-HOUSE, n (council, n III - house)   413 counsel   2
            house

164 COURTLY, a.2   2039 courtly   7

165 COVENANT, n.1   1381 couenant, 1860 couenant, 2382   7
        couenant

*166 CRANNY, a   1212 cranny (A: crannied)   0

167 CRAVEN, a.A.2   2106 crauen   2

168 CROAK, v.1   2111 croke   4

169 CROSS-BOW, n.1   1947 Crosbowes (A: crossbows;   2
        C: cross-bows) 2491 Crosbowes (A: cross-bows;
        C: cross-bows)

170 CUFF, v^1.1   1934 cuff   3

171 CUMBER, v.4   654 comber   2

172 CURRENT, a.2   2153 currant   12

173 CURTAIL, v.2   1472 Curtall   1

174 CYNIC, n.B.2   666 cyncke   1

175 DART, n.1   2491 darts   11

176 DAY-STAR, n.1   316 day stars (A: day stars)   0

177 DAZZLE, v.2   513 dazle, 893 dazles   8

178 DEADLY, adv.1   2491 deadly   7

179 DECEASE, n.1   2528 decease   5

180 DECLINE, n.2 (fig)   287 declyne   0

181 DECREE, v.1; v.1   1804 decreed, 2385 decreed   12

182 DEFACE, v.3   2081 defast   11

183 DEFECTIVE, a.3   541 defectiue   5

184 DEFER, v.2; v.2   1528 deferd, 1874 deferd   3

185 DEFIANCE, n.2; n.2; n.2; n.3; n.2   92 defyaunce, 93   12
        Defiance, 385 defiance, 1824 defiance, 2001
        defiance

186 DELICIOUS, a.2   763 delitious   4

187 DELINEATE, v (ppl).3   910 delineate   0

188 DELIVERANCE, n.1   2472 deliuerance   9

189 DELUDE, v.2   2356 deluded   3

190 DELVE, v.1   337 Delue   3

191 DERIDE, v.1   188 deride   1

192 DERISION, n.1   2258 derision   5

193 DESCANT, n.3   473 descant   2

194 DESCRY, v.3; v.3; v.3   229 discry, 1109 discribde,   11
         2484 descry

195 DESOLATION, n.2   1308 desolation   11

196 DETESTABLE, a.1   703 detestable   6

197 DEVOUT, a.A.1   574 deuout   8

198 DIFFUSE, v (with meaning of diffuse, a.1)   2479 diffusd   5

199 DIGNIFY, v.1   1545 dignifie   12

200 DIM, v.2   1400 dym   12

201 DINT, n.2   2402 dynt   3

202 DISADVANTAGE, n.1   2233 disaduantage   2

203 DISBURDEN, v.2   415 disburdning   1

204 DISCOMFITURE, n.a   1188 discomfiture   1

205 DISCOURAGEMENT, n.2; n.3   2243 discouragement, 2301   0
         discouragement

206 DISDAINFUL, a.1   1351 disdainfull   9

207 DISEASE, v.2   1757 deseased   11

208 DISGORGE, v.1   674 disgorged   4

209 DISLODGE, v.2; v.2   235 dislodge, 235 dislodge   1

210 DISMAY, n   2232 dismaie   4

211 DISOBEDIENCE, n   2423 disobedience   8
212 DISOBEY, v.2   2167 disobey   4

213 DISPENSE, v.II.3   2317 dispence   12

214 DISPOSSESS, v.1   585 disposse   6

215 DISSEVER, v.1; v.1; v.2   129 disseuered, 1213 dissuuered,   3
         1919 disseuered

216 DISSOLUTE, a.5   994 dissolude (A: dissolved)   3

217 DISTAIN, v.2   748 distaine   4

218 DISTANT, a.3   1307 distant   5

219 DISTRACT, a. ppl. a.2   2216 distract   7

220 DISTRAUGHT, a.1   2231 distraught   2

221 DOLEFUL, a.1   2459 dolefull   6

222 DOMESTIC, a.A.3   1075 drum stricke (A: domestic)   8

223 DOMINION, n, 2b; 2b; 2b   87 Dominions, 829 dominions,   7
         1703 Dominions

224 DOOM, v.3   1574 dooming   11

225 DOWNY, a.4   1482 downie   4

226 DRONE, n¹.1   98 droane   5

227 DRUMMER, n.1   879 drummer   1

228 DUB, v¹.1   1497 dub   7

229 DUG, n¹   778 Dug   9

230 DUSTY, a.2   32 dusty   2

231 EAGER, a.4; a.5   203 eager, 2468 eager   11

232 EARNEST-PENNY, n   1199 earnest peny   0

233 EASTERN, a.2   1036 esterne   7

234 ECHO, v.1b   1170 eckoing   3

235 ELDER, n.B3   2255 elders   4
["No lesse than fortie thousand wicked elders,/ Haue fortie leane
slaues this daie stoned to death."   King John likens his soldi-
ery to aged dignitaries inflamed with lust.]

236 ELECT, v.1; v.3   148 elect, 1809 elect   7

237 ELSEWHERE, adv.1   903 elsewhere   10

238 EMBASSAGE, n   199 embassage, 725 embassage   6

239 EMBATTLE, v.1   2113 imbatteled   4

240 EMBOSS, v.1   2488 imbost   7

241 EMBRACEMENT, n.1   1348 imbracement   12

242 EMMET, n   1600 Emmets   0

243 EMULATE, v.1   509 emulats   1

244 ENACT, v.2   623 enacted   9
245 ENAMOUR, v.1   2306 enamored   6

246 ENCAMP, v.1   1045 incampe   5

247 ENCHANTMENT, n.2   285 enchantment   2

248 ENCLOSE, v.1; v.4   136 inclosd, 1204 inclose   11

249 ENCOMPASS, v.5 [SOED cites Wiv.2.2.158]; v.2; v.2   776 encom-   8
               passed, 1591 incompast, 2143 incompast

*250 ENCOUCH, v   420 encouch   0

251 ENCROACH, v.2   1369 incroach   1

252 ENDAMAGEMENT, n   735 indammagement   1

253 ENDLESS, a.A.1; A.1   816 endles, 953 endles   10

254 ENGENDER, v.3   48 engendred   12

255 ENGIRD, v   2006 ingirt   5

256 ENGRAVE, v.3   1449 ingraud   4

257 ENJOIN, v.2; v.2   74 inioynd, 1656 enioynd   11

258 ENKINDLE, v.2   1435 inkindled   5

259 ENLARGE, v.5   1326 inlarge   12

260 ENSIGN, n.5; n.5   1115 Ensignes, 2284 Ensignes   8

261 ENSNARE, v   1849 insnard, 1912 insnard   5

262 ENTAIL, v².2   63 entayld   2

263 ENTANGLE, v.1b   1602 Intangled   3

264 ENTHRONE, v.1   1470 inthrone   5

265 ENTIRELY, adv (entire, a.3 - ly)   198 intirely   9

266 ENTOMB, v.1   1493 intombed   8

267 ENTRAIL, n¹.1   1442 entrailes   11

268 ENTRAP, v.1   1885 intrapt   6

269 ENTRENCH, v.1; v.1   1650 intrencht, 1740 intrench   2

270 ENVENOM, v.2   778 inuennometh   7

271 ENVIRON, v.1   771 inuierd   10

272 EPICURE, n.2   1067 Epicures   2

273 EPITHET, n.3   380 epithites   5

274 EQUALITY, n.1   1979 equalitie   3

275 EQUALLY, adv.2   1123 equally   9

276 ESQUIRE, n.2; n.2; n.2; n.2   1789 Esquire (A: squire), 1985   9
Esquires (A: squires), 2416 Esquire, 2419 Esquire

277 ETERNALLY, adv (eternal, a.3 - ly)   1873 eternally   1

278 EVIDENCE, n.6; n.6   913 euidence, 987 euidence   12

279 EXCLUDE, v.2   30 exclude   1

280 EXCOMMUNICATE, v (ppl)   689 excommunicat   2

281 EXECRATION, n (from execrate, v.3)   1420 execrations   2

282 EXHALATION, n.2   1175 exalations   4

283 EXPEDIENT, a.A1   1924 expedient   8

284 EXPULSE, v   1288 expulsd   1

285 EXTEMPORAL, a   2032 extemporall   3

286 EYELESS, a.2   1923 eie lesse   5

287 EYE-SIGHT, n.1   757 eie-sight   7

•288 FACELESS, a   258 facelesse   0

289 FALTER, v.1   1657 faulter   2

290 FAMINE, n.1   1743 Famine   12

291 FASTEN, v.6   2498 fasten   9

292 FATHER-IN-LAW, n.1   154 Father in law   4

293 FATHERLESS, a.1   1538 fatherles   2

294 FEALTY, n.1   83 fealty   5

295 FEATHER-BED, n.1   1482 feather-bedes   1

296 FEATHERED, a.1; a.3; a.1   1896 fethered, 2220 feathered,   6
2221 feathered

297 FELL, v.2   1656 fell   6

298 FELONIOUS, a   2373 fellonious   1

299 FENCE, v.5; v.5   1512 fenst, 2253 fenst   12

300 FERVENT, a.2   114 Feruent   0

301 FESTER, v.2   808 fester   6
302 FIG, n²int   2220 fig   5
303 FIGURE, v.2   1119 figuring   5
304 FINAL, a.A1   119 finale   0
305 FIRST-FRUIT, n.1   1647 first fruit   1
306 FLANKER, n.2   540 flankars   0
307 FLESH, v.3   1773 fresh (A: flesh)   11
308 FLEUR-DE-LIS, n.2   1126 Flewer de Luce,   1282 fluerdeluce   5
309 FLINT, a   423 flynt   3
310 FLINTSTONE, n   1897 flint stones   0
311 FLOCK, v.1   1053 flocke   5
312 FLOOR, n.2   2115 flower   (A:flower,   C:floor)   4
313 FLOWER, v.1   1287 flowring   6
314 FLUENT, a.4   377 fluent   1
315 FOEMAN, n   1229 foemens   5
316 FOG, n².II.1   2114 fog   9
317 FOIL, v¹.II.2   1399 foile (A: soil)   9
318 FOOLISHNESS, n.1   390 foolishnes   1
319 FOOTMAN, n.2   146 footemen   6
320 FOOTSTOOL, n.2   454 footstoole   1
321 FORAGE, v.1   1909 forrage   3
*322 FORAGEMENT, n   753 forragement   0
323 FOREFRONT, n.1   1561 forefront   0
324 FOREIGNER, n.1   1466 forrener   1
325 FOREPASSED, ppl.   2046 forepast   1
326 FORTIFY, v.II.1   1052 fortified   12
327 FORTITUDE, n.2   1506 fortitude   5
328 FORTNIGHT, n   821 fortnight   10
329 FOSTER, v.2   110 fostred   8
330 FOWLER, n.1   1848 fowlers   1
331 FRAGRANT, a   17 fragrant,   517 fragrant   5
332 FRANC, n.b   1714 Francks   0
333 FRANTICLY, adv   1603 Frantiquely   2
334 FRAUD, n.3   2137 fraude   6
335 FRAUGHT, n (= freight, n.2)   1644 fraught,   2431 fraught   3
336 FRAUGHT, ppl. a.2   2022 fraught   (= 342)   ex
337 FRIVOLOUS, a.1   1911 fryuolous   3
338 FROSTY, a.1   393 frosty   9
339 FROTHY, a.3   1068 frothy   1

340 FRUITLESS, a.1; a.1   191 fruitlesse,   334 fruictles   5

341 FUGITIVE, n.B.2; B.2   1374 fugitiue,   1476 fugitiues   2

•342 FULL-FRAUGHT, a   2022 full fraught   2

343 FUME, v.2   2507 fuming   3

344 FURNITURE, n.2   1048 furniture   5

345 FURTHERANCE, n   1697 furtherance   2

346 GALE, n³.1b   1124 gale   ᵤ4

347 GALLOP, v.2   299 gallop   10

348 GARNISH, v.3   342 garnisht   4

349 GARRISON, n.4   1558 garrison   2

350 GARRISON, v.3   2412 garrison   2

351 GAUDINESS, n (from gaudy, a².2)   1935 gaudinesse   0
352 GAZER, n.1   513 gazers   5

353 GHASTLY, adv. (from ghastly, a.1)   2108 gastly   1

354 GIMMALED, ppl. (from gimmal, n.2)   207 Gymould   1

355 GIN, n¹.4   1848 gin   4

356 GIRDLE, n¹.1   2178 girdle   11

357 GIVER, n   2295 giver   4

358 GLAIVE, n.3   1652 glaues   0

359 GLIDE, v.2   1752 glyding   9

360 GLITTER, v.1   1306 glittering   9

361 GLOOMY, a.3; a.1; a.3   550 gloomy,   [805 gloomie, A: glory] 3
        1203 gloomy,   2411 glomy

362 GORE, n¹.2   1210 gore   8

363 GRACELESS, a.1; a.1   730 gracelesse,   786 gracelesse   6

364 GRAINED, ppl. a². 2   208 grayned   3

365 GRASSHOPPER, n.1   1255 Grashopper   1

366 GRATULATE, v.1   268 gratulate   4

367 GRIEVOUSLY, adv (from grievous, a.2)   1793 greouously   6

368 GRUDGE, v.2; v.2   88 grudging,   1560 Grudging   6

369 GUARDIAN, n.1; n.2   642 gardion,   2179 gardion   6

370 GUIDE, n.III   1319 guide   10

371 GULF, n.4; n.4   1643 gulphes,   1851 gulfe   11

372 GUSH, v.1   1211 gushing   1

373 HABITATION, n.2   1310 habitation   5

374 HALF-MOON, n.2   1945 halfe Moone   3

375 HALFPENNY, n.1   2075 halfepenie   6

376 HALTER, n¹.2   1817 halter   9

377 HANDFUL, n.2; n.1; n.2   1273 handfull,   1957 handful,   2
        2264 handfull

378 HANDIWORK, n.2   2126 handie worke   3

379 HANDMAID, n.2   1121 handmaides   6

380 HAPLESS, a   1567 haplesse, 1899 haples   8

381 HARDY, a.3; a.3   275 hardie, 1090 hardie   6

382 HARE-BRAINED, a   1097 hare braind   2

383 HAVEN, a (= haven, n.1 attrib.); (same)   1682 Hauen,   0
        2596 hauen

384 HAVEN, n.1   1101 Hauen   8

385 HAVOC, n.2   1292 hauock   8

386 HAY, n.1   747 heye   7

387 HAZEL, a (= n.1 attrib)   2495 Hasle   1

388 HEARSE, n.2b   2523 hearse   5

389 HEART-BLOOD, n   984 hart bloods   7

390 HEARTEN, v.1   2123 harten up   2

391 HEART-SICK, a.1   445 hart sicke   2

392 HEARTY, a.4   1640 harty   9

393 HELMET, n.1   1511 helmet   10

394 HELPLESS, a.2   675 helples   7

395 HERALDRY, n.1   1941 heraldry   6

396 HEREAFTER, a.4   2585 hereafter   2

397 HERETOFORE, adv.1   49 heretofore, 1062 heeretofore   0

398 HEREWITHAL, adv   2553 heerewithall   0

399 HERMIT, n.1   1895 Hermyt   8

*400 HIGH-SWOLLEN, a   1178 high swolne   1

401 HINDMOST, a   234 hindmost   2

402 HITHERWARD, adv   228 hitherward, 1125 hitherward   8

403 HOLLOW, n.1   478 hollowes   4

404 HONEY-SWEET, a   1395 hony sweete   3

405 HOOP, v.1   2204 Hoopt   4

406 HORIZON, n.1   2493 horison   1

407 HORN, v.1   1119 horned   5

408 HOST, v.2   349 host   2

409 HOUSE, v.1   739 housd   8

410 HOVER, v.1   2111 houer, 2133 houer   8

411 HUGY, a   759 hugie   0

412 HUSH, v.1   2083 husht   10

413 IDIOT, n.1   2069 idiot   11

414 IDOL, n.2   709 idoll   8

415 IGNOBLE, a.2   142 Ignoble   9

416 IMMODEST, a.2; a.1   365 immodest, 1425 immodest   6

417 IMMOVABLE, a.1   1451 immouable   0

418 IMMURE, v.2   530 emured   6

419 IMPALE, v.1   1504 impall   3

420 IMPERATOR, n   861 imperator   1

421 IMPOTENT, n.4   1446 impotent   1

422 INCONSTANT, a.2   352 inconstant   ex

423 INDIRECTLY, adv   40 in directly   8

424 INFANCY, n.1   110 infancy   11

425 INFERIOR, a.2   1384 inferior   9

426 INFLAME, v.2   2587 inflamd   11

427 INFRINGE, v.2; v.2; v.2   624 infringe, 1380 infringed,   8
        1869 infringe

428 INHABITANT, n   1300 inhabitants, 1756 inhabitants   2

429 INHERITOR, n   19 inheritor   7

430 INLY, adv., a   330 inly   2

431 INNER, a.1   327 inner   0

432 INSCRUTABLE, a   1575 inscrutable   1

433 INSINUATE, v.2   1402 insinuate   11

434 INSOLENT, a.2   2420 insolent   8

435 INSOMUCH, adv.4   1380 insomuch, 2400 insomuch   1

436 INSTALL, v.1   2552 Install   5

437 INTELLECTUAL, a.2   590 intellectual   2

438 INTERCESSION, n.4   2593 intercession   6

439 INTERRUPT, v.2   835 interrupt   11

440 INTOLERABLE, a.1   251 intollerable   8

441 INTRICATE, a.1; a.2   1840 intricate, 2505 intricate   1

442 INTRUSION, n.3; n.1   544 intrusion, 1373 intrusion   4

443 INVASION, n.1   133 inuasion   2

444 INVECTIVE, n.1   1419 inuectiues   1

445 INVOCATE, v.1   416 inuocate   3

446 IRE, n   1070 ire, 2590 ire   5

447 IRREVOCABLE, a.2   2563 irreuocable   3

448 JAW, n.2   752 jawes   12

449 JENNET, n.1   2007 iennet   2

450 JIG, n.1   189 giggs   5

451 JOINTLY, adv   159 joyntly   6

452 JOLLITY, n.1   1256 iollitie   6

453 JUICE, n.1   640 vice   7

454 KEN, v. II.1   1112 ken   3

455 KNELL, n.b fig; n.b fig; n.a   2310 knell, 2499 knell,   12
         2525 knell

456 LAMENT, n.2   421 laments   5

457 LANGUISHMENT, n.3   445 languishment   3

458 LANTHORN, n.1   914 lanthorne   10
459 LAUREL, a   1514 lawrell   3
460 LAVISH, a.2b; a.2b   38 lauish, 662 lauish   5
461 LAWFULLY, adv   1866 lawfully   3
462 LAWLESS, a.2   1861 lawlesse   7
463 LAWN, n¹.1   406 lawne   6
464 LAY, n²   449 layes   5
465 LAZY, a.1   98 lazy   10
466 LEAK, v.1   1298 leaking (some edd. reeking)   3
467 LEATHERN, a.1   210 leatherne, 940 Letherne   5
468 LEPROUS, a.1 fig   777 leprous   1
469 LESSEN, v.3   668 lesned   5
470 LET, n¹   961 lets   2
471 LIABLE, a.4   224 liable   7
472 LICENCE, n.2   2174 lisence   10
473 LIEGEMAN, n.1   68 liegeman   4
474 LIEUTENANT-GENERAL, n.1   828 leiuetenant generall   0
*475 LIGHTNING-FLASH, n (= LIGHTNING, vbl.n attrib as a.)   807   2
                 lightning flash, 1176 lightning flash
476 LIKEN, v.1   507 likened   1
477 LINEAGE, n.2b; n.1   21 lynage, 1455 linage   0
478 LINEAL, a.2c   39 lyneal   8
479 LINEN, A.adj   1816 linnen   2
480 LITTER, n.2a   2344 Litter   3
481 LIVELY, a.4   1223 liuely   4
482 LOIN, n.2b   12 loynes   12
483 LOP, v.2b   2308 lopt   12
484 LOTTERY, n.2   2066 lotterie   7
485 LOUR, v.2   2299 louring   12
486 LOVESICK, a   1677 loue sicke   4
487 LOVINGLY, adv   517 louinglie   1
*488 LOWLY, adv (= lowly, a.1, adverbially)   2535 lowly   2
489 LUCKLESS, a.1   1430 luckles   2

490 MAIL, n¹.2   207 mayle   1
491 MAIM, v.a   1210 maymed   6
492 MAJESTICAL, a   1118 Maiesticall   8

```
493 MALCONTENT, A.adj      833 malcontent                          2
494 MALCONTENT, B.n     1055 malcontents                           4
495 MALE, B.n.2    28 male                                         5
496 MANAGE, n.5     1548 manage                                   11
497 MAN-AT-ARMS, n    147 men at arms                              2
498 MANFULLY, adv     1393 manfully                                2
499 MARBLE, II adj.c    1653 marble                                8
500 MARTIAL, a.1    1037 Marshall, 1048 marshiall                 11
501 MARTIALIST, n.2    1496 Martialists                            0
502 MASSY, a.2     487 massie                                      5
503 MASTER, v.2    919 master, 2401 master                        5
504 MASTERSHIP, n.2    1820 masterships                            3
505 MATCHLESS, a.1    1506 matchlesse                              2
506 MAW, n.1    1136 mawe                                          9
507 MEADOW, n.1    1116 meddow                                     3
508 MEAGRE, a.1    1526 meger                                      6
509 MEDICINABLE, a (= medicine, v + able)    678 medicinable       5
510 MEDITATE, v.4 intr; v.4    401 meditate, 2024 meditate         8
511 MENACE, n.a    2582 menaces                                    1
512 METAMORPHOSE, v.1    2119 metamorphosd                         2
513 MICKLE, a.1    2550 mickle                                     5
514 MIDNIGHT, a.3 attrib    2092 midnight                          6
515 MIDST, n.1    1306 midst, 2492 midst                          11
516 MIGHTINESS, n    456 mightines, 957 mightines                  5
517 MILK-WHITE, a    2043 milke white                              5
518 MIRTHFUL, a.1    1256 mirthfull                                1
*519 MISCONSTER, v    2571 misconster                              6
520 MISDEED, n    761 misdeeds                                     4
521 MISDO, v.2    751 misdoo                                       0
522 MISGIVE, v.2    1185 misgiues                                  5
523 MODEL, v.1    900 Modeld                                       0
524 MOISTURE, n.3    1211 moysture                                 3
525 MOON, attrib. and comb    506 moone                            0
526 MOONLIGHT, attrib. a    518 moonelight                         1
527 MOTE, n.1    793 mote                                          8
528 MOTTO, n.1b    1690 motto                                      3
529 MOULD, n¹.1    1350 mould, 2524 mould                          1
530 MOURNER, n.1    2521 mourners                                  7
531 MURMUR, v.3    2085 Murmure                                    7
532 MUSTER, n.3    147 muster                                      7
```

533 NARROWLY, adv.4   1583 narrowly   3

534 NAVY, n.2   1043 Nauie, 1130 Nauy, 1192 Nauies, 1247 Nauy   10

535 NEEDY, a.1   1375 needie   7

536 NEGLIGENT, a.1   1409 negligent   7

537 NEIGHBOUR, attrib.a   202 neighbor   9

538 NEIGHBOURHOOD, n.1   1086 neighborhood   3

*539 NIGGARD, v niggard,B.a.3 used as vb   306 niggard   2

540 NIGHTINGALE, n   116 nightingale, 458 nightingale, 461   12
                nightingale, 462 nightingale

541 NIP, v.4   1258 nipt   9

542 NORTH-EAST, a   259 North-east,   1

543 NORTHERN, A.a   2419 Northern   11

544 NUMB, a.1   1540 numb   3

545 NUMBERLESS, a   1301 numberles   2

546 OBJECTION, n.3   947 obiection, 1840 obiections   3

547 OBSTINATE, a.1   1347 obstinate, 2421 obstinate   5

548 OFTEN, B.adj   1654 often   2

549 OPERATION, n.3   760 operation   7

550 OPPOSITE, B.n.2   534 opposite, 810 opposite   12

551 OPPOSITION, n.1   971 opposition   9

552 ORATORY, n².1   323 Oratorie   6

553 ORDAIN, v.II.4   1607 ordaynd   12

554 ORDERLY, adv.1   1499 orderly, 1551 orderly   5

555 ORDNANCE, n.1   2488 ordynaunce   4

556 ORDURE, n.1   338 ordure   1

557 ORE, n.1   332 Ore   2

558 ORIENT, B. adj. 3   2379 Orient   4

559 ORIENT, A.n.1   360 oryent all red (some edd. oriental red)   2

560 ORISON, n.a.   1993 orizons   5

561 OUTCRY, n.1   2099 outcrie   3

562 OUTRAGEOUS, a.2   1893 outragious   7

*563 OUTSCOLD, v   2223 outscolde   1

564 OUTSHINE, v.1   499 outshine   1

565 OVEN, n.1   1297 ouen   4

566 OVERBEAR, v.2   958 ouerbeare   ex

567 OVERCAST, v.2   280 ouercast   3

568 OVERREACH, v.5   2376 ouerreach   6

569 OVERRIDE, v.5   1484 ouerridden   1

570 OVERSPEND, v.1   2411 orespent   0

571 OVERWEEN, v.1   1104 ouerweaning   10

572 PACIFY, v.1   2351 pacifie   3

573 PAINFUL, a.3; a.3; a.3; a.3;   1642 paynefull, 1784   10
          painefull, 2586 painfull, 2593 painfull

574 PALPABLE, a.3 fig   493 palpable   5

575 PARADISE, n.2   1871 paradise   10

576 PARCEL, v.1   1955 parcelling   2

577 PARCHMENT, a (parchment, n.1 attrib)   872 parchment   1

578 PARTI-COLOURED, a   336 party colloured   1

579 PASSIONATE, a.2   444 passionat   7

580 PASSPORT, n.2; n.2; n.2; n.2   779 pasport, 1718   3
          pasport, 1844 pasport, 1880 pasport

581 PATRONAGE, v. trans   1538 patronage   2

582 PEDIGREE, n.2; n.2   8 pedegree, 1155 pedegree   4

583 PEISE, v.4   659 peise   3

584 PELICAN, n.1b   1686 Pellican   2

585 PENDANT, n.7 (= PENNANT)   1934 pendants   0

586 PENDENT / PENDANT, a.1/n.7 1940 pendant (A: pendants, n)   0

587 PENETRABLE, a.1   885 penytrable   3

588 PERPLEXED, ppl. a.1   2545 perplext   9

589 PERSECUTE, v.2   1390 persecute   1

590 PERSIST, v.1   202 persist   3

591 PERSUASIVE, A.a   404 perswasiue   0

592 PERVERSE, a.3   1774 peruerse   4

593 PICTURE, v.3   1223 pictured   2

594 PIECEMEAL, adv.2   104 peecemeale   0

595 PIKE, n^5.1   231 pickes, 1301 pikes, 1939 pikes,   12
          2490 pikes

596 PILFER, v.2   1379 pilfering   2

597 PILLAGE, n.2; n.2   1393 pillage, 1416 pillage   6

598 PILLAR, n.2   2523 pillers   7

599 PINE, n^2.1   1113 pines, 2495 Pynes   12

600 PITCH, v.I.4, I.3 spec; PITCHED, ppl.a.2   1144 pitch,
          1801 pitch, 1495 pitched   ex

601 PLANK, n.1   1212 planks   2

602 PLATE, n.3b; 3b   231 plate, 1931 plate   11

603 PLAYFELLOW, n   945 plaiefellow   9

604 PLEA, n.II.3   1995 plea   10

605 PLENTEOUS, a.1   510 plenteous   11

606 PLENTIFUL, a.3   1095 plentiful   4

607 PLOUGH, v.4   1125 plough   9

608 PLUME, n.3   89 plumes   11

609 POETRY, n.II.1b; II.1.c   403 poetrie, 479 poetrie   9

610 POLLUTE, v.1   790 polluted   5

611 POMPOUS, a.1   2094 pompeous   3

612 PONDEROUS, a.1   1652 ponderous   4

613 POOL, n¹.2   1438 poole   4

614 PORTION, n.I.4   2381 portion   7

615 POTION, n   762 portion (A: potion)   12

616 POWDER, n¹.3   2507 pouder   8

617 PREACH, v.2b   712 preacht   7

618 PRECEDENT, n.2b (metaphorical)   2187 presidents   3

619 PRE-EMINENCE, n.2   2427 preheminence   2

620 PRESAGE, v.2; 1; 1b   330 Presageth, 1533 persaging,   10
          2102 presage

621 PRESCRIBE, v.2   782 prescribes   5

622 PRESUMPTUOUS, a.1   2416 presumtious   5

623 PRETEND, v.I.2   1427 pretended   10

624 PREVENTION, n.4c   1006 preuention   7

625 PREY, v.3   2127 praie   12

626 PRINT, v.I.2b; II.b metaphorical; I.2b   488 print,   8
          1520 print, 2108 printed

627 PROFFER, n.2   2063 proffer   4

628 PROFFER, v.1   655 proferest, 1345 poffered, 1738   9
          profered, 1765 proffered, 1991 profered,
          2582 proffered

629 PROGENITOR, n.1   618 progenitour   4

630 PROGRESS, v.1   1343 progresse   1

631 PROSPECT, n.I.3   1439 prospect   6

632 PROSTRATE, a.1   1818 prostrate   6

633 PROUDLY, adv   1951 proudly, 2345 proudly   11

634 PROVIDENCE, n.3   1574 prouidence   6

635 PUISSANT, a   1100 puissant, 1977 puissant, 2252 puisant   8

636 PURPLE, n.B.1b   2379 purple   1

637 PURSUIVANT, n.2   1794 Pursueaunt   4

638 QUADRANT, a   2490 quadrant   0
639 QUAIL, v.II.1   2263 quaile   6
640 QUARRY, n.1   1932 quarrie   1
641 QUARTER-DAY, n   1242 quarter daie, 1244 Quarter day   0
642 QUARTER, v.3; 1; 3; 1   1123 quartred, 1244 quartering,
          1942 Quartred, 2387 quartering   ex
643 QUIETLY, adv   1695 quietly   10
644 QUIETNESS, n   2398 quietnes   7

645 QUITTANCE, v. trans   2477 quittance   1

646 QUIVER, n¹.1   2217 quiuers   1

647 QUOIT, v   2254 quait   1

648 RACK, v¹   353 racke   1

649 RACK, v³.3b   49 rakt   8

650 RANCOUR, n.1   20 rancor, 1178 rancor   8

651 RANSACK, v.2; 4; 4b   504 ransack, 1021 ransackt,   6
         1289 ransackt

652 RARITY, n.3   939 rarieties   6

653 RASH, adv.3   674 rash   1

654 RAVENOUS, a.2   2129 rauenous   6

655 REARWARD, n.1   1550 rereward   5

656 REAVE, v¹.4   1205 reft   10

657 REBATE, v¹.2c   43 rebate   1

658 REBEL, v   2238 Rebell   ex

659 REBELLIOUS, a.1   20 rebellious   10

660 REBOUND, v.4; 1   93 rebound, 471 rebounde   0

661 RECALL, v.5; 3   1825 recall, 2236 recalling   7

662 RECANTATION, n   711 recantation   2

663 RECOURSE, n.6; 2   1720 recourse, 2444 recourse   4

664 RECOVERY, n.I.1   746 recouerie   ex

665 REDOUBLE, v¹.1   2584 redoubled   4

666 REDOUBT, v   2531 redoubted   5

667 REDUCE, v.III.4   876 reduce   3

668 REEL, v¹.1   1217 reeling   8

669 REFLECT, v.II.1   230 reflicting   6

670 REFLECTION, n.1b   471 reflection   6

671 REFRESH, v.2   2594 refresh   7

672 REGAL, a.A.a1   11 regall   12

673 REGENERATE, A.ppl.a.3   109 Regenerate (A:Degenerate)   1

674 REGIMENT, n.7   1964 regements   8

675 REGISTER, n¹.I.1 (metaphorical, = thesaurus)
         939 register   4

676 REGREET, v.1   1640 regreet   3

677 RELATION, n.6   2445 relation   10

678 REMORSELESS, a.1   1422 remorseles   4

679 REPAST, n.1   1162 repast   3

680 REPLENISH, v.1b   1934 replenisht   4

681 REPLETE, a.2   26 repleat   9

682 REPORTER, n.1   1193 reporter   1

683 REPOSSESS, v.1   70 repossesse   4

684 REPULSE, n.1   313 repulse   5

685 REPULSE, v.1   161 repulse   0

686 REQUISITE, a.A   452 requisit   1

687 RESOLUTE, a.4; 4; 4   162 resolute, 993 resolute,   12
        994 Resolute

688 RESOLVE, n.2   2587 resolue   5

689 RESOUND, n   882 resounds   0

690 RESPITE, n.1   2365 respit   5

691 RESTORATIVE, a.A   2315 restoritiue   0

692 RESTY, a.2   1487 resty   3

693 RETAIN, v.3c; 3c; 3c; 1b   6 retayne, 593 retaine,   10
        1066 retayna, 1715 retayne

694 RETREAT, n.1   1179 Retreae, 1630 retreat   9

695 REVERENCE, v.2b   198 reuerence, 2409 reuerence,   5
        2437 reuerence

696 RIDER, n.1   204 riders   11

697 RIOT, v.1b   943 ryot   1

698 ROBBER, n   2373 robbers   9

699 ROUND, v.II.3   1946 rounds   9

700 ROYALIZE, v.1   1951 royalized   1

701 RUST, v.1   205 rust in (A:rusting)   9

702 RUTHLESS, a   1218 ruthlesse   11

703 SADDLE, v   236 saddle   5

704 SAFE-CONDUCT, n.1; 2   2185 safe conduct, 2464 safe   2
        conduct

705 SALUTATION, n.1   1395 sallutation   9

706 SANDY, a.1   1801 sandy   6

707 SAPLESS, a.1   1541 saples   2

708 SATIRICAL, a.2   463 satyrical, 1397 satiricall   1

709 SAVOUR, v.III.1   1610 sauor   7

710 SCANDALOUS, a.2; 3; 3; 2   774 scandalous, 1426   2
        scandalous, 1492 scandalous, 1839 scandalous

711 SCAR, v.1   116 scard   4

712 SCARLET, B.a.1c   359 scarlet   10

713 SCORNFUL, a.2   184 scornefull   9

714 SCOUR, v.1b   1031 Scoure   11

715 SCOUT, n³.3   1132 scouts   6

716 SCURRILOUS, a   97 scurrylous   1

717 SECURELY, adv (from secure,a.1)   1413 securelie   7

718 SEDITIOUS, a.1   1056 seditious   2

719 SEED, v.I   2055 seed   2

720 SEIGNIORY, n.2b   6 Seigniorie   5

721 SERE, a.1; 1   334 sere, 2522 sere   2

722 SERVICEABLE, a.1   2463 seruiceable   5

723 SERVILE, a.2b   2372 seruile   11

724 SERVILELY, adv (from servile, a.3)   78 seruilely   1

725 SERVITOR, n.3; 3   1091 seruitors, 2532 seruitor   6

726 SESSION, n.4   991 Sessions   10

727 SEVERITY, n.1   2375 seuerity   4

728 SHADOW, v (used in two contradictory senses, 7 paint the   7
    likeness of, and 4 obscure with a shadow)
    406 shadow

729 SHAFT, n.1; 1   2217 shafts, 2220 shafts   11

730 SHALLOW, B.n   1320 shalow   2

731 SHARPLY, adv (here in sense of 'explicitly' and 'energ-
    etically'; perhaps adv of sharp, a.3e)
    181 sharpely   5

*732 SHARPNESS, n (sharp,A.a.1 + ness)   113 sharpnes   3

733 SHARP-POINTED, a.2   1011 sharpe poynted   1

734 SHEEPSKIN, n.2   871 shipskin   1

735 SHELTER, v.2   1313 Shelter   6

736 SHIRE, n.2   148 shire   1

737 SHOWER, n¹.1   45 shewers   10

738 SICKLE, n.1   1434 sickles   2

739 SILKWORM, n.1   466 silke wormes   0

*740 SIT, v. trans   2012   0

741 SKIRMISH, v.1   1416 skirmish   1

742 SKITTISH, a.2   1352 skittish   3

743 SLACK, a.I.1   1410 slacke   6

744 SLAUGHTER-HOUSE, n.2   1439 slaughter house   7

745 SLENDER, a.3a   2492 slender   10

746 SLYLY, adv   1402 slylie   6

747 SMOKY, A.a.1   1201 smoky   6

748 SNAFFLE, n   206 snaffles   1

*749 SNAILY, a   144 snailie   0

750 SNARE, n.1   1600 snares   7

751 SOAR, n.1   438 soare   0

752 SOLACE, n.1   552 solace   2

753 SOLDER, v.3   586 souldered   1

754 SOLEMNLY, adv (from solemn, a.3)   1061 sollemnly   6

755 SOLICITOR, n.1   774 soliciter   2

756 SOLITARINESS, n (from solitary, a.2)   1343 sollitarines   0

757 SOOTHE, v.6 1049 soothing	9
758 SOT, v.1a 432 sots	0
759 SPEEDILY, adv (from speedy, a.3) 232 speedely	12
760 SPENDTHRIFT, n.1 1057 Spend thrifts	2
761 SPLENDOUR, n.1 (metaphorical) 508 splendour	4
762 SPOUSE, n.1 2329 spouse	4
763 SQUADRON, n.1; 2 540 squadrons, 1964 squadrons	4
764 SQUARE, n.II.6 2112 squares	5
765 STABLE, a.5a 2162 stable	2
766 STABLISH, v 2390 stablish	1
767 STALL, v^1.I.2 1072 stalls	5
768 STAR-CHAMBER, n.2 990 Starre-chamber	0
769 STARVELING, n.A 2251 staruelings	2
770 STEALTH, n.3 99 stelth	10
771 STEELY, a.2 1643 steely	2

772 STEER, v.1c "Stir angry Nemesis the happie helme,/ That   6
with the sulphur battels of your rage,/ The English Fleete
may be disperst and sunke,", i.e. King John prays that
Nemesis shall take a guiding hand; the emendation of stir
to steer seems to be demanded by authorial intention.
      1167 Stir (A: Stir)

773 STERNLY, adv (from stern, a.2)   1163 sternly   0

774 STIFF, a.8 fig; a.2 (1451 "these graue schollers of experi-
ence, / Like stiffe growen oakes, will stand immouable, /
When whirle wind quickly turnes vp yonger trees."; the oak
has not stiffly grown, but has grown stiff, a, in the sense
of a.8, 'steadfast, resolute, firm, constant'. For resty
stiff of 1483 Crawford, but not Armstrong has resty-stiff.)
      1451 stiffe (A: stiff-grown), 1483 stiffe   12

775 STIRRUP, n.1 2535 stirop	5
776 STONE, v.1 2256 stoned	4
777 STRAGGLE, v.1b 1160 stragling	2
778 STRAIGHT, a.A.2 1940 Streight	9
779 STREAM, v.3a; 1 1115 streaming, 1210 streaming	5

•780 STRONGER, adv (from strong, a.8, comparative, as adverb)
      1928 stronger   ex

781 STRUGGLE, v.4 fig 1936 struggles	7
782 STUBBORNNESS, n (from stubborn, a.1) 1774 stubbornnes	3
783 STUDENT, n.2 1724 students	3
784 SUBJUGATE, v.1 1267 subiugate	0
785 SUBMISSIVE, a 1993 submissiue	4
786 SUBORNATION, n.1 801 subbornation	4
787 SUBVERT, v.1 1371 subuert	1

788 SUCCESSFULLY, adv   10 successefully,   1338 successfullie   3

789 SUCCOUR, n.3   179 souccour   12

790 SUCCOUR, v.2; 2; 2   1590 succour,   1606 succour,   1742
             succour   5

791 SUCH-LIKE, a.A.a   1283 such like   8

792 SUGAR, v.2. fig   763 sugred   1

793 SULLY, v.2 intr   280 sullied   5

794 SULPHUR, a.II attrib   1168 sulphur   0

795 SUNBURN, v.2 / SUNBURNT, a   460 sunburnt   4

796 SUNDRY, a.3; 3   1116 sundry,   1942 sundy   5

797 SUNSHINE, n.1c   588 sunshine   8

798 SURMISE, n.4   1283 surmises   10

799 SURRENDER, n.2   1791 surrender   3

800 SURRENDER, v.2   106 surrender,   1704 surrendred,   2433
             surrendred   2

801 SWEET, v.1   924 sweete   0

802 SWEETNESS, n (from sweet,a.A.1)   532 sweetnes   9

803 SWIFT, adv.1   2231 swift   12

804 SWILL, v.3   1069 swill   2

805 TAPESTRY, n (fig)   333 tapestrie   6

806 TARGET, n.1   1523 target   9

807 TASK, v.3   1021 taskt   12

808 TAUNT, n.3a   1398 tants   7

809 TAWNY, a.A   210 tawny   7

810 TESTAMENT, n.I   2338 testament   12

811 TEXT, v.1   2047 texted   0

812 THAW, v.1b fig   511 thaw   9

813 THEREWITHAL, adv.1   2009 therewithall   9

814 THICK, adv.3; 2   1651 thicke,   2488 thicke   7

815 THIEVISH, a.3; 2   901 theeuish,   1375 theeuish   7

816 THIRST, n.1; 2   1103 thirst,   1385 thirst   3

817 THIRSTY, a.1   1443 thirstie   8

*818 THORNY, adv (thorny, a.2, adverbially)   115 thornie   0

819 THOUSANDFOLD, adv.B   1566 thousandfold   4

820 THREESCORE, a(b) 1890 threescore   8

*821 THRICE-DREAD, a   572 thrice dread (A: thrice-dread)   0

*822 THRICE-GENTLE, a   555 thrice gentle (C: thrice-gentle)   1

*823 THRICE-GRACIOUS, a   543 thrice gracious   2
                     (C: thrice-gracious)

*824 THRICE-LOVING, a   967 thrice loning (A,C: thrice-loving)   0

•825 THRICE-NOBLE, a   819 thrice noble (C: thrice-noble)   5

•826 THRICE-VALIANT, a   897 thrice valiant   2
(A, C: thrice-valiant)

•827 THROUGH-SHOT, a   1212 through shot (A,C: through-shot)   0

828 TIGHTLY, adv.1   1124 titely   2

829 TIMOROUS, a.1   1408 timerous   8

830 TIP, v³   658 tip   3

831 TISSUE, n.1a   802 tissue   1

832 TONGUE-TIED, ppl.a.2   2092 tongue-tied   12

833 TOPGALLANT, n.A.1   1120 top gallant   1

834 TOPLESS, a.2   2198 toplesse   1

835 TOTTER, v.2; 2   1218 tottering, 1316 tottering   9

836 TRAFFIC, n.3 fig   2586 traffike   11

837 TRAGIC, a.3   1303 tragicke   7

838 TRAGICAL, a.1b   2458 tragicall   5

839 TRAITOROUS, a   161 trayterous   9

840 TREASURER, n.2   538 treasurer   1

841 TREASURY, n.2 fig; 1   1021 treasurie, 1096 Treasory   7

842 TREBLE, a.A.1c; A.1c   810 treble, 1098 trebble   8

843 TRENCH, n.3   2486 trenches   7

844 TRIANGLE, n.2   2112 triangles   0

845 TRUDGE, v.1b   852 trudge   6

846 TRUE-BORN, a   1447 true borne, 1458 true borne   2

847 TUMULT, n.1   167 tumult   6

848 TURF, n.2   335 turfe   6

849 TWENTIETH, a.A.2   2262 twentith   2

850 TWIST, n.II.1   466 twist   1

851 TYPE, n.1   1497 tipe   4

852 UNADVISED, ppl.a.2   2029 vnaduised   7

853 UNBRIDLED, ppl.a.1   1305 vnbridled   2

854 UNCIVIL, a.1; 2   189 vnseuill, 881 vnciuill   8

855 UNCOMFORTABLE, a.1   2098 vncomfortable   1

856 UNCOUPLE, v.1b   273 vncupple   3

857 UNDECKED, ppl.a.1   333 vndect   1

•858 UNDER, a (cf. Tim.1.1.165 "Sir, your jewel / Hath suffered under praise!" "What, my lord, dispraise?";
Lr.2.2.163 "thou beacon to this under globe";
Cor.4.5.92 "with the spleen / Of all the under
fiends"; Son.7.2 "each under eye"; TNK.4.2.24
"the under world"; so here "the under earth".
2097 vnder   4

859 UNDER, adv.4   342 vnder   2

860 UNDERPROP, v.3   1653 vnderprop   3

861 UNDOUBTEDLY, adv.1   838 Vndoubtedly   1

862 UNENDED, ppl.a.1   490 vnended   0

863 UNFEIGNEDLY, adv (from unfeigned, ppl.a.2 + ly)   3
            1734 vnfaynedly

864 UNFERTILE, a (un - fertile, a.1)   334 vnfertill   0

865 UNFOUGHT, ppl.a (un - fought, ppl. fight,v.4)   1
            1461 vnfought

866 UNHEARD OF, ppl.a.2   2518 vnheard of (A,C: unheard-of)   0

867 UNHOLY, a.1   1009 vnholie   4

868 UNITE, v.1, ppl.a   1122 vnite   11

869 UNIVERSE, n.2   619 vniuerse   2

870 UNLAWFUL, a.2   938 vnlawfull   11

871 UNMASK, v.1   499 vnmaskt   4

872 UNNECESSARY, a.A.1   1049 vnnecessary   3

873 UNPOLISHED, ppl.a (un-polish,v.2.fig-ed)   80 vnpolisht   3

874 UNRELENTING, ppl.a (un-relent,v.2b-ing) 1505 vnrelenting   3

*875 UNREPUTED, ppl.a (un-repute,v.4-d)   793 vnreputed   0

876 UNRESTRAINED, ppl.a.1   1292 vnrestrained   1

877 UNSAY, v.2   788 vnsaie   4

878 UNSPOTTED, ppl.a.2   595 vnspotted   6

*879 UNSWEAR, v   682 answere (A: unswear)   2

880 UNTAMED, ppl.a (un-tame,v.1-d)   1352 vntamed   0

881 UNTIMELY, adv.1; adv.2   1232 vntimly, 2562 vntimely   9

882 UNTOUCHED, ppl.a.2   2559 vntoucht   2

883 UNTUNED, ppl.a (un-tune,v.1-d)   185 vntuned   5

884 UNWILLINGNESS, n (unwilling,ppl.a.2 + ness)   3
            955 vnwillingnes

885 UPPER, a.6   335 vpper   6

886 UPRIGHTLY, adv.1   1858 vprightly   0

887 UPSHOT, n.1   1683 vpshot   3

888 UPSTART, n.A.1   1160 vpstarts   1

*889 URE, v (= ure,n.3 used as v)   165 vre   0

890 UTTERANCE, n¹.2   351 vtterance   8

891 VAIL, v².2; v².1b   366 waile, 2430 vale   12

892 VALE, n¹   2201 vale   9

893 VALLEY, n.1   1926 vallie, 1949 valleie, 2485 vallie   6

894 VANTAGE, v   680 vantage, 1927 Vantagd   0

895 VASSAL, a (= A.2c attrib)   754 vassell   6

```
*896 VASTURES, n      759 vastures                                   0
 897 VAWARD, n.1      1544 vowarde                                   5
 898 VEHEMENT, a.II.3      182 vehement                              6
 899 VEIL, n.5 fig      406 vaile                                    7
 900 VERDICT, n.2 fig      988 verdict, 2162 verdict                 6
 901 VERIFY, v.3      2298 verefied                                  8
 902 VIA, int.1      830 via                                         4
 903 VICEGERENT, n.A.1      1778 vicegerent                          1
 904 VICIOUS, a.II.1      1404 vitious                               9
 905 VICTUAL, n.2.pl.; n.2; n.2      1741 vituals, 1760 victuals,
             1770 victuals                                           4
 906 VIGOUR, n.2      47 vigor                                      12
 907 VINEYARD, n      1297 vineyards                                 7
 908 VIOLATE, v.1; 1      615 violating, 1854 violate                9
 909 VIPER, n.2 fig      109 viper                                   7
 910 VIZARD, n.1      81 visard                                     12
 911 VOLUNTARY, a A.I.1b; II.2; I.1b      107 voluntarie,
             474 voluntarie, 655 voluntary                           9
 912 VOMIT, n.2 (fig)      674 vomit                                 2

 913 WAKEN, v.II.1      388 wakened                                  8
 914 WALL, v².2      1506 wald                                       7
 915 WAN, a.2      2479 wan                                          3
 916 WAND, n.1      2495 wand                                        3
 917 WANTONNESS, n.1      1478 wantonnes, 1676 wantonesse            8
 918 WARDEN, n.3b      1029 Warden                                   0
 919 WARY, a.2      151 warie                                       11
 920 WATCHFUL, a.2      1110 watchfull                              11
 921 WATCHMAN, n.2      39 watch men (A: watchman)                   5
 922 WAVER, v.2      916 wauering                                    5
 923 WEALTHY, a.1; 3      1815 welthiest, 2432 wealthie             12
 924 WEDDING, a attrib      998 wedding                              4
 925 WESTERN, a.A.3      2377 western                               10
 926 WESTWARD, adv.A.1      2196 westward                            4
 927 WHENAS, conj. (= when,II.1)      1281 When as (A,C: Whenas)
             1535 When as (A,C: Whenas)                              0
 928 WHERETOFORE, re. pron.      1876 wheretofore                    0
 929 WHEREWITH, rel. pron.      30 Wherewith, 1512 Wherewith        10
 930 WHINYARD, n      211 whinyards                                  0
 931 WHIRL, v.5 (fig)      888 wherle                                9
 932 WHIRLWIND, n.1; 1      1215 wherle winde, 1452 whirlewind       6
```

933 WHOLE, n.B.1   1928 whole   5

934 WHOLLY, adv.1   2319 wholie   6

935 WILDERNESS, n.3 fig   90 wildernes   9

936 WILFULNESS, n (wilful, a.1 + ness)   1613 wilfulnes   2

937 WILLINGNESS, n (willing, ppl.a.2 + ness)
              2325 willingnes, 2366 willingnes   2

938 WINTER, a (n'.3 attrib)   935 winter   4

939 WISE, n'.I   209 wise, 2490 wise   1

*940 WISTLY, adv   912 wistely, 1684 wistlie   2

941 WOLFISH/WOLVISH, a.2   1401 woluish   4

942 WOODMAN, n'.2   1655 Wood-mans   4

943 WORMWOOD, n.1   1394 wormwood   5

944 WOVEN, ppl.a.3   1603 wouen   10

945 WREATH, n.II.a   2549 wreath   7

946 YEW, n.1b   2226 Ew   4

947 YOUNGLING, n.2   1166 younglings   3

948 ZEALOUS, a.1   1658 zealous   6

Edward III's once-only nouns with their relationship to *Tamburlaine* and *Henry VI*

The following is a list of all the nouns appearing once and not more than once in *Edward III*, excluding proper names, nouns with an initial capital and hyphenated words, as so shown in *SOED*. The material is taken from Crawford's *Marlowe Concordance*. All words which are also catch words in Appendices I and II are marked by *. Against each word is entered the number of its appearances in Marlowe's *Tamburlaine* plays (1T and 2T) and in Shakespeare's *Henry VI* plays (1H, 2H and 3H).

NO APPEARANCES IN TAMBURLAINE 1, 2 OR IN HENRY VI 1, 2 or 3

abbey	*arbour	*barbarism
accents	*arrogance	*barons
access	*ash	*barricado's
accomplements	*attirement	*belts
*allies	*avail	*bequeath
*amber	*babble	*besiege
*anchorage	bag	boldness
*anvil	*baggage	*bonnet
ape	banner	bough
*application	*bannerets	*bravery
*brief	*commonplace	debts
*bubble	*compulsion	*decline
*burgesses	*concept	defects
*cabinet	*conduit	*derision
*canon	*consort	*descant
carriage	*consummation	*dint
*certainty	contemplation	*disadvantage
*chess	cornfield's	*dismay
*cleftures	corruption's	*elder
*cockney	*cynic	*embracement
*emmets	*forefront	gravity
*endamagement	*foreigner	growth
*epicures	*fortnight	*habitation
errand	*fowler	*halfpenny
*eyesight	*francs	*handywork
*flankers	gage	hazard
*floor	gaudiness	heaviness
*fog	*girdle	*heraldry
*foolishness	*glaives	*hollows
*foragement	*grasshopper	honey

*idiot
*idol
 impediment
*imperator
*inheritor
 instant
*invasion
 jacks
*jennet
*jigs

 moral
*motto
*mourners
 mourning
*muster
 negligence
*neighbourhood
*opposition
 orchard
*ordure

 restraint
*salutation
*sessions
*shallow
*sharpness
*shire
*sickle
*signiory
*silkworm's
*snaffles

*treasurer
*topgallant
*triangles
*turf
*twist
*universe
*unwillingness
*upshot
*utterance
 vanity

*jollity
*juice
 languishment
*laurel
*lawn
 learning
*lets
 lilies
*lottery
*malcontents

*outcry
*oven
*pelican
*pebdant
*plea
*powder
*preeminence
 property
*providence
*purple

*soar
*solicitor
*solitariness
*spendthrifts
*splendour
*spouse
*squares
 stamp
*starvelings
*stealth

*vasture
*vicegerent
*vineyards
*viper
*visard
*vomit
*warden
*whinyards
*wilfulness
*woodman's

*manage
 mansion
*martialists
*masterships
*maw
*meadow
 melancholy
*menaces
 metal
 middle

*quarry
*quiver
 rarieties
*recantation
*relation
*repast
 reply
*reporter
 reproof
*resounds

 strain
*students
 stuff
*surmises
 surprise
*surrender
*tapestry
 tenders
 testimony
*tissue

*wormwood
*yew
*younglings

ONE APPEARANCE	1T	2T	1H	2H	3H		1T	2T	1H	2H	3H
*abstract		1				breakfast				1	
*advocate	1					*brick				1	
*alteration			1			bud				1	
*armado		1				*chaplain					1
*attendance			1			*chines				1	
*bane				1		clamours				1	
*beak				1		*clangour					1
beef				1		*coil		1			
*booty					1	coin				1	
bread			1			*colt		1			

	1T	2T	1H	2H	3H
*conspirator			1		
*conventicle				1	
*coral	1				
*deliverance				1	
dénial				1	
*desolation				1	
dinner			1		
*discomfiture			1		
*disobedience			1		
division			1		
*fig				1	
flatterer			1		
*fortitude			1		
friar			1		
*furtherance			1		
*gale				1	
*goddess		1			
*gore			1		
habit	1				
*halter			1		
*mail	1				
*misdeeds				1	
*mote	1				
*operation	1				
*oratory		1			
orb	1				
*orisons				1	
pace	1				
*paradise		1			
path	1				
*invectives				1	
punishment		1			
quality			1		
*rearward			1		
*reflection	1				
*register		1			
rein	1				
*repulse			1		
*respite			1		
retire				1	
*stubbornness	1				
*target				1	
*testament			1		
throng	1				
*traffic			1		
*type				1	
*upstart			1		
*vale				1	
*vaward			1		
*vigour	1				
*drone			1		
*drummer					1
*dug				1	
earnest			1		
*enchantment	1				
epitaph	1				
*epithet	1				
exchange	1				
*execrations				1	
fashion				1	
*havoc	1				
*hay					1
*hermit			1		
*horizon					1
infirmity			1		
*intercession			1		
*lament			1		
*license	1				
*liegeman			1		
*litter			1		
pattern			1		
performance				1	
petition			1		
*planks		1			
*playfellow				1	
*potion		1			
poverty		1			
*prevention					1
*prospect					1
proverb		1			
*rider	1				
sacrifice		1			
scholar				1	
school					1
seal				1	
season				1	
*severity		1			
shirts				1	
*solace				1	
*stirrup				1	
voyage		1			
ward				1	
*watchman		1			
*lantern				1	

	1T	2T	1H	2H	3H
Totals	12	20	37	29	16

Grand total 114

251

TWO APPEARANCES	1T	2T	1H	2H	3H
accidents	1		1		
adversaries			1		1
*adversity			1		1
*arrival	1		1		
author		1			1
bay (at a)		1	1		
beard			1	1	
bee				2	
beer				2	
*bower	1	1			
*gazers			1	1	
*gin			1	1	
*handmaid	1		1		
*haven	1				1
*hearse		1	1		
height		1	1		
herb		1		1	
honesty					2
horns	1	1			
ignorance				2	
*progenitor		2			
purse			1	1	
*pursuivant			1	1	
*quietness			1		1
recompense			2		
record		1		1	
red			1	1	
*regiment	2				
*resolve			1		1
ring		2			
*wilderness			1	1	
wish	1			1	
*wreath	1			1	

	1T	2T	1H	2H	3H
characters	1			1	
chastity		1		1	
crime			1	1	
departure		2			
difference		2			
entertainment	1			1	
entrance		2			
expense		2			
fancies		2			
*fraud			1		1
innocence				2	
journey		1		1	
lute		1	1		
*male					2
net		1			1
party		2			
penny	–			2	
*precedents	1				1
price		2			
*proffer		2			
*robbers					2
roof	1		1		
statutes				1	1
stead		2			
strumpet's		2			
*subornation				2	
*sunshine					2
thread			1	1	
toys	1		1		
visage		1		1	

Totals | 15 20 40 29 22   Grand total   126
(for 63 words)

THREE APPEARANCES	1T	2T	1H	2H	3H			1T	2T	1H	2H	3H
*bit		3					creature			1	1	1
brook				2	1		date	1	1	1		
*burgonet			3				*decease			1	1	1
canker			2	1			destiny	2				1
*cates	1	1	1				device	1		1		1
commission			1	2			dragon	1	1	1		
*confederates		1	1	1			*entrails	1	1			1
conference				1	2		*exhalations	2	1			
contempt	1			2			fleet	1	1			1
content				3			*foemen			1		2
friendship			2		1		*lays		1	2		
*furniture	2			1			load				3	
*guide	1	1		1			map	1	1	1		
harvest		1	1	1			merchants	2	1			
helm				1	2		miles		2			1
*helmet	1	1			1		morn		1	1	1	
homage	1		1	1			naught	1	2			
hounds		1	1		1		pangs	1			1	1
*infancy	1		1	1			*portion	1	1	1		
*jaws	2			1			*recovery		1		1	1
redress				2	1							
riches	1	1		1								
*snares			1	2								
*sweetness	3											
tiger					3							
token		3										
*tumult				2	1							
worms			1	1	1							

Totals (for 48 words)	29	24	28	37	26		Grand total	144

FOUR APPEARANCES	1T	2T	1H	2H	3H
act	1		1	2	
*anchor	1				3
blot	2		1	1	
*captivity		1	1	1	1
circumstance			1	3	
commonwealth			1	3	
compass	1	1	1	1	
coronation			2	1	1
dam			1	1	2
empire	1	2	1		
humour	1			3	
infant	2		1	1	
knowledge	1		1	2	
leisure			4		
*loins	1	2			1
ministers	1		1	2	
mirror	2		1		1
*moisture	1	2			1
parentage	1		2	1	
*plumes	2	1	1		
work	1		1	2	

	1T	2T	1H	2H	3H
enterprise		1	2		1
envy			1	2	1
falsehood				2	2
*famine		1	1	2	
*footmen	4				
freedom	2		1	1	
*gale	1		1	2	
grass				4	
greatness	2			2	
grove				4	
*pool	2	2			
privilege			4		
readiness	1		1		2
regard		1	3		
reverence	1		1	2	
streamer	2	2			
*taunts		1	1		2
threats	2				2
trunk		1		3	
vapour		2	1		1

Totals
(for 41 words) 36 20 41 46 21

Grand total 164

FIVE APPEARANCES	1T	2T	1H	2H	3H
*artillery		3	2		
blade		3	1		1
blossom		1	3	1	
branches			1		4
channel		3		1	1
extreme	2		1		2
foxes	1			3	1
grooms			1	4	
legion	2	2	1		
oracles	4			1	

	1T	2T	1H	2H	3H
penance		1		4	
picture		3	2		
*pillars	1	2		1	1
pirate	1			4	
proportion	1		2	2	
religion		3	2		
*scouts			2		3
sire			1		4
*succour	1		3	1	
talk	1		2		2
vassal	2	1	1	1	

Totals
(for 21 words) 16 22 25 23 19
Grand total 105

SIX APPEARANCES

	1T	2T	1H	2H	3H
ashes			4	1	1
aspect	2	3	1		
circle	2	2	2		
council		1		4	1
*darts	1	3		2	
destruction	2	1	2	1	
faction			5		1
*footstool	3	2			1
iron		1	2	1	2
joints	4	1		1	
style		1	3	2	
supply	1	2	2		1
territories	1	1	2	2	
tomb		1	2	2	1
*veil	2	3			1
mate		2	2	1	1
measures		2			4
meat	5		1		
*ordnance		5	1		
prophet		2	2	1	1
question			2	4	
rain	1		2	1	2
reign	1		1	3	1
sleep		1		2	3
stake		1	3	2	

Totals (for 25 words)

	1T	2T	1H	2H	3H
	25	35	38	31	21

Grand total 150

SEVEN APPEARANCES

	1T	2T	1H	2H	3H
actions	5		2		
corn			4	2	1
cowardice	1	2	1		3
discipline	5		1	1	
garden			3	4	
moon	3	3	1		
ocean	4	1		1	1
pitch	1	1	3	2	
proof		2	4	1	
purpose	1	1	3	1	1
robe	1	3	2	1	
serpents	1	1		4	1
temples	2	2	2		1
*trenches	1	5	1		
wine		4	1	2	
witch			4	3	

Totals (for 16 words)

	1T	2T	1H	2H	3H
	25	25	29	25	8

Grand total 112

EIGHT APPEARANCES

	1T	2T	1H	2H	3H
babe			4	2	2
*bullet	4	3	1		
*carcasses	3	5			
crest	4	1	2	1	
defense	2		1		5
foil	3	3	2		
groans	1			5	2
instrument	1	3	2		2
labour	1	3		1	3
misery	2		3	2	1
remorse	2	1	1	2	2

Total (for 11 words)

	1T	2T	1H	2H	3H
	23	19	16	13	17

Grand total 88

NINE APPEARANCES

	1T	2T	1H	2H	3H
*coach	3	6			
haste		2	2	2	3
health		5	1	3	
limbs	2	2	4		1
prey	1	1	1	3	3
stomachs	3	1	3	2	
strife			7	1	1
tide		1	2		6
towers	1	4	4		
veins	2	5	1		1

Totals (for 10 words)

	1T	2T	1H	2H	3H
	12	27	25	11	15

Grand total 90

TEN APPEARANCES	1T	2T	1H	2H	3H			1T	2T	1H	2H	3H
heat	2	4	1	2	1		shadow	1		5	1	3
leg	1	1	1	4	3		*showers	4	3		1	2
morning	5	1		1	3		slaughter	1	3	3	1	2
pearl	4	6					streets	1	4	1	4	
prize	4		1	3	2		wretch			2	5	3

Totals (10 words)	23	22	14	22	19		Grand total	100

ELEVEN APPEARANCES AND OVER

	1T	2T	1H	2H	3H				1T	2T	1H	2H	3H	
argument	1	3	4	2	2	12		help			3	3	6	12
birth	4	4	9	4	2	23		justice		3		5	4	12
brain	5	5	2	2		14		maid	4	1	7	1	1	14
brows	8	4	2	3	3	20		marriage's	1		4	2	11	18
cannons	3	8			1	12		nature	7	5	3	2	4	21
conqueror	8	4	4		2	18		order	1		6	5	1	13
fiends	4	2	3	2		11		palace	1	4	2	3	6	16
governor	3	4	3	1		11		passage	7	3	3		3	16
hair	3	3		5	2	13		policy	1	1	2	6	3	13
heir		2	4	11	17	34		province	8	1	1	1	1	12
regent	2		6	8		16		traitor	2	10	6	24	13	55
regions	4	5	3			12		triumph	7	3	1	2	2	15
rocks	3	5		2	3	13		truth	1	1	12	5	7	26
rose			19	1	3	23		wound	5	14	4	3	7	33
sceptre	3		2	5	4	14		wrath	9	9	1	3	4	26
sirrah	1	7	3	10	1	22								
spear	8	2	1	2		13								
speech	4	6	4	7	2	23								
staff	1	1		9	1	12								
thief	7	2		2	1	12								

Totals

1T	126
2T	122
1H	124
2H	141
3H	117

Grand total 630

Rare words from *Edward III* and their links with Parts 1, 2 and 3 of *Henry VI, Titus*, and *Edmund Ironside*

In his article on *Edmund Ironside* (*T.L.S.*, 13 August 1982) Eric Sams proposed the consideration of this anonymous play as an early work of Shakespeare. His arguments were countered by Richard Proudfoot (Letters, 17 September 1982), and the discussion continued in further letters from both parties (24 September and 8 October). Reference was made to another anonymous play, *Edward III*, and to my work on it. The effect of my thesis was to show that words, rare in Shakespeare's vocabulary, which occurred in *Edward III* clustered to a statistically highly significant degree in Shakespeare's earliest works, particularly the *Henry VI* plays and *Titus Andronicus*. Dr Sams drew attention to similarities between *Edmund Ironside* and *Edward III*; and the question arose whether the rare-word vocabularies of the two plays showed a corresponding relationship with Shakespeare.

It has now become possible to put the matter to the test. Louis Ule has made available computer-read texts, concordances and word counts both for *Edmund Ironside* and for *Edward III*. In 'The problem of *The Reign of King Edward III* (1596): a statistical approach', I listed 940 words appearing in that play, which appeared either not at all in Shakespeare's plays and major poems, or from one to twelve times and not more. Mr Ule's concordance for *Edmund Ironside* has enabled me to count how many of these 940 words occurred also in that play, with comparison counts for Parts 1, 2 and 3 of *King Henry VI* and *Titus Andronicus*. It was found that 481 of these words appeared in one or more of these five plays, namely:

	Words	Appearances
1 Henry VI	204	254
2 Henry VI	157	184
3 Henry VI	139	191
Titus	125	152
Ironside	140	185

From this it appears that *Edward III*'s rare words show their highest frequencies of appearance in the *Henry VI* plays, especially *1 Henry VI*, in *Titus* and *Ironside* to a lesser degree but in *Ironside* more commonly than in *Titus*. All these numbers are of roughly comparable magnitude.

We can now carry out a further test by counting the numbers of specified words with coincidental appearances in both members of any pair of these five plays. Of each word we note whether it appears both in play *A* and play *B*, or in *A* but not *B*, or in *B* but not *A*, or in neither. The numbers of coincidental appearances of words should be proportionate to the numbers in the Words column of the above table. For instance, 204 of *Edward III*'s 940 words are found in *1 Henry VI*; 140 are found in *Ironside*. The number which one can expect to find in both *1 Henry VI* and in *Ironside* as a chance effect will be 204 × 140/940 = 29.081. The actual number so found is 44, which is half as much again, and is in statistically significant excess. Proceeding in this way we reach the figures of the following table, where the numerals 1, 2 and 3 stand for the three parts respectively of *Henry VI*, T for *Titus* and I for *Ironside*.

	1	2	3	T	I
1	—	52	47	39	49
2	0.00025	—	39	35	27
3	0.00025	0.00025	—	26	28
T	0.005	0.00025	0.05	—	27
I	0.0025	0.20	0.05	0.025	—

The observed numbers of coincidences are shown above and to the right of the table. All numbers are in excess of random expectation, some of them in very large excess. To test their statistical significance we can use a chi squared test (one tail) with Yates's correction. The probabilities of the values of chi squared are less than the decimal numbers shown below and to the left in the table.

These results indicate that the rare-word vocabulary of *Edmund Ironside* is particularly closely related to that of *1 Henry VI*, but also to a statistically significant degree to that of *Titus Andronicus*, and less so, but still significantly, to that of *3 Henry VI*. They can be regarded as providing evidence which tends to support the hypothesis maintained by Dr Sams.

Rare words from Edward III with the numbers of their appearances in Parts 1, 2 and 3 of Henry VI, Titus and Edmund Ironside, respectively:-

abandon, v 0 0 1 1 0; abject, a 1 3 0 0 2; accordingly, adv 1 0 0 0 0; admiral, n 0 0 1 0 0; adorn, v 1 0 0 1 0; adverse, a 1 0 0 0 0; adversity, n 1 0 1 0 0; aloft, adv 0 2 0 3 2; alteration, n 1 0 0 0 0; anchor, n 0 0 3 1 0; anchorage, n 0 0 0 1 0; apparel, v 1 1 0 0 0; array, n 1 1 1 0 0; arrogant, a 1 1 0 0 0; artificial, a 0 0 1 0 0; artillery, n 2 0 0 0 0; assault, v 0 0 0 0 2; astonish, v 2 1 0 0 0; attaint, v 3 1 0 0 0; attendance, n 0 1 0 0 1; attorney, n 1 0 0 0 0; attract, v 0 1 0 0 0; augment, v 0 1 1 0 0; avail, n 0 0 0 0 3;

bandy, v 1 0 1 1 0; bane, n 0 1 0 1 0; baron, n 0 1 0 0 0;

basely, adv 1 0 0 4 2; beak, n 0 1 0 0 0; beautify, v 0 1 0 1 0;

bemoan, v 0 0 1 0 0; beneath, adv 0 0 0 0 1; betake, v 0 1 0 0 0;

bewail, v 0 1 0 0 0; blaze, v 0 0 2 0 0; bloodless, a 0 1 0 1 0;

bloodthirsty, a 1 0 0 0 1; bonny, a 0 1 0 0 0; booty, n 0 0 1 1 0;

bravery, n 0 0 0 0 1; brazen, a 0 2 2 0 0; brick, n 0 1 0 0 0;

broad, adv 1 0 0 1 0; bruit, v 1 0 0 0 1; bullet, n 1 0 0 0 0;

burgonet, n 0 3 0 0 0; buzz, v 0 1 2 2 0; cannon-shot, n 1 0 0 0 0;

caper, v 0 1 0 0 0; captive, a 0 0 2 1 0; captivity, n 1 1 1 0 0;

cate, n 1 0 0 0 0; certify, v 2 0 0 0 1; chain, v 1 1 1 0 0;

chaplain, n 0 0 1 0 0; character, v 0 1 0 0 0; cheerfully, adv 1 0 0 0 0;

chine, n 0 1 0 0 0; choice, a 1 0 0 0 1; city, n 0 0 0 1 4;

clangor, n 0 0 1 0 0; cloak, v 0 0 0 0 1; cluster, v 1 0 0 0 0;

coach, n 0 0 0 1 0; coil, n 0 0 0 1 0; comb, n 0 0 0 0 1;

combat, v 1 1 1 0 0; commence, v 1 1 0 0 0; compulsion, n 0 0 0 0 1;

conduit, n 0 0 0 1 0; confederate, n 1 1 0 3 0; conflict, n 1 2 0 1 0;

conjoin, v 1 0 0 0 1; consort, n 0 1 0 0 0; conspirator, n 1 0 0 1 0;

contemplate, v 0 0 1 0 0; contemptuous, a 0 1 0 0 0; contradict, v 0 1 0 0 1;

conventicle, n 0 1 0 0 0; coronet, n 2 0 0 0 0; council-house, n 0 1 0 0 0;

courtly, a 0 1 0 0 0; covenant, n 2 0 0 0 0; craven, a 1 0 0 0 0;

cross-bow, n 0 0 1 0 0; cuff, v 1 0 0 0 0; dart, n 0 2 0 0 0;

dazzle, v 1 0 1 1 0; deadly, adv 0 0 1 0 0; decease, n 1 1 1 0 0;

decree, v 0 0 0 1 0; deface, v 2 2 0 0 0; defer, v 1 1 0 0 0;

defiance, n 0 0 0 0 1; delicious, a 0 0 0 1 0; deliverance, n 0 0 1 0 0;

delude, v 1 0 0 0 0; descry, v 1 0 0 0 1; desolation, n 0 1 0 0 0;

detestable, a 0 0 0 1 0; dignify, v 0 0 0 0 1; dim, v 1 3 1 1 0;

disadvantage, n 0 0 0 0 1; discomfiture, n 1 0 0 0 0; disdainful, a 0 0 0 0 1;

disobedience, n 1 0 0 0 0; disobey, v 1 0 0 0 0; dispense, v 1 1 0 0 0;

distract, a 0 1 0 1 0; distraught, a 0 0 0 0 1; dominion, n 0 0 0 0 1;

doom, v 0 0 0 2 0; downy, a 1 0 0 0 0; drone, n 0 1 0 0 0;

drummer, n 0 0 1 0 0; dub, v 0 0 1 0 1; dug, n 0 1 0 0 0;

eager, a 1 0 2 0 1; echo, v 0 0 0 1 1; elect, v 1 0 0 1 1;

elsewhere, adv 0 0 1 0 0; embracement, n 0 0 0 1 0; enact, v 3 0 0 0 0;

encamp, v 0 0 1 1 0; enclose, v 1 1 0 0 0; encompass, v 2 0 2 0 0;

encroach, v 0 1 0 0 0; endless, a 1 0 0 0 1; engender, v 2 0 1 0 0;

engird, v 0 2 0 0 0; engrave, v 1 0 0 0 0; enlarge, v 1 0 0 0 0;

ensign, n 1 0 0 1 0; entail, v 0 0 2 0 0; entrail, n 0 0 1 2 0;

entrap, v 1 0 0 0 1; entrench, v 1 0 0 0 0; envenom, v 0 1 0 0 0;

environ, v 1 0 3 1 0; equality, n 0 0 0 0 1; esquire, n 0 2 0 0 0;

evidence, n 0 1 0 0 0; execration, n 0 1 0 0 0; expedient, a 0 1 0 0 0;

expulse, v 1 0 0 0 0; extemporal, a 1 0 0 0 0; falter, v 0 0 0 0 1;
famine, n 1 2 0 0 0; fealty, n 0 1 0 1 0; fell, v 0 1 1 0 0;
felonious, a 0 1 0 0 0; fence, v 0 0 2 0 0; fester, v 1 0 0 0 0;
fig, n 0 1 0 0 0; figure, v 0 0 0 1 0; flesh, v 1 0 0 0 0;
fleur-de-lis, n 2 1 0 0 0; flock, v 0 0 1 0 0; flower, v 1 1 0 1 0;
foeman, n 1 0 2 1 1; fog, n 0 0 0 1 1; foil, v 0 0 1 0 2;
footman, n 0 0 0 1 1; footstool, n 0 0 1 0 0; forefront*,n 0 0 0 0 2;
foreigner, n 0 0 0 0 1; fortify, v 2 0 1 0 0; fortitude, n 1 0 0 0 1;
foster, v 0 0 0 1 0; fragrant, a 0 0 0 2 0; franticly, adv 0 0 0 1 0;
fraud, n 1 0 1 0 2; fraught, a 0 0 0 1 0; frivolous, a 1 0 1 0 0;
frosty, a 0 1 0 2 0; fugitive, n 1 0 0 0 0; furniture, n 0 1 0 0 0;
furtherance, n 1 0 0 0 0; gale, n 0 0 1 0 0; gallop, v 0 1 0 1 0;
garrison, n 1 1 0 0 0; gazer, n 0 1 1 0 0; ghastly, adv 0 1 0 0 0;
gin, n 0 1 1 0 0; girdle, n 0 0 0 0 1; glide, v 0 1 0 1 0;
gloomy, a 1 0 0 1 0; gore, n 1 0 0 0 1; graceless, a 1 1 0 0 1;
gratulate, v 0 0 0 1 0; grudge, v 2 0 0 0 0; guide, n 0 1 0 0 0;
gulf, n 0 0 1 0 0; halter, n 0 1 0 1 0; handmaid, n 1 0 0 1 1;
hapless, a 1 1 2 0 0; hardy, a 0 0 1 0 3; hare-brained, a 1 0 0 0 0;
haven, n 0 0 1 0 1; hay, n 0 0 1 0 0; hearse, n 1 0 0 0 0;
heart-blood, n 1 1 1 0 0; hearten, v 0 0 1 0 0; hearty, a 1 0 0 0 1;
helmet, n 0 0 1 0 1; helpless, a 0 0 0 0 1; hereafter, a 1 0 0 0 0;
hermit, n 1 0 0 1 0; hindmost, a 0 0 0 0 1; hitherward, adv 0 1 1 0 1;
hollow, n 0.0 0 1 0; horizon, n 0 0 1 0 0; horn, v 0 0 0 1 0;
hover, v 0 0 0 1 0; idiot, n 0 0 0 1 1; ignoble, a 2 2 1 0 0;
immodest, a 1 0 0 0 0; immovable*, a 0 0 0 0 1; impale, v 0 0 2 0 0;
infancy, n 1 1 0 0 0; inferior, a 2 0 1 0 0; inflame, v 1 0 0 0 1;
infringe, v 0 0 1 0 0; insinuate, v 1 0 0 1 3; insolent, a 0 1 0 0 0;
install, v 2 0 2 0 0; intercessor, n 1 0 0 0 0; interrupt, v 0 0 1 0 0;
intolerable, a 1 2 0 1 0; invasion, n 0 0 0 0 1; invective, n 0 0 1 0 0;
invocate, v 1 0 0 0 0; ire, n 1 0 1 0 0; irrevocable, a 0 1 1 0 2;
jaw, n 0 1 0 0 0; jointly, adv 0 1 0 0 0; ken, v 0 1 0 0 0;
knell, n 0 0 0 0 1; lament, n 1 0 0 2 0; languishment, n 0 0 0 1 0;
lanthorn, n 0 1 0 0 0; laurel, a 0 0 1 1 0; lavish, a 1 0 0 0 0;
lawless, a 0 0 0 1 1; lazy, a 0 0 1 0 0; licence, n 0 1 0 0 0;
liegeman, n 1 0 0 0 1; lightning-flash, n 0 0 0 1 0; liken, v 0 0 1 0 1;
lineal, a 1 0 0 0 0; litter, n 1 0 0 0 0; loin, n 0 0 1 0 1;
lop, v 1 1 1 2 1; lour, v 0 1 0 0 1; lovesick, a 0 0 0 1 0;
lovingly, adv 0 0 0 1 1; luckless, a 0 0 2 0 0; maim, v 0 1 0 0 0;
majestical, a 1 0 0 0 0; malcontent, a 0 0 2 0 0; male, n 0 0 2 0 0;
man-at-arms, n 0 0 0 0 1; manfully, adv 0 0 0 1 0; marble, a 0 0 1 0 0;

martial, a 3 0 0 0 0; massy, a 0 0 0 0 1; mastership, n 0 0 0 0 1;

matchless, a 0 0 0 0 1; maw, n 0 0 0 0 1; meadow, n 0 0 0 1 0;

meagre, a 0 1 0 0 0; meditate, v 1 0 0 0 0; menace, n 0 0 0 0 1;

mickle, a 1 1 0 0 0; midst, n 0 0 1 0 1; mightiness, n 0 0 0 1 1;

milk-white, a 0 1 0 1 0; mirthful, a 0 0 1 0 0; misconster, v 1 0 0 0 1;

misdeed, n 0 0 1 0 0; misgive, v 0 0 1 0 0; moisture, n 0 0 1 0 0;

narrowly, adv 0 0 0 0 1; navy, n 0 0 0 0 1; needy, a 0 1 0 0 1;

negligent, a 1 0 0 0 0; nip, v 0 1 0 1 1; northern, a 0 1 2 1 2;

numb, a 1 0 0 1 0; objection, n 1 1 0 0 0; obstinate, a 1 0 0 0 0;

operation, n 0 0 0 0 1; opposite, n 0 1 0 0 0; oratory, n 1 0 0 1 0;

ordain, v 3 1 2 1 0; ordnance, n 1 0 0 0 0; orison, n 0 0 1 0 0;

outrageous, a 2 0 0 1 0; oven, n 0 0 0 1 0; overcast, v 0 0 0 0 1;

overreach, v 0 0 0 1 0; overween, v 0 2 1 1 0; pacify, v 0 0 0 0 1;

paradise, n 0 0 0 0 1; passionate, a 0 1 0 0 0; patronage, v 2 0 0 0 0;

pedigree, n 1 0 2 0 0; perplexed, ppl a 1 0 0 0 0; perverse, a 2 0 0 0 0;

piecemeal, adv 0 0 0 0 3; pike, n 1 0 1 0 0; pillage, n 1 1 0 1 0;

pillar, n 0 1 1 0 0; pine, n 0 1 0 0 1; playfellow, n 0 1 0 0 0;

plenteous, a 0 1 0 0 0; plough, v 0 0 0 1 1; plume, n 1 0 0 0 2;

poetry, n 0 0 0 1 0; pollute, v 1 0 0 0 0; portion, n 1 0 0 0 0;

powder, n 0 0 0 1 0; preach, v 1 0 0 0 2; presage, v 1 0 2 0 1;

presumptuous, a 2 1 1 0 1; pretend, v 2 0 1 1 0; prevention, n 0 1 0 0 0;

prey, v 0 0 0 2 1; print, v 0 2 0 1 0; proffer, n 2 0 0 0 0;

proffer, v 2 0 0 0 2; progenitor, n 2 0 0 0 0; prospect, n 0 1 0 0 0;

prostrate, a 1 1 0 0 0; proudly, adv 2 0 0 0 1; puissant, a 0 1 3 0 0;

pursuivant, n 1 1 0 0 0; quail, v 0 0 1 0 1; quietly, adv 2 0 1 1 0;

quietness, n 1 0 1 0 0; quittance, v 1 0 0 0 0; rack, v 0 0 1 0 0;

rancour, n 0 2 0 0 0; ravenous, a 1 1 0 2 0; rearward, n 1 0 0 0 1;

reave, v 0 1 0 0 0; rebellious, a 2 1 0 0 1; recall, v 1 1 0 0 1;

redouble, v 0 0 0 0 1; redoubt, v 1 0 0 0 0; reel, v 0 0 0 0 1;

reflect, v 0 0 0 1 0; refresh, v 0 0 0 0 1; regal, a 1 1 7 0 0;

remorseless, a 0 1 1 0 0; replete, a 3 1 1 0 0; repossess, v 0 0 4 0 0;

repulse, n 1 0 0 0 0; resolute, a 2 2 2 0 0; resolve, n 1 0 1 0 0;

respite, n 1 0 0 0 0; retain, v 1 0 0 0 0; retreat, n 1 1 1 0 2;

reverence, v 2 0 0 0 0; robber, n 0 0 2 0 0; rust, v 0 1 0 0 0;

ruthless, a 1 1 5 2 0; sandy, a 1 2 0 1 0; sapless, a 2 0 0 0 0;

scar, v 0 0 0 1 0; scarlet, a 2 0 0 0 0; scour, v 0 1 0 0 1;

scout, n 2 0 3 0 0; securely, adv 0 0 0 1 1; seditious, a 0 1 0 0 0;

serviceable, a 0 0 0 0 1; servile, a 1 1 0 2 0; servitor, n 1 0 1 1 0;

severity, n 1 0 0 0 1; shadow, v 0 0 0 1 0; shaft, n 0 0 0 1 0;

shower, n 0 0 1 1 0; skirmish, v 1 0 0 0 1; slack, a 1 1 0 0 1;

APPENDIX VI

slaughter-house, n 0 2 1 0 0; slyly, adv 0 1 3 0 0; snare, n 1 2 0 0 0;
solace, n 0 1 0 0 2; solemnly, adv 0 0 0 0 1; soothe, v 0 0 1 0 1;
speedily, adv 0 0 1 0 0; squadron, n 1 0 0 0 0; stablish, v 1 0 0 0 0;
steely, a 0 0 1 0 0; steer, v 0 1 0 0 0; stiff, a 0 1 0 0 0;
stirrup, n 0 1 0 0 0; struggle, v 0 1 1 0 0; submissive, a 2 0 0 0 0;
subornation, n 0 2 0 0 0; subvert, v 1 0 0 0 0; successfully, adv 0 0 0 1 0;
succour, n 3 1 0 0 1; succour, v 0 2 3 1 5; sugar, v 0 0 0 0 1;
sully, v 1 0 0 0 0; sunshine, n 0 0 2 0 1; surmise, n 0 0 0 1 0;
swift, adv 1 0 0 3 0; target, n 0 0 1 0 0; taunt, n 1 0 2 0 0;
tawny, a 1 0 0 1 0; testament, n 1 0 0 0 0; thirst, n 0 0 1 0 1;
thirsty, a 0 0 1 0 1; thousandfold, adv 0 0 2 0 0; threescore, a 0 0 1 0 1;
thrice-noble, a 0 1 0 1 0; thrice-valiant, a 0 0 0 1 0; timorous, a 2 0 1 0 0;
tongue-tied, a 1 0 1 0 0; totter, v 1 0 0 0 0; traffic, n 1 0 0 0 0;
tragic, a 0 1 1 1 0; tragical, a 1 0 0 0 0; traitorous, a 1 1 0 4 3;
treasury, n 0 2 0 1 1; treble, a 0 0 0 1 0; trench, n 1 0 0 1 0;
true-born, a 1 0 0 0 1; tumult, n 2 0 1 0 0; type, n 0 0 1 0 0;
unadvised, a 0 0 0 1 2; uncivil, a 0 1 0 0 1; uncouple, v 0 0 0 1 0;
under, adv 0 0 0 0 1; unheard (of)*, a 0 0 0 0 1; unite, v 1 1 0 0 1;
unlawful, a 1 0 0 0 0; unpolished, a 0 1 0 0 0; unrelenting, a 1 0 1 1 1;
unspotted, a 1 1 0 0 1; untimely, adv 0 0 2 0 0; upper, a 0 0 0 0 1;
upstart, n 1 0 0 0 1; utterance, n 0 0 0 1 0; vail, v 1 0 0 0 0;
vale, n 0 1 0 2 0; valley, n 0 0 0 1 0; vaward, n 1 0 0 0 0;
veil, n 0 0 1 0 0; verdict, n 2 0 0 0 0; verify, v 2 0 1 0 3;
via, int 0 0 1 0 0; vicious, a 1 0 0 0 0; vigour, n 0 0 0 1 0;
violate, v 0 0 0 0 1; viper, n 0 0 0 0 1; waken, v 0 0 1 0 0;
wall, v 2 0 0 0 0; wan. a 0 0 0 1 0; wand, n 0 1 0 0 0;
wary, a 2 0 0 0 1; watchful, a 0 0 0 0 1; watchman, n 1 0 0 0 0;
waver, v 1 0 0 0 1; wealthy, a 0 2 1 0 0; wedding, a 1 0 0 0 0;
western, a 0 0 1 0 0; whenas, conj 0 0 3 1 11; wherewith, pron 2 1 1 0 0;
whirl, v 1 0 0 2 1; whole, n 1 0 0 0 0; wilderness, n 0 1 0 2 0;
willingness, n 0 0 1 1 0; winter, a 0 1 0 0 0; woven, a 0 1 0 0 0;
wreath, n 0 0 0 1 0; yew, n 0 0 0 1 0; youngling, n 0 0 0 2 0;
zealous, a 0 0 0 0 1.

* Words so marked are not found in Shakespeare.

	Words	Appearances
1 Henry VI	204	254
2 Henry VI	157	184
3 Henry VI	139	191
Titus	125	152
Ironside	140	185

COINCIDENCES

	1	2	3	T	I
1H6	–	52	47	39	49
2H6	.00025	–	39	35	27
3H6	.00025	.00025	–	26	28
Tit	.005	.00025	.05	–	27
Ir	.0025	.20	.05	.025	–

To the top and right, observed numbers of words

Below and to the left upper probability limits
of χ^2, one tail, with Yates's correction

References

1. THE RAIGNE OF KING EDWARD III

1 Armstrong, R. L. (ed.) 1965 *Edward III*, in *Six Early Plays Related to the Shakespeare Canon*, ed. E.A. Everitt, Copenhagen.

2 Armstrong, W. A. (ed.) 1966 *Elizabethan History Plays*, London.

3 Bell, M. 1959 'Concordance to the Shakespeare Apocrypha', Dissertation, University of Liverpool.

4 Brooke, C. F. Tucker (ed.) 1908 *The Shakespeare Apocrypha being a collection of fourteen plays which have been ascribed to Shakespeare*. Oxford.

5 Crundell, H. W. 1939 'Drayton and *Edward III*', *Notes and Queries* 176, 258–260.

6 Dobson, W. B. 1957 '*Edward III*: a study of its composition in relation to its sources', Dissertation, University of Texas. Reported in *Shakespeare Newsletter*, May 1957, 7, 19.

7 Farmer, J. S. (ed.) 1910 *The Reign of King Edward III*. Tudor Facsimile Texts, vol. 78. Edinburgh and London.

8 Golding, S. R. 1928 'The authorship of *Edward III*', *Notes and Queries* 154, 313–15.

9 Hart, A. 1934 'The vocabulary of *Edward III*', in *Shakespeare and the Homilies*, 219–41. Melbourne.

10 Horn, F. D. 1969 '*The Raigne of King Edward III*: a Critical Edition'. Dissertation, University of Delaware. *Dissertation Abstracts* 30, 2969A.

11 Jackson, McD. P. 1965b '*Edward III*, Shakespeare and Pembroke's men', *Notes and Queries*, n.s. 41, 329–31.

12 Jackson, McD. P. 1971 'A note on the text of *Edward III*', *Notes and Queries* 216, 423–4.

13 Koskenniemi, I. 1964 'Themes and imagery in *Edward III*', *Neuphilologische Mitteilungen* 65, 446–80.

14 Lapides, F. R. 1966 'A critical edition of *The Raigne of Edward III*', Rutgers Dissertation, *Dissertation Abstracts* 27, 1788A.

15 Melchiori, G. 1976 *Shakespeare's Dramatic Meditations, an Experiment in Criticism*. Oxford.

16 Muir, K. 1953 'A reconsideration of *Edward III*', *Shakespeare Survey* 6, 39–48.

17 Muir, K. 1960 and 1969 'Shakespeare's hand in *Edward III*', in *Shakespeare as Collaborator*, 10–30. London.

18 O'Connor, F. I. 1961 *Shakespeare's Progress*. New York.

19 Østerberg, V. 1929 'The "Countess scenes" of *Edward III*', *Shakespeare Jahrbuch* 65, 45–91.

20 Platt, A. 1911 '*Edward III* and Shakespeare's Sonnets', *Modern Language Review* 6, 511–13.

21 Ribner, I. 1957 *The English History Play in the Age of Shakespeare*. Princeton.

22 Schaar, C. 1962 *Elizabethan Sonnet Themes and the Dating of Shakespeare's Sonnets*. Lund.

23 Schoenbaum, S. 1966 *Internal Evidence and Elizabethan Dramatic Authorship*. London.

24 Smith, R. M. 1911 '*Edward III*. A study of the authorship of the drama in the light of a new source', *Journal of English and German Philology* 10, 90–104.

25 Tillyard, E. M. W. 1944 *Shakespeare's History Plays*. London.

26 Wentersdorf, K. P. 1960 'The Authorship of *Edward III*', Dissertation, University of Cincinnati. *Dissertation Abstracts* 21, 905–6.

27 Wentersdorf, K. P. 1965 'The date of *Edward III*', *Shakespeare Quarterly* 16, 227–31.

2. THE STATISTICAL STUDY OF LITERARY VOCABULARY

1 Hart, A. 1943 'Vocabularies of Shakespeare's plays', *Review of English Studies* 19, 128–40.
2 Hart, A. 1943 'The growth of Shakespeare's vocabulary', *Review of English Studies* 19, 242–54.
3 Spevack, M. 1973 *The Harvard Concordance to Shakespeare* (one-volume edn). Cambridge, Mass.
4 Yule, G. U. 1944 *The Statistical Study of Literary Vocabulary*. Cambridge.
5 Zipf, G. K. 1932 *Selected Studies of the Principle of Relative Frequency in Language*. Harvard.

3. THE ADVENT OF THE COMPUTER

1 Bailey, R. W. 1969 'Statistics and style: a historical survey' in (4) Doležel and Bailey, pp. 217–36.
2 Bennett, P. E. 1969 (originally published *Shakespeare Quarterly* 8, 1957, 33–50) 'The statistical measurement of a stylistic trait in *Julius Caesar* and *As You Like It*' in (4) Doležel and Bailey, 29–41.
3 Carlyle, T., quoted by (6) Ellegård.
4 Doležel, L. and Bailey, R. W. (ed.) 1969 *Statististics and Style*. New York. See also Bailey, R. W. and Doležel. L., 1968 *An Annotated Bibliography of Statistical Stylistics*. Ann Arbor.
5 Ellegård, A. 1962 *A Statistical Method for Determining Authorship. The Junius Letters, 1769–1772*. Göteborg.
6 Ellegård, A. 1963 *Who Was Junius?* Stockholm.
7 Hart, A. 1934 'The vocabulary of *Edward III*: a re-appraisal' in *Shakespeare and the Homilies*, 219–41. Melbourne.
8 Junius 1978 *The Letters of Junius*, ed. John Cannon. Oxford.
9 McCurdy, H. G. 1953 *The Personality of Shakespeare*. New Haven.
10 Mosteller, F. and Wallace, D.L. 1964 *Inference and Disputed Authorship: 'The Federalist'*. Reading, Mass.
11 Popper, K. R. 1968 (1st edn 1959) *The Logic of Scientific Discovery*. London.
12 Spevack, M. 1969 *The Harvard Concordance to Shakespeare*. Cambridge, Mass.
13 Tallentire, D. R. 1971 'Mathematical modelling in stylistics: its extent and general limitations' in (14) Wisbey, 117–28.
14 Wisbey, R. A. (ed.) 1971 *The Computer in Literary and Linguistic Research*. Cambridge.
15 Yule, G. U. 1944 *The Statistical Study of Literary Vocabulary*. Cambridge.

4. STYLE AND STYLOMETRY

1 Barton, A. 1980. 'Leontes and the spider: language and speaker in Shakespeare's Last Plays', in (5) Edwards *et al.*, 131–50.
2 Brooke, N. 1980 'Language most shows a man…? Language and speaker in *Macbeth*', in (5) Edwards *et al.*, 67–77.
3 Clemen, W. 1980 'Some aspects of style in the *Henry VI* plays', in (5) Edwards *et al.*, 9–24.
4 Edwards, P. 1980 'The declaration of love', in (5) Edwards *et al.*, 39–50.
5 Edwards, P., Ewbank, I.–S. and Hunter, G. K. (eds.) 1980, *Shakespeare's Styles. Essays in honour of Kenneth Muir*. Cambridge.
6 Foakes, R. A. 1980 'Poetic language and dramatic significance in Shakespeare', in (5) Edwards *et al.*, 79–83.
7 Herdan, G. 1956 *Language as Choice and Chance*. Groningen.
8 Hibbard, G. R. 1980 '*Feliciter audax. Antony and Cleopatra*, I.i.1–24', in (5) Edwards *et al.*, 95–109.
9 Knights, L. C. (1980) 'Rhetoric and insincerity', in (5) Edwards *et al.*, 1–8.
10 Langworthy, C. A. 1931, 'A verse-sentence analysis of Shakespeare's plays', *Publications of the Modern Language Association* 46, 738–51.
11 Maxwell, J. C. 1950 'Peele and Shakespeare: a stylometric test', *Journal of English and German Philology* 49, 557–61.

12 Maxwell, J. C. (ed.) 1969a *The Works of Shakespeare: King Henry the Eighth*. Cambridge.

13 Merriam, T. 1979 'What Shakespeare wrote in *Henry VIII*', *The Bard* 2, 81–94.

14 Michaelson, S., Morton, A. Q. and Hamilton-Smith, N. 1978 *To Couple is the Custom*. University of Edinburgh, Department of Computer Science: Internal Report. October 1977, revised November 1973.

15 Michaelson, S., Morton, A. Q. and Hamilton-Smith, N. 1979 'Fingerprinting the mind', *Endeavour*, New Series 3, no. 4, 171–5.

16 Michaelson, S., Morton, A. Q. and Hamilton-Smith, N. 1979 *Justice for Helander*. University of Edinburgh, Department of Computer Science: Internal Report.

17 Morton, A. Q. 1978 *Literary Detection: How to prove an authorship in literature and documents*. United Kingdom (Bowker Publishing Co.).

18 Morton, A. Q. 1980 'The comparison of three plays of Shakespeare: *Julius Caesar, Pericles* and *Titus Andronicus*'; 'The habits displayed in *Titus Andronicus*'; 'The comparison of *Titus Andronicus* with *Pericles*'; 'A comparison of the punctuation of the three plays of Shakespeare'. 'The comparison of the plays of Peele'; 'The comparison of Peele and Shakespeare'. Privately circulated.

19 Morton, A. Q., Winspear, A. D. *et al.* 1971 *It's Greek to the Computer*. Montreal.

20 Partridge, A. C. 1949 *The Problem of Henry VIII Reopened*. Cambridge.

21 Slater, E. 1975b 'Some psychological aspects of the *Sonnets*', *The Bard* 1, 1–8.

22 Williams, C. B. 1970 *Style and Vocabulary*. London.

5. THE STATISTICAL WORK OF ALFRED HART

1 Hart, A. 1934 'The vocabulary of *Edward III*', in *Shakespeare and the Homilies and Other Pieces of Research into the Elizabethan Drama*, 219–41. Melbourne.

2 Hart, A. 1943 'Vocabularies of Shakespeare's plays', *Review of English Studies* 19, 128–40.

3 Hart, A. 'The growth of Shakespeare's vocabulary', *Review of English Studies* 19, 242–54.

4 Slater, E. 1975b 'Some psychological aspects of the *Sonnets*', *The Bard* 1, 1–8.

6. RARE WORDS AND SHAKESPEARE'S CHRONOLOGY

1 Baldwin, T. W. 1957 *Shakespeare's Love's Labor's Won: New evidence from the account books of an Elizabethan bookseller*. Carbondale, Southern Illinois.

2 Brigstocke, W. O. (ed.) 1904 *The Arden Shakespeare: All's Well That Ends Well*. London.

3 Hotine, M. 1977 '*Troylus and Cressida*: historical arguments for a 1608 date', *The Bard* 1, 153–61.

4 Hunter, G. K. (ed.) 1962 *The Arden Shakespeare: All's Well That Ends Well*. London.

5 Jackson, MacD. P. 1965 *Shakespeare's A Lover's Complaint: its Date and Authenticity*. University of Auckland Bulletin 72, English Series 13.

6 Maxwell, J. C. (ed.) 1968 *The Works of Shakespeare: Timon of Athens*. Cambridge.

7 Maxwell, J. C. (ed.) 1969 *The Works of Shakespeare: The Poems*. Cambridge.

8 Muir, K. 1964 '*A Lover's Complaint*: a reconsideration', in *Shakespeare 1564–1964*, ed. E. A. Bloom. Providence, RI.

9 Muir, K. 1973 '*A Lover's Complaint*: a reconsideration', in *Shakespeare the Professional and Related Studies*. London.

10 Oliver, H. J. (ed.) 1971 *The Arden Shakespeare: The Merry Wives of Windsor*. London.

11 Schäfer, J. 1980 *Documentation in the O.E.D.: Shakespeare and Nashe as Test Cases*. Oxford.

12 Slater, E. 1973 'A statistical note on *A Lover's Complaint*', *Notes and Queries* 218, 138–40.

13 Slater, E. 1975a 'Shakespeare: word links between poems and plays', *Notes and Queries* 220, 157–63.

14 Slater, E. 1975c 'Word links with *The Merry Wives of Windsor*', *Notes and Queries* 220, 169–71.

15 Slater, E. 1977 'Word links with *All's Well That Ends Well*', *Notes and Queries* 222, 109–12.
16 Slater, E. 1978a 'Word links between *Timon of Athens* and *King Lear*', *Notes and Queries* 223, 147–9.
17 Slater, E. 1978b 'Word links from *Troilus* to *Othello* and *Macbeth*', *The Bard* 2, 4–22.

7. THE RARE-WORD VOCABULARY OF KING EDWARD III

1 Donow, H. S. 1969 *A Concordance to the Sonnet Sequences of Daniel, Drayton, Shakespeare, Sidney, and Spenser*. Carbondale.

Bibliography

Armstrong, R. L. (ed.) 1965 *Edward III*, in *Six Early Plays Related to the Shakespeare Canon*, (ed.) E. A. Everitt. Copenhagen.

Armstrong, W. A. (ed.) 1966 *Elizabethan History Plays*. London

Bailey, R. W. 1969 'Statistics and style: a historical survey' in *Statistics and Style*, (ed.) L. Doležel and R. W. Bailey, 217–236. New York

Bailey, R. W. and Doležel, L. 1968 *An Annotated Bibliography of Statistical Stylistics*. Ann Arbor

Baldwin, T. W. 1957 *Shakespeare's Love's Labor's Won: New evidence from the account books of an Elizabethan bookseller*. Cardondale, Southern Illinois.

Barton, A. 1980 'Leontes and the spider: language and speaker in Shakespeare's Last Plays' in Edwards, Ewbank and Hunter 1980 131–50

Bell, M. 1959 'Concordance to the Shakespeare Apocrypha', Dissertation, University of Liverpool

Bennett, P. E. 1957 'The statistical measurement of a stylistic trait in *Julius Caesar* and *As You Like It*', *Shakespeare Quarterly* 8 33–50

1969 above republished (without word lists) under same title in Doležel and Bailey 1969, 29–41

Brigstocke, W. O. (ed.) 1904 *The Arden Shakespeare: All's Well That Ends Well*. London

Brooke, C. F. Tucker (ed.) 1908 *The Shakespeare Apocrypha being a collection of fourteen plays which have been ascribed to Shakespeare*. Oxford

Brooke, N. 1980 'Language most shows a man...? Language and speaker in *Macbeth*' in Edwards, Ewbank and Hunter 1980, 67–77

Clemen, W. 1980 'Some aspects of style in the *Henry VI* plays' in Edwards, Ewbank and Hunter 1980, 9–24

Crundell, H. W. 1939 'Drayton and *Edward III*', *Notes and Queries* 176, 258–60

Dobson, W. B. 1957 '*Edward III*: a study of its composition in relation to its sources', Dissertation, University of Texas, reported in *Shakespeare Newsletter*, May 1957, 7, 19

Doležel, L. and Bailey, R. W. (eds.) 1969 *Statistics and Style*. New York.

Donow, H. S. 1969 *A Concordance to the Sonnet Sequences of Daniel, Drayton, Shakespeare, Sidney, and Spenser*. Carbondale, Southern Illinois

Edwards, P. 1980 'The declaration of love', in Edwards, Ewbank and Hunter 1980 39–50

Edwards, P., Ewbank, I.-S. and Hunter, G. K. (eds.) 1980 *Shakespeare's Styles. Essays in honour of Kenneth Muir*. Cambridge

Ellegård, A. 1962 *A Statistical Method for Determining Authorship. The Junius Letters, 1769–1772*. Göteborg

   1963 *Who Was Junius?* Stockholm

Farmer, J. S. (ed.) 1910 *The Reign of King Edward III*, Tudor Facsimile Texts, vol. 78. Edinburgh and London

Fisher, R. A. 1925 *Statistical Methods for Research Workers*. Edinburgh

Foakes, R. A. 1980 'Poetic language and dramatic significance in Shakespeare', in Edwards, Ewbank and Hunter 1980, 79–93

Golding, S. R. 1928 'The authorship of *Edward III*', *Notes and Queries* 154, 313–15

Hart, A. 1934 'The vocabulary of *Edward III*', in *Shakespeare and the Homilies and Other Pieces of Research into the Elizabethan Drama*, 219–41. Melbourne

   1943 'Vocabularies of Shakespeare's plays', *Review of English Studies* 19, 128–40

   1943 'The growth of Shakespeare's vocabulary', *Review of English Studies* 19, 242–54

Herdan, G. 1956 *Language as Choice and Chance*. Groningen

Hibbard, G. R. 1980 '*Feliciter audax. Antony and Cleopatra*, 1.i.1–24', in Edwards, Ewbank and Hunter 1980, 95–109

Horn, F. D. 1969 '*The Raigne of King Edward III*: a Critical Edition', Dissertation, University of Delaware. *Dissertation Abstracts* 30, 2969A

Hotine, M. 1977 '*Troylus and Cressida*: historical arguments for a 1608 date', *The Bard* 1, 153–61

Hunter, G. K. (ed.) 1962 *The Arden Shakespeare: All's Well That Ends Well*. London

Jackson, MacD. P. 1965a *Shakespeare's A Lover's Complaint: its Date and Authenticity*. University of Auckland Bulletin 72, English Series 13

   1965b '*Edward III*, Shakespeare and Pembroke's men', *Notes and Queries*, n.s. 41, 329–31

   1971 'A note on the text of *Edward III*', *Notes and Queries* 216, 423–4

Junius 1978 *The Letters of Junius*, (ed.) John Cannon. Oxford

Knights, L. C. 1980 'Rhetoric and insincerity', in Edwards, Ewbank and Hunter 1980, 1–8.

Koskenniemi, I. 1964 'Themes and imagery in *Edward III*', *Neuphilologische Mitteilungen* 65, 446–80

Langworthy, C. A. 1931 'A verse-sentence analysis of Shakespeare's plays', *Publications of the Modern Language Association* 46, 738–51

Lapides, F. R. 1966 'A critical edition of *The Raigne of Edward III*', Rutgers Dissertation, *Dissertation Abstracts* 27, 1788A

Maxwell, J. C. 1950 'Peele and Shakespeare: a stylometric test', *Journal of English and German Philology* 49, 557–61

   (ed.) 1968 *The Works of Shakespeare: Timon of Athens*. Cambridge

   (ed.) 1969a *The Works of Shakespeare: King Henry the Eighth*. Cambridge

   (ed.) 1969b *The Works of Shakespeare: The Poems*. Cambridge

McCurdy, H. G. 1953 *The Personality of Shakespeare*. New Haven

Melchiori, G. 1976 *Shakespeare's Dramatic Meditations, an Experiment in Criticism.* Oxford

Merriam, T. 1979 'What Shakespeare wrote in *Henry VIII*', *The Bard* 2, 81–94.

Michaelson, S., Morton, A. Q. and Hamilton-Smith, N. 1978 *To Couple is the Custom.* University of Edinburgh, Department of Computer Science: Internal Report. October 1977, revised November 1978

    1979 'Fingerprinting the mind', *Endeavour*, n.s. 3, no. 4, 171–5

    1979 *Justice for Healander.* University of Edinburgh, Department of Computer Science. Internal Report

Morton, A. Q. 1978 *Literary Detection: How to prove an authorship in literature and documents*, United Kingdom (Bowker Publishing Co.)

    1980 'The comparison of three plays of Shakespeare: *Julius Caesar, Pericles* and *Titus Andronicus*'; 'The habits displayed in *Titus Andronicus*'; 'The comparison of *Titus Andronicus* with *Pericles*'; 'A comparison of the punctuation of the three plays of Shakespeare'; 'The comparison of the plays of Peele'; 'The comparison of Peele and Shakespeare'. Privately circulated

Morton, A. Q., Winspear, A. D., *et al.* 1971 *It's Greek to the Computer.* Montreal

Mosteller, F. and Wallace, D. 1964 *Inference and Disputed Authorship: 'The Federalist'.* Reading, Mass.

Muir, K. 1953 'A reconsideration of *Edward III*', *Shakespeare Survey* 6, 39–48

    1960 and 1969 'Shakespeare's hand in *Edward III*', in *Shakespeare as Collaborator*, London

    1964 '*A Lover's Complaint*: a reconsideration' in *Shakespeare 1564–1964*, ed. Edward A. Bloom, Providence RI

    1973 *Shakespeare the Professional and Related Studies.* London

O'Connor, F. I. 1961 *Shakespeare's Progress.* New York

Oliver, H. J. (ed.) 1971 *The Arden Shakespeare: The Merry Wives of Windsor.* London

Østerberg, V. 1929 'The "Countess scenes" of *Edward III*', *Shakespeare Jahrbuch* 65, 45–91

Partridge, A. C. 1949 *The Problem of Henry VIII Reopened.* Cambridge

Platt, A. 1911 '*Edward III* and Shakespeare's Sonnets', *Modern Language Review* 6, 511–13

Popper, K. R. 1968 (1st edition 1959) *The Logic of Scientific Discovery.* London

Ribner, Irving 1957 *The English History Play in the Age of Shakespeare.* Princeton

Schaar, C. 1962 *Elizabethan Sonnet Themes and the Dating of Shakespeare's Sonnets.* Lund

Schäfer, J. 1980 *Documentation in the O.E.D.: Shakespeare and Nashe as Test Cases.* Oxford

Schoenbaum, S. 1966 *Internal Evidence and Elizabethan Dramatic Authorship.* London

Slater, E. 1973 'A statistical note on *A Lover's Complaint*', *Notes and Queries* 218, 138–40

    1975a 'Shakespeare: word links between poems and plays', *Notes and Queries*, 220, 157–63

1975b 'Some psychological aspects of the *Sonnets*', *The Bard* 1, 1–8

1975c 'Word links with *The Merry Wives of Windsor*', *Notes and Queries* 220, 169–71

1977 'Word links with *All's Well That Ends Well*', *Notes and Queries* 222, 109–12

1978a 'Word links between *Timon of Athens* and *King Lear*', ibid, 223, 147–49

1978b 'Word links from *Troilus* to *Othello* and *Macbeth*', *The Bard* 2, 4–22

Smith, R. M. 1911 '*Edward III* A study of the authorship of the drama in the light of a new source', *Journal of English and German Philology* 10, 90–104

Spevack, M. 1969; one-volume edn, 1973 *The Harvard Concordance to Shakespeare*. Cambridge, Mass.

Tallentire, D. R. 1971 'Mathematical modelling in stylistics: its extent and general limitations' in Wisbey 1971, 117–28

Tillyard, E. M. W. 1944 *Shakespeare's History Plays*. London

Wentersdorf, K. P. 1960 'The authorship of *Edward III*', Dissertation, University of Cincinnati. *Dissertation Abstracts* 21, 905–6

1965 'The date of *Edward III*', *Shakespeare Quarterly* 16, 227–31

Williams, C. B. 1970 *Style and Vocabulary*. London

Wisbey, R. A. (ed.) 1971 *The Computer in Literary and Linguistic Research*. Cambridge

Yule, G. U. 1944 *The Statistical Study of Literary Vocabulary*. Cambridge

Zipf, G. K. 1932 *Selected Studies of the Principle of Relative Frequency in Language*. Harvard

Index

www.ingramcontent.com/pod-product-compliance
Ingram Content Group UK Ltd.
Pitfield, Milton Keynes, MK11 3LW, UK
UKHW030900150625
459647UK00021B/2720